SUBURBAN WARRIORS

POLITICS AND SOCIETY IN TWENTIETH-CENTURY AMERICA

SERIES EDITORS

William Chafe, Gary Gerstle, and Linda Gordon

A list of titles

in this series appears

at the back of

the book

SUBURBAN WARRIORS

The Origins of the New American Right

Lisa McGirr

PRINCETON UNIVERSITY PRESS

PRINCETON AND OXFORD

Library of Congress Cataloging-in-Publication Data
McGirr, Lisa, 1962–
Suburban warriors : the origins of the new American Right /
Lisa McGirr
p. cm. — (Politics and society in twentieth-century America)
Includes bibliographical references and index.
ISBN 0-691-05903-9 (alk. paper)
1. Conservatism—United States—History—20th century. 2. United States—
Politics and government—1945–1989. 3. Right and left (Political science)—
History—20th century. I. Title. II. Series.
E839.5 .M32 2001
320.52'0973—dc21   00-056508

This book has been composed in Sabon.

The paper used in this publication meets the minimum requirements
of ANSI/NISO Z39.48-1992 (R1997) (*Permanence of Paper*)

www.pup.princeton.edu

Printed in the United States of America

10   9

ISBN-13: 978-0-691-09611-7 (pbk.)

ISBN-10: 0-691-09611-2 (pbk.)

For Joan and William McGirr
and for Sven

Contents

Illustrations

Acknowledgments

Numerous individuals and institutions have contributed to bringing this book to fruition. Archivists and librarians in many places were generous with their time and expertise. I would like to thank the staff of the Bancroft Library at the University of California, Berkeley; the Hoover Institution on War, Revolution and Peace; the University of California Special Collections divisions at Irvine and Los Angeles; California State University, Fullerton Oral History Program and Special Collections; and the National Archives, Pacific Southwest Region. I am grateful to the Anti-Defamation League of B'nai B'rith in New York and Los Angeles for providing assistance. The librarians of the numerous branches of the public libraries of Orange County I visited, along with the staff of the Sherman Library in Corona del Mar, also provided vital help.

I would also like to thank the many women and men of Orange County who granted me oral history interviews. Without their willingness to share their memories of conservative politics in the 1960s, this book would not have been possible. In retelling their stories to a wider audience, I have placed them within a historical and analytical framework and drawn conclusions that they will, at times, take issue with. I am therefore especially grateful that they opened their homes and shared their recollections with me.

Other kinds of help have been essential to this book. The Pew Program in Religion and American History provided a generous faculty grant for the final year of writing. Harvard University's Joseph H. Clark Fund provided a much-needed travel grant. In addition, my department chair, William Kirby, facilitated my academic leave year and, more broadly, has provided gracious support to young faculty members at Harvard University.

At the early stages of this project, Elizabeth Blackmar, Joshua Freeman, Ira Katznelson, and Jonathan Rieder provided encouragement, insights, and criticisms. Alan Brinkley generously offered suggestions, and his advice proved invaluable to the direction this project took. I also owe a special debt to Eric Foner. His own work has stood as a model of engaged scholarship, but most of all, his commitment to my intellectual development made my dream of becoming a historian a reality; for this, I will be forever grateful.

In addition, I am indebted to several scholars who have read the manuscript in its entirety. Jerome Himmelstein and Michael Kazin offered rigorous criticisms and identified a number of areas that needed more depth and clarification. So, too, Bill Chafe and Gary Gerstle have helped to make this a better book through their numerous suggestions for improving the narrative and sharpening the interpretations I wished to present. At Princeton University Press, Brigitta van Rheinberg has skillfully guided the book from unrevised manuscript to production. Several friends and colleagues consented to read portions of the manuscript at various stages. Aaron Brenner, Liz Cohen, Ruth Feldstein, Tami Friedman, Joan Roe, Bruce Schulman, Jonathan Soffer, and Cyrus Veeser have all offered useful criticisms. Charles Forcey deserves special mention. His unsurpassed editing skills and keen insights have proven invaluable to this project. I have also relied on a number of skilled research assistants at Harvard. I would like to thank Adam Beaver, JuNelle Harris, Luke McCloughlin, Andrew Owen, Rebecca Shapiro, and Jennifer Tattenbaum.

Friends and family have sustained me emotionally through the early stages of this project, as well as its completion. Lisa Badner, Julien and Marcela Kalina Bonder, Janet Braun, Sadhana and Devesh Kapur, Petra Kaufhold, Linda McLean, Bill McGirr, Maureen McGirr, Constance Newman, Rosemary Rice, Donna Roberts, Julia Rodriguez, and Mindy Roseman have provided love, diversion, and a constant reminder that there is more to life than history. I am especially grateful to my dear friend Maria Jebari-Carrillo, who, in many ways, made the writing of this book possible; she is truly one in a million. And the energy and unwavering support of my parents, Joan and William McGirr, have helped me in ways impossible to measure.

The past years of research and writing have been indelibly marked by the birth of my sons, Noah and Pascal, whose coming into the world taught me what really matters in life. This has been the greatest of all possible gifts. I have also been lucky enough to share the odyssey of academic life (and parenting) with Sven Beckert. His incisive criticisms and careful reading of drafts of this manuscript have made an enormous contribution to this project. Above all, his love, support, laughter, and friendship have made it all a joyful adventure and much, much more. This book is dedicated to him and to the future journeys we take together and to my parents for their inspiration.

SUBURBAN WARRIORS

Orange County, 1960. Inset: Southern California region.

INTRODUCTION

ON MARCH 4, 1964, Estrid Kielsmeier, a mother of two young children and the wife of an accountant, rose bright and early at her home on Janet Lane in one of the newer suburban developments of Garden Grove, California. She made her way into the kitchen to set out coffee, putting dozens of cups on the table. Mrs. Kielsmeier was expecting visitors. But this was not to be an ordinary suburban coffee klatch. Next to the coffee, she placed blank nominating petitions to qualify Barry Goldwater as a candidate for president in her state's Republican primary. Starting at six o'clock, the first neighbors arrived to sign the petitions. Throughout the morning they came alone, as families, and in small groups. Goldwater was their candidate.

On this spring day, Kielsmeier and thousands of grassroots conservatives worked feverishly in a show of support for their standard-bearer. They had set up "Operation Q" for the March 4 opening, in the words of one commentator, "as meticulously drilled and planned as an expeditionary force waiting for D-Day."[1] Some, like Kielsmeier, set up "coffees." Others pounded the pavement. Doorbells rang throughout Southern California as volunteer cadres gathered signatures. In a remarkable organizational feat, before noon on the first day of their drive, these volunteers had gathered over 36,000 names, about three times as many as were needed to qualify their candidate for the ballot. Yet despite their having accomplished their goal, the torrent of support for Barry Goldwater continued, and by March 6, they had gathered another 50,000 names.[2]

Kielsmeier's effort on behalf of Goldwater that early spring morning was just one step in her deepening conservative activism—an activism spurred by her strong conviction that the world's first "Christian Republic" was in danger. America was, in her eyes, on a course of political, economic, and moral decline; a course steered by the nation's liberals. To counter the tide, Kielsmeier, and many men and women like her, sought to create, as she put it, a "mini-revolution . . . in the true sense of the word . . . a revolving back . . . to the foundations of the country."[3] It was a revolution quite different from those we usually associate with the 1960s.

Indeed, Kielsmeier and "suburban warriors" like her built a vibrant and remarkable political mobilization during the 1960s, and it is their history that this book seeks to chronicle. It was in suburbs such as Garden Grove, Orange County (the place Kielsmeier called home), in conjunction with the backing of regional entrepreneurs, that small groups of middle-class men and women met in their new tract homes, seeking to turn the tide of liberal dominance.[4] Recruiting the like-minded, they organized study groups, opened "Freedom Forum" bookstores, filled the rolls of the John Birch Society, entered school board races, and worked within the Republican Party, all in an urgent struggle to safeguard their particular vision of freedom and the American heritage. In doing so, they became the ground forces of a conservative revival—one that transformed conservatism from a marginal force preoccupied with communism in the early 1960s into a viable electoral contender by the decade's end.

This book is a history of the conservative movement, using Orange County as the lens through which to explore the social base and ideological waters of one of the most profound transformations of twentieth-century U.S. politics. Orange County, as contemporary newspaper commentators never tired of emphasizing, was a real center and symbol of American conservatism in the 1960s.[5] Its conservative movement was the nucleus of a broader conservative matrix evolving in the Sunbelt and the West that eventually propelled assertive and unapologetic conservatives to national prominence.[6] Political analyst Kevin Phillips, noting the national significance of the conservative political traditions of Southern California suburbanites, observed as early as 1969 that "perhaps no other political impetus in the nation is so important as the middle-class upheaval of the Sun country, and Southern California in particular."[7] The south-land's size and affluence has made it an important source of money and votes for conservative candidates and organizations, enabling it to help shape the political direction of the nation. Southland conservatives led the way in making an emerging Republican majority. Together with their conservative brethren elsewhere in the South and the West, they recast the party of Lincoln from the moderate Republicanism of the eastern Wall Street establishment into a southern and western mold of a far more conservative bent.[8]

These conservative activists and the movement they forged are essential to understanding the rightward shift in American politics since the 1960s. Far outside the boundaries of respectable politics in the early 1960s, the Right expanded its influence on the national scene in the late 1960s and 1970s and vaulted to national power with the Reagan landslide of 1980. Since that time, conservatives in Washington have transformed the relationship between federal and state power, limited the regulatory capacity of the central state, and altered the fundamental structure of the New Deal welfare state. Conservatives' successes, to be sure, were due in no small part to liberalism's foundering on the shoals of race, economic discontent, and its own internal contradictions. But just as significantly, conservatives' ability to build a powerful movement enabled them to pick up the pieces and profit politically from liberal failures.

This book, then, is not only about the making of the modern American Right but also about the forging of the late twentieth-century United States. People like Kielsmeier made history in the conservative revival, in effect recasting politics in ways comparable only to the upheavals of the New Deal. When their standard-bearer claimed the presidency in 1980, the long years of organizing in obscurity, the times when the conservative movement was ridiculed and marginalized seemed to have come to an end. "It was so exciting," one activist recalled. "People finally understood what we're about."[9] From their inauspicious beginnings in the early 1960s, these conservatives had, by 1980, helped to transform the political landscape of America. For better or for worse, these other radicals of the 1960s have had lasting influence on American politics in the late twentieth century.

These "kitchen-table" activists have fundamentally shaped the course of American politics, and yet, until now, they have lived in obscurity. They have done so in part because their mobilization has been overshadowed by the more flamboyant Left and its movement culture. Images of Martin Luther King proclaiming "Let freedom ring" on the Washington Mall, students burning draft cards at federal induction centers, and flower children gathering in Haight-Ashbury for the "summer of love" filled American television screens in the 1960s. The left-wing and liberal movements of the period dominated the airwaves and newspapers; indeed, the sixties were the heyday of liberal social change. African-Americans in the South built the most successful social movement of the twentieth century. Inspired by their example and a deepening rights consciousness, white student radicals, counterculturalists, and feminists altered the political and cultural fabric of the nation.[10] But at the same time, buffered and buffeted by these progressive gains, conservative intellectuals, politicians, and pastors—together with thousands of grassroots activists—set in place the ideas, strategies, and politics that would pave their road to national power.

It is not only because of liberalism's strength during this stormy decade that this movement has remained largely uncharted. Rather, the popular images of the 1960s grassroots Right as a band of emotional, irrational "kooks" contributed to their obscurity. Orange County's vibrant conservative movement, for example, earned the county the reputation, according to a *Fortune* magazine article in 1968, as America's "nut country."[11] Such pejorative labels resulted in part from liberal disdain for the unappealingly exclusionary aspects of conservative politics, but they were also given substance by the Right's apocalyptic and conspiratorial rhetoric. Robert Welch, the leader of the John Birch Society, for example, made the preposterous suggestion that Dwight D. Eisenhower was a "crypto-Communist" whose actions were driven by "Communist bosses who count on him merely for the execution of their planning," and Congressman James B. Utt of Orange County made national news in 1963 with his suggestions that "a large contingent of barefooted Africans" might be training in Georgia for what he hinted could be part of a United Nations military exercise to take over the United States.[12] Such outlandish statements by right-wing politicians and leaders were easy to lampoon and gave the popular press reason to dismiss the mobilization as "fanatical" and "extremist" without further examination. The kitchen-table activists and their motivations remained unchronicled.

Contemporary scholars amplified the tendencies of the popular press. In the wake of McCarthyism and the rise of right-wing groups in the early 1960s, Daniel Bell, Richard Hofstadter, and Seymour Martin Lipset turned their attention to explaining the roots of popular support for right-wing politics. Sharing a vision of the United States as fundamentally shaped by the liberal pluralism they so strongly sought to uphold, they viewed right-wing activists as motivated less by any coherent set of ideas or rational politics than by psychological distress. Bell and Lipset, in particular, argued that status anxieties of both an older, dispossessed middle class and an upwardly mobile group of white ethnics explained support for the Right. Hofstadter, in turn, borrowing from clinical psychology, suggested that a sense of "persecution" and a "paranoid style" characterized the Right's adherents. In effect, these influential scholars cast the Right as a marginal, embattled remnant fighting a losing battle against the inexorable forces of progress.[13] The Right, they concluded, was prone to episodic outbursts similar to those of other "extremist" movements in American history that ran counter to the fundamental direction of change in American life—the tireless forward march of American liberalism.[14] While they correctly argued for paying attention to the ordinary people who populated the ranks of the Right, their excessively psychological interpretation distorted our understanding of American conservatism.

This book's exploration of the world of Orange County activists and the movement they built, however, produces a picture of the Right that is at odds with both the contemporary media images and the explanations of conservatism put forth by the consensus-school scholars.[15] While a segment of the Right appealed to traditional ideas, embraced a fundamentalist religious worldview and apocalyptic strands of thought, challenging some of the basic assumptions of modernism, these ideas took hold among a highly educated and thoroughly modern group of men and women. Conservatives in Orange County enjoyed the fruits of worldly success, often worked in high-tech industries, shared in the burgeoning consumer culture, and participated in the bureaucratized world of post–World War II America.[16] Their mobilization, then, was not a rural "remnant" of the displaced and maladapted but a gathering around principles that were found to be relevant in the most modern of communities. Post–World War II American conservatism thus explodes any easy dichotomies between tradition and modernity. Indeed, an exploration of this movement highlights the dual nature of modern American conservatism: its strange mixture of traditionalism and modernity, a combination that suggests the adaptability, resilience, and, thus perhaps, intractability of the Right in American life.

The question of how conservative political ideology, often considered an antimodern worldview, attracted a large number of people in the most technologically advanced and economically vibrant of American locales is one of the central puzzles this book tries to solve. The vibrant conservative milieu in which these activists flourished, of course, owed its strength, in part, to Orange County's established cultural patterns and traditions. But its real rise was linked to the region's breathtaking transformation after World War II. Propelled by the Cold War military-industrial complex, Southern California's ways of life and work changed radically, disposing many of its inhabitants to embrace a radicalized form of politics. The largely white-collar, educated, and often highly skilled women and men who embraced right-wing politics saw their own lives and the flowering communities where they made their homes as tributes to the possibilities of individual entrepreneurial success. Regional business leaders, moreover, promulgated a vigorous libertarianism that helped to lead Orange County citizens to an unabashed celebration of the free market. The people who came to Orange County were often steeped in nationalism, moralism, and piety that were part of the warp and woof of the communities from which they hailed. While, in other settings, this conservatism had been tempered by an earlier link to the political traditions of the New Deal, here it took on different meanings, a transformation sharpened by Orange Countians' new affluence and discomfort with the growing liberalism in state and national politics in the 1960s. Compounding the attraction of the Right was the sense of coherence, community, and commitment that conservative churches and right-wing organizations provided—a sense otherwise absent from the larger world of Orange County. For these middle-class men and women, Western libertarianism, combined with a theoretically incompatible social and cultural conservatism, came to make "common sense."[17]

The pejorative labels that served in the past to dismiss this movement have led me to be cautious in choosing terminology. The slipperiness of these older labels is evinced by their lack of durability. Whereas in 1965 William F. Buckley, Jr., was touted by *Life* magazine as "the enfant terrible of the Far Right" and Barry Goldwater was often labeled a dangerous extremist by his contemporaries, more recently these individuals have been regarded as representatives of respectable conservatism, despite the fact that their politics did not change significantly during the past decades.[18] This not only shows how much the political spectrum has shifted but also complicates the question of how to talk about grassroots conservatives of the 1960s. I have chosen not to use the terms "ultraconservatism," "Radical Right," or "Far Right" when referring to the movement. I have done so first because these terms are fraught with psychological overtones and dismissive connotations. Second, they do not accurately reflect the politics and ideas of the conservative movement as a whole. Instead, they brand the entire movement with a dismissive label that may, at most, be said to fit a small segment of it. The "Radical Right" or "extreme Right" label might be usefully applied to that segment of the Right that engaged in conspiratorial thinking—organizations, for example, like the John Birch Society. Yet, even here, such terminology is problematic. Even the most militant John Birchers in Orange County sought to work through constitutional channels to forward their goals.[19] Additionally, many conservatives who joined such conspiratorial organizations as the John Birch Society did not share the paranoid theories of their leader. Rather, they saw the society as the only organized voice for the right wing. More important, conservatives who embraced conspiratorial thinking shared a sufficient set of complaints, assumptions, and common enemies that united them with their more "respectable" cohorts in one movement. They swam in the same ideological waters as the broader conservative movement as a whole and, above all, participated in building one mobilization out of their common grievances against American liberalism. For definitional precision, then, the terms "Far Right" and "Radical Right" should be limited to white supremacist, paramilitary, and fascist fringe groups like the Ku Klux Klan and the Minute Men, groups that stepped outside of democratic political processes to achieve their goals. The Minute Men did have a small organized presence in Southern California in the 1960s, but they remained marginal.[20]

I use the terms "conservatism" and "the Right" interchangeably to characterize the movement under investigation here, but these terms still require definition. The Right, after all, was composed of distinct groups whose priorities, worldviews, and political strategies differed. Despite important internal divisions, however, conservatives in the 1960s shared a number of concerns. First, they were united in their opposition to liberal "collectivism"—the growing tendency of the state to organize social and economic life in the name of the public welfare and the social good. Libertarians sought to limit the intrusiveness of the nation-state in economic matters (although their antistatism stopped at the door of a strong-armed defense), and normative conservatives opposed what they perceived to be a decline in religiosity, morality, individual responsibility, and family authority—a decline, they argued, that went hand in hand with the growth of centralized federal power. In Orange County, both groups championed virulent anticommunism, celebrated laissez-faire capitalism, evoked staunch nationalism, and supported the use of the state to uphold law and order. America, they believed, had an organic, benevolent order that would function well if not for tampering by liberal elites.[21]

The triumph of Ronald Reagan in 1980 and the new respectability of conservative ideas in national discourse thereafter brought a renewal of interest in the origins of the conservative movement. Indeed, historical and sociological studies on the post–World War II American Right have proliferated in recent years.[22] Historians have charted the conservative intellectual movement, traced the odyssey of the Right in the Republican Party, offered biographical treatments of national conservative leaders, and outlined the history of organizations such as the Young Americans for Freedom.[23] Sociologists have argued for the importance of understanding the Right as a social movement, taking into account its ideas and its coalition building.[24] These scholars and political observers have identified important factors that contributed to the rise of the Right.[25] Yet these studies have focused exclusively on the national level, leaving unexamined and unexplained the dynamic social base that propelled the movement and gave it its endurance and strength.[26] We still lack a deep understanding of the women and men who built the movement and of the communities from which they sprang.[27]

The few studies that have explored single settings have focused on grievances and discontent among lower-middle-class, urban, eastern ethnics: the "Reagan Democrats," once considered locked into the New Deal coalition, whose shifting allegiances helped pave the road to national power for the Right.[28] Although they were undeniably important, such disgruntled Democrats were not the driving force of the conservative movement. The issues of race and welfare indeed alienated swing voters and, as this study confirms, were important motivators at all levels, but the conservative grassroots mobilization predated the

height of urban violence and "white backlash" and had its ideological roots in a more thoroughgoing, anti-egalitarian, conservative worldview.

This book, then, advances a new perspective on the conservative insurgency of the recent past. It touches on all the existing
narratives that have contributed to our understanding of the rise
of the American Right, but it has a central dynamic that lies
outside of them. Telling the story of Orange County's "suburban
warriors" requires more attention to social forces, to regionalism, to enduring political traditions outside the liberal consensus, and to the political movements that ordinary men and
women at times create.[29] I suggest that it is only within the context of the Cold War; postwar demographic transformation; the
dynamics of economic, cultural, and political change; and their
cumulative impact on the values and beliefs of ordinary people
that we can uncover the process by which the modern American
Right was made. This perspective moves beyond the realm of
pure politics to explore the social forces that created political
opportunities for the Right. It seeks to illuminate the world of
the men and women who rejected the liberal vision and instead
championed individual economic freedom and a staunch social
conservatism.

In short, then, this book explores the Right as a social movement, distinguishing the distinct but intersecting levels at which
right-wing mobilization occurred.[30] Locally, mobilization involved the grassroots leaders and rank-and-file men and women,
the broader ideological waters in which they swam, as well as
regional business elites who offered resources and institutional
support. At the national level, it involved the formation of an
intellectual leadership that sought to give cohesion to the ideas
underpinning the movement, as well as a political leadership that
offered direction to channel conservative sentiment.

While this book addresses the conservative movement at
the state and national levels, it is primarily a local study. A thick
description of right-wing politics in one locale, I believe, best
reveals the process of conservative mobilization, the Right's
means and mechanisms of recruitment, and the movement's evo-

lution. It allows me to describe the interplay between local and national political movements. Such a perspective, moreover, permits a rich understanding of the complex interaction between individuals and their social milieu, as well as the broader institutions and structural forces that informed their world. It provides a microscopic view of processes that are often left to the realm of abstraction: the sources of right-wing support, the creation of the Sunbelt, suburbanization, and white backlash. Such a study can best reveal the social setting, the economic forces, and the impulses, prejudices, and ideas that nourished popular conservatism in recent American history.

Although this is a local study that helps to explain the rise of a national movement, I make no claims that Orange County was "typical." Indeed, what makes Orange County worthy of attention was the atypical vibrancy of its conservative movement. But while Orange County differed in the degree and visibility of its mobilization, the socioeconomic, cultural, and political patterns that contributed to conservatism's success there were symptomatic of the patterns and forces that contributed to its appeal in other Sunbelt and western communities. In California itself, the neighboring counties of Los Angeles and San Diego also provided fertile soil for right-wing growth. In contrast to these areas, however, Orange County politics were not tempered by the presence of influential counterbalancing forces: liberal Jewish Democrats, organized workers, and vocal minorities. Orange County exaggerated trends occurring elsewhere—trends that were harbingers of future national change.

Orange County might best be understood as a prototype: the first functional form of a new conservative milieu that appeared less distinctly elsewhere. While studies remain to be written that would fully describe the details, the most cursory examination of postwar settings in the Sunbelt and the West where conservative cultures have flourished since the 1960s—places like Fort Worth ("Free Enterprise City") and the northeast suburbs of Dallas, Texas; Scottsdale and Maricopa County, Arizona; Cobb and northern Dekalb Counties, Georgia; the affluent suburbs of Jefferson Parish, Louisiana (towns like Metairie); or

Colorado Springs, Colorado—suggests that they had much in common with Orange County. They have shared an older regional identity that defined itself against northeastern power, a model of growth based on "clean development," a socially homogeneous group of highly skilled, affluent inhabitants, and, often, the powerful presence of defense and military. Taken together, these large, prosperous communities have had a tremendous influence on the national scene, providing many of the rank-and-file supporters of the libertarian and Christian Right.

In telling the story of the making of the national Right through the lens of Orange County, my study will necessarily emphasize certain features of modern conservatism while downplaying others. As part of the American West, Orange County has had distinctive patterns of development and political and cultural traditions that have propelled a regional ethos and a staunch antistatist libertarianism significant in modern American political history.[31] The modern West has drawn on a sense of identity rooted in notions of the self-made, individualist frontiersman counterposed to an older, corrupt East. The themes of local control and of the threat of intrusion by a distant federal center of power have resonated powerfully in a region long dependent on East Coast financiers and federal funds to propel economic growth, an area where federal government bureaucrats have controlled vast amounts of land and resources.

These demands for local control and opposition to federal power (despite the region's simultaneous embrace of federal funds for internal development) were not unique to the West. They have been at the core of modern conservatism and are central to a distinct southern and western regional identity. Yet the forces underlying these concerns have varied. Racial issues were far more central to the texture and fabric of southern politics and to that region's conservatism. While Orange County's southwestern location links it geographically to the South as well as the West, making it a central part of the distinctive regional identity that has come to be known as the Sunbelt, racial issues did not occupy the same prominence in the life, ideas, and politics of Southern California as they did in the former confederate states in the 1960s. Opposition to government action to bolster the constitutional rights of African-Americans did contribute to the Right's appeal, but it was only one of a host of issues in a broader conservative package. Focusing on western conservatism, then, tells a somewhat different story that cannot be subsumed under the North-South civil rights dichotomy that has so much dominated our narratives of the 1960s.[32]

This book traces the transformation of the modern American Right from a marginal force tagged as "extremist" in the early 1960s into the mainstream of national life by the decade's end. This transformation happened in four distinct steps, and the book is organized to highlight the ideas and strategies that characterized each of them. While a core set of assumptions informed all the stages, the package of conservative concerns shifted from a discursive preoccupation with public, political, and international enemies (namely, communism) to enemies within our own communities and families (namely, secular humanists, women's liberationists, and, eventually, homosexuals). Chapter 1 sets the stage for these developments, describing the Southern California that proved such a fertile seedbed for right-wing growth; painting a broad picture of the region's socioeconomic character in 1960, it argues that the process of rapid suburbanization, the Cold War economic boom, regional business entrepreneurs, and a particular group of in-migrants reinforced an already existing conservative ethos. Chapter 2 charts the first and second moments of mobilization: first, the movement's birth in the late 1950s, a time when conservatives, disheartened with their lack of power on the national stage, struck back by founding journals and organizations, creating the core around which the movement would grow. The period of the early 1960s, the second phase of conservative mobilization, was a time of deepening grassroots activism that drew from the ideas, symbols, and targets of McCarthyism. Chapter 2 lays out the history of this mobilization, paying close attention to its beginning, its leaders, its rank-and-file activists, its strategies, and its movement culture. This second stage led activists to enter the electoral arena in order to take over the local and state Republican Party apparatus—the subject of chapter 3. Here, I explore the intersection of the grassroots Right with a broader national political movement. Culminating with the successful nomination of Barry Goldwater for the presidency in 1964, this "moment" ended when the Right's extremist and apocalyptic rhetoric almost doomed conservatism as a national movement. Chapter 4 links this phase of conservative mobilization with the next one by analyzing the ideology of the Right, looking at the core strands of right-wing thought—namely, libertarianism and social conservatism—that transcended the different political strategies of its activists. The third stage of conservative mobilization was the birth of a new populist conservatism in the wake of Goldwater's defeat, the subject of chapter 5. Piloted by Ronald Reagan, who became the new standard-bearer in 1966, conservatives refashioned their discourse, moving away from tirades on socialism and communism, and toward attacks on liberal "permissiveness," "welfare chiselers," "criminality," and "big government." This shift in emphasis, which coincided with the dramatic events of the decade so familiar to us, produced the Right's first significant triumph: the election of Ronald Reagan to the governorship of California in 1966. The fourth and final stage, the rise of new social issues and the resurgence of evangelical Christianity in the late 1960s and early 1970s, is charted in chapter 6. Here, the book explores the decline of older organizations on the Right that had been important early in the decade and the shifting lines of battle driven by concerns over sexual liberation, liberalized abortion laws, and the women's movement. Along with these new initiatives, large-scale and growing evangelical churches in the region brought conservative social concerns to new prominence. The confluence of a middle-class economic backlash over taxes and state spending with Christian conservative hostility toward "Big Brother" stoked a fiery brew that would nourish conservative fortunes nationally. The book ends by following the trajectory of a group of core conservative activists into the late twentieth century, highlighting the evolution of the movement since the 1960s.

This study examines how a group of people in one county of the nation responded to the social, economic, and cultural changes of the 1960s—a time when national leaders foresaw a major expansion of federal functions to improve the lives of citizens; a time when personal freedoms vastly expanded, when racial hierarchies came tumbling down, and when gender relations were fundamentally reworked. In chronicling the meaning of these changes for the women and men of Garden Grove, Santa Ana, Anaheim, and Newport Beach, and, in particular, the way these people organized to assert the dominance of their beliefs and values in politics, this book provides a case study of how the New Right was made. But it is also my hope that this study of how the men and women in Orange County came to act collectively in politics in the 1960s will further our understanding of the deep, tenacious roots of popular conservatism in twentieth-century America. The conservative movement in Orange County, after all, did not emerge sui generis in the 1960s. It formed but one stage in a much longer history of the contest between conservatives and progressives for public power in American life in the twentieth century. Conservatives in the 1960s drew from an older font of ideas. Indeed, until the New Deal, conservative ideas had occupied a central, if not dominant, place in American culture and national life. In conservatives' eyes, then, the period from 1933 to 1980 was a trying time of displacement, marginalization, and struggle. It was a time when they had to adjust to their new position as simultaneous insiders and outsiders to the realms of power. Eventually, as this book demonstrates, their posture as outsiders enabled them to build a self-conscious movement to develop a critique of liberal elites. The world of the New Deal state, thus, first marginalized, then reshuffled, and eventually reinvigorated American conservatism. By the 1960s, conservatives had organized a cohesive movement with institutions, networks, and a broad grassroots following.

This movement, combined with growing opportunities, eventually enabled conservatives to obtain a central position in the halls of national power once more.

In the largest sense, then, this book probes the shifting nature of twentieth-century American conservatism. When, where, and how have conservative political cultures been generated? To what extent has a self-conscious conservative movement advanced and defined itself in reaction to social change? And, most of all, how do we explain the staying power of the Right in American life? In the wake of conservative upheavals—from the fundamentalist mobilizations of the 1920s and the Red-baiting crusades of the 1950s to the Goldwater movement in the 1960s—liberal commentators argued that the Right was in disarray and retreat. With the spread of national liberal culture, education, and modernization to the rural areas and small towns that had once formed the heartland of conservative mobilizations, so the argument went, the Right would become increasingly marginalized. But conservative forces have instead flourished, and they have done so most recently in areas considered least conducive to them: modern suburban regions. They have been able to do so because, in Orange County and elsewhere, conservatives have meshed preservationism with adaptation. While embracing ideas often thought of as incompatible with modernity—in particular a rejection of secularism, egalitarianism, liberal relativism, and the tendency toward a centralized state—conservatives have conceived of themselves, in many ways, as a modern force. Just as importantly, they have accommodated aspects of American pluralism and jettisoned older unpalatable ideas (of anti-Semitism, biological racism, and anti-Catholicism, for example) in the face of new circumstances. At the same time, however, they have carried forward a core set of older assumptions about the nation, God's place within it, law and order, and limited government precepts that resonated with the new circumstances of life of many post–World War II middle- and lower-middle-class (especially white) Americans— Catholics and Protestants alike—particularly in the South and the West. They have addressed real dilemmas that faced Americans in the post–World War II period: concerns about the erosion of local autonomy, of community, of individualism, and a disparagement of tradition in a familiar language. They have done so, moreover, in a way that seemed to safeguard a way of life and a set of power relations its adherents wished to preserve. Conservatism has been both a reactive and a proactive force, a mixture that helps explain its strength and endurance.

CHAPTER ✦ 1.

THE SETTING

O N July 17, 1955, Walt Disney opened his visionary new amusement park in Anaheim, California. After years of planning, Disneyland stood ready to provide packaged and planned family fun to hosts of tourists from around the nation and to the growing number of Americans who made Southern California their home. Women, children, and men crowded the sidewalks to witness the festivities: Life-size cartoon characters paraded through the streets of a sentimentalized "Main Street, U.S.A.," "Frontierland," "Tomorrowland," and "Fantasyland."[1] In keeping with its founder's vision of Disneyland as an alternative to the chaotic Coney Islands of the East, with their "tawdry rides and hostile employees," clean-cut employees strove to maintain order and a friendly attitude.[2]

Walt Disney could not have found a more fitting home for his ambitious theme park, with its mixture of nostalgia for a simple American past and its bright optimism about the future, than this booming western locale at midcentury. No state in the nation in the mid–twentieth century represented the promises of the United States more than California, and no part of California stood for this dream more than the southland—the stretch of towns and cities extending from Santa Barbara to San Diego. Having packed their bags and said good-bye to their families and friends and the old "Main Streets" of their childhoods, millions of migrants settled in Southern California in the decades following World War II to realize their American dream. They took new jobs in high-tech industries, professions, and services, settled in single-family homes, and raised their children. In so doing, they formed part of a seismic demographic shift that would eventually forge the Sunbelt. Los Angeles stood as the prime destination in this migration, but just to the south of the City of Angels, Orange County came into its own in the 1960s as the land of promise for hundreds of thousands of Americans drawn by its job opportunities, climate, and suburban lifestyle. One of the thousands of migrants to Orange County noted years later that "it was God's country. . . . It was the dream of being able to get somewhere."[3]

This suburban heartland was not only home to Walt Disney's visionary new park, to thousands of new California families and new towns and cities; it was also the birthing ground of a powerful grassroots political movement. A revitalized and militant Right—fueled by a politics of antistatism, virulent anticommunism, and strict normative conservatism—burst onto the scene nationally in the early 1960s, and nowhere more forcefully than Orange County. At living room bridge clubs, at backyard barbecues, and at kitchen coffee klatches, the middle-class men and women of Orange County "awakened" to what they perceived as the threats of communism and liberalism. Sensing an urgent need for action, they forged study groups, multiplied chapters of national right-wing organizations, and worked within the Republican Party to make their voices heard. In so doing, they became the cutting edge of the conservative movement in the 1960s. But before we examine the movement these people built, it is necessary to understand the setting in which it grew: the region's history, political and cultural traditions, and its economic development. The characteristics of Orange County's development—its specific form of economic growth, the domination of its politics by an antiliberal and anti-eastern business elite, and the experiences of the people who settled there—created a favorable context for virulent right-wing beliefs.

✧✧✧

Orange County lies at the geographic center of the Southern California basin, bounded by Los Angeles County to the northwest, Riverside and San Bernardino to the northeast, San Diego County to the southeast, and the Pacific Ocean to the southwest. Approximately 800 square miles in size, about 575 square miles of which are inhabitable, it is a geographically diverse region. In its easternmost recesses to the north and south, beautiful mountains, rolling hills, and forests break the monotony of the thousands of acres of plains that made Orange County so well suited to farming. On its westernmost reaches, the sparkling waters and soft, sandy beaches of the Pacific Ocean beckon Orange Countians to enjoy its pleasures.

A migrant family from a small town or urban center in the Midwest or border South moving into one of the many new suburban tracts in 1960 would likely have been first struck by the county's lack of internally bounded towns and communities. Towns flowed together with little spatial distinction, intersected by a complex web of superhighways. It had not always been so. Only twenty years earlier, the county consisted of distinct small townships and cities, surrounded by ranches large and small. But spiraling growth led to a centrifugal form of development that lessened the importance of city centers and town units. Individuals and families may have resided in Garden Grove, Fullerton, Anaheim, Huntington Beach, or Costa Mesa, but, more important, they lived and increasingly worked in Orange County, a cohesive spatial unit with a self-definition distinct from neighboring Los Angeles.[4]

Despite its centrifugal growth, Orange County did have distinct geographic areas defined less by the twenty-two cities incorporated there by 1960 than by three differentiated regions.[5] In the northwest, the rapid growth of suburban tract housing in the 1950s and the commercial and industrial establishments that sprang up in their wake created unending miles of suburban sprawl. Here, cities such as Anaheim, Garden Grove, Buena Park, and Santa Ana provided affordable, albeit uninteresting, single-family homes for the middle classes. While this region was predominantly lower-middle- and middle-class, north Fullerton and east Tustin were home to some of the wealthiest enclaves within the county, and central and southern Santa Ana contained some of the county's poorest areas.

The coast made up the county's second distinct region. In contrast to the inland north, the central and south coast grew more slowly due to its distance from Los Angeles and its controlled development. The beaches of Orange County, extending forty miles from Seal Beach in the north to San Clemente in the south, had long been a favored retreat for weary Angelenos. Consequently, resort towns and beautiful homes dotted the Orange County coastline as early as the 1920s.[6] But a large portion of this land was owned by the Irvine Company and released for development only in the 1950s and 1960s.[7] Its setting, and the exclusive homes the company built on the land, made it a playground of the wealthy, who leased or bought the expensive properties of Newport Beach and Balboa Island, creating exclusive townships and some of the most valuable houses within the county.[8]

Agribusiness gave the southeast, the county's third region, a distinctive rural flavor throughout the 1960s. Suburban home construction proceeded slowly and, as in the coastal areas, only in a highly controlled fashion. This area was home to the 60,000-acre Cleveland National Forest and to vast working farms owned by a few modern-day land barons. In 1959, only ten landowners held more than 200,000 acres. The Irvine ranch alone covered almost one-fifth of the county.[9] These landowners slowly sold their land to developers or went into development themselves, transforming profitable working farms into huge development companies that created corporate visions of the American dream and packaged communities for the wealthy.

Like much of the West, Orange County's history was one of contest and conquest, of winners and losers, of boom and bust. In its early days, before the United States' conquest of California in 1848, the area's economy was dominated by a small number of cattle rancheros who had been given massive land grants under Spanish and Mexican rule. When California was admitted as a state in 1850, legislators eager to assert control over the region nullified all land titles and forced landowners to spend exorbitant sums of money to defend their property. Anglo-American entrepreneurs bought land at cheap rates from the ruined Mexican ranchers and quickly became the new ruling class of the southland.[10]

A host of other colonists, ranging from merchants to small farmers to religious utopians who bought up the property so avidly hawked by local real estate speculators joined the few large ranching families who dominated the economy.[11] Unified in their desire for local control over their new townships in the wake of the speculative boom of the 1880s, they broke away from neighboring Los Angeles in 1889.[12] The county experienced the boom-and-bust cycles the old West was famous for—with town maps filed for cities that have long since been forgotten. But Anaheim, Santa Ana, Orange, and Tustin thrived, and other towns, such as Buena Park, Fullerton, and Laguna Beach, plotted during the real estate boom of the 1880s, just managed to survive. By 1890, Orange County's population stood at 13,589.[13] While developers broke up the holdings in the western part of the county, the new American ranch owners in the east and south passed their holdings almost intact to their heirs. As a consequence, landholdings remained extremely concentrated.[14]

Agricultural crops had replaced the cattle industry as the driving force of the local economy in the 1870s and remained a basic source of income into the mid–twentieth century. Farmers produced sugar beets, truck crops, beans, and dairy, but no crop proved more important to the county's economy than citrus fruits.[15] By 1930, lemon and orange groves covered the soft hills, slopes, and plains of Orange County. Small, thriving commercial centers and townships, along with packinghouses and the cottages and shacks of Chinese, Japanese, and Mexican laborers, dotted the landscape. The slightly pungent scent of oranges permeated the air, and the balmy climate and small townships lent an idyllic atmosphere to the place. Although an oil boom in the 1920s brought in an important second industry, the county remained a prosperous, though sleepy, agricultural region. As late as 1940, only 113,760 people lived in the area.[16]

World War II transformed the American West and, with it, Orange County. A watershed in the region's development, it set in motion a chain of developments that would eventually turn Orange County into a sprawling metropolis.[17] Taking advantage of their strategic location on the Pacific Coast, local business- men, real estate speculators, and boosters who had long envi- sioned a bright future for the county sought to entice the U.S. Army, Navy, and Air Force to locate bases there. To encourage the military to settle in Orange County, the Santa Ana City Council obtained an option to lease a 412-acre berry ranch south of the city and offered to subcontract the property to the War Department for the symbolic sum of one dollar per year.[18] The War Department accepted the offer and built the United States Air Corps Replacement Training Center, later renamed the Santa Ana Army Air Base. Two years later, the navy added a Naval Ammunition Depot at nearby Seal Beach and, in 1942, the United States Naval Air Station moved from Long Beach to Los Alamitos.[19] El Toro became the home of the U.S. Marine Corps Air Station, an installation that remained important dur- ing the Cold War.[20]

The military was thoroughly entrenched by 1950, and the bases provided one of the county's main sources of income. Thousands of military personnel moved to the area, enticing some farmers, battling a destructive plant disease and facing stiff competition from Florida, to take advantage of the new demand for housing and development and subdivide their land.[21]

World War II foreshadowed other, even greater, changes for Orange County and the nation. Rising tensions with the Soviet Union meant that the development model that had spurred the economy during wartime could serve as a catalyst for growth, even in times of peace. The Cold War and its close relative, the military-industrial complex, shaped U.S. economic development in the postwar years.[22] New industries sprouted up to feed the voracious appetite of Uncle Sam for new weapons in a spiraling arms race. From 1950 to 1959, contracts by the Department of Defense amounted to the staggering sum of $228 billion nation- ally.[23] This was an increase of 246 percent over these ten years;

during the same period, the nation's business as a whole expanded by only 76 percent. By 1962, defense had become the nation's largest business, and from 1946 to 1965, 62 percent of the federal budget went to defense.[24] These huge expenditures catalyzed the "affluent society" and directly and indirectly affected the lives of every American.

While defense money drove national economic growth, the regions that profited most directly were the Sunbelt South and West, and the biggest beneficiary was Southern California. The federal funds that poured into California created the nation's largest urban military-industrial complex.[25] In 1953, California topped New York as the leading state in net value of military prime contracts awarded. Throughout the next decade, awards to the Golden State amounted to twice as much as the annual amount any other state received. These federal funds, plus the annual military and civilian payroll of the Department of Defense in California, funneled more than $50 billion in defense dollars into California for approximately the ten-year period from 1950 to 1960.[26] And no region received more funds than Southern California. With the exception of Santa Clara in the north, Los Angeles County, San Diego County, and Orange County received the lion's share of defense moneys.[27] As a result, whereas virtually no Orange Countians worked in defense-related industries in 1950, there were 31,000 workers on their payrolls twelve years later.[28]

World War II and subsequent defense spending transformed Los Angeles and Southern California into a new regional power.[29] Los Angeles, at the heart of the initial growth, received 61 percent of California defense outlays in 1959, making it a "world city" and a leading international industrial center.[30] It grew from a population of 1.5 million in 1940 to close to 2.5 million by 1960. The metropolitan region included more than 6 million inhabitants by 1960. The phenomenal growth of Los Angeles spilled over into sleepy Orange County, turning it into a sprawling suburban region.[31] Los Angeles's new bedroom community soon attracted its own manufacturing base (with defense leading the way), making Orange County the second most populous county in California by 1967.[32]

By the early 1960s, Orange County had become an important center for defense-related industries in its own right. Between 1957 and 1961, Hughes Aircraft moved into the county, employing 10,000 people; Autonetics made its home in Anaheim, adding 10,000 workers to its payroll; Ford Aeronutronics set up facilities in Newport, bringing 2,800 jobs. American Electronics came to Fullerton, generating 380 jobs; Beckman Instruments also chose Fullerton when it moved its headquarters into Orange County, employing 3,100 workers; and Nortronics settled in Anaheim, hiring 2,300 employees.[33] By 1960, more people worked in manufacturing than in any other sector. Orange County had become a "military-related suburb."[34] Electronics was the fastest-growing manufacturing industry, accounting for about 40 percent of all manufacturing employment in the county.[35] By 1964, of the thirteen manufacturing firms in Orange County employing 500 or more workers, nine were in the electronics-instruments-missile-aircraft classification.[36] The growth of these industries, as Spencer C. Olin has argued, was the result not only of the vast defense outlays but also of the availability of a pool of technical and scientific labor, low rates of unionization, and the existence of venture capital.[37] These factors drew the burgeoning new growth industries in defense and electronics not only to Orange County but also to other regions in the West and South. At the same time, the older northern industrial cities of the East and Midwest saw a decline in their manufacturing base.[38] The resulting demographic and economic changes would eventually help shift the balance of economic and political power in the nation increasingly southward and westward.

The military-industrial complex brought equally impressive employment gains in other sectors. Retail sales and service industries that provided the amenities, the fast food, the household furnishings, and the appliances for the growing suburban communities trailed closely behind manufacturing in providing jobs. The demand for housing and commercial buildings brought a frenzied construction boom, along with phenomenal profits for the building industry.[39] New lots and rising land prices brought with them a mushrooming real estate industry as property development became a vast business. Together with retail and services, these three sectors employed the majority of workers in the county, more than manufacturing itself.[40] The underpinning of the local economy, however, was the defense-related manufacturing sector.

The rapid growth and affluence of the region drew scores of entrepreneurs whose ventures, in turn, spurred new development. Walt Disney and his engineers, for example, decided to locate Disneyland in Orange County after scouring the country for the choicest location.[41] They counted on the region's pleasant climate and future growth to draw crowds and profits. The park, in turn, brought hotels, restaurants, and other service establishments to Anaheim.[42] By 1963, tourist expenditures counted for approximately 20 percent of retail sales in the county.[43] Professionals, small businessmen, doctors, and dentists, moreover, moved into the region to service the new suburban communities. Even ministers saw opportunities in Southern California, becoming religious entrepreneurs bent on preaching the word of God in the new promised land.

The Sunbelt economic boom brought new people into the area at a dizzying pace. While in 1940, 130,760 people made their homes in Orange County, by 1960, 703,925 people resided there—a growth of an astounding 385 percent. In individual cities, these gains ranged from 25 percent (Cypress) to an astronomical 18,000 percent (Garden Grove) in the decade after 1950. With growth rates three times the state average and eleven times the national average, Orange County ranked among the fastest-growing counties in the nation.[44] In the 1960s, the spiraling growth continued, though at a slower pace. By the decade's end, the population stood at close to 1.5 million.[45]

This growth was, in a very real sense, a modern-day version of the California gold rush—making Orange County the new frontier West of the second half of the twentieth century. Entrepreneurs found unending opportunities to try their hands and stake their capital, betting on the continued growth of the region. Their success and the resulting prosperity reaffirmed many Orange Countians' faith in the American dream. Notwithstanding that economic growth took place as a result of the largesse of Uncle Sam, for many this link was indirect, since they made their fortunes in private businesses, in construction, and as professionals serving the new communities. For others, particularly a segment of regional businessmen who experienced the link more directly, the presence of the federal government—and the bureaucracy, red tape, and control it brought with it—deepened their resentment against Washington regulators. But for everybody, the hundreds of individual success stories, the thousands of new businesses—ranging from medical and dental practices to new construction firms—reinforced an ethos of individualism that boded favorably for the Right.

By 1960, Orange County's economy and social structure had become remarkably complex. Rapid growth had deepened and magnified elements of social strain. Moreover, the community's very newness meant that its values and mores were, to some extent, up for grabs—to be determined in the cultural battles that would be fought in the decade to come. Yet these factors do not, in themselves, explain how the Right found a home, since many communities shared the region's experience of rapid growth, yet few witnessed a conservative mobilization of the strength and magnitude of that in Orange County during the 1960s. Rather, it was the convergence of a particular set of social, economic, and political forces within the region that contributed to the germination of a conservative culture.

The county's cultural traditions, its conservative regional elite, its mode of development, and the kinds of migrants who made their home there provided the ingredients from which the Right would create a movement. First, there were the "old-timers," the large ranchers and small farmers, merchants, shop owners, and middle-class townspeople who had embraced a strong individualism and strict moralism for many years. Added to this older conservatism were the southland's "cowboy capitalists," the new boom-time entrepreneurs who made their fortunes in the post–World War II era of affluence and spent their capital and their energy spreading the gospel of laissez-faire capitalism and an anti-Washington ethos. Together with ranchers-turned-property-developers, county boosters, and real estate speculators, they created a built world that affirmed the values of privacy, individualism, and property rights and weakened a sense of cohesive community, providing an opening for organizations, churches, and missionary zealots that could provide one. Into this setting came the homogeneous group of migrants who populated Orange County. Although they had not necessarily embraced right-wing politics before they came West, the environment of Orange County reinforced strands of social conservatism they had brought in their cultural baggage. Finally, the specific economic dynamics of the Cold War–related industries reinforced the connection between anticommunism and prosperity in the minds of both newcomers and old-time residents.

Taken together, these forces magnified conservative strands of political culture within the region, creating a fertile ground for right-wing growth. Once catalyzed, this fermentation developed a dynamic of its own. The conservative ethos of the county, for example, drew like-minded folk to settle there, making it more likely that large numbers of Orange Countians would hear the Right's message and heed its call. Still, it was only when a combination of local and national events in the early 1960s ignited this tinder that a conservative movement blossomed.

Staunch individualism, Protestant piety, and resentment against Washington "collectivists" had already made a deep impact on the political culture of the region in the first half of the twentieth century. The strict moralism of the overwhelmingly Protestant population led to prohibition ordinances long before the federal government took action against drinking in the 1920s. In Huntington Beach, large magazine advertisements promoted the city by boasting that "there are no saloons or drinking in Huntington Beach and the moral atmosphere is of the highest order."[46] In Orange County, the Women's Christian Temperance Union was, according to a local historian, "an important political institution."[47] Strict moral norms led not only to regulations against drinking but also to the enforcement of rules regarding public displays of sexual behavior. In nearby Long Beach in the 1920s, ordinances forbade "caresses, hugging, fondling, embracing . . . kissing or wrestling with any person or persons of the opposite sex in or upon or near any public park, avenue, street, court . . . or any other public place." Violators of this measure faced a $500 fine or up to six months in prison.[48]

Orange County's strict moralism reflected the influence of conservative Protestantism within the region. At the turn of the twentieth century, Southern California had already earned a reputation for its fundamentalist proclivities. By the 1920s, the region's numerous small Christian churches gave the impression, as one observer put it, that "Christianity ranked as the city's leading industry after real estate and motion pictures."[49] The region not only boasted many small conservative churches but also was home to some of the most important figures and developments in twentieth-century evangelicalism. For example, the region was the birthplace of the *Fundamentals*, the influential series of pamphlets published from 1910 through 1915 that has become the symbolic reference point for identifying the beginnings of the fundamentalist movement.[50] And during the 1920s, when the City of Angels became better known as a mecca for movie stars, it also spawned the Azusa Street Pentecostal revival, the founding moment for twentieth-century Pentecostalism.[51] The Los Angeles region also proved receptive to fundamentalist Reverend Bob Shuler's fire-and-damnation preaching against Jews, Catholics, and the teaching of evolution; in the 1920s his congregation numbered 42,000.[52] And Placentia, Orange County, was the home of the rancher Charles Fuller, whose born-again experience led him to build the Christian radio empire that would make him, in the 1940s, the nation's most well-known radio evangelist.[53] Further reflecting the influence of the region's conservative Christianity, the first four-year college in Orange County was the evangelical Southern California Bible College.[54]

Orange County proved hospitable not only to conservative religious evangelicalism but also to right-wing organizations such as the Ku Klux Klan. The first "klavern" in Anaheim, started by a local Baptist minister in a men's Bible class in 1923, mushroomed to the point that Klan supporters won local government positions in Anaheim, Fullerton, Brea, and La Habra.[55] While the Klan lost its influence in the late 1920s, the conservative Protestant political culture that had nourished it continued to shape the community.[56]

While historically evangelical Protestantism has not always brought with it political conservatism, in Orange County the two seemed to go hand in hand. Electoral politics reflected the conservative political beliefs of the county's farmers and middle-class citizens. Orange Countians had, for example, voted heavily Republican in the years prior to 1960.[57] In 1928, Herbert Hoover carried the county by a resounding four-to-one majority. But embittered by hard times during the Great Depression, many Orange Countians moved briefly to vote for the Democratic Party. For the first and last time in the county's history, voters supported a Democrat in the two presidential elections of 1932 and 1936.[58] But this move was temporary, and in 1940, Orange Countians once again voted heavily for the Republicans.[59]

The Great Depression also witnessed the emergence of a number of populist movements in Southern California: Technocracy, the Utopian Society, End Poverty in California (EPIC), Townsendism, and "Ham and Eggs." Conservative Orange Countians proved indifferent to plans like Upton Sinclair's EPIC, which, in their eyes, smacked of "socialism."[60] But schemes that combined odd forms of utopianism with conservative populism were greeted more favorably.[61] Nearby Long Beach was the home base of Dr. Townsend's Old Age Revolving Pension scheme; many lower- and middle-class Southern Californians were receptive to Townsend's populist notion of solving the national crisis by infusing money into the pockets of the nation's elders—a prospect that promised to solve the crisis by promoting consumption without massive government regulation of the economy. One in six San Diegans became members of Townsend Clubs.[62] And while a majority of Orange Countians came out against "Ham and Eggs" or the "Thirty Dollars Every Thursday" plan (a proposal for the state to pay life payment pensions), they did so only by a slim margin.[63]

While certain elements of these movements paralleled the mobilization in the 1960s—with their basis among white-collar workers, as well as newcomers, and their scapegoating tactics—they articulated ideas and politics quite removed from the right-wing mobilizations of the 1960s.[64] The mobilizations of the 1930s represented a populist politics of economic desperation. Because the decade brought economic ruin to so many citizens, it witnessed the "radicalization of the middle classes," according to scholar Mike Davis, and "bizarre political fermentations" arose.[65] In contrast, the growth of the Right in the 1960s was fueled by an economic boom, drew a younger and more affluent constituency, and articulated a radically different political message.

But while the 1960s Right disseminated a different message, it did draw on the ideological inheritances of an earlier anticollectivist conservatism. This "antisocialist" outlook brought James B. Utt to Capitol Hill in 1952. Utt, the son of a prominent rancher from Tustin, became Orange County's congressional representative, winning a joint Orange County and San Diego County seat by attacking his opponent—Lionel Van Deerlin—for "preaching the gospel of socialism in glowing terms." Utt rattled off a laundry list of denunciations, arguing that Van Deerlin stood "for many things which are socialistic pure and simple," including such programs as public housing, government ownership of the Tidelands, controlled agriculture, public ownership of power, and a "planned economy."[66] The district's electorate responded enthusiastically: Utt won by a two-to-one majority.[67]

The region's conservatism, as Utt's tirades suggested, had consisted not only of a staunch Protestant moralism but also of

libertarianism. The area's businessmen had railed against government planning, state socialism, and the Washington bureaucracy since the days of the New Deal. They had a strong influence on the political climate of the region.[68] The Southern
California business community, moreover, produced individuals
who made important contributions to the postwar libertarian
movement. Leonard Read, who in 1945 would organize the
Foundation for Economic Education, an institution devoted to
promulgating the message of "free market, private property, and
the moral principles which underlie these concepts," converted
to libertarianism during his tenure as the manager of the Los
Angeles Chamber of Commerce in the 1930s and 1940s.[69] Read
had been influenced by William C. Mullendore, who was then
vice president of the Southern California Edison Company and
a board member of Spiritual Mobilization (a conservative group
of Los Angeles businessmen and clergymen) and also, in 1959
and 1960, was one of twenty-five to thirty prominent businessmen invited by Robert Welch to organize the John Birch Society
on the Pacific Coast.[70] The Los Angeles Chamber of Commerce
set the tone of the Southern California business community and
proudly publicized its libertarian sentiments in its publication,
Southern California Business.[71]

The southland's large agricultural ranchers, as well as
urban industrial interests, contributed to the antistatist and anti-
regulatory impulses of the region's capitalists. Powerful industrial farmers feared the impingement of government regulations
on their large monopolistic marketing cooperatives, their labor
relations, and their land. Having successfully battled California
Grange proposals for limiting corporate farming and "economic
monopoly" through taxation, and having triumphed over the
unionization efforts of their pickers and packers during the
1930s, California farmers were wary of the regulatory capacity
of the state. The Associated Farmers of California and the California Farm Bureau, dominated by Southern California membership, allied with reactionary and conservative Republican
Party politicians and fostered a staunch conservative ethos.[72]

The reactionary disposition of many Southern California business leaders was driven, in no small part, by the state's vibrant progressive and radical movements in the 1930s and 1940s.[73] Business leaders in the interwar years established institutions to combat "subversive elements inimical to the ideals of our country." Organized as the Better American Federation, they kept tabs on all "identified communists" in the region, building massive lists of names, as well as "2,000,000 cards as a working research index . . . the largest and most complete aggregation of its kind in civilian hands."[74] For the Los Angeles area, the records included the names and occupations of more than 2,000 workers—from electricians and utility workers to gas workers and engineers—who had at one time been members of the Communist Party.[75] According to the Los Angeles Police Department, which made liberal use of the federation's records, they provided "information on Communism and allied activities which are invaluable to the Los Angeles Police Department and frequently furnish the background for necessary action." The federation's files also supplied requested information to the federal, state, and local governments.[76] In the 1950s, business leaders established the American Library of Information as an auxiliary to the Better American Federation, an anti-"subversive" organization that later housed the American Security Council.

While anticommunism was driven in part by the real growth of the Communist Party in California in the 1930s and 1940s, and while it transcended party divides, making it a Cold War consensus ideology, Southern Californians championed a right-wing variant. This variant was a broad rubric that encompassed not simply a rejection of a Soviet-style organization of society but also a rejection of "collectivism" in all its forms, including federal regulations, the welfare state, and liberal political culture. In Orange County, "anticommunism" often meant opposition to the United Nations, agricultural controls by the federal government, or any sort of planning. Anticommunism provided the symbolic glue that united conservatives with divergent priorities, concerns, and interests, bringing social and religious conservatives together with libertarians.

California anticommunism led to the establishment of the Joint Fact-Finding Committee on Un-American Activities.[77] First established by Jack B. Tenney, then a New Deal Democrat, California's investigative committees soon became a tool of attack by conservative Republicans against liberalism in the state.[78] Tenney, moreover, quickly moved into the conservative wing of the Republican Party and eventually became a virulent right-wing anti-Semite, running as the vice presidential candidate on the Christian Nationalist Crusade ticket in 1952.[79]

Anticommunist Red-baiting became a cloaked means of attacking unionists and the labor movement along with other progressive causes, such as civil rights and civil liberties, as well as a vehicle through which ambitious politicians launched their careers. Riding the tide of popular anticommunism, Orange Countian Richard Nixon, backed by a group of prominent southland businessmen, was ushered to Capitol Hill in his 1946 campaign against Jerry Voorhis by denouncing Voorhis for "toeing the communist party line."[80] Using the same tactics and again backed by the strong support of southland business, Nixon rode to the U.S. Senate in 1950 by smearing Helen Gahagan Douglas with his infamous "pink sheet," which listed her votes along with those of New York congressman Vito Marcantonio, the American Labor Party representative from New York.[81]

Allied with urban industrial and agribusiness interests, regional media boosted the region's libertarian proclivities. The media were indeed, at times, on the cutting ideological edge of the region's conservative politics. Raymond Hoiles's Santa Ana *Register* had provided the main source of daily news for most Orange Countians since the 1930s, railing against government schools and roads. To Hoiles, taxation was "robbery." The *Register* supplied Orange Countians with a heavy dose of its "freedom philosophy" in its editorial pages.[82] But Hoiles's paper gave voice not only to thoroughly libertarian views but also to a broader spectrum of right-wing opinions, and introduced its readers to conservative writers from around the nation. It was, moreover, part of a broader conservative press axis in the region. Just to the south, James Copley's *San Diego Union* adhered to staunch Republican lines, and in Los Angeles, the *Los Angeles Herald-Examiner* gave voice to vociferous Red-baiting. The *Los Angeles Times*, which had been a strong anti-union paper since the early twentieth century, adhered to its conservative positions until the 1960s, and even with its reformed centrism in the mid-1960s, it remained tightly linked to the Republican Party in its editorial pages.[83]

The anti-eastern bias of the southland's elites was infused with a western consciousness that had long been fostered by the region's deep dependence on the East Coast for capital. Even after the West's economy took off during and after World War II, ending this "colonial relationship" (and replacing it with a deepening dependency on federal funds to spur internal development), western regional consciousness remained strong. Western resentment against the East, however, shifted from attacks against private corporate capitalists to tirades against Washington bureaucratic fat cats. The region's newly powerful "cowboy capitalists" resented perceived eastern dominance and the power easterners purportedly wielded within Washington political circles. They railed against federal interference in the West, championed individual initiative, and sought to control western resources, even while eagerly contending for federal funds for internal development projects.[84] They battled to assert a political influence equal to their economic weight, and they chose as their vehicle the Republican Party.[85]

But while a broad segment of the southland's business community railed against Washington and resented federal interference, its growing economic power was a product of federal government largesse. Washington provided funds for infrastructure projects, such as irrigation systems and dams. It awarded defense contracts, built army installations, and granted FHA loans for new housing. Nowhere in the nation was the federal government more directly responsible for economic growth than in the building of the West. Although it seems paradoxical that a region so dependent on the federal government decried governmental influence, conservative westerners did not see this tension as problematic. The fact that their actions did not square with their beliefs did not take away from the fervor with which these beliefs were held.[86] Indeed, in the period after 1945, in Orange County as well as the West and Sunbelt more broadly, the very presence of the federal government often led to hostility against the bureaucracy and regulations that went along with federal money. Moreover, the government's role as the greatest landowner in the West, as well as its control of resources such as the Tidelands, army bases, and national forests in California and the West, led many westerners to perceive the government as an "intrusive presence."[87] This perception led to conflicts between regional entrepreneurs and the government and made the issue of federal control very real.[88] These conflicts deepened an already prevalent libertarian sentiment.

Conflicts over growth within the county further fostered libertarianism. Efforts by county government officials to direct planning ran into vociferous opposition by those who would be adversely affected by development: oilmen and small farmers in developing areas. When the county sought to pass a zoning measure in 1949, its efforts were attacked by the Western Oil and Gas Association, local oilmen, and the Orange County Farm Bureau, representing smaller and midsize ranchers who opposed designating areas within the county as residential.[89] While they lost their call for "no planning" at all, the county boosters, developers, and large ranchers who favored growth embraced a limited planning model of development.[90]

This model promised to create a supportive climate for business. Officials worked to "ensure that industry will continue to look favorably upon this community" by "preventing the encroachment of deterring factors . . . which may be questioned by our industries and cause them to seek locations elsewhere." Among the influences they felt would attract industries were "a sensible tax picture and a community climate, both political and civic, favorable to industry and its employees"—and the near

absence of unions.[91] In both words and deeds, county government was deeply concerned with maintaining the boom. County
Supervisor William J. Phillips remarked in 1961, for example,
that "the attitude of government exerts a commanding influence
on any business climate." Phillips especially stressed that Orange
County's 4,000 government employees represented one of the
lowest relative rates of public employment in the state of California and that the county's tax rate was low compared with those
of other metropolitan counties in the state.[92] Expressing his optimism, he asserted that "as the world is only now feeling the full
impact of communism, it is also just reaping the bonanza of reborn capitalism."[93]

If regional entrepreneurs celebrated the private over the public
and championed laissez-faire capitalism, the model of development they embraced mirrored these values. County officials
largely left the control of development in private hands. This
resulted in a built environment that reinforced privacy, individual property rights, home ownership, and isolation at the expense of public space and town centers that could have created
a sense of public and community responsibility. While many
communities throughout the United States embraced similar
models of development without becoming strongholds of the
Right, the built landscape is nonetheless the stuff of one's everyday environment, not only reflecting an ethos but also affecting
the consciousness of its inhabitants. This was even more the case
for women and men who had left friends, family, and old associations behind and consequently were more likely to be looking
to establish new community ties. The physical landscape, therefore, contributed to creating a hospitable terrain for the Right
by reinforcing a search for alternative forms of community. A
segment of its middle class found a sense of community in the
politics and social interaction proffered by local businessmen,
right-wing ideologues, and conservative church leaders. Thus,
one woman said of conservative activism that "it became . . . a
social thing."[94]

Much of the county followed the "planned sprawl" model of development.[95] This led to chaotic spatial arrangements, with one tract developed after another. Streets were bisected by new housing tracts, increasing a perception of discontinuity and chaos. This form of growth created what one may term "free-enterprise cities," with a strong emphasis on private development and growth and little regard for public and community spaces. By neglecting public space in favor of growth, such arrangements weakened the sense of community.[96] In fact, even the existing central spaces in the old downtowns were undermined in favor of convenience, privacy, and shopping malls. The most extreme result of this pro-growth attitude was the eventual demolition of the old downtown city center in Anaheim to make room for development.[97]

While development in the northwestern portion of the county followed the anarchy of the market, a second form of growth seems, at first glance, to be its antithesis. Along the south coast and in the southeast, development was undertaken by large property holders who responded to the sprawl, blight, and congestion of uncontrolled growth by building fully planned communities that would maintain order and green space. Yet these spatial arrangements also reinforced privacy, individualism, and private property rights—and again accentuated the need to search for alternative forms of community.[98] Although it sought to create more desirable and sustainable communities, this new form of development did not bring public accountability or collective approaches to growth. Controlled by private entrepreneurs, many of them former ranchers, these artificial communities were constituted by developers who had a free hand in constructing their own visions of "community," visions that emphasized individual privacy, private property, and public spaces defined by consumption.

In many ways, Orange County represented a developer's dream come true. Businessmen built their particular vision of an American middle-class utopia, and entire communities were shaped by the desires and profit considerations of developers. Among the extreme examples were walled communities, the first of which was built by developer Ross Cortese in 1960, aptly named the "Walled City of Rossmoor" and now known as Rossmoor City.[99] In 1961, Cortese opened a walled community in Seal Beach, specifically targeting adults aged fifty-two and older.[100] His final dream for an adult retirement community was fulfilled with the creation of Leisure World in Laguna Hills.[101] These were amenity-packed and fully planned guarded housing developments that included churches and clubs. Such designs reinforced the sense that one needed to protect oneself and, also, the sanctity of private property. These communities became increasingly popular during the 1960s, with one established at Newport, one at Balboa, and many more since then.

An even more extreme version of this form of development was the creation of an entire city by one developer. The vast tracts of land under individual ownership, an inheritance of the agribusiness history of the county, meant that large companies could direct such growth. Irvine, a city incorporated within the county in 1973, was entirely planned by one company. Starting out first by building houses on small coastal patches of land in the 1940s (with the land on which they were built leased rather than sold to homeowners), the Irvine Company moved into larger-scale development in the 1960s. Even when the city of Irvine was incorporated, development was maintained and directed by the Irvine Corporation, which had by then evolved from a multi-million-dollar farming operation into a huge real-estate corporation.[102] It was social engineering on a grand scale.

The Irvine Company reacted to the blight and congestion of the northwest by attempting to construct more sustainable communities. Working with architect William Pereira, company officials had created a "master plan" for development.[103] The plan was created in the venerable tradition of garden city principles, including notions of "balanced communities" to foster social heterogeneity. But under the auspices of the company, developments were sheared of the progressive aspects of the original master plan. While planners included greenbelts and community parks for the city, these, along with amenities such as tennis courts, clubhouses, and swimming pools, were packaged as consumer

products for the well-to-do. Housing developments were designed to maintain property values, and fat profits for the company.[104] Residents, for example, had to join homeowners' associations organized by Irvine executives. By paying the mandatory
assessment fees—and by following the rules and regulations—
they were entitled to use association property and to vote for
association officers.[105] The company maintained total control
over architectural standards. Convenience, privacy, and decen-
tralization were the keys to the master plan, with few central public spaces except those dominated by consumption activities.[106]
Irvine executives, with a good sense for business, consciously created solidly middle-class neighborhoods. They preferred to forgo
federal government subsidies that would have required them to
open their developments to poorer residents, and they did not
incorporate open-housing provisions into their master plan.[107]
Their desire to build high-priced homes helped to reinforce an
already existing social homogeneity in Orange County.[108]

The result of development along these lines, of both the corporate and the free-market models, was spatial isolation and an
absence of community, which, in a complicated way, helped to
reinforce a conservative ethos.[109] One Santa Ana resident, for
example, who in 1961 criticized the lack of neighborliness in
housing developments and called for "more community recre-
ational activity . . . where people can get to know one another,"
linked the depletion of community to government centralization.[110] He believed that the growing scale and scope of the federal government was "being born in a community that don't [sic]
care what happens to Joe Smith or Bill Jones who just happen
to live in the same block as us but we never had the time to be
neighborly." He called, as a result, for "getting government back
in the hands of the people."[111]

The peculiar form of mixed-market anarchy and corporate planning that shaped the built landscape also created an exceptional
degree of economic and racial homogeneity, which further contributed to a favorable setting for the Right. For if the spatial
and physical landscape reinforced privacy and lack of commu-

nity, the middle-class character of the population helped to assure that the people there could find common solutions to their grievances, solutions that spoke to their particular class and racial group interests. The lack of a large organized working class and the near absence of racial minorities made it likely that Orange County's political rainbow would consist of relatively few colors.[112] In 1960, 80 percent of the families in the county had annual incomes falling between $6,000 and $9,000.[113] The median family income was $7,219, about 27.5 percent more than the national median. Orange Countians were, in other words, a privileged group. Their annual median family income in 1963 was greater than that of all but four California counties and more than that of all the states except Alaska.[114] In this age of the middle class, Orange County had an exceedingly strong specimen of a middle class.

Hence the circumstances of most of these middle-class men and women were quite similar. Approximately seven out of ten Orange Countians, for example, owned their own homes in 1960. Home ownership, with its emphasis on "not in my backyard," or "NIMBY," politics, as Mike Davis has written, reinforced a stake in property rights and a conservative political ethos.[115] Orange County had a higher proportion of homeowners than the nation as a whole—and this high rate of home ownership contributed to a germinating conservative political culture.[116] The weekends spent remodeling, landscaping, and improving property, along with concerns over property taxation, all reinforced a conservative ethos.[117] Indeed, Walter Knott, the county's homegrown conservative, once explained the region's conservatism with reference to home ownership: "People come to Orange County and buy a home. They then have a little piece of America and begin to think a lot differently about their government."[118]

Orange County was also remarkably racially homogeneous, and the lack of diversity weakened Orange Countians' stake in government remedies to rectify inequality and racial discrimination. The approximately 60,000 nonwhites residing within the country's borders accounted for less than 10 percent of the population.[119] The most sizable nonwhite ethnic group consisted of Hispanics of Mexican ancestry, many of whom had lived in the area for a long time and worked as tenant farmers.[120] Until the mid–twentieth century, they attended segregated schools and lived in segregated communities.[121] For African-Americans, the situation was even more restrictive. There were only a minute number of blacks—3,171 in the entire county in 1960—or less than .5 percent of the population. Minorities were largely segregated in neighborhoods in south and central Santa Ana and in the southern portion of the county in the El Toro area and San Clemente.

The county's lack of racial diversity was hardly a historical accident. Restrictive housing covenants and institutional redlining made it extremely difficult for minorities to obtain housing and jobs. In 1954, Dr. Sammy Lee, a world-famous Korean-American athlete and two-time Olympic gold medal winner, was twice unable to purchase a home in Garden Grove, succeeding only after the international media condemned the incident.[122] Lieutenant Harold Bauduit of the U.S. air force, an African-American, faced a hostile group of more than fifty people at his new Garden Grove home after a fellow air force captain had sold it to him. His neighbors hastily organized a homeowners' association to "keep undesirable elements out of the community" and sought to raise money to purchase the home and to find one of "equal value" for the lieutenant elsewhere.[123] In a similar incident, Dr. Vincent A. Mark of Santa Ana filed suit in 1961 against the Santa Ana Board of Realtors and a private development corporation after they refused to sell him a home.[124] Another African-American, Joshua White, faced extreme difficulty in finding a job in the area. After he finally succeeded in landing employment through his church contacts, he met a wall of opposition in finding housing. When he finally rented an apartment, his windows were shot out shortly afterward.[125] An African-American woman, the first African-American schoolteacher in the Magnolia School District, was forced to quit one year later because she could not obtain housing.[126]

Racism, of course, was endemic to new suburbs throughout the country, many of which were ostensibly "liberal" in other ways, and thus does not in itself explain right-wing politics. Racial diversity, however, might have broadened the spectrum of politics within the county. As such, its lack fostered a favorable climate for right-wing politics. The configuration of Orange County politics was also affected by a different kind of homogeneity. Many of the county's citizens shared the experience of migrating. From 1950 to 1960, a full 85 percent of the population increase was due to in-migration. As a result, in 1960, only 39 percent of residents in Orange County had been born in California; the rest came from other parts of the nation.[127] Who came to Orange County, and the expectations and beliefs they brought with them, deeply influenced the texture of the region's politics in the 1960s.

Orange County in-migrants differed from their nineteenth-century California gold rush predecessors. First, they came not as single men but as families. The typical new Southern Californian was a member of a family of two adults and three school-age children.[128] It was on average a young group; in 1960, more than 25 percent of the population consisted of children under ten years old, with their mothers and fathers (adults between the ages of thirty and forty-four) making up another 25 percent.[129]

The new citizens of Orange County also differed from their nineteenth-century predecessors in that many came to the county with prior knowledge of the West Coast. Many had passed through the Southern California region on Pacific tours of duty during World War II or had been stationed there. Their exposure to the mild climate and the beauty of the region encouraged them to take up the job opportunities that became available in the postwar years.[130] Indeed, the war experience was no minor element in drawing people to the county; in 1960, half of all civilian male residents fourteen years of age or older were veterans, significantly higher than the figure for the nation as a whole.[131]

But the most important thing to understand about the new settlers in explaining the political ethos of the region was their premigration experience. Traditionally, migrants to Southern California were drawn from the "heartland" states of the country: the Midwest, the border states, and the near South. The values and religion they brought with them had a strong influence on the political culture of Southern California. Nearby Long Beach, in fact, became known in the postwar period as "Iowa's seaport."[132] While the region continued to attract migrants from these states during the postwar period, the picture was broadening. Of persons registering a motor vehicle in Orange County between January and April 1962, in-migrants came from numerous states in almost equal numbers, with Iowa, Indiana, Ohio, Illinois, Florida, Michigan, Kansas, New York, Pennsylvania, Texas, and Virginia all accounting for 9 to 13 percent of registrants.[133] The Midwest, the most important place of origin, contributed 35.5 percent. The states of the Northeast now accounted for 13.9 percent, with the western and southern states contributing 20.4 percent and 24.9 percent, respectively.[134] Looking at the birthplaces of California residents in 1960 reinforces the picture: Most residents from outside the West were born in the Midwest, followed by the southern states, and finally the East. While there is no simple correlation between the place where people spent their formative years and conservatism— after all, the Midwest was the heartland of progressive reform and a stronghold of American unionism—segments of the population in the Midwest, South, and West did harbor strong strains of Protestant individualism, unbending anticommunism, and hostility toward the presumed national dominance of eastern elites. This had fueled McCarthyism in the 1950s, and in the 1960s it enabled the Right to draw on an established and understood set of symbols, language, and targets. Along with their suitcases and packed cars, migrants brought the cultural baggage of their hometowns, helping to shape the political culture of Orange County. Certainly, a good many were heirs to conservative cultural beliefs. But migration also broadened the political spectrum in the county and even brought in some newcomers whose strong liberal beliefs and values resulted in a culture clash that informed the political battles of the 1960s.

At first, new migrants seemed to shift the political proclivities of the region's citizens toward the Democratic Party. In 1956, Orange County elected a Democrat to the state assembly for the first time since 1892.[135] Democratic registration, moreover, reached a high point in 1960 and topped Republican registration by a small percentage. In 1962, Orange County sent its first Democrat ever to the House. Enough Orange Countians voted Democratic to allow Congressman Richard T. Hanna to hold his seat for more than a decade.[136]

The correlation between increased Democratic registration and the peak of in-migration points to the political loyalties of migrants before they came to the county. The fact that Republicans soon regained their lead, and continued to win elections, supports the notion that the politics of many migrants changed after they settled in Orange County. It was, in an important sense, the experience of starting a new life—with social mobility, social and cultural upheaval, and the explanations proffered by conservative elites—that transformed migrants' politics, creating a new right-wing political formation.

Yet it is also important to note that previous Democratic loyalties were not necessarily liberal Democratic loyalties. Indeed, there is a good deal of evidence that many of the Democrats who came to Orange County embraced socially conservative values. The candidates they chose to elect in the 1960s, such as Congressman Richard T. Hanna or Assemblyman William Dannemeyer (who eventually moved into the Republican Party), were not liberal Democrats. Still, Democratic loyalties did point to a more positive vision of the role of the state in the economic realm than that proffered by Republicans. Nevertheless, many of these Democrats slowly but persistently were sheared of their prior attachments to New Deal statism and embraced conservatism, finding their values better articulated by the Republican Party.

✧✧✧

The men and women who moved to Orange County, Democrats and Republicans alike, encountered a set of existing social, cultural, and political institutions. Building on these networks, they expanded the scope and number of these institutions and added new ones. Life in Orange County had long revolved around work, family, and church; but there were also service clubs, meeting clubs, and informal networks that formed much of the sense of community that existed for the middle class. As in many towns and cities throughout the country, Orange County had its share of Elks, Kiwanis, Rotary, and "Ebel" clubs, as well as chambers of commerce and posts of the American Legion. Just as important to creating a sense of belonging were the informal networks that new residents forged in their neighborhoods and at their places of work. Attending informal neighborhood meetings and participating in bridge clubs were some of the ways people sought to create a sense of community for themselves, eased by their shared socioeconomic backgrounds.

But the cornerstone to developing a sense of community and the most important cultural contribution of the new migrants were the churches. In a region with many uprooted residents and few organic milieus, churches provided a strong sense of belonging and fellowship. They were places where one could find friends and establish roots. As a result, from 1950 to 1960, churches mushroomed throughout the county. Protestant denominations experienced the greatest growth, maintaining a long-standing dominance. Mainline Protestant churches flourished: Where there had been six Episcopal churches in 1950, by 1960 there were thirteen; where there had been eight Presbyterian churches, there were now fourteen. Congregational churches grew from three to six, Methodists gained seven new churches, and Lutheran churches more than quadrupled, to thirty-five churches in 1960.

Even more impressive than the growth of these mainline Protestant congregations was the growth of conservative Protestant churches. The conservative Baptist churches grew especially rapidly. There were six Baptist churches in the incorporated cities of Orange County in 1950; the number increased to fifty-seven by 1960. These churches played a leading role in spreading a fundamentalist Protestant message, preaching a strict mor- 🖉 alism and antiliberalism.[137] Twenty-six of the new Baptist churches were affiliated with the conservative Southern Baptist Convention, while only three listed themselves as members of the moderate American Baptist Convention. Many of the other Baptist churches were independent or conservative churches that favored local autonomy, individual salvation, and strict moralism, all of which boded well for a right-wing politics.

In addition to the Baptists, theologically conservative churches included other Pentecostal, evangelical, and fundamentalist sects. Orange County counted two Assembly of God congregations in 1950; by 1960, that number had risen to thirteen. The fundamentalist Church of the Nazarene grew from three to fourteen congregations. Clearly, conservative religious sects grew rapidly with in-migration, a trend that would continue through the next decades. Even mainline Protestant churches witnessed strong conservative growth within their ranks. For example, while the number of Lutheran churches reached thirty-five in 1960, fifteen of these belonged to the Missouri Synod, the theologically conservative segment of the Lutheran Church.[138]

Certainly, a belief in conservative Protestant doctrine did not make a right-wing political activist; many adherents to conservative Protestantism abstained from politics, seeking separation from a sinful world. Still, these adherents' normative conservatism, firm religious convictions, and moral values helped infuse a socially conservative political culture.

Why were so many Orange Countians attracted to these churches? Given that many in-migrants grew up in regions of the country where conservative Protestantism was strong, it is very likely that many of them grew up embracing conservative religious beliefs and were simply carrying them through to their new communities. But for some new migrants, the solid moorings and feeling of community these churches provided also renewed and deepened the attraction of these churches. They provided a familiar cultural setting in these very new communities. In a privatized, physically isolated landscape, among people who had only recently arrived in their new communities, conservative churches offered a sense of stability and a space for intensive social interaction. Their emphasis on personal salvation instead of social gospel probably appealed not only because it was familiar but also because it fit particularly well with the life circumstances of entrepreneurial and individualist Orange Countians.

Protestant religious institutions were not the only ones that experienced growth. While the Jewish community had been minuscule in Orange County in 1950, represented by only one synagogue, the growing strength of the Jewish community led to the building of Jewish community centers and institutions. In 1960, the Jewish community in Orange County was represented by one Conservative and one Reform congregation: Temple Beth Emet of Anaheim and Temple Beth Sholom of Santa Ana.[139] The increased, though still small, Jewish presence broadened the religious and cultural rainbow in Orange County and helped shape the political and cultural battles of the 1960s.

Migration also created a burst of growth in the number of Catholic parishes and schools in the region, turning the once-small Archdiocese of Los Angeles into a vast and important see. *The Official Catholic Directory* of 1951 listed 1,812 students in diocesan or parochial schools in Orange County; by 1960, that number had jumped to almost 10,000.[140] Presided over by Francis Cardinal McIntyre, the most right-wing member of the American Catholic hierarchy, the institutions of the Catholic Church contributed to the virulent anticommunist ethos.

Like-minded Orange Countians met through churches, clubs, and informal networks. More inclusive, however, were the schools—the one locale where residents of various political stripes came together. With young families moving into the region in large numbers, the Orange County school system grew rapidly during these years. Enrollment in 1960 was 200,000, an increase of 368 percent over a ten-year period.[141] By 1962, the school system had twenty-seven elementary school districts (encompassing 215 elementary schools), eight high school districts, and four unified school districts (with 12 junior high schools and 24 high schools).[142] As one of the few public spaces, schools were vibrant arenas of political contest during the 1960s. For many of those moving to Orange County, the disjuncture between what children were learning in schools and the values their parents had embraced at home led to deep concerns. This cultural clash led residents to be acutely aware of a growing liberalism and convinced them that the country was changing culturally and socially.

The combination of conservative political traditions deeply embedded in Orange County, the particular kind of economic boom the county experienced in the post–World War II years, and the heritage of many newcomers, along with their experiences in Southern California, provided a hospitable context for a surge of right-wing politics during the 1960s. Yet one more factor needs to be considered before we have a satisfactory explanation for the particular political trajectory of the county: the peculiar political climate that resulted from the fact that the Cold War was so close to the lives and livelihoods of many Orange Countians. The dependence of the economy on defense and the military deeply penetrated the consciousness of local elites, reinforcing the sense of connection between capitalism, prosperity, and anticommunism. According to Maurice H. Stans, former president of Western Bancorporation, "What happens in Southern California is so totally dependent on events on the national scene. . . . California trend lines cannot be foretold without considering the national backdrop of political, economic and military involvements." "It is assumed," he continued, "that the Cold War will continue without significant change, . . . that there will be no agreements on disarmament or on limitation of nuclear weapons, . . . that Castro will continue in power, with Communist economic support, and that any free-world gains in Vietnam or elsewhere will be countered by new Soviet or Chinese thrusts in other places." According to Maurice Stans, the future prosperity of the region depended on these conditions.[143]

More broadly, the centrality of the Cold War to the daily lives and livelihoods of so many Orange Countians heightened their consciousness of foreign policy matters and deeply affected the political culture in the region. In the West, the Cold War had a definite impact on people's psyches. Bombs and fallout shelters were, in 1961, of "prime interest," according to the Orange County Research Institute. The institute's eastern and midwestern surveys "indicate a much lower degree of concern . . . than here in the West. . . . Southern Californians, in particular, have a higher interest and concern in foreign affairs than in other sections of the country . . . due in part to our defense-oriented business climate."[144]

This pro-defense climate reinforced a discourse of anticommunism that was already present among the region's elites and a socially conservative grass roots. Linked with the anticommunism of conservative churches, this discourse created a fertile climate for right-wing growth.

✧✧✧

From its roots as a frontier community of Mexican and Anglo-American rancheros, Orange County had emerged in the postwar era to become one of the fastest-growing of American communities. For the hundreds of thousands of upper-, middle-, and lower-middle-class men and women who made it their home, it symbolized the American dream. Here was the heartland of suburban utopia with its ranch homes, tract housing, and two-car garages. Here also was the heartland of American technical know-how—home to the engineers, researchers, scientists, and skilled workers who provided the physical and mental labor driving America's Cold War economy. And here was the last bastion of the frontier, where individualism remained the ruling ethos of the day and where new entrepreneurs, from small businessmen to powerful cowboy capitalists, made their dreams come true. In some sense, Orange County was a true "frontier," although its growth was generated by federal government contracts rather than the East Coast financiers who had sponsored California's gold rush booms in the nineteenth century.

The underside of this American dream was a form of development that depleted bonds of community. The middle-class men and women who populated Orange County found meaning in a set of politics that affirmed the grounding of their lives in individual success and yet critiqued the social consequences of the market by calling for a return to "traditional" values, local control, strict morality, and strong authority. Hence, when Fred Schwarz's Christian Anti-Communism Crusade came to Orange County and when Robert Welch brought the John Birch Society to the West Coast, they encountered fertile terrain. This terrain sparked a grassroots social movement in the early 1960s—a movement that, after careening through a series of transformations through the decade, helped to reshape the political direction of the nation.

CHAPTER 2

"A SLEEPING GIANT IS AWAKENING":
RIGHT-WING MOBILIZATION, 1960–1963

IN La Palma Park Stadium in Anaheim, more than 7,000 Orange County young people gathered to attend a special session of Fred Schwarz's School of Anti-Communism. It was an early spring morning in 1961, and the students, many of them excused from regular classes by their school boards, listened to Schwarz and other national right-wing figures rail against communist subversion in the schools, the government, and the nation. The event had been planned for months by prominent local citizens with the help of such organizations as the Kiwanis Club, and it culminated a five-day Orange County School of Anti-Communism.[1] At the weeklong school, "educational" sessions detailed the Communist Party's "treasonous" networks in the United States, classified communist philosophy as "Godless materialism," linking it with a "faith" in progress and change, and outlined the networks in Washington that purportedly had contributed to Soviet gains since World War II. In a concluding session, participants were treated to a dinner banquet with the program theme "Design for Victory."[2] Attendance at the "school" surpassed its organizers' expectations. "The tremendous response" required them to hold "double sessions" and to send overflow crowds from the original site at the Disneyland Hotel to the Anaheim High School auditorium.[3] According to the *Register*, the school "brought the largest attendance ever reported in an effort of this type."[4]

"Youth Day" at the Orange County School of Anti-Communism. The school symbolized the new mobilization among Orange Countians toward a perceived threat of communism. Many local schools released their students to allow them to attend the session. (Reprinted by permission of the *Orange County Register.*)

Fred Schwarz's school was just one sign of the awakening in Orange County to the perceived dangers of "communism" in the early 1960s, an awakening that initially drew on the legacy of 1950s McCarthyism for its language, targets, and ideology. Before the school arrived, and even more so in its wake, local anticommunist initiatives flourished. These initiatives cloaked conservative concerns with American liberalism—fears of federal government centralization and apprehensions over the penetration of liberal ideas into the nation's schools, churches, and communities—under an overarching discourse of "communist subversion." Numerous organizations were formed to thwart the "Red menace," ranging from the Orange County Freedom Forum and the California Free Enterprise Association to the Californians' Committee to Combat Communism and the Citizens for Fundamental Education.[5] Orange Countians also swelled the ranks of the John Birch Society, opened numerous right-wing bookstores, and worked within their churches, schools, and communities to roll back liberal gains that, in their eyes, threatened the nation.

While this mobilization was small when compared with the vibrant national liberal movements, it had a significant regional base of support. In the South and West, resentment and suspicion of federal control and the federal government's perceived allegiance to eastern elites had long run deep.[6] Emboldened by the economic boom of the Cold War, which transformed the Sunbelt and West into the economic frontier of the second half of the twentieth century, regional business leaders, editors, and a large segment of its middle class now opposed "communistic" control based on a reborn entrepreneurial philosophy. While nearly all Sunbelt regions experienced a rise in conservative political activity, nowhere was it more powerfully felt than in Southern California, and especially in Orange County.[7] Orange County doctors, dentists, housewives, and engineers, in effect, gave birth in the early 1960s to a movement that would help shape the future of the American Right and, eventually, the political direction of the nation. It was here, in the mundane yet complex world of school battles, evangelical churches, and local politics, that the grassroots New Right asserted itself.

On June 24, 1960, the first spark of grassroots mobilization ignited when Joel Dvorman, an Anaheim resident and an elected school board trustee, held a meeting of the Orange County chapter of the American Civil Liberties Union (ACLU) in his backyard. The ACLU had earned the wrath of the Right in the past for its defense of liberals and nonconformists and now came under fire for its opposition to the activities of the state and federal investigating committees on un-American activities. The meeting Dvorman had called centered on a proposal to abolish the committees. Long a thorn in the side of progressive organizations, the committees were under increasing attack by a vocal group of Southern California liberals. Joel Dvorman had invited Frank Wilkinson, director of the Los Angeles–based Citizens Committee to Preserve American Freedoms (CCPAF) and a leader in the national effort to abolish the House Un-American Activities Committee (HUAC), to speak on the issue.[8] The response was swift and forceful: Angry neighbors denounced Dvorman for importing "communist ideas" into their suburban enclave. Heeding their neighbors' call, citizens whose lives had previously revolved around work, church, and family became involved in a contentious political battle.

Dvorman and Wilkinson personified what conservative Orange Countians feared most. Dvorman, New York–born, liberal, Jewish, and Yale educated, had worked as a college student with American Youth for Democracy, a progressive student organization. A young family man, Dvorman brought his liberalism with him to Anaheim in 1953.[9] He was an active Democrat and a strong supporter of civil liberties, serving as a membership chairman of the Orange County ACLU chapter.[10] Wilkinson, the speaker Dvorman had invited, had been even more prominently involved in progressive causes. Called before the California Senate Committee on Un-American Activities, he had refused to answer questions about Communist Party membership, leading to his dismissal from his position with the Los Angeles Housing Authority.[11] Wilkinson was a leading opponent of HUAC. Most recently, he had helped organize the San Francisco City Hall protests against the House Un-American Activities Committee in May 1960, which, according to one demonstrator, "was the start of the sixties for me."[12] In the wake of the protests, Wilkinson was prominently featured as one of a "handful of hardcore, trained communist agents" in a controversial film released by the committee.[13]

The politics of these two men and, above all, their hostility to HUAC provoked bitter opposition among many Orange Countians who considered the committees a sacred cow, their chief protection against "internal subversion" and an appreciated way of attacking liberal and progressive organizations. So widely had the California committee cast its net that in 1943 the ACLU, for example, had been declared a "communist front or transmission belt organization."[14] A few years later, the committee had agitated against sex education in public schools, accusing these programs of following "the Communist Party line for the destruction of the moral fiber of American youth."[15] While the committees had lost a good deal of prestige since their halcyon days in the early 1950s, their elaborately staged investigations into subversive activities continued. But the committees were increasingly vulnerable to attack, with a series of 1957 Supreme Court decisions that circumscribed the powers of congressional investigating committees and restricted the antisubversive activities of state agencies, providing liberals with powerful ammunition. With opposition against the committees gathering steam in the early 1960s, conservatives feared losing an authoritative ally in government and fought to save what they believed to be one of the last effective tools against "communist subversion."[16]

Meetings of the ACLU were not new to Anaheim, but the affront of an "identified communist," bent on abolishing HUAC, speaking in their community outraged a number of residents who heard about the meeting and decided to attend. James Wallace, a production supervisor at Autonetics, a local aerospace firm, was one of them. He learned of the meeting about an hour before it started: "Having heard many derogatory things about the ACLU, and being mildly curious about what an identified communist might have to say, I decided to attend. I was very upset to find this thing going on in our neighborhood."[17] Returning home, he wrote a letter to the editor of the *Register* in which he described the meeting, calling Wilkinson a "traitor" and issuing a call to action: "I wonder what we would have done in 1942 if Mr. Dvorman had a German-American Bund meeting at his home."[18]

Concerned Anaheim residents heeded Wallace's call. Aware that Dvorman was a school board trustee, they descended on school board meetings, demanding that Dvorman reveal whether he was or had "ever been a member of the Communist Party."[19] Declaring that his ACLU activities were incompatible with his service as a trustee, opponents requested that the school board censure Dvorman and put a halt to his political activities. Rebuffed by the board, they formed a committee for the recall of Dvorman from the school board.[20] R. Dickson Miles, an engineer at Nortronics, another local aerospace firm, became the leader of this group. Arguing that "Dvorman embraces opinions to which most loyal Americans are vigorously opposed," the group claimed that "it was the duty of all Americans to recognize the . . . threat to our heritage, to expose it and to combat it with every weapon at our command."[21] And fight they did—organizing meetings, petitions, and, on November 4, 1960, a "ladies auxiliary," whose purpose was to carry the recall petition block by block through the Magnolia School District.[22] One resident remembers answering her doorbell to find a person with petition in hand, informing her that a "comm-symp" was on the school board and requesting that she offer her signature.[23] Hundreds of letters poured in to the *Register*, explaining why Joel Dvorman was "guilty" and how this sort of vigilance was necessary to defend the nation against subversion.

Many of these activists had, until then, led quiet suburban family lives. This is not to say that they had not held strong anticommunist beliefs. But it was only during the 1960s that they saw the need to actively involve themselves in the struggle against "subversion," and they left a deep institutional impact. According to its founder, the first Anaheim chapter of the right-wing John Birch Society was born as a result of the Dvorman conflict and grew so rapidly that it eventually split into several chapters. Underlining his newfound activism, James Wallace asserted that his only earlier civic engagements were professional activities: "The only ultra-conservative radical right-wing reactionary organizations in which I held membership at that time were the National Management Association and Precision Measurements Association."[24] By the fall of 1960, a group of Orange Countians were thanking God and Robert Welch, the founder of the John Birch Society, for "awaken[ing] us out of our selfish apathy and indifference to what is happening in America."[25]

The sense of urgency concerning the "Red menace" snowballed in early 1961. In January, six months after Dvorman's ACLU meeting had galvanized a band of zealots, Orange County State College and Fullerton Evening Junior College sponsored a series of talks, "scheduled by popular demand," titled "Understanding the Goals and Techniques of World Communism." The talks supplemented "History of Communistic Aggression," an adult education course already offered by Santa Ana Junior College that drew an enrollment of 250, four times the expected number.[26] In March, civic and business leaders incorporated the Orange County Freedom Forum to "educate the people of our community to threats against our national security, threats against our nation's form of government, and threats against our nation's way of life."[27] But it was the promotion of the Orange County School of Anti-Communism, held some days later, that symbolized most clearly the new awareness and new networks among conservative suburbanites.[28]

The Orange County School of Anti-Communism was sponsored by a local committee made up of more than 100 prominent local citizens and headed by conservative Walter Knott, owner of a successful recreation park, Knott's Berry Farm. Meeting each Wednesday in space provided by Knott, citizens worked for several months, organizing more than eighteen subcommittees to ready their community for the "school," including a religious committee, a youth committee, a military committee, a veterans' committee, and a regional committee to head mobilization in each city in Orange County. Led by Dr. Fred Schwarz of the Christian Anti-Communism Crusade, the school brought in "faculty" from around the nation to warn of an imminent communist takeover.[29]

Schwarz, a lay pastor and former physician from Australia, had given up a medical career to devote himself to battling communism. In 1950, his skillful orations against communist philosophy as an enemy to Christianity, individualism, and class harmony earned him the attention of Carl McIntire, the leader of the right-wing fundamentalist American Council of Christian Churches, who invited him on a two-month lecture tour. Returning to the United States in 1953 and speaking at small Protestant churches throughout the country, Schwarz developed the idea of a mass Christian anticommunism crusade.[30] After settling in nearby Long Beach, California, Schwarz traveled extensively, spreading his message especially in the Southwest, where he was best known.[31] A gifted orator, he drew on his medical training in describing the "evils" of communism, comparing communism to a disease with many symptoms, a disease that would have to be studied, diagnosed, and treated.[32] Describing a monolithic force on a march toward world domination, Schwarz stressed both the external threat of communism and the susceptibility of modern American society to internal subversion.[33]

Schwarz was influential in shaping the agenda of the Orange County School of Anti-Communism. The organizing committee echoed Schwarz's most apocalyptic utterances, ominously noting "communist plans for a flag of the U.S.S.R. flying over every American city by 1973."[34] As William Brashears, a dentist, staunch Baptist, and general chairman of the organizing committee, put it, "What we are trying to do [is] to wake people up. . . . We must realize that we are at war NOW, and HERE, in Orange County." The war, he asserted, was a battle of "capitalism against communism," and communism, he warned direly, was winning.[35]

The School of Anti-Communism decisively shaped the future of right-wing politics in Orange County. It recruited new activists to the cause and linked them together in networks that remained active throughout the decade. More than one activist attributed the beginnings of the conservative mobilization in Orange County to "Dr. Schwarz and the Christian Anti-Communism

Crusade that came through Orange County."[36] Through the preparations for the "school," an optometrist who had recently moved to Orange County met the core group of people who would later help him build the California Republican Assembly, a mass-membership conservative organization that would play an important role in Barry Goldwater's 1964 presidential campaign. Another group in Huntington Beach founded Citizens Combating Communism. Members of the Anaheim Chamber of Commerce established an "Americanism Committee": "As leaders in the community," they argued, "we must lead the way in the fight to the death against the international conspiracy called communism."[37] Study groups sprouted up throughout the county, anticommunist films were shown in churches and halls, and conservative literature was shared. One local doctor from Garden Grove alone was reputed to have organized forty-four study groups.[38]

So rapid was the spread of right-wing activity during this period that, in any one week, an interested citizen might have chosen from two, and possibly three, showings of such films as *Communism on the Map* or *Operation Abolition*, a controversial film put together by the House Committee on Un-American Activities, which declared that students were "toying with treason" when they demonstrated in 1960 against the committee.[39] It is likely that other unadvertised "neighborhood showings" were offered in private homes, encouraged by the Orange County Freedom Forum, which lent out these films.[40] By 1962, Freedom Forum bookstores had been opened in Fullerton, Costa Mesa, Garden Grove, and Anaheim.[41] The stores, which stocked items ranging from books on "the menace of communism" and studies of "education and religion" to Bibles and American flags "in assorted sizes," served as a "kind of meeting place for conservatives."[42] One activist described the atmosphere quite vividly: "We would go to meetings and people would find out about it, and we would share it all. . . . Newsletters were copied and spread around, if you didn't have the money to order a newsletter from the Christian Anti-Communism Crusade or *Human Events* . . . that was a big thing that went around . . . people just shared all these things."[43] This stirring activism led one Costa Mesa conservative, Michael Owalube, to confidently proclaim, "Here . . . in [the county] of Orange, a sleeping giant is awakening. Men and women of all walks of life are pledging a fight to victory for God and America."[44]

✧✧✧

While the "sleeping giant" awoke in Orange County, the county was not alone in witnessing a revival of the Right. In the wake of Democratic victories at the national and state levels in the late 1950s and early 1960s, conservative activity quickened throughout the nation. The intellectual and national organizational foundation had already been laid in the 1950s, in effect constituting the first stage in the making of the conservative movement. Two new journals announced the birth of a conservative intellectual movement. William F. Buckley, Jr., began publishing *National Review* in 1955, to help usher in a "new era of conservatism." Russell Kirk followed in 1957 with the more scholarly quarterly *Modern Age*, to "forthrightly oppose . . . political collectivism, social decadence and effeminacy."[45] Following these journals' efforts to formulate a cohesive set of conservative ideas and policies, a spate of new national organizations translated ideas into politics. In 1958, conservative Republican Party politicians and business leaders created Americans for Constitutional Action, to help repeal "the socialistic laws now on our books."[46] A group of conservatives meeting in Indiana in December of the same year founded the John Birch Society, which by the early 1960s boasted 300 chapters in its "banner state" of California and an estimated membership of 60,000 throughout the nation.[47] Finally, in 1960, Buckley, together with a group of conservative students, founded Young Americans for Freedom (YAF) to provide a vehicle for conservative youth to work for "economic freedom," "states' rights," and "the destruction of international communism."[48] Older groups also grew by leaps and bounds. The Christian Anti-Communism Crusade, conceived in 1953, held its first weeklong "Anti-Communism Schools" in

Ronald Reagan was one of the speakers at the Southern California School of Anti-Communism held in the wake of the Orange County Schools in August and September 1961, with approximately 15,000 in attendance. (Courtesy of Department of Special Collections, Charles E. Young Research Library, UCLA.)

1958. On the upswing in the late 1950s and early 1960s, the crusade doubled its receipts each year. In 1961, sparked by its successes in places like Orange County, where sympathizers were able to back their support with money, the organization took in more than $1 million.[49]

The Southern California School of Anti-Communism "Design for Victory" banquet, with about 3,500 southlanders in attendance. (Courtesy of Department of Special Collections, Charles E. Young Research Library, UCLA.)

The size and scope of this conservative activity alarmed American liberals, who warned of the threat it posed to American democracy.[50] Arnold Forster and Benjamin Epstein, two leaders of the Anti-Defamation League of B'nai B'rith, alerted Americans to the "dangers on the right," and sociologist Daniel Bell warned that the right wing's commitment and its methods threatened to disrupt the "fragile consensus that underlies the American political system."[51] In 1963, spurred by the deepening right-wing organizing, a group of prominent liberal scholars published an updated collection of essays (originally written in the wake of McCarthyism) titled *The Radical Right*, which surveyed the revival and characterized its supporters as dangerous, paranoid, and status-anxious men and women.[52]

These liberal scholars were confident that this new wave of conservative mobilization was of fleeting importance, a necessary if painful adjustment of some Americans to the recast world of "modernity."[53] Because they misunderstood the motivations of right-wing activists, however, they failed to accurately predict the future of the movement. The right-wing revival was not an irrational, momentary outburst of psychologically maladjusted men and women, as liberals hoped and believed. Michael Owalube, and thousands like him, felt compelled to enlist in battle, rather, because of their sense of a widening chasm between the world of the New Deal liberal state and the values they found meaningful. Thoroughly modern in their ways of life and work, these people were threatened by social and cultural changes under way in the nation. The first years of the 1960s were, after all, a time of effervescent liberalism. While the student rebellions and antiwar protests that would so strongly mark the decade had yet to heat up, the staid consensus of the 1950s had given way to a climate of change boosted by the energy, dynamism, and youth of the Kennedy administration and a blossoming civil rights movement. It was a time when a deepening atmosphere for reform promised change on the horizon. It was a time, most of all, when the Right felt bereft of power and influence.

Ironically, given liberal fears of the increase in right-wing activity, the resurgence of grassroots mobilization on the Right was a result not of strength but of a lack of political power and influence within national politics, and even conservatives' chosen party. The political strength conservatives had enjoyed during the early 1950s in the national Republican Party, through their champions Senator Robert Taft of Ohio and Senator Joe

McCarthy of Wisconsin, had vanished by the mid-1950s. It was Dwight D. Eisenhower, not Robert Taft, who won the Republican Party primary battle of 1952. The death of Taft one year later, and McCarthy's censure in 1954, left conservatives without powerful spokesmen in Washington.[54] The moderates' triumph within the Republican Party was symbolically confirmed when the new president appointed Earl Warren to the Supreme Court, thereby opening the door for school desegregation and restrictions on the scope of state activity against "communist subversion."[55]

Not only was the Right marginalized within its own party, but the Republican Party itself was losing important elections to a reinvigorated Democratic Party. In the 1958 midterm elections, Democrats substantially increased their majorities in both houses of Congress. And in 1960, John F. Kennedy won the nation's highest office in a neck and neck race against Republican candidate Richard Nixon. Democratic victories on the national scene were mirrored on the state level. In California's 1958 gubernatorial campaign, liberal Democrat Edmund Brown defeated conservative William Knowland in a landslide vote. Democrats also won control of both houses of the California legislature for the first time in the twentieth century.[56] Vital center liberal, Adlai Stevenson, in his 1956 primary campaign, remarked on the new assertive spirit of youthful liberalism in California.[57] Even in Orange County, traditionally a stronghold of the GOP, a Democrat won an assembly seat in 1956 that had been Republican since 1892.[58] While, for liberals, the string of Democratic victories breathed new hope into the possibility of extending the liberal promise to all Americans through an expanded welfare state and civil rights, for conservatives, the Democratic resurgence heightened fears that the nation was on the road to "collectivism."

In conservatives' eyes, Eisenhower's middle-of-the-road Republicanism was disturbing enough, but liberal Democrats' even more optimistic embrace of the federal government to solve social and economic ills posed a dire threat to individual liberties. While capitalism and freedom were synonymous for both liberals and conservatives, the Right's vision of capitalism implied strict limits to government planning and little, if any, regulation of the economy. In its eyes, the welfare state was not a means of bolstering capitalism but was in itself "socialistic" and, in the words of one leading intellectual in the conservative movement, the "road to serfdom."[59] As James Townsend, who joined Orange County's Conservative Coordinating Council in 1961, put it, "We could see that they [the Democrats] were headed right toward socialism all the way. . . . [It] deeply disturbed us and we wanted to do something to reverse that trend."[60] Linking any expansion of federal responsibilities with "collectivism," "socialism," or "communism," conservatives sought to tap popular touchstones and appeal to the tradition of American anti-statism.[61] While Townsend vastly exaggerated the extent to which liberal Democrats wished to extend federal power, the president's circle of prominent liberal advisers and his espousal of the "New Frontier" implied change from the moderate Republicanism of Eisenhower and suggested a positive vision of the central state as a tool for redressing social and economic ills. Additionally, Kennedy's brand of newly assertive liberalism, with its internationalism and emphasis on individual rights and personal freedoms, represented a departure from the past and shook conservatives to the core.

It was not only Democratic victories and the ascendancy of moderates within the Republican Party that worried conservatives; equally troublesome was the penetration of liberal ideas into the nation's cultural, educational, and religious institutions. The liberal faith in the capacity of social engineering to create a more equitable and inclusive nation and liberals' championing of economic security threatened, in conservatives' eyes, traditional American values of competition, entrepreneurship, and individualism. Just as important, liberals' embrace of cultural pluralism and the marketplace of ideas denigrated adherence to "traditional morality," a belief in moral absolutes, and a God-centered vision of the nation. It was all the more disturbing, then, that even the National Council of Churches, representing all of the nation's mainline Protestant denominations, embraced liberal ideals, calling for federal action for racial justice and to resolve economic ills.[62] To add insult to injury, the nation's schools, backed by liberal foundations and government funds, experimented with new curricula and challenged "the status quo in every area of endeavor."[63] While the halcyon days of "progressive education" were long dead, schools in states like California had not returned to "traditional methods" with an emphasis on the "three R's," but instead introduced experimental curricula. To conservative parents, the abandonment of an emphasis on phonics, subject matter, and competition and the introduction of textbooks with liberal ideas represented a shift that undermined the religious and cultural values they held dear.

To conservatives, the liberal influence in the nation's schools, pulpits, and politics endangered what they perceived as the "traditional American way of life." As one staunch right-wing proponent in Anaheim put it,

> Customs, traditions and mores have too often been considered obsolete, old fashioned, and hence, discarded or minimized by a powerful faction of sincere but misguided Americans who have attempted to indoctrinate the American public through every possible media of communications and weapons of propaganda . . . to the benefits of change and "modernism". . . without . . . an appreciation and understanding of the basic foundations of our country.[64]

Inheriting the language of McCarthyism, conservatives identified these values with communist internal subversion. One local conservative thus ominously remarked that "the American People have been inflicted with the plague of communism. It has spread through our school system, our social groups and political offices."[65]

The Right's obsession with communism and its concern with liberal "subversion" were also closely linked to the unfolding Cold War. Conservatives had blamed American liberals for the spread of communism since World War II, and these fears gained urgency as socialism triumphed only ninety miles from

U.S. shores with the successful Cuban revolution of 1959.[66] Third World liberation struggles and anticolonial revolutionaries, such as those in Vietnam and Laos, moreover, looked toward the Soviet Union for support and guidance. When this rapid spread of socialism coincided with serious foreign policy debacles under the Kennedy administration, preeminently the Bay of Pigs invasion in April 1961, conservatives felt vindicated in their belief in the bankruptcy of liberal foreign policy efforts. To them, America was adrift. With the ascendancy of liberals in the nation in general, and in California in particular, the future seemed bleak. Some on the Right felt so threatened by these developments that they suspected that a sinister plot was under way to undermine the American nation and American freedoms. As Rufus Pearce, a Fullerton aerospace engineer, observed nearly forty years later, "All those things really indicated to us that there was something rotten in the U.S. government."[67] Seeking to reverse the international, national, and local "collectivist" gains, Orange County citizens, along with Americans across the Sunbelt and across the nation, embraced political mobilization. Their sense of urgency and passion can be compared only to that of the New Left students, who began to organize at the same time.

Conservative businessmen, politicians, and intellectuals were the first to act. Perceiving their weakness within the halls of power in Washington, as well as in the Republican Party, they saw the need for new strategies to make their influence felt. Some sought to effect a revolution of ideas, and the burgeoning number of conservative books and journals testify to their efforts.[68] Others turned to grassroots organizing in an effort to educate and mobilize the population. They were hopeful that their initiatives would be welcomed by those Americans who shared their concern with the rising tide of liberalism and were willing to "do something" to shift the political direction of the nation.[69] They offered discontented citizens right-wing organizations, such as the John Birch Society, as a means of articulating their politics; in so doing, they helped give grassroots antiliberal and anticommunist sentiment direction and molded it into a broader right-wing ideology. Grassroots politics in the 1960s did not develop in isolation.

In the rising Sunbelt, and in Orange County in particular, these wielders of movement resources encountered a receptive group of men and women who were alert for their clarion call. Housewives, doctors, dentists, engineers, and ministers in Orange County heeded the message and forged a vibrant, zealous mobilization, built on the networks and fabric of their daily lives. In the process, they created their own movement culture. While the scope and scale of this mobilization were obscured, particularly in the second half of the decade, by the far more visible, powerful, and flamboyant liberal and Left movements, these conservatives' ideas, politics, institutions, and networks provided the scaffolding for the future house of the American Right. Their movement, emerging out of the world of the new affluent suburbs and the complicated intersections between local school battles, culture wars, and national and international politics, set out to remake the world.

But to win the war, many battles had to be fought. In Orange County, right-wing activists employed the organizations and networks that had sprung up in the wake of Dvorman's ACLU meeting to influence the county's school board. They flexed their muscles first in the Magnolia School District when they succeeded in recalling Joel Dvorman and two of his fellow liberal school board trustees and replacing them with three archconservatives in April 1961. Rallying conservatives, activists reaped rewards when residents turning out at the polls voted more than three to one in favor of the recall.[70] The removal of Dvorman owed most to the grassroots men and women who rallied against him, but the support from prominent individuals and city officials bolstered their efforts. Congressman James B. Utt, of the Thirty-fifth District in Orange County, came out with a strong attack on the ACLU and argued that "such activities have no place in our school system, and every effort should be made to purge our school boards and our teaching personnel of the element."[71] Costa Mesa's school board refused the ACLU the use of its facilities for meetings, and the county superintendent of schools rebuffed the ACLU's efforts to block the recall.[72] Lawsuits filed by the ACLU, which argued that it was not a subversive organization and therefore the recall was based on false information, failed to convince an Orange County Superior Court judge to halt the election.[73] Never before had a public official been recalled from office because of membership in the ACLU.[74]

The successful removal of Joel Dvorman as a school board trustee and the heightened anticommunist atmosphere spurred other school boards to prove themselves on the "right" side of the political spectrum. In April 1961, the elementary school district in Garden Grove, a rapidly expanding community of close to 90,000 residents adjacent to Anaheim, issued a special flyer stressing that "love of country counts high among the district's points of emphasis. . . . All classes in all twenty-seven schools start each day with the pledge of allegiance." The flyer further noted that "Americanism in district schools is based on a firm official basis [and] any type of propaganda in conflict with county, state and national laws is prohibited."[75] Dr. Doss, assistant superintendent of educational services, pointed out that "kindergartners start by singing the Star-Spangled Banner, or some other patriotic song. Eighth graders must pass a test on the U.S. constitution, first graders study the importance of the family in the American scheme of things, sixth graders learn the relation of their country to its neighbors in this hemisphere, and fourth graders concentrate on their California heritage."[76]

While, in the wake of the recall, other boards sought to publicly affirm their "Americanism," the most serious consequences were felt in the Magnolia School District, where Dvorman had been a trustee. In April 1961, the district's voters elected a new majority school board, whose right-wing proclivities were matched only by the ideological zeal with which it sought to implement them. Over the next three years, the board introduced a new "American heritage program," an eight-point curriculum to "promote a deep devotion to the American Way of Life," and replaced the first-grade reading instruction with a program centered on phonics, a traditional reading method that many schools had abandoned. More radically, the school district sent home monthly bulletins with its more than 6,400 pupils that meshed fundamentalist religion and a hostility toward modern experimentalism with a call for conservative renewal.[77] Typical of these public school bulletins was the controversial December 1963 essay "The Meaning of Christmas," which, critics charged, undermined the legal separation of church and state:

> The world is in a state of confusion, turmoil and crisis upon crisis. It is a divided battleground between two ideologies striving to capture the mind, the heart and the very soul of mankind. Country after country have disappeared behind the iron curtain and these unfortunate people have been engulfed . . . by a political philosophy that is atheistic and denies the existence of a divine being. . . . There is ONE . . . ETERNAL TRUTH defying the power of man to pervert or time to diminish its message. "For unto you is born this day in the city of David a Savior, which is Christ the Lord."[78]

To implement its educational politics, which emphasized the "*duty*, the *responsibility*, and the *privilege* of the public schools to teach our children . . . to just plain love their country," a country, it asserted, that "was, is and *must always be* a God-centered nation," the board required that new teachers supply information about all past political affiliations. The superintendent also laid down a district policy that declared the United Nations a topic not fit for class discussion. Opponents were informed that if they disagreed with the district's educational philosophy, they should go elsewhere.[79] These unconstitutional actions and authoritarian tactics led to the eventual resignation of seven of the district's eight principals and a threat by the district's teachers to follow suit.[80]

When the board eventually drew the entire professional staff of the schools into a battle that promised chaos for the education of the district's children, however, it went too far, even in conservative Orange County. With the upheaval in the schools reaching crisis proportions, a tiny group of five liberal parents who had been fighting the board initiatives saw their opportunity. After a three-year struggle, including one earlier effort to recall the board, this group of parents finally convinced a sufficient number of voters to remove the board.[81] The highly combative conservatism of board members had proved so disruptive that it finally led to their dismissal in 1964.

The school board struggle was but one example of the grassroots battles that a small but burgeoning conservative movement launched in the early 1960s. Defeated at the national electoral level and marginalized within the Republican Party, conservatives could make their impact felt at the grassroots level. They often chose schools as a focus because they wished to inculcate in their children the religious and social values they held dear. Conservative parents expressed dismay when they encountered liberal influences in their children's schooling. One conservative, Charles Heath, was "shocked to encounter displays of the United Nations in school hallways."[82] In Fullerton, a group of 400 parents, led by William Dannemeyer, a future Christian Right congressman, expressed outrage over "sex knowledge inventory tests" given to children in health education classes in the local high school.[83] Parents in Westminster High School expressed similar dismay over the tests.[84] And at Fullerton Junior College, a student paper came under attack as subversive.[85] In California, where Max Rafferty, conservative state superintendent of public instruction, slammed away repeatedly at what he claimed was the continued influence of "progressive education" in the schools (a euphemism for liberal methods), the lines of battle were drawn. Teachers and the liberal-dominated State Board of Education clashed with Rafferty and conservative parents over their children's schooling. Because many parents had moved from places that had more conservative educational philosophies, their sense of concern was heightened. As one outraged conservative put it, "We haven't been in California quite two years and I have been fighting for good education during that time. This California system hit us like a slap in the face. . . .

Our child in kindergarten was taught evolution. Her religion was ridiculed and her confidence in her parents was shaken."[86] These men and women were bound to clash with liberal teachers and trustees like Dvorman who, they feared, were in a position to "subtly impose his beliefs upon the students through selection of textbooks, establishment of curriculum, [and] selection of teachers."[87]

To many conservatives, education was extremely important; it was therefore not surprising that it was in school struggles that some activists got their start in politics. For example, Nolan Frizzelle, a prominent local conservative, was politicized in a Pasadena struggle against progressive educational policies before coming to Orange County.[88] After thirty years of activism on the Right, he recalled that it was then that "politics began."[89]

By 1961, concerned Orange County citizens, initiated to movement politics, cast around for allies in their struggle for the control of schools and the broader struggle against liberalism. Their search for allies created an opening for organizations to channel the "awakening." Most prominent among these was the John Birch Society. John Birch Society members, in turn, encouraged by Robert Welch's command to "take over the PTA," broadened and deepened right-wing agitation in Orange County schools and the community.[90]

The John Birch Society had its roots in the national right-wing revival of the late 1950s. Candy manufacturer Robert Welch, a man long active in Massachusetts Republican Party politics and in the leadership of the National Association of Manufacturers, founded the organization in December 1958.[91] Disillusioned with the moderate leadership of the Republican Party, Welch saw the need to build an organization to thwart the growth of socialism and communism—which, in his eyes, included all aspects of the welfare state, whose progress, he claimed, was rooted in an internal communist conspiracy.[92]

Gathering a group of twelve prominent businessmen from around the country to found a new organization, Welch outlined its form and purpose. He sought to develop a national mass-membership organization of dedicated anticommunist patriots who would work to shift the political direction of the nation. Choosing the name John Birch Society, after a Baptist missionary killed by Chinese communists, Welch linked the society centrally to Cold War events, a link that would inform the organization's activities throughout the decade. To wage a successful war against domestic and international "communism," Welch organized the society with all lines of authority descending from himself. Drawing on his experience in business and salesmanship, he modeled the society on a corporate structure with little room for internal democratic decision making. Believing the Communist Party to be highly successful, moreover, Welch self-consciously adopted many of its tactics, such as secret membership and the use of front organizations, to achieve his goals.

The organization attracted men of substantial means from around the country to its leadership ranks, particularly owners of midsize industrial firms from the Midwest and South: William Grede of the Grede Foundries from Milwaukee, Wisconsin; Fred Koch of Koch Engineering and the Koch Oil Corporation from Wichita, Kansas; and A. G. Heinshohn, president of Cherokee Mills Manufacturing Corporation in Tennessee were prominent among them. While the John Birch Society never exceeded 80,000 to 100,000 members (its exact membership was always kept secret), at its height it rivaled the peak membership strength of the Communist Party, U.S.A. during the Popular Front period.[93] Moreover, like the Communist Party, the John Birch Society flourished in supportive ideological waters of "fellow travelers." Most congenial to its growth were the regions of Southern California, Texas, Arizona, and Tennessee.[94] In 1961, Welch stated that the society was growing fastest in the Southwest, contrasting the situation to his home state of Massachusetts, where it encountered much less favorable terrain.[95]

No one initiative gained such notoriety or was more important in channeling grassroots fears of liberalism than the

John Birch Society, whose resources and inspiration were crucial for right-wing mobilization. Although derided by liberals and the national media, it gained strength as one of the few conservative organizations concerned with developing a mass base and as one of the few groups actively "fighting communism."[96] Testifying to its favorable image among conservatives, a Mr. Kilgore, of the city of Orange, though not a member, viewed the organization as a "dedicated and apparently very effective anti-communist organization."[97] While some conservatives, such as William F. Buckley, Jr., were disturbed by Welch's conspiracy theories, even these critics, at least in the society's early years, carefully distinguished the membership—"some of the solidest conservatives in the country," according to *National Review* writer Frank Meyer—from the society's leader.[98]

The John Birch Society, oriented toward educating citizens to its brand of virulent anticommunism, was perfectly suited to mobilize middle-class suburban neighborhoods like those in Orange County. Concerned men and women, in turn, were attracted to the society because it enabled them to meet in their own homes and neighborhoods with like-minded people and to feel they were doing something to "fight communism." One conservative, an aerospace engineer from Fullerton and a devoted reader of *Human Events*, a national organ of libertarian journalism, had been dissatisfied with the trend of national events for some time. Learning about the society from a colleague at work, he attended a meeting in Santa Ana. Persuaded by what he saw as the organization's commitment to action, he soon founded the first chapter in Fullerton.[99] Another conservative, also a defense worker, planned to "organize a chapter in my neighborhood," since he believed the society to be "the kind of dynamic action group needed to effectively fight the conspiracy."[100] As a result of such activities, the John Birch Society spread rapidly in California, and in Orange County in particular.[101] In 1961, Pat Hitt, a moderate Republican and a member of the Republican National Committee, noted that the organization was "growing by leaps and bounds" in Orange County and the entire Southern California area: "I have been alarmed to find out how strong the John Birch Society has become, with clubs springing up like spring grass all over the county."[102] By the end of 1962, there were more than eight chapters in Santa Ana, five in Anaheim, five in Costa Mesa, three in Garden Grove, and five in Newport Beach.[103] In all of Orange County, thirty-eight chapters of the John Birch Society flourished, with an estimated membership of more than 800.[104] Three years later, membership had mushroomed, reaching, by some estimates, 5,000. This was an extraordinary number for an organization that, after all, was derided not only by liberals but also by moderates within the Republican Party and even by some conservatives.[105]

Building the John Birch Society was in some ways like building the Communist Party, testifying to the willingness of 1960s conservatives to appropriate the movement strategies of the Left. Members established individual chapters of the John Birch Society, aided by section leaders and paid field coordinators who operated at the local level.[106] When a chapter, or "cell," reached a maximum of twenty members, it would split in two so that meetings could still be held in members' homes as directed by the home office. Information about meetings often traveled by word of mouth. One La Habra resident heard about John Birch Society meetings from neighbors down the street. After she attended some meetings, however, she concluded that the society was not for her. Although she considered herself a staunch conservative, it was "too controversial."[107] Another resident of Garden Grove, a young Democrat from Ohio, had a different reaction. She described how she was recruited by her in-laws: After giving her some books to read, her mother-in-law asked her to attend a meeting. Although she did so apprehensively—"I thought they were going to be Nazis or something"—some weeks later, she and her husband decided to join.[108] Most members in Southern California, affirming a study of the John Birch Society conducted in 1968, were, indeed, recruited by friends and relatives. The remaining individuals were introduced to the society through the news media attention the organization received, as well as through John Birch Society programs.[109]

Meetings sometimes opened with an educational film or a speaker. At one large gathering in Newport Beach, for example, more than 100 Orange County residents met at the home of a wealthy member to hear a Catholic priest who had been a missionary in China.[110] After a short film or lecture, the chapter leader would try to keep the discussion focused on the agenda items set by the society; this was sometimes a difficult task, given the variety of conservative concerns.[111] Among the agenda items were, for example, strategies for impeaching Earl Warren, getting the United States out of the United Nations, and, in 1963, supporting the local police.[112] Members conducted letter-writing campaigns, showed films, and passed out recruiting literature. Their activity within the John Birch Society often led them into other arenas of political activity within their communities and eventually into Republican Party politics.[113]

The deepening support for the Right in Orange County was visible not just in the blossoming of John Birch Society chapters but also in a statewide measure "to secure California against subversion," launched by a group of California politicians and businessmen in 1962. Orange Countians D. W. Kirkpatrick and E. D. Whittier, along with a group of prominent conservative Republican politicians from around the state, organized the Californians' Committee to Combat Communism, a group headquartered in Orange County that spearheaded the initiative.[114] The Francis amendment, a proposal to amend the California Constitution, which became Proposition 24 on the November ballot, denied political party status to the Communist Party and undefined "subversive organizations," prohibited "advocates of subversive doctrines" from holding public office or public employment, and required teachers and employees of public institutions to answer congressional and legislative committee inquiries concerning communist affiliation and subversion.[115]

Critics charged that the amendment was dangerously vague and opened the way to the prosecution of any number of organizations as "un-American" by empowering county grand juries or judicial officers to designate subversives.[116] In Orange County, the ACLU had been successfully tagged with such a label, and it was not unlikely that it and other liberal organizations would be deemed subversive under the amendment. The *New York Times* called Proposition 24 a "grotesque proposal" and a "gross violation of the Federal constitution," arguing that it was "really a disguised instrument for the destruction of liberal nonconformist organizations."[117] Even the *Los Angeles Times*, which had recently undergone a change of guard that moved its editorial stance from hard-line conservatism to a more moderate Republicanism, came out in opposition to it. Labor unions, educational organizations, and diverse politicians from Edmund (Pat) Brown to Richard Nixon, both running for governor at this time, opposed the measure. Nixon made clear his support, however, "for a more effective program to combat communism in California"; yet he feared that "this important piece of legislation" would be tied up in court by "communist tactics" because of its "fatal constitutional flaw."[118]

Despite its patently unconstitutional nature, the proposed amendment received a good deal of support in Orange County and throughout the state. While a large number of statewide organizations opposed the measure, the California division of the American Legion and the Los Angeles Chamber of Commerce, along with the Associated Chambers of Commerce of Orange County, came out in its support.[119] The organizers received well over the number of signatures required for the November ballot. Indeed, if it had been up to Orange County, the Francis amendment would have become part of the California Constitution. For while the amendment went down to overwhelming defeat statewide by a margin of more than three to two (2,928,350 to 1,978,520), more than half the voters in Orange County registered their approval (130,305 to 123,007).[120]

The defeat of such a constitutionally flawed measure was not surprising, but the extent of support it received points to the strong current of conservative sentiment at the grass roots. The strength of this sentiment was made more obvious as the measure itself was qualified for the ballot not by professionals working with a large budget but, according to proposition organizers, by "fifty to sixty thousand volunteer workers."[121] The chairman of the Californians' Committee to Combat Communism called the qualification "the greatest grass-roots success story in the history of this state."[122] While this was an exaggeration, there was a good deal of footwork among anticommunist cadres to get the measure qualified for the ballot. In Orange County, petitions were widely distributed.[123] Right-wing businessmen helped the effort along by financing the publication and free distribution of the *Liberty Bell*, a magazine devoted solely to the Francis amendment; campaign organizers planned to distribute, free of charge, 50,000 copies in Orange County alone.[124] The mobilization for the Francis amendment demonstrated that virulent anticommunist and conservative ideas, while not dominant, had a broad base of active support in the population of suburban Orange County. The conservative movement there was, as local activist Ronald Rankin called his newsletter, truly *Grass Roots*.[125]

Who were these men and women who answered the call to action? After all, while the right-wing mobilization of the early 1960s drew a large number of Orange Countians into its orbit, most citizens of the region did not join the ranks. Although many more may have agreed with the message, they were not sufficiently aroused to step into public view. Furthermore, many Orange Countians directly opposed the Right. While the Francis amendment received a majority of the popular vote, nearly half of Orange Countians voted against it. Moreover, whereas Orange County sent staunch conservative James B. Utt to Congress for twenty years, it also elected Congressman Richard T. Hanna, an anticommunist Democrat who embraced welfare state programs. What, then, set apart those individuals who became active in the movement? A look at the biographies of a few activists helps us understand who joined the Orange County Right.

✧✧✧

When Bee Gathright, a Brownie leader and mother of three young girls, held a meeting at a local public school in the early 1960s so that members of her community might hear a man from Knott's Berry Farm talk about liberalism and conservatism, it was her first step on a road of grassroots activism that would shape her life and politics in the years to come. Only shortly earlier, a neighbor had asked Gathright if she would allow her patio to be used to hold a meeting led by this same speaker. Gathright agreed, and the meeting proved to her a revelation. As she put it more than thirty years later, "This is when I discovered that I was a conservative."[126] Over the following months, Gathright pored through the local newspapers and read books, "because I began to hear that [the communists] were going to bury us and . . . were going to take over the world. . . . I was afraid."[127] She soon attended study groups and eventually joined a conservative Republican volunteer organization to help bring conservative candidates into office. After working for rock-hard conservative Joe Shell in the Republican primary gubernatorial campaign against Richard Nixon in 1962, she then put her heart and soul into Goldwater's presidential campaign in 1964, establishing her Garden Grove home as a neighborhood Goldwater headquarters. Her husband was at first skeptical of her newfound activism, thinking she had "gotten into the extremist [element]," but he soon joined the fray. He even turned himself into a movement leader, something his wife did not accomplish. Neil Gathright served as the vice president of the Garden Grove California Republican Assembly, a grassroots conservative Republican volunteer organization.

The road that led Bee Gathright to Orange County and to the Right began in rural Iowa. Born during the Great Depression, one of nine children, she grew up on a family farm. Raised in a "very Christian home," Gathright remembers her father's staunch social conservatism: Members of a midwestern evangelical variant of Quakerism, her father and the family moved to the Methodist church when a "lady preacher" was brought in.[128] Upon graduation from high school, Gathright left home with her sister to work and to attend business school for training as a secretary. Opportunity soon beckoned in California, and, following in the well-trod path of many of her Iowa brethren, Gathright took up an offer to work as a secretary to the commander in charge of the air force office of Douglas Aircraft in Santa Monica, California. A magnet for Iowans since World War II, California worked its magic on Gathright: "I liked California before I even tried it," she recalled, and despite knowing that her mother "hated me to go off and live in some other state," she made the move.[129] She soon met her husband when the Douglas offices moved to Long Beach, where he worked as a plant engineer. They settled in the burgeoning new community of Garden Grove in the late 1950s, bought a small house, and started a family.

When Gathright became active in conservative circles in the early 1960s, she joined thousands of women and men who embraced the movement. These activists stuffed envelopes and walked precincts, driven by a missionary zeal to stem the tide of "collectivism" that they believed threatened the nation's future. While each of them came to the Right from his or her own unique background and no one can be considered "typical," Gathright's life is illustrative of broader trends. As such, her story says much about the conservative mobilization of the 1960s.

Gathright's story points first to the solid middle-class nature of the movement. It was made up of young and middle-aged professionals and their wives who, like Gathright and her husband, had recently migrated to California—people with bright futures who took the Right's message to heart. Most had come to Orange County because of the job opportunities in Southern California and because the county was a hospitable place to raise children. The sense of promise was vividly described by one conservative some thirty years later: "It was God's country. . . . It made you so thrilled to be an American that you wanted to do everything you possibly [could] to keep it this way."[130]

These activists, like Gathright, were central beneficiaries of the "affluent society," upcoming professionals who were members of a solid middle class. Most of them, like the Gathright family, had arrived within their immediate communities during the 1950s.[131] Indicative of the solidly middle-class nature of the Right was the leadership of four local conservative groups. Most of these leaders were drawn from the professional and managerial segments of the community.[132] Of the thirty-five leaders of these organizations, twenty-four worked in professional, managerial, and supervisory positions; of these individuals, nine were employed in the aerospace industry. Additionally, three local leaders were small-business owners, two were middle-class salesmen, and seven were lower-middle-class skilled workers or service workers. By and large, these were people benefiting from the recent emergence of new industries or the expansion of professional opportunities rooted in the growing local economy. They were new suburban settlers and were generally well educated, well read, and knowledgeable about America's foreign policy.[133]

Strikingly, doctors and dentists who settled in Orange County to provide their professional services to new suburban communities were prominent among the ranks of local activists. James Garry, D.D.S., helped form the Orange County Conservative Coordinating Council; Dr. Charles Downs, a former army surgeon, replaced Joel Dvorman as school board trustee; Dr. E. D. Whittier and William Brashears, D.D.S., cochaired the Christian Anti-Communism Crusade; Dr. Robert Ralls directed the steering committee of the Advocates for Americanism in Education; Richard Underwood, D.D.S., along with fourteen other members of St. Andrew's Presbyterian Church, sponsored W. Cleon Skousen to speak at Orange Coast College Auditorium; and Dr. Ralph E. Graham chaired the Magnolia Parents Committee supporting Dvorman's recall.[134] Fifty medical professionals went so far as to establish the group Doctors for America in Orange County, to support conservative principles. They urged support for Max Rafferty's campaign for California state school superintendent, since he believed in "local control and a return to the r's." They encouraged the distribution of their conservative mailings to patients and friends and probably played a part in getting the Orange County Medical Association offices to sell tickets to a lecture by W. Cleon Skousen, author of *The Naked Communist*.[135] Revealing the strident conservatism of a segment of the Southern California medical community in the early 1960s, the *Los Angeles Times* printed this classified ad: "Wanted: conservative pediatrician to establish practice in the Newport-Mesa area. No one worlders need apply."[136]

Like Neil Gathright, managers, supervisors, and engineers within the aerospace industries were also prominent in the movement. In the struggle to recall Joel Dvorman, three of the nine members of the recall committee were engineers, two of them employed at local aerospace firms, and another was a technical writer with Hughes Aircraft. These were members of the nation's technical elite, and their occupations directly linked them to the military-industrial complex of the Cold War. The other sponsors of the recall included an American Airlines pilot, a salesman, a gas company supervisor, a one-time mechanic at Ford Firestone, and an employee of the Collier Chemical Company.[137]

Doctors, dentists, and engineers were joined by military officers and their wives. These men and women were also closely linked to the Cold War. They made their homes in Orange County after retiring from such nearby bases as the El Toro Marine Corps Air Station.[138] Two important local right-wing leaders had been military officers. Robert Peterson, who arrived in Orange County as an elementary school principal, had been a lieutenant colonel in the air force reserve. He began teaching an adult course on world communism at Santa Ana College, helped organize the Christian Anti-Communism Crusade, and, in 1966, was elected to the post of county school superintendent on a conservative platform. John Schmitz, who won election to the California Assembly in 1964 as an outspoken member of the John Birch Society, had served as a Marine Corps captain, a pilot, and a leadership school instructor at the El Toro Marine Corps Air Station.[139] The wives of military officials also did their part to forward the conservative cause. Lois Lundberg of Yorba Linda, whose husband had been a military officer before entering the real estate business in Orange County, became a hardworking conservative Republican volunteer worker during the 1960s.[140] And Eleanor Howe of Anaheim, the wife of a retired pilot from El Toro Marine Corps Air Station, voted for Goldwater in 1964 and later became a prominent conservative activist.[141] Importantly, the influence of military settlers in Orange County extended well beyond the fact that some became activists themselves. Rather, they more broadly influenced the political culture of the county. Their direct experiences and expertise gave them an authority that helped influence the outlooks of many of their friends and neighbors. Edna Slocum of Santa Ana, a part-time college teacher, recalled the influence of a neighbor and bridge club member, a marine pilot, in bringing about her conversion to conservatism. His frustrations with the limits placed on the military in Vietnam made her "uneasy."[142] Peterson and Schmitz, the two military men who taught at Santa Ana College, spread their views to hundreds of Orange Countians through their adult education classes on communism and world events.[143]

While the most prominent activists came largely from the ranks of doctors, dentists, and engineers, small-business owners, pharmacists, city officials, plasterers, independent construction contractors, and housewives were also represented. Many had secured their middle-class and professional status in the recent boom times in Orange County. Aside from these core activists, who by and large were solidly middle-class, right-wing sentiment extended to a broader segment of the community. A sampling of the published right-wing letters to the editor of the *Register* points to a constituency on the Right that extended to lower-middle-class individuals.[144] Of a sample of 110 letter writers, 46 were professionals or managers; 26 were low-level professionals, including teachers, salesmen, and pharmacists; 5 were small-business owners; and 33 held lower-middle-class jobs in construction or in the nonunion service sector. But the majority of supporters for right-wing causes (more than two-thirds of the letter writers in the sample) came from the upper and middle reaches of society.[145] In Orange County during the first half of the 1960s, the conservative movement was, by and large, a middle- and upper-middle-class phenomenon.

Women were very much a part of the constituency of the Right, although they were underrepresented in leadership positions.[146] Among the people who wrote letters to the *Register* were 123 men, 87 women, and five couples. According to a study of the John Birch Society in California during the 1960s, women were in fact overrepresented among the rank and file of the movement.[147] Their centrality to right-wing mobilization within their communities was vividly expressed by one activist who argued that many women participated because "men were at work all the time and women had the freedom."[148] One prominent Republican Party activist even asserted that the decline of grassroots Republican Party volunteer activism in the late 1960s was due to increased numbers of women working—"you lost your volunteers, you lost your precinct workers."[149] Not only were women activists themselves, it was also not unusual for women to first become involved and then to bring their husbands into the cause.[150] They also enlisted female neighbors and friends and developed cooperative networks so that young mothers could participate in conservative activity. Jan Averill, who lived on the northern border of the county, for example, remembered a friend inviting her to a "Tuesday morning study club" in Pasadena: "There were two other gals in our neighborhood that were interested also. . . . Since we all had little kids . . . we'd get a babysitter and have all our kids at the same house. We'd pack a little bag lunch and they'd have speakers in the morning . . . and a speaker in the afternoon."[151] Women also mentioned taking their children along in precinct work, while staffing offices for conservative candidates, and even to conventions.[152] These women's identification as wives, mothers, and "moral guardians" of the family led them, as one of their cohorts called for, to "let a sink full of dirty dishes" wait in order to "safeguard . . . freedom."[153]

What these conservative Orange County activists shared was not only relative wealth but also the experience of social mobility

that affirmed their faith in the possibility of individual achieve-
ment. A close look at the careers of several activists and supporters shows that many were upwardly mobile. Neil Gathright,
who worked as a plant engineer at Douglas Aircraft when he
first moved to Garden Grove, had, by the early 1960s, established his own contracting firm, Westco Engineering, eventually
employing about twenty-five individuals.[154] R. Dickson Miles of
Anaheim, who also worked as an engineer for Nortronics in
1959, had moved into a managerial position by 1963 and had
opened up his own business venture, Miles and Associates, by
1964.[155] His ally on the Dvorman recall committee, James Wallace, started as an engineer at North American in the late 1950s
and, by 1961, worked as a production supervisor at Autonetics.[156] One activist, Cathy Sullivan, who had worked in the personnel department at Boeing in Seattle while her husband
worked for Boeing as a salesman, found better opportunities in
Orange County in the early 1960s; her husband opened his own
construction company, while she became a full-time right-wing
activist and mother.[157] These new frontier settlers of Cold War
America found their beliefs in the possibilities of entrepreneurial
success reaffirmed when they established themselves in businesses in Orange County. These men and women, new to the
land of promise, sought to hold on to the moorings they believed
were fundamental to the American success story: traditional social and normative conservative beliefs, strict moral values, unabashed individualism, and faith in free enterprise.

While new frontier settlers dominated the ranks of the Right, a
number of "old-timers" also joined the movement. These individuals had grown up in Orange County when it was a land of
farms and ranches, and they could vividly recall the scent of orange blossoms that once permeated their towns. They saw the
beauty and quiet of the land marred by housing tracts, strip
malls, and highways. One of these old-timers was James Townsend, whose rural Kentucky family had settled in Anaheim in
1936. By the time Townsend had his own family, Anaheim was
undergoing rapid changes. Housing tracts displaced orange

groves, and, when Disneyland opened, thousands of homes and businesses sprouted. As Townsend put it, "It happened all too fast for any of us to really understand."[158] The social strains accompanying such change might well have led Townsend to yearn for the small-town virtues and simple life of the past; a desire to turn back the clock to a time when life was easier might provide a neat explanation for his next thirty-five years of activism on the Right.

Such an explanation, however, does more to mislead than to enlighten us about Townsend's motivations. He was not, after all, a passive victim of change that rode roughshod over his community; like other conservative activists who had lived in Orange County for many years, Townsend often benefited tremendously from the changes around him. A closer look at Townsend's life provides an illustration of how the postwar boom that built the Southwest shaped both careers and politics.

James Townsend's mother, a widow who supported her three children from a pension earned by her husband's service in World War I, moved her family to Orange County in 1936 from the small town of Franklin, Kentucky, where they had lived on a farm. Arriving in Orange County upon finishing grammar school, Townsend spent his teenage years there, attending high school, courting his future wife, and, on rare occasions, attending the Baptist church that his mother had joined. When war broke out in 1941, he enlisted in the army and cast his first vote for Roosevelt. Returning to Anaheim briefly after the war, Townsend heard that there was land for the asking from a relative in Arizona "who put dollar signs in my eyes." Townsend moved to Yuma, getting a job as an irrigator, ditch digger, and bulldozer operator with the Bureau of Reclamation.[159] Mistaken in his belief that servicemen could qualify for 160 acres of land from the bureau, and encountering a confusing bureaucracy, Townsend found work as a laborer on a large farm, eventually leaving over a wage dispute with his supervisor. In the booming Southwest, however, he quickly found better opportunities as a salesman selling income tax and bookkeeping systems ("making more in one day than I was making all in a week") and finally, most likely with support from his "rich uncle" who had drawn him there, bought a bakery distributorship.[160] In 1949, he sold his business and moved back to Orange County because his father-in-law had just bought a "pool hall and beer joint" in Santa Ana and needed some help. Townsend soon found opportunities of his own in the gold rush atmosphere of postwar Orange County, making out well as a kind of broker matching venture capitalists with entrepreneurs seeking financial backing. He "went through a series of businesses that I owned or ran," including a power brake manufacturing company.[161] As a successful businessman, he was soon invited to join the Orange County Conservative Coordinating Council and, shortly thereafter, helped to found California Citizens for Goldwater. Having made a successful career at the heart of the postwar boom in the Southwest, the individualistic and entrepreneurial rhetoric of the Right, its championing of the rising West, and its hostility to intrusive government made sense to him, especially since they were validated by his own biography. The Right's moralism and strident nationalism, moreover, meshed well with the ideological inheritances of his southern Baptist roots.

Townsend was by far not the only activist on the Right who had deep roots in the West, and specifically in California. There were many others whose families originated from Southern California and who, unlike Townsend, had been born there. These Californians grew up in solid middle-class or, at times, even lower-middle-class communities in Los Angeles, Long Beach, and Orange County. Estrid Kielsmeier, for example, who pounded the pavement for Goldwater in 1964, grew up in a middle-class home in nearby Long Beach, her mother a staunch evangelical Christian. Tom Rogers, a dedicated worker in conservative John Schmitz's campaign in 1964, moved to Orange County from Pasadena, where his father had been a middle-level manager in an oil company before turning to property development.[162] And Nolan Frizzelle, following in his father's footsteps, took up a career as a doctor of optometry in Los Angeles. A few conservative activists hailed from the southland ranching community and had made a successful transition from ranching to new endeavors. The Muckenthaler family, supporters of the John Birch Society, for example, had been ranchers prior to the county's suburban days and had turned from ranching to property management and real estate speculation.[163] There was also the prominent Utt family, who had been longtime Orange County growers when their son Jimmy ran for Congress in 1952 with a thoroughly right-wing program. To label this group as America's "dispossessed," as some scholars have done, presents a distorted and inaccurate portrait and does not accord with these individuals' sense of themselves or their worldview.[164]

While most conservative activists had been brought up in middle-class and, in some cases, upper-middle-class families, a few, like Bee Gathright, got their starts in more modest circumstances; however, they had climbed into the ranks of the middle class before becoming active in the Right. Armstrong Dowell, who joined the John Birch Society and served on the Goldwater committee in the city of Orange, is a case in point. His father worked in a steel mill in Torrance, California. But the younger Dowell grasped better opportunities, attending college and even earning a master's degree before becoming a technician and then a materials engineer for Hughes Aircraft.[165] David Bergland, born in 1935, was another social climber. His family moved from Iowa to California in the depths of the Great Depression and was "very poor."[166] He worked his way up, going to college part-time at UCLA and finishing his degree while working and raising his three small children. In 1965, he attended law school and, by 1969, was a practicing lawyer.

The Right's staunch antistatism and its hostility to welfare programs, taxes, and regulation appealed to the circumstances of these middle-class women and men of the New West. "Big government" was linked to the "decadent ways" of eastern elites with their decaying cities. Confident in their region's affluence and their own, these women and men saw themselves and the West as the future—a future, they believed, that was most in line with the true traditions of the nation's past. But these individuals' politics were not shaped by economic class and regional pride alone. For many conservatives, a deeper set of ideological concerns fueled their politics; concerns forged out of the cultural baggage migrants brought with them to Orange County and tempered by the new places they made their homes. Like Bee Gathright, many of them came from small towns in the Midwest, border South, and Southwest, and the social values they grew up with influenced their politics. Jan Averill, who joined the Young Republicans in the early 1960s and by 1964 was a staunch Goldwater supporter, had grown up in a middle-class Republican household in Stillwater, Minnesota. Edna Slocum of Santa Ana, founder of one of the first California Republican Assembly chapters in 1962, had grown up on a farm in Missouri and moved west with her husband.[167] John Schmitz, an anticommunist instructor at Santa Ana College, hailed from a conservative middle-class Catholic boyhood in Milwaukee, Wisconsin. Cathy Sullivan joined the John Birch Society after moving to Orange County from Toledo, Ohio; while she was still a teenager, her devout Catholic mother made her read *Witness* by Whittaker Chambers before she was allowed to date.[168] And Peggy and Rufus Pearce, who helped found a chapter of the John Birch Society in Fullerton, were native Texans.[169]

When these migrants came to California, their beliefs at times clashed with the more liberal tenor of California politics and cultural life, for while Orange County had long had a strong conservative flavor, the state at large boasted vibrant progressive and liberal movements. Most recently, Governor Edmund Brown, elected in 1958, had propelled an assertive liberal vision of big government backed by organized labor. The liberal tenor of state politics and an ever more cosmopolitan and multicultural Los Angeles contrasted with the values that had been part of the warp and woof of the communities many Orange Countians had left behind. Such a cultural clash led to easily heightened fears of communist subversion of the American way of life, turning California, for some migrants, from a dream into a nightmare.

But it was not simply the values they brought with them that shaped the outlook of Orange County conservatives. New circumstances reshaped values. Orange County's conservative residents drew selectively from a font of ideas on which they were raised that resonated with the circumstances of this new home. In the new frontier environment of Orange County, the social conservative and antistatist strands of their heritage became ever more prominent. Bee Gathright, for example, did not think of herself as a conservative until the early 1960s. She registered as a Democrat upon arriving in Orange County because "we were just starting out" and Democrats, she recalls being told by the registrar who came to her door, "were for the little, poorer people."[170] Despite having grown up in a Protestant evangelical family, in a household where, she recalled, her mother "wouldn't take government aid on anything," it was only in her new environment that the social conservatism and antistatist inheritances on which she had been raised became part of a self-conscious conservative identity. Thus, her conservatism seemed, to her, natural and commonsensical: "I suppose it would be considered pretty political, but it made so much sense because, to me, it was just the way we were all trained up to live."[171] Once she was introduced to conservative ideology, it resonated with her circumstances.

Bee Gathright was not the only conservative activist who had arrived in Orange County as a Democrat. Edna Slocum remembered that where she grew up in Missouri, everyone was a Democrat. Armstrong Dowell first voted Democratic, as his family had done before him. While some of these men and women hailed from border southern and southwestern Democratic households, where the Democratic Party embraced strands of antistatism, others did not. Lois Lundberg, for example, came from "a strongly Midwestern Democrat family." Her father, a labor union member, was, in her words, "very, very Democrat-oriented."[172] Cathy Sullivan's mother had served as a Democratic ward captain for liberal Adlai Stevenson in Ohio; Sullivan herself was a Young Democrat in her college days.[173] These activists came from families that had a more nuanced view of the state and had been willing to embrace New Deal reforms. With middle-class security, their prior attachments to those reforms lost relevance, and the Right's staunch championing of entrepreneurial individualism meshed with their sense of themselves and with the strands of social conservatism they carried from their pasts. Loosened from their past associations, families, and community ties, these men and women found their new communities in the ideas and organizations proffered by the Right.

While many of these activists hailed from rural and small-town backgrounds in the Midwest and border South, it is misleading to characterize their mobilization, as contemporary observers often did, as a rearguard action against "modernity."[174] These were, after all, people who decided to leave their small towns behind. The mere fact of choosing to migrate, of leaving their homes and extended families behind for new, but distant, opportunities, implies that they were open to change and believed in the possibilities of social mobility. In Southern California, these men and women were immersed in a high-tech world. They enjoyed the fruits of consumer culture, reveled in their worldly success, and, for the most part, found the suburban world of tract homes, private developments, and decentralized living space to their liking. They were not looking to turn back the clock to a Jeffersonian world. Indeed, one activist who firmly asserted the need for "revolving back to the foundations of this country," distinguished between clinging to what she saw as timeless truths—moral absolutes and an adherence to the literal word of the Bible—and a nostalgic desire to return to the ways of life and work of the past, which she firmly opposed.[175]

These men and women embraced modernity but did so selectively. They rejected some elements usually associated with modernity—namely, secularism, relativism, and egalitarianism, believing that a thoroughly modern life could, and should, exclude them—while embracing thoroughly modern lifestyles. The new modern suburban consumer setting seemed to threaten older family and church values many had grown up with, creating an urgent realization of their importance. Indeed, we can surmise that their very embrace of geographic mobility and of change may have made them cling even more strongly to traditional moorings.

Their past ideological inheritances, then, contributed to their outlook, but it was their lives in the new suburban communities that strengthened and deepened these beliefs, making their politics very much a product of the new world in which they lived. But, as we will see, their ideology was hardly traditional. They embraced older ideas within a new context, and the meaning of the ideas themselves was transformed. Orange County conservative ideology meshed elements of traditionalism with extremely modern elements. Their worldview harked back to an older world but also called for a new one based on a highly modern technocratic defense ethos, an assertion of absolute property rights as the ultimate test of freedom, and an invigoration of the nuclear family unit as the locus of moral authority.[176]

Entering their first political battles in the early 1960s, these suburban Americans came to perceive of themselves as part of a broader national conservative movement. This sense was fostered by national political organizations such as the John Birch Society and by a burgeoning conservative intellectual culture that helped to shape their initial impulses into a coherent right-wing ideology. Orange County conservatives were, for example, avid readers of magazines like *National Review* and *Human Events*. The importance of the national intellectual movement to grassroots activists was attested to by one activist, Edna Slocum. Noting the importance of Buckley's *God and Man at Yale* to her development as a conservative, she asserted, "Reading was extremely important [to us]. . . . There had to be a coming forth of good conservative writers that could express the view, there had to be a legitimate voice of the conservative position before there could be a growth of the conservative movement."[177]

The importance of the availability of books and literature to these well-educated middle-class citizens cannot be overstated. Letters to the *Register* written by conservatives urged their fellow citizens to read, read, and read some more. Specific titles were often recommended, among them J. Edgar Hoover's *Masters of Deceit* and W. Cleon Skousen's *Naked Communist*. Letter writers frequently even included the names and addresses where readers could send away for the *Dan Smoot Report* or included passages from *Human Events* or *National Review*.

A glimpse at the content of a few of the books that were read by grassroots conservatives provides a sense of the concerns that led Orange Countians to action and of how these works contributed to building a movement. Books like *The Naked Communist, Masters of Deceit*, and Fred Schwarz's *You Can Trust the Communists (to Be Communists)* spoke urgently of dire communist plans to conquer the United States and issued calls to action. They emphasized, above all, the threat of internal subversion. As the respected authority J. Edgar Hoover, put it:

> Something utterly new has taken root in America during the past generation, a communist mentality representing a systematic, purposive, and conscious attempt to destroy Western civilization and roll history back to the age of barbaric cruelty and despotism, all in the name of "progress." Communist thought control . . . has spread the infection, in varying degrees, to most phases of American life.[178]

A key weapon in combating this menace was, in Hoover's eyes, to recall the "deep roots of religion" in American culture.[179] While Hoover spoke of the importance of faith in a "Supreme being," Fred Schwarz's *You Can Trust the Communists (to Be Communists)* stressed communism's opposition to the principles of "an absolute God" and "an absolute Truth." The modern outlook, he contended, is "materialism": "There is no God; there are no absolutes; everything is relative; Truth itself is a relative of the class struggle."[180] Schwarz further enjoined citizens to do something to oppose the menace:

> The power of individuals is limitless. The time has come for people to cease looking for great organizations afar off and to begin looking for things that can be done close at home. Every man who invites a friend into his home, gives him literature to read, and informs him of the danger, is helping to thwart the Communist program. The powers of multiplication are limitless. The principle on which to work is the recruitment of individuals one by one on a basis of knowledge, understanding and motivated service. . . . Upon such a foundation the political, legislative and cultural programs necessary can be built.[181]

While the content of conservative literature was important, providing education for the movement and fostering "a new way of looking at things," examining its distribution patterns tells us something about how the conservative movement gained adherents.[182] Many right-wing tracts, books, and magazines were passed from hand to hand through a network of friends, neighbors, and family. A core group of conservatives spread the message within their communities, bringing new recruits to the cause and, in the process, generating a movement culture. One young mother recalled how an illness led to her inadvertent introduction to conservatism: A relative promised to care for her two young children if she, in turn, would read a number of conservative books. She later attended a John Birch Society meeting and soon embarked on a career of activism on the Right.[183] Another woman, who had moved to Tustin in 1960, vividly remembered the centrality of friends in bringing about her politicization. She described the influence of a couple down the street with whom she socialized and played bridge, but the influence of another friend stood out even more strongly:

> We became friends with a couple, Marge and Stew Brown. Marge was a very intellectual lady, we were very close friends, did a lot of things together. . . . From the very first she challenged me. Statements would be made . . . about what was going on or what we thought, and she would say, "well, obviously you haven't read so-and-so . . . I'll bring it down for you." So, I was literally forced to read some opposing views and . . . if you're intellectual at all you have to start considering other views.[184]

Bridge clubs, coffee klatches, and barbecues—all popular in the new suburban communities—provided some of the opportunities for right-wing ideas to spread literally from home to home throughout the county. One neighborhood meeting could produce several recruits to the cause. The meeting where Gathright had discovered her conservatism, for example, also "brought in" a neighbor.[185] Conservative recruitment within these networks worked because of the widely available books and magazines that conservatives passed on to their friends. These publications provided seemingly authoritative voices and helped to build a new level of consciousness and politicization among recruits. Networks and the availability of outside resources thus were central to the growth of the grassroots conservative movement in Orange County.

The grassroots dissatisfaction with the trend of national politics may have come to naught, had it not been for the institutional support provided by strategically placed local organizations. Successful mobilization needs access to resources and information, and although it is conceivable that grassroots activists could have built their own institutions, they did not have to; instead, local businessmen, churches, and the libertarian *Register* provided the infrastructure and ideas essential to the movement's success.

No one played a more pivotal role in fostering the grassroots conservative revival than Walter Knott. A prominent businessman from Buena Park, Knott had been a key sponsor of the Orange County School of Anti-Communism, serving as its honorary chairman.[186] His name lent prestige and legitimacy to the cause, but his support extended well beyond the symbolic. He gave money and resources that were invaluable in spreading the conservative gospel.

Born in San Bernardino in 1889, Knott had deep roots in the West. His grandparents had migrated from Tidewater Virginia to Texas to plant cotton and, after the Civil War, went on to California.[187] His father had been an evangelical Methodist preacher and a successful rancher. While Knott grew wealthy on the changes wrought in the West by the New Deal liberal state, he saw himself as a twentieth-century individualist in the pioneering mold and retained the staunchly conservative religious values of his family. He held deep attachments to his pioneer heritage, which were mythologized in the tourist attractions on his farm. In addition to establishing a church on Knott's Berry

Farm, he continued his membership in his father's conservative Methodist church.[188]

Concerned with the political direction of the nation, Knott became involved in politics in the mid-1950s, leaving his multi-million-dollar amusement park and restaurant increasingly in family hands.[189] By the early 1960s, he was at the core of right-wing activity, both in Southern California and nationally.[190] He served on the national advisory board of Billy James Hargis's Christian Crusade, as national treasurer of the Liberty Amendment Committee, as well as on the board of trustees of Constructive Action, Inc., which provided "the American public with educational material exposing socialist and communist inroads into the American system."[191] Furthermore, he played an important role in conservative Republican Party politics in Orange County by serving on the Republican Central Committee throughout the decade. By 1966, his influence expanded when he became a member of Ronald Reagan's finance committee. But, most important for the conservative revival in Orange County, Knott served as honorary chairman for the arrival of Dr. Fred Schwarz and the Orange County School of Anti-Communism and founded the California Free Enterprise Association in 1960.[192]

Knott's Free Enterprise Association started out small and eventually expanded to become a critical right-wing institution in Orange County. Knott began by sending monthly letters to his approximately 1,000 employees on topics such as taxes, economics, and lessons in "the American capitalist system."[193] He decided to expand to other regional businesses, so he enlisted some businesspeople—such as Charles Pearson, who owned the Anaheim Truck and Transfer Company, and Adolph Schoepe, owner of the Kwik-Set Lock Company—to form the California Free Enterprise Association.[194] They circulated 20,000 pamphlets per month through employees' pay envelopes, reading racks, and educators and ministers.[195] To spread their message even further, the association, under Knott's leadership, hired a staff of five employees, bought books, tapes, and films, and started a library to provide resources and direction for the grassroots activists.[196] Knott, in fact, developed a whole "Freedom

Center" on his Berry Farm during the early 1960s, which was home not only to the California Free Enterprise Association but also to two other nonprofit organizations: the Libres Foundation, whose goal was to place patriotic books in supermarkets and disseminate educational material, and the Americanism Educational League, "Walter Knott Branch," which offered speakers on problems related to the "preservation of the Constitutional Republic and American Freedom."[197]

The California Free Enterprise Association, the most visible and successful of the "Freedom" enterprises, published a catalog offering films, such as *Communism on the Map*, and books and pamphlets by right-wing authors, such as Ludwig Von Mises, Russell Kirk, and Leonard Read of the Foundation for Economic Education.[198] In its brochures, the association made it clear that free-enterprise capitalism could not allow for even the most minimal welfare state. As stated in one pamphlet:

> The difference between a free nation and a slave nation can be very simply stated. In a free nation, the people accept the responsibility for their own welfare; while in a slave nation the responsibility is turned over to the government. . . . They will want their government to . . . guarantee them minimum wages . . . full employment . . . good prices for their produce . . . good housing . . . medical care. . . . such people are . . . choosing slavery rather than freedom . . . for this is the security of the penitentiary.[199]

The association's literature linked the welfare state with a communist conspiracy, an analogy common to the Right. One pamphlet, under the caption "The Socialist Plan for Conquest," showed an evil-looking conspirator gloating, "THE WELFARE STATE is what we socialists will call our government although the right name should be MASTER STATE where we socialists are the masters and the rest of the people are the servants."[200]

Actively working to stimulate grassroots activity, the California Free Enterprise Association put out a detailed "Freedom Study Clubs Guide" to help citizens, churches, and neighborhoods establish study groups. The association suggested speakers and provided detailed guidance on conducting such groups, urging interested parties to use Hoover's *Masters of Deceit* as a "basic textbook" and to obtain copies of Skousen's *Naked Communist* "to gain insight into communist conspiracy."[201] The guide contained an outline of local resources available for the cause of "freedom," listing the Orange County Freedom Forum and suggesting such speakers as Dr. Fred Schwarz, the Reverend Bob Schuller of the Garden Grove Community Church, and the Reverend Bob Wells of the Central Baptist Church of Orange County.[202] Knott was pleased with the "progress we are making in our little Free Enterprise Association," asserting one year after its founding that "this work toward conservative thinking and government is growing here in Orange County faster than we could have hoped a year ago."[203]

Knott was not the only businessman who supported regional right-wing activism; he was also part of a broader conservative business community in Southern California. Support for the conservative cause came from Orange County companies such as the Fluor Corporation, Kwik-Set Lock, John B. Kilroy Construction, Anaheim Truck and Transfer, Carl's Jr. Burgers, and nearby Los Angeles–based and Southern California–based companies such as Schick Razor, Technicolor Corporation, Coast Federal Savings, Kohlenberger Engineering, and numerous other firms.[204] The seventy-member Orange County Industrial Committee was part of a group that coordinated county participation in the All-Southern California School of Anti-Communism.[205] The five-day school, held from August 28 through September 1, 1961, in the Los Angeles Sports Arena, not only featured Schwarz, W. Cleon Skousen, and Herbert Philbrick but also drew Rear Admiral Chester Ward, Senator Thomas J. Dodd of Connecticut, and prominent actors John Wayne, Ronald Reagan, Pat Boone, Roy Rogers, and George Murphy onto the stage. The school was supported by large and small businesses from Orange County and the greater Los Angeles area.[206]

The biographies of the Orange County businessmen who supported the Right seemed to confirm their strong belief that hard work, individual entrepreneurship, and intelligence paved the road to success. They saw themselves as twentieth-century Horatio Algers, and, indeed, there was some truth to their perception. Walter Knott started out as a farmer in San Bernardino. During the Depression years, he successfully introduced the boysenberry to the market and, in 1934, entered the restaurant business. During and after World War II, Knott expanded his restaurant into a theme and amusement park, eventually establishing his business as the state's second-largest tourist attraction.[207] Carl Karcher, of Carl Karcher Enterprises, started out hawking hot dogs from a stand across from the Goodyear plant in Los Angeles during World War II. With the money he earned, he bought a small restaurant in Anaheim in 1945. He parlayed this thirty-three-seat restaurant into a six-establishment chain by 1961, and eventually into a restaurant empire.[208] Adolph Schoepe of the Kwik-Set Lock Company also established his manufacturing business shortly after the war, moving the company to Anaheim in 1948. These men started out with small amounts of capital and transformed their businesses into large and growing fortunes. Their success depended as much on the vastly expansive opportunities and the growth of the corporate economy in Southern California during and after World War II as it did on individual effort, but central to their worldview was the fact that their success did not depend on the government— except, of course, indirectly, as the government fueled the growth of the California economy.

Local businessmen-ideologues fostered right-wing mobilization, but they were not alone in providing institutional backing for the region's conservative movement. As the reference to local ministers in the California Free Enterprise Association's "Freedom Study Clubs Guide" suggests, conservative religious leaders were also critical to spreading the gospel of right-wing anticommunism. Many evangelical and Catholic churches played a supportive role in fostering a climate of virulent anticommunism, not least because the Soviet Union's antireligious policies seemed to threaten their institutions. Within American fundamentalism, the Soviet Union had been regarded since the 1930s as the "Antichrist" of biblical prophecy. Anticommunism within evangelical churches ran the gamut from moderate evangelicals like Billy Graham, who warned of communism's satanic character, to the fundamentalist followers of Carl McIntire, who tied anticommunism to extreme right-wing beliefs.[209] These evangelists shared a belief in Bible inerrancy and conservative social values, but they differed fundamentally on tactics. It was the more militant fundamentalists who most visibly provided important support for right-wing revival in the early 1960s.

Conservative Christianity had found a home in Southern California, with its long history of religious fundamentalist, evangelical, and Pentecostal movements.[210] While many believers in conservative Protestant doctrine abstained from politics, seeking separation from a sinful world, their values did help infuse a conservative political culture; and some of the churches that established themselves with the vast influx of new migrants into Orange County from the Midwest and Bible Belt regions of the near South took an active political stance.

One important group in Orange County was the Baptists. Southern California Baptists had long been known as a conservative group, and the new Baptist churches that mushroomed with the growth of the county played a leading role in spreading a fundamentalist Protestant message, combining strict Protestant moralism and antiliberal politics.[211] By the 1960s, there were at least thirteen churches within Orange County that actively supported right-wing activities within the community; most of them were Baptist.[212] These churches offered their places of worship as sites for right-wing speakers and for showing virulent anticommunist films. Reverend Salvaggio of the First Baptist Church of Tustin, for example, announced the showing of *Communism on the Map*.[213] Dr. P. G. Neuman, pastor of the First Baptist Church of Costa Mesa in 1961, spoke on the topic "Why Did God Permit the John Birch Society?" and brought in the Reverend Jesse Cochran, who was a close friend and seminary classmate of John Birch, as a special guest.[214] Some of the churches voiced anti-Semitic ideas, evincing that right-wing attitudes that had been important for the old Christian Protestant

Right in the 1930s and 1940s were alive and well within the new mobilization. The Temple Baptist Church in Westminster sponsored a series of talks on such topics as "Communism in the USA," "Where Did the Jew Come From and Where Is He Going?" and "Are Jews to Blame for the Present-Day Crisis?"[215] Anti-Semitism, while not a core component of the movement as a whole, was present in the discourse and language of a segment of the grassroots religious Right.

A militant white Christian identity infused a segment of Protestant fundamentalism in Orange County, laced with racist and anti-Semitic ideas.[216] Pastor Bob Wells of the Orange County Central Baptist Church was its champion. No religious leader played a more vocal role in the revival of the Right than "Fighting" Bob Wells, a close ally of the Reverend Carl McIntire and his American Council of Christian Churches.[217] In his "fundamental down on your knees Bible-preaching church," Wells preached a strong dose of hellfire and damnation for the liberal "traitors."[218] Although Wells had moved to Orange County only in 1956, by 1967 he led a congregation of 3,000 members and 565 students at his Heritage High School.[219] Styling himself as a West Coast Billy James Hargis, Wells was, according to his supporters, a "real fighter against the enemies of Jesus Christ— socialism and communism."[220] He brought national right-wing figures to his church to "defend the savior in action as well as speech."[221] And he supported the more extreme edge of the conservative movement from the pulpit by arguing, for example, that "John Birch Society members are for basic Americanism . . . for old fashioned principles of truth, righteousness and freedom."[222] To make sure his congregation was politically informed, Wells spread out literature on tables after his services to "awaken the people to the dangers of communism."[223] These tables offered his "Truth and Freedom Pamphlets" such as "The United Nations, a Smoke-Screen for Communist Aggression" and "Disarmament, an Invitation to Communist Take-Over."[224] Wells spread his message even further through his Saturday morning radio broadcasts of *The Truth and Freedom Program*.

Fundamentalist churches, like Wells's Central Baptist Church, supported right-wing groups for good reason. Robert Welch, the leader of the John Birch Society, proclaimed in *The Blue Book of the John Birch Society* that "the true fundamentalists in our midst . . . are the moral salt of the earth."[225] In his terms, a member of any religion could be a fundamentalist, and the John Birch Society drew broad nonfundamentalist support. Still, the society's absolute division of the world between good and evil fit well with religious fundamentalist beliefs, and Welch chose as his hero John Birch, a fundamentalist Baptist preacher.[226] Additionally, the society, which had barely addressed moral and spiritual issues in its early years, increasingly stressed the importance of Christianity as the backbone of Americanism.[227] The close relationship between fundamentalism and the right-wing revival was also evident in Fred Schwarz's Christian Anti-Communism Crusade. Schwarz had served as a fundamentalist minister under the tutelage of Carl McIntire before founding his crusade. For Schwarz, faith in an absolute God was critical to combating communism. Although he later played down his fundamentalist preaching, his ideology drew upon a fundamentalist worldview.

But not all politically conservative churches were old-time fundamentalists. The Reverend Edward W. Greenfield, for example, whose church was located on Knott's Berry Farm, limited himself to expounding a probusiness ideology and fiscal conservatism, and to warning Orange Countians of the "fascist threat in America . . . the threat of centralized governmental control over the economic, education and cultural life of the nation."[228] Other churches also played a role in spreading a pro-capitalist, entrepreneurial message favorable to the growth of the Right; while they did not embrace a political stance from the pulpit, their message of individual success blended well with conservative politics.

This more moderate gospel was best symbolized by Robert Schuller, a pastor affiliated with the Reform Church of America. In March 1955, Schuller established the first drive-in church in the world, in Garden Grove, California, with his message "Worship as you are in the family car."[229] He started out by holding services on top of a snack bar in a drive-in theater, but his success led him to eventually establish the world's first combined walk-in and drive-in church in the fall of 1961. Located at the corner of Chapman Avenue and Lewis Street, across from Disneyland, this unique church could accommodate 1,000 people who desired to "walk in" and provided space for an additional 500 cars in the parking lot. It was equipped with a mechanical glass door so that Schuller could step outside and address the drive-in members of the congregation.

Schuller preached a message that he coined "possibility thinking," inspired by the ideas of Norman Vincent Peale. Schuller emphasized the possibilities of individual success through positive thinking. From his theology of self-esteem was born his theology of economics, the belief that the welfare state diminishes man's initiative and self-esteem.[230] He explicitly espoused the gospel of private wealth in his 1963 book *God's Way to the Good Life*, in which he stated, "You have a God-ordained right to be wealthy. You're a steward of the goods, the golds, the gifts, that God has allowed to come into your hands. Having riches is no sin, wealth is no crime. Christ did not praise poverty. The profit motive is not necessarily unChristian."[231] It was no wonder that his teachings appealed to many Orange County residents, who saw their own lives as confirmation of the truth of Schuller's philosophy.

Schuller's message fit well with Orange Countians' conservative Republican politics. His gospel implicitly affirmed the politics of the anticommunist and pro–free enterprise revival in Orange County. Testifying to the link between his church and the conservative movement, Schuller served on the religious committee of the Orange County School of Anti-Communism and joined the Californians' Committee to Combat Communism to sponsor the Francis amendment.[232] Schuller also placed himself on the conservative side of the battle in the Magnolia School District. When the board came under attack for the Christian religious and "American heritage" messages the superintendent sent home at school expense, Schuller wrote to the school board, expressing his support for the policy.[233] Schuller's support was appreciated by those working in conservative circles.[234] It is not surprising, then, that, according to one Garden Grove conservative activist, "many of the active people went out there to church."[235]

Another important ally of the conservative resurgence was the Catholic hierarchy in Southern California. The American Catholic clergy was politically divided regarding the right-wing resurgence of the early 1960s. At their annual meeting in 1961, for example, Catholic bishops denounced reckless Radical Right charges, and a host of powerful clergy within the church attacked John Birch Society membership as inconsistent with Catholic ideals. Still, there was support for the Right among a broad segment of the Catholic Church. Nowhere was this more strongly felt than through the leadership of Francis Cardinal McIntyre, western America's first cardinal, and the most extreme right-wing member of the American Catholic hierarchy.[236]

McIntyre, who had presided over the growing Catholic flock in Orange County since 1953, sought to lead his large and growing diocese in a thoroughly conservative direction.[237] Breaking all records for church and school growth, he expanded his see into a huge development corporation.[238] He used his rising power "to mobilize the archdiocese against every liberal cause in Southern California and to build a regional hierarchy which followed his conservative orthodoxy."[239] He sent his priests to meetings of right-wing forums addressed by Welch and other conservative leaders. And his archdiocese newspaper, the *Tidings*, firmly announced its opposition to secular liberalism, forwarding a message that closely paralleled the fulminations of the John Birch Society. Indeed, the paper was decidedly pro-Birch, recommending subscriptions to *American Opinion* and other Birch publications.[240]

The *Tidings*, available to churchgoers in every parish, provided fodder for Catholic participation in conservative activism. Given the presence of Catholics among the grassroots activists, it seems to have had an impact.[241] Word about the *Tidings*, for example, was spread by one activist in a letter to the *Register*, which asserted that "this is an excellent conservative newspaper and is read by people of many faiths. Anyone wishing to subscribe . . . can do so by calling the local Catholic school."[242] The newspaper also legitimized those local priests who provided active support for conservative social issues. Father Paul Peterson of St. Boniface Parish, Orange County's intended diocese seat and its largest parish, educated his parishioners to the anticommunist struggle through Sunday bulletins. In the November 19, 1961, issue he published eleven steps to combat communism.[243] Father Peterson also provided support and leadership for those with concerns over sex education in the early 1960s, an issue that would break into the open later in the 1960s. At least one of his parishioners took up his mantle after Peterson left Orange County, becoming a key local leader of the mobilization against sex education in Orange County during the late 1960s.[244]

The support of religious institutions in Orange County for the right-wing mobilizations of the early 1960s was significant, yet this does not mean that all, or even most, churches in the county supported the Right. To the contrary, many churches were theologically and politically quite liberal, some of them urging citizens not to go overboard in their anticommunist zeal. The Fullerton Ministerial Association, a group of about twenty ministers from liberal churches, for example, came out in support of Joel Dvorman.[245] Various other local churches strongly supported civil rights and liberal social reforms.[246]

The liberalism of some churches was not taken lightly by conservatives.[247] One conservative complained that the First Methodist Church "brushed aside . . . the communist menace . . . as of little or no consequence." He wished to see his church follow the "forthright attacks" against communism being waged by some other community churches.[248] And a group of parishioners of the First Methodist Church in Santa Ana complained about the "political statements" of their minister when he took Congressman James B. Utt to task for his opposition to the United Nations. Progressive churches even became the target of attack by conservative religious zealots. Religious conservatives hung an effigy at the Unitarian church in 1962, charging that communists had invaded the church: "Arise!" said the note, which demanded the resignation of the minister, "help us throw out the tools of Satan before they lead more innocent souls to the slaughter."[249]

The regional daily newspaper, the *Register*, broadly and proudly publicized these activities within the churches and the community. Owner and editor Raymond Cyrus Hoiles had moved from Ohio in the 1930s to take over the Santa Ana *Register*, and by 1964 he had built a small empire of fourteen "Freedom Newspapers" throughout the Midwest, Texas, and California.[250] His paper was the largest circulating daily in the county, selling approximately 70,000 copies per day in 1960 and providing the main source of news for most Orange County residents.[251] While Hoiles had been printing his libertarian views in the Santa Ana *Register* even prior to World War II, he found a new mission in the revived conservative atmosphere of the early 1960s. He played a crucial role in the mobilization through publicizing anticommunist activities and giving voice to a broad spectrum of socially conservative and libertarian ideas in the newspaper's editorial pages. Conservatives recognized the *Register*'s contribution, and many wrote in to thank its editors for the "battle you are waging against communism."[252] H. E. Boldizer of La Mirada, a "proud and new member" of the John Birch Society, was thrilled with the editorials his coworkers at Autonetics brought in to work, leading him to eventually buy a subscription to the paper.[253]

The *Register* helped move Orange Countians' thinking on their schools, government taxes, and foreign policy in a conservative direction. Edna Slocum of Santa Ana attributed her politicization to her neighbors and the friendly press. "You start reading some of the writers in the Santa Ana *Register*, and getting another point of view from what we'd had, and you begin to wonder and question."[254] Moreover, the large space the *Register* offered to its readers in its "Clearing House" section served as a community billboard for conservative discussion, debate, and announcements, helping to foster conservative networking and mobilization. In this section, the Californians' Committee to Combat Communism announced when and to whom petition collectors should return their completed petitions. Even conservative activists from outside the region wrote in with news on conservative mobilization. One man from Ohio, for example, announced the formation of a "Committee to Save the Connally Amendment" in the columns of the *Register*.[255]

Hoiles's *Register*, along with local businesses and churches, provided critical institutional support for the Right. Financial and organizational help from conservative businessmen who circulated right-wing books, films, and pamphlets, the moral and material support of right-wing preachers, and the role of Hoiles's "Freedom Newspapers" in giving voice to conservative ideas were all indispensable for the heightened and sustained anticommunist atmosphere in Orange County during the early 1960s.[256] They provided the mechanisms of widespread internal communication within the movement, as well as the methods of education that forged the movement culture.

This institutional backing helped a galvanized group of citizens to build a strong local movement, which, because of its striking vitality, gained national attention. Although relative to the entire population of Orange County only a small band of men and women became active, their numbers were significant, and they swam within broader supportive waters. With the later upheavals of the decade, they would adjust their rhetoric and their concerns to attract more citizens to their cause. Mobilized in the early 1960s by single issues within their school districts and communities, they soon saw that political power could most easily be exerted through an established institution—the Republican Party. Using their networks and experiences to reinvigorate Republican volunteer organizations, these activists worked within the party to achieve their goals. Here, they joined forces with others throughout the nation to become part of a burgeoning conservative resurgence. Their opportunity to make their influence felt came with the campaign for Barry Goldwater in the 1964 presidential election.

Chapter ✧ **3**

THE GRASSROOTS GOLDWATER CAMPAIGN

O N SATURDAY, March 13, 1964, 600 delegates of the California Republican Assembly (CRA) gathered in Fresno to choose a slate of leaders for the coming year and to endorse a candidate for the November presidential election. The assembly, an unofficial body that included in its ranks most of the party's leadership in California, had been formed in the 1930s to bypass a state law prohibiting endorsement of candidates by county and state central committees in party primaries.[1] It had long been under the sway of moderate Republicans, but conservative activists had gained support in the early 1960s among the organization's approximately 14,000 members. Now the conservatives had come to Fresno to challenge the moderate leadership.[2] In two days of factional infighting, conservative supporters of Barry Goldwater, led by Newport Beach optometrist Nolan Frizzelle, challenged the forces favoring Nelson Rockefeller.[3]

By the early morning hours of March 15, the battle was over. The Right had installed Frizzelle as the new president of the statewide CRA and endorsed the senator from Arizona to carry the Republican banner in November. So hard-fought and significant was the victory that, according to the *CRA Enterprise*, "there were few dry eyes as the 1964 convention finally adjourned."[4] William Nelligan, the moderate outgoing CRA president from San Francisco, grimly conceded: "The 'Rampart Right' did their homework, came prepared to win, and they did. It was as simple as that."[5] Across the nation, conservatives cheered, and liberals warned of the takeover of the California Republican Party by the Right.[6]

Bolstered by their capture of an important Republican volunteer organization and its endorsement for their standard-bearer, the activists returned to their communities to work toward Goldwater's victory in the general California Republican Party primary set for early June.[7] The Goldwater forces concentrated their efforts in Southern California, where 40 percent of the state's Republicans lived. Now the rank-and-file cadres in Orange County and nearby Southern California communities— the housewives, doctors, engineers, dentists, and businessmen who had come into public view some years earlier to fight the collectivist menace in their schools, churches, and towns— walked precincts, made phone calls, and spread the conservative word. In the end, they played a decisive role in Goldwater's California triumph: Although Goldwater lost fifty-four of the fifty-eight California counties, his wide margins in Los Angeles, Orange, and San Diego Counties won him the election. Victory in California, a large state with eighty-six delegates, virtually guaranteed him the 1964 Republican nomination. Goldwater's success, according to one scholar of the postwar Republican Party, was due to the "volunteer army" that had mobilized in the southland.[8] Thus did Southern California's conservative mobilization, and its core activists from Orange County, for the first time make a national mark, decisively shaping the nation's politics by helping to bring conservatism onto the national political stage.[9]

The rise of Southern California's right wing to national prominence was a process that unfolded in several distinct stages. First, conservatives moved into the California electoral arena by drawing on earlier local activism. Once attuned to electoral politics, these local activists intersected with a national conservative movement and, in particular, the insurgent Goldwater wing of the Republican Party. The resulting symbiotic link between a mobilized grass roots and the national and regional conservative elites enabled the movement to reach new heights of success in

1964. If this relationship aided the movement, it also undermined its viability, as the national campaign became ever more securely yoked to extremism, leading it to certain national defeat. Consequently, a transformed conservative movement struggled to understand why a high degree of mobilization did not result in victory.

Ironically, the grassroots mobilization of the Right in the early 1960s was a result of the conservatives' lack of influence in Washington. Moderate Republicanism had triumphed under Eisenhower, and old-time spokespersons of the Right, such as Robert Taft and Joseph McCarthy, had died. At the same time, the ascendancy of the Democratic Party in 1960 and a blossoming rights-based liberalism, given life in Freedom Rides and sit-ins, magnified conservatives' sense of displacement. As a result, they mobilized at the grass roots. According to a conservative directory, for example, the number of right-wing groups more than doubled between 1957 and 1965—the largest number of which operated out of Southern California.[10] These initiatives were diverse, uncoordinated, and largely nonpartisan. Beyond the local struggles, however, they provided the activists who eventually would work in electoral politics when the opportunity arose.

While the burgeoning number of initiatives at the national and grassroots levels reflected a deep dissatisfaction with the choices the two parties were offering, most conservatives remained conscious of the importance of electoral politics in achieving their goals. For most of them, this meant the Republican Party. Even though the grassroots activists were hardly party loyalists, they saw electoral politics as a vehicle to influence the national government. As Walter Knott, owner of Knott's Berry Farm and a staunch backer of conservative causes, put it, "I'm not a fanatical Republican. It's not party that's the main thing . . . although I think that you have to work through a party. . . . [I]f you don't, you would be pretty ineffective."[11]

Right-wing organizations operating in Orange County—and nationally—also sought to influence the Republican Party. The John Birch Society, under the leadership of Republican Party loyalist Robert Welch, was dedicated to infiltrating the party. Although never formally endorsing political candidates, its members often played key roles in Republican Party activism.[12] Welch and his followers believed that the Republican Party alone "could not save the country . . . unless it has strong help and backing from forces outside of the straight political organization," which, presumably, included his own organization.[13] As national conservative leaders sought to coordinate and build grassroots activism and bring it into the party, local activists themselves, even those who organized outside of party channels, had never entirely given up on the electoral arena.

Some state and national conservatives, skeptical of the possibility of influencing the Republican Party, organized third-party movements, but these movements generally came to naught for lack of a mass commitment. Howard Jarvis, disappointed in his own bid to unseat Senator Thomas Kuchel, the moderate incumbent, in the Republican primary in 1962, organized the Conservative Party of California late that year, arguing that "we do not believe . . . that any conservative can win the Republican nomination for the presidency."[14] Such an argument resonated with some conservatives, and the party gained 60,000 members. But when Barry Goldwater announced his candidacy in January 1964, more than half of these members jumped ship and reregistered Republican, effectively destroying the new party.[15] Similarly, Conservative Party members from twenty-five states came together at a convention in Richmond, Virginia, in February to plan a national conservative party, but their efforts dissipated after Goldwater won the Republican nomination.[16]

Even after Goldwater's defeat and the seeming collapse of the conservative Republican movement, southland activists would largely ignore third-party conservative movements. George Wallace's American Independent Party, the most successful third-party movement in the 1960s, won 13.5 percent of the national electoral vote in 1968.[17] But Wallace, a staunch segregationist who spoke the language of a lower-middle-class populism, held deep attachments to New Deal programs, the welfare state, and unions—attachments that were anathema to most Southern California (as well as national) conservatives.[18] As a result of these inclinations, the Right—in Orange County and nationally—remained, to a large extent, tied to working within the Republican Party.

Although the extent of the grassroots mobilization in the California Republican Party in the 1960s was unprecedented, right-wing efforts to influence the party were hardly new. The party had long been divided between its moderate and conservative wings. Even in 1952, Earl Warren's "favorite son" status in the Republican presidential primary was challenged by California conservatives who, in a bitter contest, ran a separate slate of delegates.[19] And, in 1958, Senator William Knowland, the state's leading conservative, gained enough support in his bid for the party's nomination for the governorship that incumbent Goodwin Knight gave up his bid for reelection, running instead for the Senate. This infamous switch—along with Knowland's embrace of "right-to-work" laws—led to the party's debacle in the 1958 elections.[20]

In the 1940s and 1950s, however, the Warren strategy of downplaying ideological differences to capture Democratic votes essential for a Republican victory and the cross-filing system (whereby a candidate was allowed to enter the primaries of both parties) by and large held the field.[21] The California party sent staunch liberal Republicans like Thomas Kuchel to the U.S. Senate, and even in Orange County, moderates like Bruce Sumner were elected to the California assembly.[22] Yet moderate control proved to be built on a fragile foundation. The abolition of the cross-filing system in 1959, large Democratic electoral victories in 1958 and 1960, and the burgeoning grassroots conservative movement left the moderate leadership vulnerable to attack by well-organized conservatives in the 1960s.[23]

These conservatives—the men and women who first mobilized in civil society against the "collectivist menace" in their schools and communities—knew that in order to exert significant political power their movement had to gain influence over the institutions of the state. For this purpose, already in 1961, a group that included William Brashears, a dentist and conservative Baptist who had helped organize the Orange County School of Anti-Communism, and R. Dickson Miles, who had headed the drive to remove Joel Dvorman from the Magnolia school board of trustees, established the Conservative Coordinating Council to help elect conservatives to office. By 1962, they were mailing 150,000 sample ballots, listing the candidates the council had endorsed, to registered Orange County voters.[24] Conservatives also ran for the Orange County Republican Central Committee (which included such prominent men as Walter Knott throughout the decade), school board positions, and other local offices. While there was a high degree of electoral activism by the early 1960s, Orange County activists moved to extend their reach beyond local politics by capturing a statewide organization.[25]

As early as 1961, a few local activists had turned toward the California Republican Assembly as a means to shift the Republican Party to the right. In the words of Nolan Frizzelle, a key organizer and future president of the organization, "I thought, well, if I could take this liberal organization and convert it to becoming conservative instead, we could help in electing conservative Republicans to the state legislature."[26] The CRA, under the leadership of Earl Warren, had for decades endorsed centrist or moderate Republicans.[27] Made up largely of the party leadership and Republican Party workers, the organization remained small, claiming 6,346 members in 1959.[28] But because it was a volunteer group, where numbers and organization counted, it was vulnerable to infiltration from the grass roots. It was therefore very attractive to newly mobilized conservatives, who saw it as a means to make themselves the "voice of California Republicans."[29] The organization dangled like a ripe fruit before conservatives' eyes.

If conservative activists hoped to use the endorsement powers of the CRA, they first needed to control it. Building a base within the assembly by recruiting new members and organizing new chapters, they hoped to eventually challenge the moderate Republican hold. According to Nolan Frizzelle, they "chartered units of the assembly very much against the leadership of the state organization. . . . [M]y idea was to have control from the bottom up." Frizzelle himself had become a charter member of the Costa Mesa assembly in 1960 and, during the next three years, diligently created the Newport Harbor, Tustin, Santa Ana, Anaheim, Brea, Rossmoor, and La Habra assemblies, as well as reorganized the old Garden Grove assembly.[30] Encountering little resistance, Frizzelle and his fellow activists had an easy time taking over the largely dormant CRA in Orange County and, by 1963, it had mushroomed into a dynamic base for local conservative campaigning.[31] In 1963, Orange County activists even established their own newspaper, the *CRA Enterprise*, which highlighted Orange County CRA activities and propounded the organization's conservative philosophy.[32] The *CRA Enterprise* strongly linked itself to a broader national conservative movement, quoting from *Human Events* and carrying articles by Tom Anderson, a frequent writer for the John Birch Society mouthpiece *American Opinion*.[33]

Capturing control of the Orange County CRA depended on the networks conservatives had established through previous activities, among them the Dvorman struggle, the Orange County School of Anti-Communism, the John Birch Society, and the mobilization to pass the Francis amendment. Nolan Frizzelle vividly recalled the vital role these networks played in building the CRA:

> I got a list of people. . . . I started out in the Christian Anti-Communism Crusade and out of the 5,000 to 6,000 people that were there, there were 100 people that I came to know fairly closely in helping to organize that crusade. Ultimately some of those 100 people became the source of verification of the viewpoints of others we asked to join.[34]

Recruiting new activists also relied heavily on personal contacts. One conservative from Tustin, for example (who founded a CRA chapter there), remembered that she and her husband, with the help of another couple, "built up membership to . . . around 400 or 500 members within two or three years just by telephone contacts and personal contacts."[35] The activists expanded the ranks of the Republican grass roots through these organizational methods, but within an ideological spectrum with little room for liberal or moderate Republicans to join. As Frizzelle noted "We'd get together in my living room, about thirty people, and we would recruit those people by telephone, one person would lead us to another—they'd lead us only to people who were conservative."[36] Peggy Pearce, one of the first sponsors of the Orange County School of Anti-Communism, was one of them. She received a phone call from Frizzelle, asking her to head the formation of a CRA chapter in Fullerton. Having worked hard for the school's success and being "on fire to do something," she now poured her energies into building the CRA.[37]

These activists' reliance on prior networks and neighborhood contacts to recruit new members meant that the socioeconomic composition of the CRA closely resembled that of Orange County's conservative movement more generally: They were solidly middle-class men and women, including housewives, ranchers, small businessmen, engineers, doctors, and dentists.[38] CRA leadership and that of the other local mobilizations also overlapped notably: Frizzelle had been active in the Christian Anti-Communism Crusade, Ronald Rankin had been on the board of the Orange County Conservative Coordinating Council and was publisher of the conservative newsletter *Grass-Roots*, John Schmitz had served as a political science instructor of the popular course "Communist Aggression" at Santa Ana College, and Peggy Pearce had helped to recruit Fred Schwarz and his School of Anti-Communism to come to Orange County.[39] But some Orange Countians also mobilized for the first time through their work in the CRA: Edna and Joe Slocum, for example, had participated only in Republican Party precinct work prior to forming a unit of the CRA. Referring to new members, Edna Slocum even contended that "probably for 90 percent of them . . . it was their first political organization."[40]

These activists' zeal did not translate, however, into success in endorsing their cohorts at the state level. Indeed, in 1962, while the CRA in Orange County supported Joe Shell, a wealthy Los Angeles manufacturer and staunch conservative, for the Republican Party gubernatorial nomination, the statewide convention endorsed Richard Nixon. In a sign of what was to come, however, the convention—much to Nixon's dismay—rejected a strong resolution condemning the John Birch Society.[41]

While Shell's primary loss against Nixon proved that the Right in 1962 was still too weak to challenge moderate control of the party, it nonetheless announced the presence of a strong conservative current within the Republican Party.[42] The new grassroots movement, especially in the southland, had supported Shell with money, time, and votes, thus enabling him to give Nixon a hard fight for his nomination. One of these new activists, Estrid Kielsmeier, felt so strongly about the campaign that she ran the candidate's headquarters in Buena Park despite her responsibilities as a young mother. Her baby played in a playpen next to her desk while Kielsmeier participated in what she called, more than thirty years later, her first real involvement in politics. "Up to that time . . . it was education and just kind of . . . networking, really."[43]

Building on this zealous grassroots base, many influential groups and leaders came out in support of Shell. The Californians for Goldwater Clubs, the California Young Republicans, the Los Angeles Republican Central Committee (a previous Nixon preserve), and Orange County CRAs supported him.[44] Important southland leaders, such as Walter Knott, also sided with the Shell camp.[45] Even Ronald Reagan, a longtime friend and supporter of Nixon, told Nixon's campaign managers that he would stay out of the primary fight between Nixon and Shell because "he feels he can then be more effective in the final campaign on your behalf."[46] Even though he did not gain a majority, Shell's 33 percent of the primary vote showed that hard-core conservatives had to be reckoned with.[47]

Considering Nixon's staunch anticommunist credentials and his later rapprochement with the Right, the hostility of some conservatives to him might seem surprising; but there was a logic to this stance. Many conservatives recoiled from Nixon's close association with the Eisenhower administration, which they considered "me-too" Republicanism. Nixon's infamous "sellout of Fifth Avenue," a compromise worked out with Rockefeller to gain the support of the eastern wing of the party for the presidential nomination in 1960, also cost him a good deal of support among conservatives nationally and in his native Southern California.[48] Nixon earned more enmity from the Right in California when he attacked the "extreme Right" and the John Birch Society. Congressman James B. Utt informed Nixon that "your denunciation of the Birch Society because of what Robert Welch has said is just . . . ridiculous."[49] And although Walter Knott reaffirmed an earlier promise that he would support Nixon in the general election, he asked him to "lay off the Birch Society and refrain from depreciating the conservative movement."[50]

The contentious and hostile nature of this 1962 primary campaign created bitter divisions within the party. Because of his opposition to the John Birch Society, Nixon earned the unbending hostility of many grassroots Republican workers who otherwise may have been willing to work for him.[51] Estrid Kielsmeier, for example, who had campaigned hard for Shell, refused to expend her energies working toward Nixon's election, despite Walter Knott's pleas.[52] Nixon's challenger, Joe Shell, moreover, refused to back Nixon in the general election unless he provided "proof that [he] could espouse the principles of conservatism" and committed to cutting $200 million out of the state budget. Nixon, not surprisingly, refused to bend to such demands, and the campaign remained divided. Meanwhile, Democratic candidate Edmund Brown, with a united party behind him, waged a cautious and upbeat campaign. In November, Nixon was defeated, drawing 2,740,000 votes to Brown's 3,037,000. According to an important state leader in the Republican Party, "We lost . . . because Joe Shell and the conservatives sat on their hands."[53] Yet while conservatives failed to work for Nixon, damaging internal party unity and probably leading at least a few conservatives to sit out the election, responsibility for Nixon's loss lay with his inability to draw in enough Democratic voters, which was necessary in California for a Republican to win election.[54]

The 1962 primary campaign showed, for the first time, the emergence of the new conservative grassroots movement within electoral politics. Nixon was too formidable a figure to defeat outright—particularly given his spotty but undeniably conservative record and his extensive national experience.[55] Yet the zealous crop of right-wing activists were not easily deterred: "We were like bull-dogs," one of them later remarked, and another recalled their slogan, "Never retreat."[56] After the 1962 debacle, they redoubled their efforts to influence the party. The heart of this movement was to "take over" the statewide CRA.

Conservative party volunteers made their first bid to gain control over the CRA at the organization's March 1963 convention, held at the Disneyland Hotel in Anaheim. The self-described "political neophytes," mostly newcomers to politics and certainly to party organization, staked their claim to control of the CRA, but they lost.[57] Parliamentary wrangling led to the seating of a majority of liberal delegates, who voted into office a liberal state leadership with William Nelligan, a San Francisco telephone worker and member of the Communication Workers of America, as president.[58] With conservatives angry over what they saw as unfair manipulations of the proceedings, bitter infighting broke up the convention.

Convinced that the CRA would remain in the hands of liberals, a small group of conservatives formed a separate endorsing organization: the United Republicans of California. Under the leadership of Joseph Crosby, a Pasadena industrialist, Joe Shell, the former gubernatorial candidate, and Bruce Reagan, a California assemblyman, this conservative offshoot grew rapidly, winning 12,000 members statewide by December 1964.[59] Other conservatives, however, convinced that they indeed could gain control of the organization, stayed within the CRA.[60] The 1964 presidential campaign for Barry Goldwater proved them right.

✧✧✧

Barry Goldwater's rock-ribbed conservative record and unrelenting schedule of public appearances had brought him to the attention of some national and regional conservative leaders as early as 1960, and they urged the Arizona senator to make a bid for the Republican Party presidential nomination that year. A small Draft Goldwater Movement spread quickly throughout the country.[61] In California, Los Angeleno Paul "Tex" Talbert, a member of the John Birch Society National Council and a wealthy insurance man, headed the regional drive. Under his direction, the Southern California Draft Goldwater Movement worked feverishly right up to the convention.[62]

These efforts bore little fruit at the 1960 convention, but they did lay the groundwork for 1964. Goldwater was well aware that with centrist forces firmly in control and Vice President Nixon standing as the heir to Eisenhower, he had little chance of winning, and he stepped aside to support Nixon.[63] Yet he called on conservatives to "get to work" to "take this party back."[64] National conservative leaders set their sights on the party's nomination four years later, and by 1961, *Time* and *Newsweek* were portraying Goldwater on their covers as the standard-bearer of a broad movement.[65] The senator from Arizona soon became known around the nation as "Mister Conservative," a symbol of the ambition and growing power of the newly mobilized Right.[66] Asserting the significance of Goldwater's leadership for conservatives, William Rusher, publisher of *National Review*, prophetically asserted that when "the conservative movement found Senator Goldwater, Senator Goldwater found the movement; it was like the meeting of the Blue and the White Nile."[67]

The national movement that Barry Goldwater had activated in 1960 now began to plan for 1964.[68] Patrick Buchanan, for example, marked the beginning of his life commitment to the movement after Goldwater's speech at the 1960 Republican convention: "I enlisted," he later remarked.[69] In the fall of 1961, a group of conservative political enthusiasts led by F. Clifton White plotted a "constitutional coup" in the Republican Party.[70] A little over a year later, the press reported on secret

Several hundred supporters attended the opening of Orange County Goldwater headquarters in Orange on February 8, 1964. (Reprinted by permission of the *Orange County Register*.)

meetings of the Draft Goldwater Movement that evolved out of this ad hoc committee. Finally, on February 16, 1963, a body of fifty-five conservatives organized the National Draft Goldwater Committee.[71] Initially, they drew on local conservative networks to encourage conservative party members to run for precinct, county, and state party positions in caucus states. This way, only bona fide conservative delegates would be selected for the 1964 convention.[72] In the old South, these young Republican leaders easily swung their delegations for Goldwater, whose opposition to the Civil Rights Bill of 1963, along with his strong states' rights position, conformed with southern white sentiments. As a result, Goldwater won a number of uncontested primary and caucus states in 1964. Their delegates made him a strong competitor against Nelson Rockefeller and Henry Cabot Lodge for the Republican Party nomination. By the beginning of June 1964, the Arizonan had secured some 300 delegates from the caucus states. According to journalist and political observer Theodore White, the Goldwater movement's "planning was more useful, more determined, and earlier begun than that of any previous presidential campaign; it was a masterpiece of politics."[73]

Yet Goldwater's success in the caucus states was not matched by his record in the open primaries. While he won the midwestern states of Indiana, Illinois, and Nebraska, he was defeated in New Hampshire and Oregon. By the spring of 1964, it was clear that Goldwater would have to win a large state with a contested primary to secure his nomination. That large state was California, with its eighty-six delegates in a winner-take-all primary.[74] Caspar Weinberger, chairman of the California Republican Central Committee, described the stakes succinctly: "If Goldwater wins here . . . he practically wins the Republican nomination. And if he loses, he won't get it."[75]

California polling statistics did not offer the senator much hope, placing his support as low as 33 percent in May 1964, less than one month before the primary.[76] But the polls underestimated the commitment of zealous southland conservatives and their drive to gain the nomination for their standard-bearer. Already in February, Goldwater volunteers launched "Operation Q," a vast and highly efficient campaign to secure enough qualifying signatures to get their candidate's name on the ballot. Goldwater troops throughout Orange County worked weeks stomping precincts and reminding conservatives of the March 4 qualifying day. In the early morning of opening day, in neighborhoods throughout the county, conservative volunteers swung open the front doors of their homes. Coffee, doughnuts, and nominating petitions were on hand for the large number of supporters who came to sign their names for Goldwater.[77] While CRA activists organized "coffees" in Orange County, volunteers elsewhere swarmed throughout the state ringing doorbells. In an amazing organizational feat, they managed to gather more than 36,000 names before noon on the first day of their drive, far surpassing the necessary 13,000 signatures. Within two days, they had gathered 86,000 names. Rockefeller, in contrast, relied on pay-per-signature professionals and was still working to acquire the necessary number of signatures the week before the deadline.[78]

While Goldwater's candidacy drew on a preexisting mobilization, it also advanced it, in effect vastly broadening the scope of grassroots conservative influence. The efforts of these Orange County activists to take over the CRA were, for example, boosted by the Goldwater candidacy. The increasingly real prospect that one of their own might have a shot at the White House drew new recruits to the CRA. As one Garden Grove activist, Cathy Sullivan, declared, Goldwater "lit a fire here in the county."[79] Membership surged, and new chapters mushroomed as fresh recruits joined the CRA. By the end of 1964, the Orange County CRA topped 2,600 members, and statewide membership reached 20,000. Between March and December 1964 alone, 6,000 new members had joined the organization.[80]

Spurred by their success, southland CRA leaders sought to flex their muscles once more in the statewide organization. After the conservative defeat at the statewide convention in 1963, Fred Hall, the assembly's retiring president, had optimistically asserted that the failure of conservatives to gain control of the organization signaled "the turning point against the conspiracy of the John Birch Society and its supporters to capture control of the Republican Party."[81] His predictions proved wrong: Conservatives, inspired in large part by the Goldwater campaign, returned in 1964 stronger in number and wiser in parliamentary and organizational tactics. As one Orange County activist recalled, "Now we [were] beginning to get a little tough. We [were] not so naive anymore . . . we got battle scars to show it."[82] Led by four southland conservatives, three of whom were from Orange County, they made a second bid to take over the California Republican Assembly in March 1964.[83]

On March 13, 1964, after a solid year of planning, conservatives came to the convention in Fresno prepared to take over the CRA. According to William Nelligan, then president of the statewide organization, "bus-loads of die-hard conservatives came up from Orange County and the deep South."[84] Moderate Republicans, however, also arrived in Fresno fully intent on maintaining their hold. Prior to the convention, a subcommittee, under centrist leadership, already had put through a resolution in favor of a neutral stance, rather than endorsing either Rockefeller or

Goldwater.[85] Nelson Rockefeller had approved this strategy, but the Right would settle for nothing less than the nomination of Goldwater.

After days of bitter factional infighting, the conservative slate won by a large majority (60.6 percent to 39.4 percent), and Orange County's Nolan Frizzelle acceded to the presidency of the statewide organization. The new CRA endorsed Goldwater—an influential and important gesture for the Goldwater forces.[86] Conservatives, moreover, had won lasting control over an important Republican organization. As the *CRA Enterprise* explained their success: "Last year's political neophytes had evolved into self-disciplined, well-organized exponents of their philosophy."[87]

Not surprisingly, moderates bitterly denounced the right-wing takeover and openly fretted about the direction of their party. After his loss at the Fresno convention, Nelligan categorized the struggle as "a fight with extremist guerrillas sniping at our flanks. . . . The fanatics of the Birch variety have fastened their fangs on the Republican Party's flank and are hanging on like grim death."[88] Nelson Rockefeller, who had given a speech at the convention, asserted in equally strong language that the convention demonstrated that "sinister forces are at work to take over the whole Republican apparatus in California."[89] Republican moderates had reason to be concerned with the developments in the party. After all, the CRA was not the only Republican organ under conservative leadership. At their 1963 convention, the California Young Republicans had elected Robert Gaston, a strong Birch supporter, to their leadership.[90] True to form, at their 1964 convention, the conservative Young Republicans refused to commit to working for a Republican ticket if their candidate, Barry Goldwater, failed to win the nomination.[91] One moderate Republican was so concerned by the developments in California that he left his post with the Republican National Committee in the spring of 1964 to work for Rockefeller.[92] Expressing the fears of moderates, Republican National Committee member Joseph Martin warned that "if Goldwater wins the June 2 California primary, the voice of the party will be the voice of the Birchers and the Minutemen."[93]

In the wake of the conservative success at the CRA state convention, moderate Republicans, as well as Democratic liberals and the Left, frequently characterized the conservative movement with reference to its most extreme component, the conspiratorial John Birch Society. And, indeed, John Birch Society members played an important role within the leadership and rank and file of the CRA, as well as the Goldwater movement.[94] As Armstrong Dowell, one of the leaders of the Goldwater committee in the city of Orange, asserted, "There were quite a few Birchers in our precinct organization. None of us . . . were hard-and-fast Birchers. We joined because it seemed to be an organization that might be doing something."[95] Moreover, while most conservatives were not members of the John Birch Society, many still perceived the organization as loyal and patriotic. As one leading local conservative, who was not himself a member, put it, "I don't consider the John Birch Society extremists, except maybe extremely American." Instead he, and many other conservatives, lumping the Far Right together with liberals and the Left, insisted that it was the "Communist Party, the Ku Klux Klan, the ADA and the California Democratic Council and black Muslims that are really extreme."[96]

While the John Birch Society was the most vital organized grassroots conservative force of the era, it is misleading to equate the movement as a whole with the society. Conservatives within the Republican Party certainly had beliefs that meshed well with those of the John Birch Society—virulent anticommunism, laissez-faire economics, and a staunch moralism. But many right-wing proponents were repelled by the conspiratorial aspects of the Birch philosophy and felt that Welch's erratic leadership of the society had damaged the movement as a whole. Frank Gaude of Santa Ana, for example, a self-described supporter of "rock-hard" conservatives, lamented that "Welch's unsubstantiated accusations . . . had done enough damage to conservatism." Indeed, he contended, if Welch's assertions about Communist influence were accurate, "I cannot see what the 'one-worlders' are waiting for. They could take the U.S. over and have their world government under communism now."[97] Even such a staunch conservative as Orange County's James B. Utt disassociated himself from some of Welch's utterances.[98] While some conservatives criticized the Society's conspiratorial vision, other conservatives (including James B. Utt, William F. Buckley, Jr., Barry Goldwater, and Ronald Reagan) were quick to distinguish between the leadership of the society and its membership, whom they considered "some of the solidest conservatives in the country."[99] After all, as they well understood, Welch's movement was the only national right-wing organization with a mass base. As the right-wing publicist Marvin Liebman put it, "There now exists in this country a conservative-anti-Communist apparat[us] that we all have hoped for. It is controled [sic] by Robert Welch."[100]

The Birch, or "extremist," tag would hound the conservative movement through the mid-1960s, a constant reminder that its ideas lay outside the bounds of respectable political discourse. And, indeed, the rhetoric of the John Birch Society and the ideas expressed in its journal, American Opinion, were, despite some conservatives' claims to the contrary, extreme. At their more radical edge, its writers evinced a mixture of blood-and-soil nationalism and traditionalism with an anti-Democratic free-market ethos.[101] The Birch Society's calls to "impeach Earl Warren," its "scoreboards of Communist conquest," its exposés of "treasonous networks in the State Department," its calls for "getting the U.S. out of the U.N.," and its tirades against what one American Opinion writer asserted was the liberal goal of "One World: One Race, One World: One Government" smacked of a zaniness that was easily lampooned by liberals and that contributed to marginalizing the conservative movement.

Only the Right's own muting of its more militant ideas and more radical edge would enable it to widen its appeal to a broader public by building a new conservative respectability. The mainstream political spectrum in the 1960s, after all, agreed that the federal government was needed to address problems that free-market capitalism could not. In a decade of liberal achievements, right-wing pronouncements on turning back the welfare state and conservatives' belief that the government had no place in redressing social and economic inequities were considered among liberal Democrats, moderate Republicans, and the Left alike as "extremist." They seemed far-fetched and radical.

Yet however accurate the "extremist" label might have been for the John Birch Society—and for the movement more broadly within the context of the post–World War II liberal consensus—it discouraged opponents of the Right from taking the potential appeal of these movements seriously. This was important, as quick judgments led to overconfident pronouncements about the limited future of these ideas. In hindsight, it is obvious that these were clearly not a marginal set of archaic beliefs that had some-how survived into the modern age, but rather ideologies birthed and nourished in the most modern of communities. They were ideas that would outlive the John Birch Society's effectiveness and emerge again more powerfully a few years later.

The core beliefs and issues that the movement embraced in the midsixties drew on older ideological inheritances with deep roots in American political culture to express concern with so-cial, political, and cultural change in the 1960s. These concerns presaged some of the themes that have become such a familiar part of conservative discourse in more recent years. By looking at the principles adopted by the newly elected conservative lead-ers of the California Republican Assembly, we can uncover the motivating concerns that drove their political involvement. Their concerns meshed libertarianism and social conservatism—a combination that had constituted diverse segments of Ameri-can conservatism in the past and that would propel its future.

Tellingly, CRA leaders adopted the "Sharon Declaration," the founding document of William Buckley's Young Americans for Freedom, suggesting the linkages between the broader na-tional movement and the activists in California. These principles affirmed a strong commitment to economic freedom, states' rights (hinting at the importance of civil rights to conservative concerns), and the destruction of international communism, as well as affirming the belief that a divine intent ruled society.[102]

Along with a strong commitment to values of the free market—expressed, for example, through resolutions calling for the repeal of the personal property tax—the CRA expressed concerns about broader social issues. The governing board passed resolutions calling for "freedom from filth" in film and television and "vigorous law enforcement . . . at the local, state and federal levels to obtain . . . the arrest, prosecution and conviction of filth peddlers whose contaminating products constitute a detailed course of instruction on perversion and act as a catalyst agent of moral decay across the length and breadth of our beloved nation."[103] These conservatives thus not only stressed their concern over "moral issues" and cultural and social change but also linked these values with the heritage of the Founding Fathers. They embraced, in other words, a staunch nationalism along with a jealous concern for U.S. sovereignty in international affairs.

Concern over social and cultural change was also expressed through the wrath CRA leaders rained down on the civil rights movement and growing student protests. While the race issue did not inform Southern California's conservative mobilization to the extent it did in the South, concerns over sustaining white racial privileges propelled right-wing mobilization well before the civil rights movement moved north and the New Left gained strength. The CRA board "opposed the efforts of pressure groups . . . to extend the activity of the FBI into acting independently of local law enforcement agencies in providing federal protection to civil rights workers . . . as an unconstitutional extent[ion] of federal power." The language of states' rights and concerns over government centralization bespoke white Orange Countians' deep hostility toward liberals' desire to extend rights, as one writer for *American Opinion* put it, to "the black and brown peoples of the world."[104] As much of a concern as the blossoming civil rights movement were events in the northern portion of the state. The CRA went on record as "urging the administration of the University of California to use all resources of law enforcement against any recurrence of disorder" and supported the dismissal of faculty who supported "rebellious students."[105] Sustaining "law and order," and thus preventing radical social change, was high on the agenda of conservatives.

Finally, the new board expressed a deep ambivalence toward popular democracy, an ambivalence that bespoke their minoritarian status. Barry Goldwater, along with the John Birch Society, had trumpeted the notion that "this is a Republic, not a Democracy," evincing a deep hostility to liberals' concerns with equality, and the CRA board agreed. Regarding the Supreme Court's 1964 decision on apportionment, the board resolved:

> The principle of one man, one vote violates the very promise of a representative Republican form of government and . . . since the further this concept of Government is implemented, the closer we come to mob rule, now therefore be it resolved the Board of Directors of the CRA inform the Legislature that sound Republican principles will be destroyed by the recent incursion of the judiciary into the . . . field of apportionment.[106]

Conservatives feared that the Supreme Court decision would lead to empowering urban, liberal, and minority constituencies in favor of more rural conservative ones—and voiced skepticism that the court should not be thought of as "a general haven for reform movements."[107]

The CRA resolutions were the direct product of the right-wing grassroots revolt, expressing some of the issues that brought conservative Southern California middle-class men and women of the new suburban communities into public view. The conservatives' favorite son, Barry Goldwater, spoke to these concerns better than any other prominent political figure of the day. After their victory at the CRA convention, they moved to clinch the general California Republican primary nomination for Goldwater. They returned to their communities ready to work, and there they encountered fertile ground.

✧✧✧

Orange County, not surprisingly, proved a stronghold of Gold-waterism. If Barry Goldwater was, as publisher William Rusher astutely observed, "the mid-wife of modern conservatism," then without doubt its birthplace was the Southwest—and specifically Southern California.[108] The epicenter of Southern California conservatism—Orange County—took the lead in mobilizing the groundswell for Goldwater: In 1964, the region from Fullerton to Laguna Beach, Yorba Linda to Irvine was Goldwater country.

Goldwater's entrepreneurial individualism and his references to the West as the repository of true American values elicited a strong regional appeal. As he boasted: "Out here in the West and the Midwest, we're not constantly harassed by the fear of what might happen. . . . sure there are risks, but we've always taken risks."[109] This mythology of risk-taking individualism and Goldwater's anti-Washington, anti-regulatory ethos resonated forcefully with Orange Countians' sense of themselves, their experiences, and their aspirations in a period of boom-time affluence. As one southland Goldwater supporter spouted: "It is time that we have a fine candidate for President from the *west* for a change and not permit a few Republicans in the east to keep control of our party."[110] Goldwater's uncompromising warriorlike attitude toward the Soviet Union, moreover, his call "not to end the Cold War but to win it," and his advocacy of "peace through strength" resonated well in a region where the lives and livelihoods of so many individuals were closely linked to the continuation of the Cold War.[111]

Goldwater also spoke to the concerns of the region's many religious conservatives.[112] While his militant anticommunism frightened many citizens, particularly his willingness to use "low-yield" nuclear weapons in battle, among religious conservatives—who saw the Soviet Union as the "Antichrist"—this stance was the only form of principled anticommunism they could accept.[113] Goldwater, in contrast to Lyndon Johnson, also forcefully referred to the "decline of morality" and the breakdown of the family. He blamed moral decay and a decline in family authority on the reliance on government largesse over individual responsibility.[114] This message resonated among both Catholic and Protestant religious conservatives concerned about shifting cultural and social norms.

Finally, Goldwater's position regarding states' rights and his vote against the 1964 Civil Rights Act found favor in a region where sentiment against "government centralization" and "collectivism" ran strong. Above all, his support of "property rights" over civil rights as the ultimate test of freedom resounded among white middle-class property holders in a state whose Democrats had recently passed fair housing legislation.[115] Fair housing was a particularly contentious issue in California's 1964 elections, with a proposition measure backed by the California Real Estate Association that, if passed, would rescind the Rumford Act—the state law prohibiting housing discrimination on the basis of race. The mobilization in favor of Proposition 14 bolstered conservatives' cause. Indeed, one activist, Tom Rogers of San Juan Capistrano, who served as the campaign finance manager for John Schmitz's state senate run in 1964 and who shortly afterward served as a coeditor of the national Catholic traditionalist paper, the *Wanderer*, asserted years later that for him and many others, Proposition 14 was what the movement was all about.[116] Goldwater's frequent references in favor of "freedom of association," his belief that "prejudice is a moral issue that cannot be legislated," and his strong advocacy of property rights placed him firmly on the side of those opposing the Rumford Act.[117] Moreover, Goldwater's determination to fight "lawlessness," his references to rising crime rates, and his linkage of crime to "lawlessness of other sorts" (a reference to the civil rights and student movements) appealed to the white middle classes in Orange County.[118]

Yet Goldwater's appeal to Southern Californians cannot be reduced merely to a "white backlash." If it had been simply that, he would very likely have won a good deal more votes than he did. The strong potential of the "white backlash" vote became clear in November, when Californians voted two to one in favor of repealing the state's fair housing laws.[119] But Goldwater's hard-and-fast conservative agenda led many of these same individuals to vote against him. Elements of the Right's message in 1964 were unpalatable to the majority of voters. Except in the Deep South, where racial issues and the preservation of white privilege overrode other considerations, Goldwater won the votes only of those individuals who embraced a broader conservative worldview based on limits to federal government control and a strong defense, as well as states' rights in the arena of civil rights.[120] Always and unendingly he referred to his central message, "Government is not your master, it must be your servant."[121] To supporters in Fullerton, he warned that a "government that is big enough to give you everything you want is also strong enough to take it away."[122]

Just as important, Goldwater's politics resonated among a powerful group of regional businessmen—and their strong backing of his campaign, in turn, helped to generate his grassroots support. Goldwater's appeal in the southland, in other words, should not be read simply as a spontaneous outpouring of sentiment from the bottom up. Goldwater was also the standard-bearer for a newly powerful segment of capital that had risen out of the Sunbelt postwar economic boom and that now sought to assert its power nationally within the Republican Party against the dominance of the eastern Republicans.[123] These elites supplied his campaign with funds and helped, through numerous channels, to spread the conservative word.[124]

By 1960, powerful businessmen had organized Goldwater Clubs in the southland. They founded the Advisory Committee for Goldwater in 1963 and finally, on January 15, 1964, changed its name to the California Goldwater for President Committee.[125] Some of the individuals involved had already played a prominent role in backing the regional anticommunist mobilizations of the early 1960s. From Orange County, there was Walter Knott of Knott's Berry Farm, who had founded the California Free Enterprise Association. From nearby Los Angeles came Patrick Frawley, president of Eversharp and chief executive of Technicolor, who had helped sponsor the Christian Anti-Communism Crusade and the All-Southern California School of Anti-Communism, as well as Joe Shell, who had run against Nixon in the Republican Party primary in 1962. Finally, two individuals who would soon become known as members of Ronald Reagan's "Kitchen Cabinet" lent their support: Henry Salvatori of Western Geophysical, a strong supporter of a right-wing southland initiative, Project Alert, and president of the Anti-Communist Voters' League, served as the finance chairman of the California Goldwater for President Committee; and Cy Rubel, retired chairman of Union Oil, sat on the committee.[126]

These businessmen not only provided funds and leadership for the regional Goldwater drive, but also spread the Arizonan's message to the grass roots. Conservative businessmen, who had distributed books and pamphlets on "freedom," now used the same networks to spread the word for the Sunbelt senator. Insurance executive Tex Talbert, who headed the southland's Goldwater Clubs, distributed and sold *Conscience of a Conservative*, Goldwater's ghostwritten autobiography, as early as 1960.[127] Citizens for Constructive Action, the right-wing southland educational organization, with Walter Knott as its top officer, distributed 500,000 copies of John Stormer's *None Dare Call It Treason*, a book that warned of a State Department clique that allegedly sought to unilaterally disarm the nation.[128] And before the primaries, a half-million copies of Phyllis Schlafly's *A Choice, Not an Echo* circulated throughout the southland, proclaiming that eastern Republicans had conspired since the 1930s with "left-wing" Democrats to assure that neither party's nominee would threaten the "hidden policy of perpetuating the Red Empire."[129] Rockefeller, as the eastern Republican "kingpin," Schlafly lamented, offered little alternative to Lyndon Johnson; the only real choice for conservatives was thus Barry Goldwater. By 1964, the southland was saturated with pro-Goldwater tracts that passed from house to house. A leader of the Goldwater committee of the city of Orange recalled that "there was literature coming out in every way. Hard-cover books to soft-cover books, tracts, one-page sheets. You couldn't imagine the stack. . . . It was incredible."[130] These books and tracts were no minor force in drawing conservatives to Goldwater. Just like the study groups before them, they generated a process of widespread internal economic and political education.[131] According to one activist, they provided interpretations of Barry Goldwater that enabled conservatives to view him in a light very different from the portrayals in much of the national press:

> Goldwater was a mystery to us. Because the press, what did the press say about him? "Well he's against Social Security, he's a war-monger," that's what we heard. She [Phyllis Schlafly] wrote a book, *A Choice, Not an Echo* and she . . . made us familiar with this person and what he was about. . . . Then we identified with him.[132]

Conservative leaders, moreover, held events to drum up support for Goldwater. One of them, a Memorial Day kickoff for Goldwater sponsored by Walter Knott, was especially successful. It was held on Knott's Berry Farm in Buena Park on a sunny, warm Southern California day, with crowd-pleasing conservatives like John Wayne and Ronald Reagan, along with a band of Goldwater "folksingers," entertaining the huge crowd. The approximately 28,000 supporters who came no doubt were strengthened in the conviction of their cause by the large numbers.[133]

In addition to business elites, religious leaders provided institutional backing for the campaign. In Orange County, a group of conservative pastors organized Clergymen for Social and Political Conservatism. They sought to provide a "voice in rebuttal to the massive political efforts of the liberal left" and to show that "among clergyman there is large support for political and social views . . . along lines most prominently symbolized by Senator Barry Goldwater." While they did not officially endorse either political party, they made clear their preference for "candidates and legislative measures associated with the conservatism of Senator Barry Goldwater."[134] The pastors who entered the public view in support of Goldwaterite conservatism included Robert Schuller of the Garden Grove Community Church (and later the Crystal Cathedral), who represented the optimistic, entrepreneurial variety of religious conservatism, along with the

One entrepreneurial group of Orange Countians marketed Goldwater cloth for rallies and meetings. This advertisement by Organizational Research Associates of Garden Grove appeared in the national conservative news journal *Human Events*, demonstrating the links between the local and national conservative movement. (© *Human Events*, 1963.)

Reverend Edward Greenfield of the United Presbyterian Church. They were joined by evangelical ministers such as the Reverend Walter Price of the Assembly of God and Paul M. Alleman of the United Brethren church, as well as Baptist ministers such as Dr. Paul Peterson.[135] Not only Protestant conservative pastors entered the conservative fray. The *Tidings*, the newspaper of the Catholic Arch-Diocese of Los Angeles that circulated in all the parishes of Orange County, continued its conservative line, carrying articles by Dr. Fred Schwarz of the Christian Anti-Communism Crusade and Frank S. Meyer of *National Review.* Their positions strongly mirrored Goldwater's foreign policy agenda. The *Tidings* also ran opinion pieces by Catholic conservative Erik von Kuehnelt-Leddihn that surpassed Goldwater's own conservative rhetoric in their advocacy of "traditionalism."[136]

The third pillar of Goldwater's support in Orange County was the press. R. C. Hoiles's libertarian *Register*, the daily newspaper of most Orange Countians, set a positive tone for Goldwater's campaign, printing biographical items extolling him as "the Man from the West." On its editorial pages, it articulated strong support for his political philosophy. When Goldwater was attacked for his controversial comments in favor of "extremism" at the Republican National Convention, for example, the *Register* offered a "different view," arguing that "the signers of the Declaration of Independence were . . . extreme as were Socrates and Jesus Christ."[137]

The local press, together with business leaders and conservative religious institutions, generated a cultural milieu in Orange County that strongly favored Goldwater. Residents could join a large number of conservative Republican clubs to work for Goldwater, volunteer for the Citizens for Goldwater-Miller, or even express their support through consumption: Entrepreneurial Goldwaterites in Orange County sold "conservative cotton" with the choice of AuH_2O (the chemical symbols for gold and water) or "Goldwater '64" woven into fabric "with gold colored thread to make shirts, bow ties, tote bags, skirts, dresses . . . to wear to meetings, rallies, parties or conventions."[138]

In the week before the primary, the "tremendous grass-roots surge of Republicanism" peaked, spilling scores of volunteers into the streets.[139] Goldwater's management team and F. Clifton White's Citizens for Goldwater-Miller organized a massive drive to get out the vote, staffed by volunteers from the California Young Republicans, the California Republican Assembly, and the United Republicans of California (UROC). Using official lists of voters supplied by the state, volunteers targeted GOP supporters by street, the side of the street, and the house address. Community chairmen handed out cardboard information kits with detailed maps and the names of known Goldwater voters circled in red. Volunteers made a last complete door-to-door check on election day to make sure that the voters had gone to the polls.[140]

Their efforts bore fruit when the returns came in on June 2: Goldwater beat Rockefeller in the June primary by 51.6 percent to 48.4 percent. His sweeping pluralities in the southland—in Los Angeles, Orange, and San Diego Counties—brought him the victory.[141] In Orange County, Goldwater won by a large margin of two to one (101,636 to 51,878).[142] His slim margin statewide meant that the volunteer efforts had made the crucial difference.[143] According to a delighted Richard Kleindienst, who headed the Goldwater organization, "All those little old ladies in tennis shoes that you called right-wing nuts and kooks . . . they're the best volunteer political organization that's ever been put together." Political observer John Kessel attributed Goldwater's California win largely to the "Goldwater groups in Los Angeles and Orange Counties," noting that "the activity of Goldwater groups in contacting their fellow suburbanites was the most crucial episode in the process of coalition formation in 1964."[144]

Moderate Republicans who had fought hard for Rockefeller were now even more concerned about the direction of their party. Indeed, they had reason to worry: Committed rightists now controlled the CRA and the UROC, as well as the Young Republicans—and they had won the primary, signaling, according to the national press, a "swing to the Right in California Party" and the "end of [the] Warren Era" for the party.[145] Moderates feared a right-wing takeover not only in California but also across the nation, and their fears were confirmed as Goldwater triumphed at the Cow Palace in San Francisco on July 14, 1964. The Goldwater forces, in effect, now controlled the party.

Resentful of moderate control ever since Eisenhower had beaten Taft eight years earlier, Goldwaterites now sped ahead with their program, failing to pay attention to the importance of unifying the party. Goldwater's acceptance speech set the tone for the uncompromising ideological direction of his campaign. Even though the Arizonan faced attacks by moderate Republicans, who urged him to distance himself from extremism, he refused to do so. Yoked to the grassroots constituency that had made his nomination possible, Goldwater pandered to these voters with his militant rhetoric. In words penned by Harry Jaffa in a Palo Alto Hotel room, he uttered his infamous words:

> Anyone who joins us in sincerity we welcome. Those who do not care for our cause, we do not expect to enter our ranks in any case. . . . And let our Republicanism, so focused and dedicated,

not be made fuzzy and futile by unthinking and stupid labels. Let me remind you: *Extremism in the defense of liberty is no vice!* . . . *Moderation in the pursuit of justice is no virtue.*[146]

His speech made clear that this was a campaign based on clear-cut, black-and-white principles of "tyranny and freedom." "The Good Lord," he remarked, "raised up this mighty Republic to be a home for the brave and to flourish as the land of the free . . . not to stagnate in the swampland of collectivism."[147]

The right-wing Republicans' staunch ideological line and their lack of concern with unifying the party were also evident in the platform they passed. Controlled by Goldwater adherents, it drew firmly on Goldwater's militant posture in foreign policy, calling for "not only the preservation but the expansion of freedom—and ultimately its victory—everyplace on earth." To contend with "the one supreme challenge . . . an atheistic imperialism—Communism," the platform advocated a "dynamic strategy aimed at victory—pressing always for initiatives for freedom, rejecting always appeasement and withdrawal." This would reduce "the risk of nuclear war."[148] Turning the rhetoric of extremism on its head, the platform condemned "federal extremists." Against a dominant liberalism, the Goldwaterites championed the expansion of free enterprise, competition, as well as state and local over federal control; spoke out against "moral decline and drift"; supported the right to "exercise religion freely in public places"; and promised to curb the flow of "obscenity."[149] On civil rights, the platform trod a finer line. While it supported the "full implementation and faithful execution of the Civil Rights Act of 1964," it firmly opposed "federally-sponsored inverse discrimination whether by the shifting of jobs or the abandonment of neighborhood schools for reasons of race."[150] When moderate Republicans proposed platform amendments on civil rights, the use of nuclear weapons, and extremism, Goldwater supporters voted the amendments down.[151] Finally, instead of seeking ideological balance on the ticket by bringing in a moderate as a running mate, the Goldwater forces picked Congressman William E. Miller, a Catholic conservative from upstate New York.

This rigid adherence to principle may have won Goldwater favor among those already committed to his program, but it angered and frustrated moderate Republicans and struck fear into the hearts of liberals and the Left. In the wake of the convention, Governor Edmund G. Brown of California warned that Goldwater's speech had the "stench of fascism." He was convinced that Goldwater was the "hand-picked candidate" of the John Birch Society.[152] Nelson Rockefeller warned at the convention of the dangers of extremism, and William Scranton's staff wrote a letter to Goldwater branding "Goldwaterism" as a "crazy-quilt collection of absurd and dangerous positions," accusing him, in effect, of inviting "racial holocaust."[153] Scores of prominent Republican liberals refused to stand behind Goldwater, among them Jacob Javits of New York, George Romney of Michigan, and Nelson Rockefeller, as well as other eastern Republican governors who avoided "appearances with Goldwater as if he were cursed with political halitosis."[154]

Other Republicans, however, positioned themselves to bridge the deep rift within the party: After Goldwater's nomination, Richard Nixon vigorously campaigned for him to the accolades of conservatives, thus beginning a long campaign to become the GOP compromise candidate in 1968. Yet for the 1964 election, the rift was too large to bridge. Liberal Republicans abandoned Goldwater in droves, and even some prominent national businessmen, who had until now found a hospitable home in the Republican Party, came out publicly for Johnson, helping to seal the party's defeat in November.[155]

The problem of unifying the party around Goldwater was coupled with an even graver problem: the difficulty of building electoral support for Goldwater's candidacy that reached beyond his core constituencies in the Deep South and the Southwest. This proved an insurmountable obstacle: Goldwater forces may have captured the California primary and the Republican Party in 1964, but they could not capture a majority of the national electorate. His strident rhetoric, bolstered by the enthusiastic support he received among his core supporters, not only failed to appeal to a broader constituency but also scared many people. "When in all our history," prominent historian Richard Hofstadter asked only weeks before the election, "has anyone with ideas so bizarre, so archaic, so self-confounding, so remote from the basic American consensus, ever gotten so far?"[156] Goldwater's pronouncements on "conventional nuclear weapons" and "low-yield nuclear bombings" shocked a nation already anxiously living under the threat of atomic warfare; nor did his unmitigated hostility to the welfare state and to Social Security resonate in an era of affluence. Goldwater's staff saw the debacle coming, and they desperately sought a means to counter his image as a warmonger and the man who would ruin Social Security. But his record was too well known, and his frantic disavowals ultimately backfired.

From the vantage point of Orange County, this may have not seemed so obvious: Eleven days before Election Day, Goldwater swung through the southland. Stopping in Santa Ana, he was able to drum up considerable enthusiasm from a huge crowd:

> What kind of a country do you want? Are you satisfied with a government . . . that tends more and more and more to take the powers away from your city, your state and from yourselves? "NO!!" Are you satisfied with a government that has not yet recognized that the one enemy to peace in this world is Communism? "No!!!"[157]

But this was Orange County, not the nation. On November 8, the broader electorate made their sentiments known: Johnson won 61 percent of the popular vote to Goldwater's 39 percent. In the Electoral College, the count was 486 for Johnson and a measly 52 votes for Goldwater. Never had a president won as decisively as Johnson.

True to its leading role in the grassroots conservative movement in California, Orange County reversed the national trend and sided resoundingly with Goldwater. Orange Countians voted 56 percent for Goldwater, his highest plurality in any large California county.[158] Outside the Deep South, Orange County enjoyed the highest plurality for Goldwater of any metropolitan region in the nation with a population above 400,000.[159] Not only did Goldwater win a strong majority, but John Schmitz, a John Birch Society member and virtual political unknown, was also swept into office as a California state senator.[160] Yet even in Orange County, Goldwater's failure to unite the party, his militant and shrill rhetoric, and the hostile media attention he received cut into his support. Goldwater received fewer votes than Eisenhower had in 1956 or Nixon in 1960.

The November election was, in many ways, a debacle for conservatives. Goldwater's defeat was monumental: a loss by a margin of 15,951,220 votes.[161] Johnson won the greatest vote, the greatest margin, and the greatest percentage any president has ever drawn from the American people, confirming that most citizens in 1964 optimistically embraced the possibilities of the liberal promise in a period of national affluence. Indeed, of the six states Goldwater carried, five were Deep South states whose votes could be attributed to his strong states' rights stance rather than to his broader conservative agenda. Conservatives in 1964 were left with few illusions about the attractiveness of their politics to most of the nation's voters. Goldwater and Goldwaterism almost doomed conservatism as a national movement.

Nevertheless, not all was lost. Goldwater's campaign had other, more positive, implications for the future of American conservatism. First, conservatives had achieved a major victory in winning the 1964 Republican Party nomination, and thus had demonstrated that they could control one of the most powerful political vehicles in the nation. Since the triumph of Eisenhower's moderate Republicanism and the death of strong national conservative stalwarts such as Senator Robert Taft and Joseph McCarthy in the mid-1950s, conservatives had been marginalized within their own party. Indeed, political observers had sounded the death knell of American conservatism since Taft's rebuff in 1952 and McCarthy's censure two years later. Now a new generation of activists, tightly organized, staked their claim to the leadership of the Republican Party. Boosted by a grassroots conservative movement with a strong southern and western regional bent, Goldwater's campaign challenged the eastern wing for control over the party, and it won. Spurred by demographic and political changes, this "takeover" signified a historic power shift in the Republican Party that, despite its November defeat, fundamentally shaped national politics for a generation.

Indeed, despite their defeat, many grassroots conservatives, at least initially, were not disheartened. Many saw the campaign and Goldwater's 39 percent popular vote as a victory. In Orange County, letters to the *Register* continually referred with hope to the number "27 million."[162] Moreover, most conservatives had been well aware of their slim chances in the November election. As one Tustin activist put it, "Most of the people that I knew were realists, and they knew that he was going to be defeated."[163] Even Barry Goldwater later said that no Republican could have won against Johnson in 1964.[164]

What many grassroots conservatives sought was a way to maintain the mobilization they had built. In the southland, some Goldwater organizations continued to operate: Six offices in the Los Angeles area refused to discontinue operations even after F. Clifton White called on them to disband.[165] Activists from around the nation wrote letters to Goldwater asking him to sustain the momentum of their movement. One local leader from Kansas suggested changing the name of Citizens for Goldwater-Miller to Citzens for Conservatives to continue mobilizing at the grass roots.[166] And a woman from California, Margaret Minek, who had organized the first Republican club in her community, explained the impact Goldwater had on those like her:

> I, like a lot of Americans, had my first encounter with politics this past campaign. . . . Because of you, I, like others, was awakened. We learned we were conservatives. . . . We have a . . . flame . . . burning and the energy it gives off needs to be utilized.[167]

These grassroots conservatives looked toward any means of staying mobilized and of affecting and changing politics in the face of defeat. This energy may account for the growth of the John Birch Society after Goldwater's failure: By the end of 1965, the estimated membership in California stood at some 12,000 to 15,000, organized in perhaps 1,200 chapters, a substantial gain from the estimated 700 chapters and 10,000 members the society could boast before Goldwater's election.[168] In Orange County, estimates for membership range as high as 5,000, although exact numbers are difficult to ascertain.[169] Jim Toft, a Goldwater supporter from Orange County who joined the society at this time, noted that when he came in, "there was a tremendous growth." He was convinced that members joined "out of frustration from the Goldwater loss."[170] And nationwide, the John Birch Society ranks reached approximately 80,000. So attractive was the Birch Society in the southland that 1,700 people attended a fifty-dollar-a-plate testimonial dinner for Robert Welch in 1965.[171]

But after the momentous defeat, moderate Republicans, along with prominent national conservatives, increasingly attacked the society.[172] It was becoming evident, even within conservative ranks, that "Republicans were being hung with the Birch albatross."[173] The John Birch Society had already lost considerable support among conservatives but now had difficulty sustaining the financial backing for its huge operations.[174] Moreover, the appeal of the society had always been based on a virulent anticommunism, but anticommunism's mobilizing power waned as concerns in the mid-1960s shifted toward domestic social issues, such as law and order, cultural changes, civil rights, and the New Left. While the national John Birch Society organization tried to pick up on these shifts—organizing, for example, Movement to Restore Decency (MOTOREDE)—its methods were increasingly ineffective.

Other conservatives looked to form respectable new groups in light of the Birch-baiting of Goldwater. To prevent the movement from becoming "decimated and disheartened," conservatives came together to form a national "brain trust" to promote and present the conservative view after the defeat and to plan for the future. Going public as the American Conservative Union in early January 1965, the group brought together prominent businessmen, national intellectuals, and politicians to forge an organization along the lines of Americans for Democratic Action. Southland conservatives who had helped organize the

Goldwater campaign, contributed to the effort.[175] They sought to promote a "respectable image," immediately going on record as "distinguishing their leadership as wholly distinct from the leadership of the John Birch Society."[176] But despite an auspicious start, by the following year, bitter factionalism, dissent, and financial trouble had brought the organization to the brink of collapse.[177]

But while national conservative elites were in disarray, southland conservatives were already gearing up for their next political battle: the gubernatorial election of 1966. And here, prospects looked brighter. In the last few weeks of the campaign, a California actor by the name of Ronald Reagan, who had been spreading his conservative philosophy since the early 1960s, had delivered a smashingly successful televised speech for Goldwater. One conservative summed up the enthusiastic response he generated: "The speech, admirably prepared and beautifully delivered, . . . was by far the finest thing the campaign produced."[178] Reagan inspired conservatives, some of whom went so far as to argue that he might have won in Goldwater's place in 1964. In one bold stroke, he had established himself as the new conservative standard-bearer. Now the California businessmen who had backed Goldwater courted Reagan to make the run for governor. Armed with the lessons learned from the recent campaign, a mobilized grassroots constituency, and tumultuous events within the state, California conservative Republicans were in a position of considerable strength. Only two years later, Ronald Reagan picked up Goldwater's mantle, sheared it of its more menacing elements, and was catapulted into the governor's mansion of the most populous state in the nation.

CHAPTER 4

THE CONSERVATIVE WORLDVIEW
AT THE GRASS ROOTS

THE MOBILIZATION of the grassroots Right in Orange County and across the nation during the first half of the 1960s did not go unnoticed by national liberal intellectuals and liberal media pundits.[1] Perplexed by the growth of "irresponsible conservatism," a set of beliefs and politics that, in their eyes, transgressed the boundaries of consensus in American life, they sought to understand why some Americans found the Right appealing. They studied the socioeconomic status of its adherents and defined the personal anxieties that they believed led to an embrace of right-wing politics. In a comprehensive and influential effort to explain the growth of conservative politics, Daniel Bell, Richard Hofstadter, and Seymour Martin Lipset located support for the Right among upwardly mobile women and men who, unsure of their "Americanism," sought security in a kind of superpatriotism. Conversely, they contended, the old middle classes, resenting the rise of new elites and a loss of social status, found a scapegoat for their decline in the Right's demonization of liberalism.[2] The "Radical Right"—a term that sometimes seemed to encompass the entire conservative end of the political spectrum and other times seemed to refer to the more marginal and extreme conspiratorial elements within the conservative fold—was, they argued, an "annoying endemic feature . . . of American political life," motivated by a variety of personality disorders and the inability to adjust to the modern world.[3]

While these explanations contained some astute observations about conservative politics, particularly in locating the social groups that proved most open to hearing the Right's clarion call, they paid little attention to the message of the movement itself or the set of ideas behind it. Postwar liberal intellectuals, writing in the shadows of Stalinism, Fascism, and McCarthyism, celebrated centrist politics and reduced ideas of both the Left and the Right, as one historian has aptly noted, "to psychological symptoms."[4] Creating an intellectual bulwark for the liberal order they championed, they cast liberalism as the sole intellectual tradition in American life. While postwar consensus scholars acknowledged the presence of conservative and reactionary "impulses," they derided them as "irritable mental gestures which seek to resemble ideas."[5] By failing to take into account the deep-seated conservative ideological traditions on which the Right drew and by refusing to closely examine the ideological universe of conservatives, liberal intellectuals underestimated the resilience and staying power of the Right in American life.

To understand the appeal of the Right in Orange County and elsewhere, we need to pay close attention to the ideas themselves and to the entire "system of beliefs, values, fears, prejudices, reflexes and commitments" that many men and women in Orange County came to embrace.[6] The constellation of conservative concerns over the United Nations, communism, liberal schooling, and "Washington planners" resonated with many Orange Countians because these issues were powerful symbols over which they fought for the dominance of a vision of a free and just society. However muddled and contradictory the content of right-wing ideology appeared to its liberal and left-wing critics, and however difficult to understand—particularly in its more extreme apocalyptic and conspiratorial forms—right-wing ideology did evoke a distinctive worldview that provided a message of real meaning to its adherents. This worldview drew on deep roots in American cultural life and rested on shared assumptions about American national identity. It provided not only a critique of the postwar American liberal order but also a vision of what the nation's future should be. The foundational elements of grassroots beliefs can be uncovered by closely examining the literature that formed the core of the movement culture—the books, pamphlets, newspapers, magazines, and speeches that conservatives consumed—along with the concerns they themselves articulated. While grassroots activists and their more numerous fellow travelers did not necessarily embrace all the various strands of right-wing thought, together they wove an ideological tapestry wide enough to encompass a broad political movement.

The women and men from Santa Ana and Anaheim, from Huntington Beach and Newport Beach, who joined the Right in the 1960s embraced a set of beliefs whose cornerstone element was opposition to the liberal Leviathan that was, in their eyes, the postwar federal government. The expansion of the scale and scope of the federal government, they believed, reduced civic autonomy and thwarted individual initiative and self-reliance, running counter to older Republican belief in the primacy of the locality and the state in determining the shape of public life. Just as important, many grassroots conservatives believed, in a somewhat contradictory vein, that the liberal state fostered "social permissiveness" by removing itself as a bulwark of "traditional" morals and values. The two central principles of the Right's message were thus an antistatist libertarianism and a normative conservatism.

This critique of liberalism resonated with many Orange Countians because, in part, it corresponded to real changes. By the end of World War II, the federal government played a central role in boosting the American economy and resolving social and economic ills. It arbitrated struggles between capital and labor, promoted domestic economic growth, and guarded international American hegemony through foreign economic and military aid. The postwar New Deal order, built on spiraling economic growth spurred by government spending and high wages, had ushered the United States into its "golden age"—a time when Americans enjoyed the highest standard of living in the world and played a critical role on the world scene.[7]

American prosperity reaffirmed liberal intellectuals' and policy makers' faith in the ability of the federal government to regulate and boost capitalism and to mitigate class differences in American life through economic growth and the welfare state. Liberals thus called for national responses to social and economic problems and emphasized centralized, bureaucratic solutions.[8] They fought to extend coverage of unemployment insurance, to expand Social Security, to establish a comprehensive public housing program, and to increase federal outlays for education.[9] Equally important, since the New Deal had largely removed the worst offenses of capitalism that had galvanized liberal reform earlier in the century, a new agenda to revitalize liberalism's future focused on the expansion of individual rights. Committed to deepening equity in American life—a core component of their vision of an American society absent of fundamental divisions—liberals also strongly supported the expansion of civil rights for African-Americans.

By 1960, John F. Kennedy and his group of Harvard advisers had brought this liberal vision to the White House. The Democratic platform on which Kennedy ran was, according to historian Steve Gillon, the most liberal in the party's history, exemplifying a faith in a triumphant American democracy at home and abroad unhampered by Republican concerns with limited spending and increased federal power.[10] Although many liberals were disillusioned with Kennedy's slow-moving progress on his campaign promises, his commitment to a liberal agenda, however abstract, earned him the ire of conservatives.

America's golden age not only brought unbounded prosperity but also was a time of far-reaching social and cultural changes to which conservative women and men responded with deep ambivalence.[11] Material prosperity, and the new cultural requirements of liberal corporate capitalism, helped to loosen and liberalize social and behavioral norms, increasingly replacing an older emphasis on the values of industriousness and frugality with a new emphasis on leisure, pleasure, consumption, and personal freedom. Liberal pluralism, the dominant ideology of the new elites, moreover, championed pragmatism, compromise, and moral relativism as positive virtues necessary to balance conflicting interests in a democratic society.[12] The liberal spirit, finally, was rooted in a secular rationalism and a faith in progress that supplanted an older emphasis within American political culture on a respect for tradition, religiosity, and a staunch puritanical moralism. Liberal elites were thus, not surprisingly, uncomfortable with the state's role as a regulator and guarantor of behavioral norms and virtues and, instead, championed a new set of individual and personal freedoms.[13] Consequently, just as national liberal policy makers were expanding their power in regulating the economy, they were seeking to remove the government as the arbiter of normative values. American liberalism thus seemed to pose a dual threat to conservative men and women. It disparaged an older set of social and cultural norms they cherished, and, in their eyes, it threatened to undermine American economic well-being and economic freedom by using state spending to distribute power and wealth more equitably downward in society.

The constellation of groups that composed the Right in Orange County and nationally in the 1960s shared a core set of assumptions in opposition to American liberalism. At the most basic level, conservatives postulated that liberal elites were responsible for America's problems. The Right, Jerome Himmelstein astutely noted, shared "the belief that American society on all levels has an organic order—harmonious, beneficent, and self-regulating—disturbed only by misguided ideas and policies."[14] Thus, America's problems were not the result of any inherent limitations of a capitalist economy or inequalities in American life, but rather were due to liberal tampering with an otherwise harmonious, self-sustaining system. Capitalism, this argument went, would run smoothly if not for an overgrown state. Family, morality, and religion would be intact if liberal elites had not encouraged permissiveness and secularism.[15]

Yet while all segments of the Right shared a staunch opposition to American liberalism, different groups of grassroots conservatives in the 1960s emphasized different critiques of American liberalism. (Complicating matters even further, by decade's end these critiques shifted focus.) For libertarians, the expanded role of the federal government and the consequent regulation of the free market, if left uncorrected, could only result in a totalitarian order and an end to individual freedom (defined at its heart as economic freedom). Social conservatives, while less philosophically wedded to notions of individual freedom, shared the concern of libertarians with the usurpation of responsibilities by a distant federal power, responsibilities they believed should rest with the family, the church, and the community. They distrusted "Washington planners" and their arbiters in national liberal culture.[16]

The distinct ideological strands of right-wing thought—libertarianism and normative conservatism—were widely in circulation at the grassroots level in Orange County. "Objectivists" championed Ayn Rand's ideas on "the virtues of selfishness"; the *Register*, in its editorial commentaries, expounded uncompromising libertarianism; the *Tidings* clarified Catholic traditionalist doctrine; and Pastor Bob Wells preached down-on-your-knees old-time fundamentalism. While these diverse strands of right-wing thought differed at their logical philosophical endpoints, they shared a belief that the tendency toward liberal "collectivism" undermined older moral principles and what they perceived as fundamental truths. For some, particularly religious men and women, these fears, shaped by apocalyptic thinking, took on hysterical overtones. But underlying their at-times-extreme beliefs were real concerns, however unpalatable some of their apprehensions may have been to their many critics.

One powerful current that ran through conservative thought in Orange County in the 1960s was a staunch libertarian anti-statism. Guided by classical liberal assumptions about the preservation of individual freedom, libertarians from local newspaper publisher Raymond Cyrus Hoiles to the national economist

Friedrich Hayek believed that state planning led inexorably to socialism, collectivism, and dictatorship. Since libertarians defined individual liberty as the absence of compulsion and coercion, and since the state monopolized the legitimate use of force, a limited state was essential to the preservation of individual liberty.[17] The increasing power of the federal government was thus, they argued, the primary threat to individual freedom. Granville Knight, a leader of California's Birch Society, warned that "we are constantly being urged to surrender our individual freedom to an all-powerful federal government."[18] At the heart of individual freedom, libertarians posited, lay economic freedom—the unrestricted right to one's property and control over one's income. The preservation of economic freedom was thus essential to the preservation of personal and political freedom. "Economic control is not merely control of a sector of human life, which can be separated from the rest," Hayek wrote, "it is the control of the means for all our ends."[19] An Orange County free-market radical echoed these sentiments, arguing that "intellectual freedom cannot exist without political freedom, political freedom cannot exist without economic freedom: a free market and a free society are corollaries."[20] Because libertarians saw property rights as absolute, the welfare state's redistribution of property through taxation was perceived as a form of socialism. Dan Smoot equated "the growth of the welfare state with Socialism and Socialism with Communism."[21] In a similar vein, *Christian Economics* called "Fabian Socialism, alias welfare statism, . . . the peaceful, pleasant road to the death of freedom and totalitarian government."[22] Echoing these sentiments, one local libertarian from Costa Mesa went so far as to argue that the welfare state, by "entitling some men . . . to the products of the work of others . . . condemned those others, . . . to slave labor."[23]

Not only were the welfare state and federal government intervention into the economy perceived as a threat to individual freedom, but libertarians also blamed social and economic problems on interference with the free market. A Dr. Brown from the city of Orange quoted from Ayn Rand to support his vision of capitalism, arguing that "all the evils popularly ascribed to capitalism were caused, necessitated and made possible only by government controls on the economy."[24] Libertarians thus, according to another staunch advocate from Orange, sought to establish "pure capitalism."[25]

This libertarian economic vision resonated among middle-class and upper-middle-class Orange Countians who believed that their success was due to their own entrepreneurial efforts and who sought to maintain total control over what they perceived as "the fruits of their own labor." As one conservative remarked years later: "I believed firmly . . . that if you worked hard you would be a success. That's true. Most all of the people I knew at that point in their career became a success. Very little welfare was involved in our lives."[26] Their attacks on the welfare state were thus directed most forcefully toward the state's distribution of wealth and power downward in society.[27] Torry Ann Truex of nearby Pomona, for example, articulated a radicalized version of these sentiments—and their moral justification—in a letter to the *Register* on April 23, 1962:

> I find many people claiming that a principle which is immoral for the individual is moral when a large number of people is involved. . . . I find many people who feel that the government is justified in taking people's property for redistribution in such fields as subsidies, medical aid for aged, . . . aid to economically distressed areas, urban renewal and so on and on and on. By what moral switch does stealing become humanitarianism? . . . This is the responsibility of churches, neighbors, families, charities, insurance programs, etc., acting in a voluntary way.[28]

At its most extreme, such logic not only called into question the use of state power to lessen social inequality but also challenged the legitimacy of the public acting collectively through government to make decisions for the community. A very small segment of the Right in Orange County, for example, went so far as to seek an end to all government services: Along these lines, the *Register* called for private police forces, firehouses, roads, and schools, arguing that they "would be more efficient were they in the employment of insurance companies than in the employ of city monopolies."[29]

This staunch libertarian antistatist ethos and unqualified celebration of capitalism carried a particular regional appeal.[30] Building on a long-standing resentment of eastern elites, southland conservatives celebrated the frontier spirit and the entrepreneurialism and individualism that came with it. This rhetoric united the interests of an ill-defined "little people" with southland entrepreneurs against an intrusive nation-state.[31] Such regionalism, however, belied the real power relations and tensions among different social groups in the West, as well as the critical role the federal government played in the West in stimulating economic growth.

Orange Countians' fear of distant national elites and concentrations of state power, and their concerns for "the people," did not translate into a critique of private economic power. Since they themselves were the beneficiaries of capitalism, they failed to see danger in private concentrations of economic power or to attribute to them the ability to destroy "freedom." Indeed, the Reverend T. Robert Ingram, rector of the Thomas Episcopal Church of Houston, Texas, went so far as to argue in a column in the *Register* that private entities such as newspapers, markets, banks, restaurants, and private schools are public institutions "belonging to the people," since "they are places and services made available on a contractual basis to the people."[32] In contrast, the "ruling power of what we call the government" operated by coercion, compulsion, and "police power."[33] Thus, he continued, government services paid for by taxes ceased to be public. Such thinking elided the coercive potential of private economic power and led many Orange Countians to instead blame whatever grievances they had with the inequities of capitalism on "Washington planners," even when concentrations of private power were responsible for their discontents. When C. Greer of Orange County complained about the power of financial moguls and real estate developers, he made this slippage evident:

Weary of city traffic, noise and confusion, I went to the country to buy me a couple of acres of land and fresh air with only mountains to bully me and make me feel small. What did I find? . . . I found that a multi-millionaire steel man and ex–movie cowboy had beaten me to it with a pocketful of money. The land was all gone, 87,500 acres, even the mountains were being tamed by the avant garde of Washington's pet developers. The Washington big planners will grab and grab to control all of America through foreclosed mortgages on what was formerly private property belonging to the little people.[34]

While a western libertarian ethos was an important component of the discourse of the Right in Orange County, it was often combined with a distinct and somewhat philosophically incompatible social conservatism. Social conservatives in Orange County were as concerned as libertarians with liberal "collectivism." They, too, opposed the aggrandizement of the state and celebrated free-market capitalism, seeing economic and spiritual freedoms as inseparable. Yet in contrast to libertarians, whose starting point was a concern with individual liberty and whose philosophy militated against community coercion of the individual not only in the realm of economics but also in social life, social conservatism was intensely normative.[35] Social conservatives' worldview was fundamentally shaped by a faith in an objective moral order ordained by a transcendent moral authority. Religion—namely, Christianity—thus loomed large in their universe. In contrast to liberals, who emphasized pragmatic rationalism, scientific inquiry, and inwardly conscious individualism, religious conservatives emphasized moral laws and the timeless truths they saw as underlying them. An editorial in the *Anaheim Gazette* argued that "there is no 'new approach' to morality. Absolutes are absolutes. We must accept them by faith."[36]

Social conservatives articulated a vision of the United States as a fundamentally Christian nation. As Joe Welchel of Huntington Beach noted, "The United States has been regarded as a Christian nation since its inception."[37] In a similar vein, Nolan Frizzelle of Newport Beach remarked that in the first 150 years of its existence, the United States "was a Christian nation; it was meant to be a Christian nation. The people and the ACLU that say otherwise have absolutely distorted the Constitution."[38] Echoing these sentiments, another grassroots conservative, Jan Averill, asserted that "our country was founded on religious principles . . . and without those religious principles we're going to be lost."[39] Indeed, conservatives believed, the American nation was the political embodiment of Christian principles.[40] Their vision of the American past and the mythic origins of the nation had implications for the present.[41] Social conservatives championed a strong respect for "tradition" and argued that politics must simply "stay the course," since it otherwise weakened the moral fiber of the nation.[42] Not surprisingly, they found the liberal emphasis on relativism, secularism, pragmatism, innovation, and experimentation abhorrent.[43]

Social conservatives were wary of state power and reliance on centralized technocratic solutions to solve social and economic problems in part because they represented a break from the past. But, they argued, such solutions also promoted immorality and undermined self-responsibility and the traditionally existing authorities within the family and church. Indeed, the centralized state, John Stormer argued in a book widely read by Orange County conservatives, was made possible only by replacing faith in God with faith in government. According to Stormer:

> The weapons of hate and fear by which the collectivists have moved a generation of Americans to sell their freedom and integrity for security would never have worked had American roots in basic Judeo-Christian traditions not first been severed. God could not be replaced by Government as the source of all blessings until moral concepts were first blurred.[44]

Social conservatives believed that liberals failed to recognize the true cause of the nation's problems—a decline in morality, religiosity, and righteous living. For them, liberals, with their emphasis on sociological explanations for social and economic problems, exorcised individual responsibility and morality. Social conservatives, moreover, placed a good deal of weight on the values of social order and authority and thus opposed the liberal emphasis on personal freedom and individual rights. Catholic conservatives, in particular, strongly emphasized the importance of "order" over personal freedom. Los Angeles Archbishop Francis McIntyre spread this doctrine to Southern Californian Catholics:

> The philosophy that I am free to do what I choose, when I choose, and as I choose, is the philosophy of the enemy of man, a philosophy that is destructive of human liberty, one that can only wreak injustice and reap tyranny. . . . It is a philosophy that can have no other end but anarchy for where law and order are disdained, not only unhappiness and misery for the individual but revolution and death for society must surely follow.[45]

For these conservatives, the liberal emphasis on personal rights and individual freedom could result only in anarchy. Their perception that liberalism fostered social permissiveness and disorder was deepened when the Supreme Court proffered a new range of fundamental constitutional protections and rights to criminal defendants in a series of pioneering decisions from 1957 to 1966.[46] Conservatives attacked the Court for making police officers work with "one hand tied behind their back," arguing that these decisions undermined "law and order" in favor of criminals.[47] Dismissing sociological explanations that focused on poverty as a cause of crime, they instead saw crime as a moral problem. The Reverend Claude Bunzel of the Colonial Research Library in Buena Park asserted, for example, that "yesterday a crime was recognized as a crime, and not some sickness for which [to] blame society."[48] Believing that resolving economic inequities would do little to solve criminal behavior, conservatives called instead for the use of discipline and authority to build an ordered and, as they saw it, just world. An opinion piece in the *Register* asserted in 1961 that "tenement kids would have a great chance if they were handled with discipline and the sure knowledge that if they get into trouble, they'll have to pay for it. . . . They might not be cozened and coddled but they'd learn to live in an orderly world."[49] Rising social conflict in the last half of the decade increased the resonance of these attacks on liberalism among California suburbanites, when the discourse of "law and order" would move into the American political mainstream.

Other Supreme Court decisions in the late 1950s and 1960s strengthened the notion that the liberal state fostered permissiveness and thus was an enemy of "traditional values." These decisions undermined long-standing accepted practices, limiting the power of the state in setting standards of morality and values. For men and women who saw their religion as the bedrock of all meaning and as the core of the moral fiber of the nation, the idea that the separation of church and state required the exclusion of religion from the schoolroom or schoolbooks seemed preposterous.[50] So when, in 1962, the Supreme Court outlawed prayer in schools, religious conservatives feared that liberals were on the road "to creating," as one Orange County woman put it, "an atheistic United States of America."[51] One conservative from Santa Ana articulated her outrage at the decision years later in terms of federal power versus community control:

> I came from a Protestant background. All the way through my grade school and high school and so forth, we didn't have prayer in school. We went to church for prayers. But we went from that to what I felt was a concerted effort to eliminate any thought of religion from our schools, which I deplore. . . . I think maybe it should be left to local decision. Some communities, if they want that, well? Too much control has been taken over by the federal government that should be left to the states and the communities. And sure, you're going to have differing views depending on where you are in the country, but then I think that's one of the strengths of the country.[52]

It was not only through the school prayer decision that the federal government appeared to be undermining "traditional" virtues. In 1962 and 1964, two Supreme Court decisions limited the government's power to prosecute "obscenity," and in the 1965 *Griswold v. Connecticut* decision, the Court recognized a right to sexual privacy, legalized the sale of contraceptive devices, and cleared the way for the widespread distribution of the birth control pill. For conservatives, already concerned about a new "permissiveness," such decisions only served further notice that the liberal state was the enemy of "moral virtue." The *American Standard*, published in Buena Park, lamented that "a nation which allows its newsstands to be flooded with salacious literature . . . is surely sowing its own seeds of destruction."[53] Goldwater claimed that "the tone of America . . . is being set too often today, by the standards of the sick joke, the slick slogan, the off-color drama, and the pornographic book."[54] And Max Rafferty, the conservative California state superintendent of public instruction, lamented, "We have a situation now where it's almost unsafe to take a child to the movies anymore. . . . No generation in all the world, even including Restoration England, has wallowed so in filth as ours has done today."[55] Such rhetoric resonated with grassroots conservatives who witnessed a loosening of personal and behavioral norms in the 1960s.

Grassroots religious and social conservatives—Catholics and Protestants alike—in contrast to libertarians, carved out a sphere of positive state action, despite their distrust of federal power. Churches and the family instilled virtue and respect for the American heritage and strengthened the nation's moral fiber. Yet conservatives' stance on social issues implied that the state also ought to guard "moral virtue." Max Rafferty, for example, emphasized "a place for God" in the schoolhouse and the importance of building moral character as part of the school's responsibility.[56]

Not only did Orange County's social conservatives differ from libertarians in their more ambivalent relationship to the state, but their worldview also contained a strong dose of apocalyptic thinking, which was relatively absent from libertarian rhetoric.[57] While libertarians tended to blame society's failures on misguided policies and ideas, social and religious conservatives tended to view them as dimensions of an all-out struggle between good and evil. Conservatives' tendency to divide the world into black and white, and their immersion in an emotive belief system, left them open to apocalyptic thinking that often contained elements of conspiracy theory.[58] Their discourse over the threats to morality and the fear of communism at times took on irrational overtones, helping to earn the Right the extremist tag that remained with it for a good portion of the decade. Granville F. Knight, a medical doctor from Santa Barbara and a prominent leader of the John Birch Society in California, echoed these apocalyptic tones:

> We have been thoroughly and expertly brainwashed. We have become soft through easy living. . . . We have lost our belief in fundamental principles. We have become amoral and irreligious. We have lost our independence of thought and action in the expectation that "Big Brother" will take care of us. . . . We tremble in fear of atomic annihilation and are told surrender is the only alternative. Like Pavlovian dogs we sit and wait for the dropped curtain and the closing gate.[59]

As we have seen, fundamentalist and evangelical churches thrived in Orange County—among a modern, young, and affluent population—and no doubt there was a relationship between the number of religious conservatives and the prevalence of apocalyptic right-wing thinking at the grass roots. Fundamentalists and evangelical pastors preached biblically foretold scenarios of the Second Coming, of the period of tribulations, of all-out war with the Antichrist, of the "rapture," and of the "end times."[60] Such apocalyptic believers wrapped their politics in an authoritative cloak of God, making them impervious to rational dispute.

While at first it seems unlikely that such an environment—one of the most modern communities in the country, if not in the world—would generate a conservative movement that harked back to traditionalism, critiqued scientific rationalism and progress, and contained powerful emotive appeals, on closer inspection it should come as no surprise: The radicalism of Orange County as a model of living and producing was reflected in the beliefs of many of its inhabitants. For middle-class men and women who made their homes in a region where change seemed constant, the Right offered a reassuring message of solidity, of moral certainties and strong moorings. In this environment—a most American of worlds—the erosion of local autonomy, tradition, and community was strongly felt. A belief in staunch conservative values provided some stability, firm grounding, and a sense of cohesive community.[61]

Perhaps it should come as no surprise, then, that Southern California produced one of the foremost traditionalist intellectuals of the post–World War II conservative movement, Robert A. Nisbet. The author of *Quest for Community* (1953) became an academic spokesperson for the rising Right in the Republican Party by the end of the 1960s. He had grown up in the suburbs of Los Angeles to the north of Orange County.[62] Nisbet scathingly attacked personal alienation, cultural disintegration, and the "intolerable aloneness" he attributed to the triumph of secularism and the rampant individualism that, he believed, resulted from the centralized state. He championed community, status, membership, and hierarchy as the only means of satisfying human need.[63] But his form of traditionalism was surprisingly modern and, indeed, as one historian has argued, tailored to the pluralist sensibilities of post–World War II America. While rejecting the rationalist, egalitarian, and centralizing tendencies of American pluralism, there were no nostalgic calls for a return to the countryside, pleas for a new aristocracy, or appeals to submission to the authority of the church. Nisbet, rather, linked libertarianism and traditionalism in his appeals for a new "laissez-faire of small groups" to lessen the power of the central state.[64]

The link Nisbet saw between the aggrandized state and the breakdown of community was mirrored, albeit in a more pedestrian and less intellectualized fashion, by Orange Countians such as J. D. Collier of Santa Ana. In 1961, Collier lamented the isolation in the new suburban tract homes and called for "help[ing] each other build a better community." He linked the absence of community to the trend toward "a centralized government, that if we allow to be completely centralized will destroy every freedom we have." "Too much centralized power," he concluded, "is not good for a man or a government."[65]

The cultural criticisms of Orange County's conservatives responded to the discontents created by the dynamics of capitalism. Orange Countians lamented the decline of family authority, the emphasis on change and innovation, the undermining of community, and the decline of the importance of locality—all of which resulted from the growth of large-scale institutions and the concentration of economic and political power that are part of the functioning of a free-market economy. Their strong stakes in this capitalist order, however, caused them to elide the very real market forces that often undercut family values and community stability, since such a knowledge would have challenged the material base on which their own lives were built. Instead, they argued that it was the deviation from a true laissez-faire capitalism, one without a strong role for the state, that was at the heart of America's problems. The strong emphasis on a market order combined with social conservative values that celebrated family values, morality, and religion validated conservatives' own lives and success, provided an explanation for their discontents, and gave them a strong sense of cohesion and community. They thus were able to avoid examining the internal contradictions within their own ideology, the ambivalence and tensions between a strong embrace of the free market and the way in which free markets often assaulted family, community, and neighborhood norms.

Thus conservative activists fused an antistatist libertarianism and normative conservatism into a single political movement. While national right-wing intellectuals battled over the relative weight of "individual freedom" versus "order and authority," Orange Countians—and eventually also the national political Right—forged a movement that meshed the moral impulses of the normative conservatives and their emphasis on religion and order with the free-market radicalism of the libertarians.

This is not to say that friction between libertarians and social conservatives was not visible at the grass roots. Extreme in-
dividualists such as newspaper publisher R. C. Hoiles prosely-
tized extending individual freedoms by "getting government off
our backs" and "out of our pockets" and opposed the use of
government "force" to restrain "evil."[66] His newspaper even
went so far as to publish editorials suggesting that it opposed
prayer in school and government restrictions on drug use.[67] Not
surprisingly, social conservatives found Hoiles's stance on
school prayer abhorrent. Anna Mae Collins of Huntington
Beach condemned the editor's stance as an indication of "muddled thinking and poor judgment."[68]

At times, libertarians and religious conservatives, as Collins's letter to the *Register* suggests, looked at one another with
discomfort and suspicion. David Bergland, educational chairman of the United Republicans of California (UROC) in Orange
County, remembered, for example, that when he and a fellow
"objectivist" (a small segment of predominantly atheist libertarians) sought to educate the membership of UROC on economics, "we were disclosed as atheists . . . and they didn't like us
anymore."[69]

Despite such disagreements and divisions on particular issues, libertarians and social conservatives shared enough grievances against their common enemy, the liberal Leviathan, to
forge a political movement. This joint mobilization was fur-
thered because they shared a set of assumptions about a properly
ordered world, assumptions that went deeper than the philosophically contradictory directives of laissez-faire versus the
"virtuous society." First, they shared a profound distrust of the
centralized state. Second, libertarians and social conservatives
shared a commitment to an objective, definable, organic authority. Such an authority, according to scholar James Davison
Hunter, defined "a consistent, unchangeable measure of value,
purpose, goodness and identity, both personal and collective."[70]
While, for social conservatives, this authority was God, for libertarians, the elevation of absolute property rights as a fundamental law of human existence served as the functional equivalent of

"the transcendent moral authority of religious conservatives."[71] Third, libertarians and social conservatives were united in their definition of freedom as primarily economic freedom. For libertarians, economic freedom and personal freedom went hand in hand, while many social conservatives believed economic freedom was, essential to building a Christian world. Fourth, their belief in economic freedom and distrust of the centralized state made them hostile toward liberal "equalitarianism." Anti-egalitarianism was an important part of the outlook of many Orange County and national conservatives in the 1960s.[72] Barry Goldwater, for example, critiqued the graduated income tax, noting that "an egalitarian society is an objective that does violence to both the charter of the Republic and the laws of nature."[73] Anti-egalitarianism was at times linked with a skepticism about democracy. Mrs. George Mackiewicz of Costa Mesa echoed these sentiments, arguing that "our constitutional fathers, familiar with the strengths and weaknesses of both autocracy and democracy, with fixed principles definitely in mind, defined a representative republican form of government."[74] Orange County conservatives thus sometimes made marked distinctions between a republic and a democracy and emphasized that the United States had been founded as a republic.

Antidemocratic right-wing rhetoric in this period had a good deal to do with the Right's political weakness. After all, the majority of the American people seemed to be willing to live with the "unfreedoms" of the welfare state. But it also developed out of deeper assumptions. Libertarians propounded a fundamental belief in a strict interpretation of the Constitution: Government ought to operate by rule of law within fixed and narrow limits. Thus, some libertarians went so far as to express deep dismay with the voting process, seeing it as a means for the majority to coerce the minority.[75] Social conservatives' belief in a natural organic order made them hostile to "collectivist" scientific engineering in the name of the "masses" or the "social welfare."[76]

Just as important, social conservatives and libertarians in Orange County shared a set of narratives about the nation's history, furthering their movement's coherence. Their antistatism, in other words, did not preclude a staunch sense of nationalism. Conservatives and libertarians endowed the Founding Founders with a respect beyond critique, and their reverential tones evoked a civic religion. They cast themselves as the true heirs to the "national heritage" and framed their political agenda as an effort to preserve this "heritage" for their children. Their mythic vision of the nation's past represented an effort to legitimize themselves as the true upholders of national good.[77] In their eyes, liberal elites and policy makers were betraying the legacy of the Founding Fathers. Martin Taylor of Anaheim took the opportunity of Independence Day, 1962, to write a letter to the *Register* expressing these sentiments:

> I cannot help but ask: where does America stand on July 4, 1962? Washington, Jefferson, John Adams, and Ben Franklin have long since left the American scene. What are we doing with the inheritance they bestowed upon us? . . . Is not our representative government, of, by, and for the people now being supplanted by a government run by sophisticated intellectuals who claim they know what is best for us?[78]

Orange County conservatives like Taylor opposed "liberal Washington intellectuals"—distant elites—in favor of the "people" and the locality; in so doing, they evoked a critique of the disempowerment of the locality by an ever more intrusive nation-state. This language of the "people" versus "sophisticated elites" presaged populist discourses that would increasingly replace right-wing minoritarian rhetoric toward the end of the 1960s. But it did not change the fundamental conservative aspect of those politics. The "people" were defined, somewhat amorphously, as middle-class, white, and Christian. And championing "local control" meant local control for particular social groups to impose their values and norms on the community.

Their mythic vision of the nation's past gave conservatives a sense of coherence and represented an effort to legitimize themselves as the true upholders of national good.[79] But in Orange County, it served an additional function. The creation of a mythical American community provided a sense of rootedness in place of the isolated, decentralized, geographic space that was Orange County. The county's social atomization encouraged these middle-class men and women to search not only for community within their churches but also for another kind of community—one that did not challenge the underpinnings of their own lives—and that fit well with their sense of themselves and their interests. The national past was such a community, and frequent references, for example, to the "early Virginia settlers" and their "desire for freedom" characterized right-wing speeches and writings.[80]

Besides sharing sufficient common ground to forge a political movement, most Orange County conservatives also meshed elements of libertarianism with social conservatism in their personal philosophies, seeing both as necessary in building the society they sought. Many Orange County conservatives, then, drank a heady and muddled cocktail of traditionalist and libertarian ideas, linking a Christian view of the world with libertarian rhetoric and libertarian economics.[81] One staunch religious conservative thus sounded very much the libertarian when she asserted that the common denominator among conservative concerns in the 1960s "was the government intrusion into the private life of the individual."[82] In a similar vein, another religious conservative announced that "we might think of ourselves, the present day conservative, as the liberal of 1776, because it is a freedom-seeking movement."[83] And R. B. Pearce of Fullerton, who labeled himself "a libertarian in politics," since "libertarianism is closer to what the Founding Fathers gave us in the Constitution," qualified this identity by declaring that "where [libertarians] get into morality and spiritual things they don't cut it."[84] Thus, while "fusionism" may have been a philosophical doctrine worked out between Frank Meyer and William Buckley to resolve the tensions between libertarians and traditionalists, as George Nash has argued, it was much more than that.[85] It was a set of ideas and of politics that many conservatives had already created for themselves. It was a belief system that, despite the tensions within it, strongly appealed to many middle-class men and women in affluent Sunbelt California in the 1960s. Moreover, while conservatives were on the outside of political power, the contradictions between the two strands of right-wing thought did not come to matter decisively. Both were united in a common opposition to liberalism, and it was that liberalism that the movement set out to fight.

While liberalism was the common enemy of all elements of the Right, this opposition was couched during the first half of the 1960s, as it had been in the 1950s, as a virulent anticommunism. In these years, anticommunism provided the discursive bond that fused libertarians and social conservatives into a united resistance to the liberal Leviathan, a bond that, by the late 1960s, would increasingly be replaced by other issues. Through their opposition to "communism," national right-wing leaders, as well as Orange County pastors, priests, and regional business executives, created a shared cast of villains. They drew on an older language—the symbols, targets, and discourse of McCarthyism—to express their apprehensions over government centralization and national liberal culture, as well as the Soviet threat. Subsuming these concerns under a discourse of a "communist menace," they reduced a variety of grievances to one highly symbolic entity and united various segments of the Right. Through positioning themselves as the true opponents of the greatest symbol of the enemy of America, and seeking to monopolize this potent symbol, they sought to legitimize their movement, which was, after all, quite marginal in an era of liberal dominance.

Of course, anticommunism was more than symbolism or political posturing. It also galvanized the Right in Orange County, in part because it represented fears about the very real struggle between the United States and the Soviet Union, the country's world political antagonist. As a political movement, communism frightened the Right, especially in the form of the socialist states of Eastern Europe, Asia, and the Caribbean. This was in itself hardly unusual, however, at a time when most Americans envisioned the world in bipolar terms, with the struggle between the United States and the Soviet Union at center stage. What distinguished right-wing anticommunism from its liberal counterpart, was the Right's messianic belief in the overwhelming magnitude of the threat and its conviction that liberal policies at home and abroad only contributed to Soviet and communist advances around the world.

The Right's extreme anxiety over communism, while resting to some degree on the material dependence of many Orange Countians on the continuation of the Cold War, also resulted from the fact that the socialist states stood in opposition to everything conservatives held dear. For both religious conservatives and libertarians, "communism" was a form of slavery. Libertarians held that communism's denial of private property extinguished the most basic human right and thus human freedom. Religious conservatives believed that its denial of God made it the enemy of Christians. And for Catholics, in particular, the reality of the struggle between Christianity and communism took on concrete meaning with the suppression of the Catholic Church in Eastern Europe.[86] For Protestant fundamentalists, moreover, communism was associated with the all-powerful Christian symbol of evil: the Antichrist.[87] Joe Welchel from Huntington Beach, for example, thought of Nikita Khrushchev and the devil as one and the same. When the Soviet leader traveled to the United States, Welchel was convinced that "we allowed Satan . . . to come here."[88]

The apocalyptic reading of contemporary political conflict was characteristic of the Right's ideological universe. Believing that communism represented a threat to the very existence of Western Christian civilization, conservatives described the contest between communism and the "free world" as "a world-wide battle, the first in history, between light and darkness, between freedom and slavery, between the spirit of Christianity and the spirit of the anti-Christ."[89] Such a vision of the magnitude of the communist threat often led to dire scenarios. "The conquest of our planet by the International Communist Conspiracy," according to Long Beach's Dr. Fred Schwarz of the Christian Anti-Communism Crusade, "lay but a few scant years in the future." Even Ronald Reagan, in comparably paranoid fashion, pointed out that "one of the foremost authorities on communism in the world today has said, we have ten years. Not ten years to make up our minds, but ten years to win or lose—by 1970 the world will be all slave or all free."[90]

In face of the immediacy of the perceived threat, conservatives blamed liberals for their "softness" in dealing with the "communist menace." Frank Meyer, in an opinion piece in the *Register*, lamented that "the fifteen years since the end of World War II have already seen the United States world position decline from one of unchallenged supremacy to a point where today a third of the world is in the camp of our enemies, and another third, the euphemistically entitled 'uncommitted nations' is basically hostile to everything we stand for."[91] Echoing such sentiments, a conservative couple from Santa Ana lamented, "We are very tired of the weak, cowardly policy of the United States for all these years. Our country that was once held in the highest honor and respect by all the world is now the laughingstock of the universe."[92] The responsibility for this retreat lay, they believed, in the failure of liberals to stand up to communism.

What, however, did conservatives mean by liberals' unwillingness to stand up to communism? American liberal policy makers and intellectuals, after all, were also wedded, as Steven Gillon has rightly noted, "to the bogeyman theory of history that placed the Soviet Union near the heart of all post-war international disturbances."[93] Democratic liberals in the early 1960s, unhampered by Republican concerns with a balanced budget, moreover, backed high levels of defense spending, and their rhetoric of freedom and slavery often mirrored the language of the Right. Yet conservatives and liberals differed dramatically in their vision of what programs and politics were best to combat communism at home and abroad. And their approaches to dealing with communism reflected the differences in their deeper assumptions about a proper world order and America's role in it.

Liberal cold warriors sought to halt the spread of communism and to extend U.S. influence in the world by shoring up American international hegemony. They emphasized not only a strong defense but also diplomacy and negotiations with the Soviet Union, foreign aid programs, and multilateral action. Upon his election, for example, John F. Kennedy combined military action and heightened defense spending with negotiations, summit talks, and strengthening the United Nations—all in order to stem the communist tide.[94] Americans for Democratic Action (ADA), the premier organized voice for liberalism, opposed unilateral military action and demanded that the United States rely on international agencies like the United Nations.[95] Believing that international prestige was as important as military might, their discourse emphasized establishing the United States as a light for democracy and freedom, which other nations would turn to in fashioning and structuring their own societies.[96] To this end, they developed new approaches toward the Third World, seeing these nations as the primary arena in which the Cold War would be fought. Their rhetoric bespoke a new concern for nationalist aspirations of colonized nations and a new friendliness toward peoples of color, part of the liberal desire to gain the allegiance of nonaligned nations in Africa and Asia.[97] Liberals' concerns with the United States' prestige abroad, moreover, contributed to their desire to bolster civil rights at home.

By the late 1950s, moreover, many liberals muted their tough stance on communism by calling for nuclear disarmament and advocating, for example, admitting China to the United Nations. Hubert Humphrey claimed that while he did not minimize the difficulties of negotiating and even living on the same planet with the Soviet Union, "the opposite of coexistence is no existence."[98] And the 1958 convention of the ADA called for the establishment of a UN inspection system as a first step toward the ultimate goal of "eliminating the manufacture of nuclear weapons, disarmament and a United Nations force displacing national armed forces."[99] Even John F. Kennedy, despite his offensive in the Cold War, abandoned, according to Steven Ambrose, "the clichés of the Cold War."[100] He, for example, elevated

the status of disarmament planning by assembling the staff responsible for it in a new Arms Control and Disarmament
Agency.[101]

For conservatives, the liberal approaches to communism
unwittingly aided their cause at home and abroad. Liberal policies, they believed, reflected an inability to understand the singu-
larity of the communist menace. Conservatives' messianic vision
of the communist threat made, in their eyes, the possibility of
compromise, of coexistence, and even of diplomacy with the Soviet Union at best stupidity and at worst treason. One anticommunist from nearby Long Beach railed that "we persist in 'negotiating' with the Russians when we know . . . that they have
never kept a treaty, and 'negotiation' with them has become synonymous with a Russian take-over. We are constantly trying to
avoid offense to the Russians who react only to naked power."[102]
In a somewhat different vein, Barry Goldwater declared that
there could be "no peaceful coexistence with Communist power
as long as they do not believe in God."[103]

While conservatives, by the early 1960s, had overwhelmingly abandoned old-time isolationism in favor of a new interventionism in the total war against communism, this reformula-
tion of their politics still emphasized unilateralism and a reliance
on military solutions.[104] Drawing on older isolationist traditions,
conservatives retained their jealous regard for U.S. sovereignty
and their distrust of entangling political alliances with other nations.[105] While the members of the Right had, by the 1960s, rejected an older anti-interventionist anticommunism, symbolized
best by the politics of Senator Robert Taft, they remained wary
of foreign entanglements and deeply hostile to the liberal internationalism symbolized best by John F. Kennedy, Dean Rusk,
Robert McNamara, and others.[106] Moreover, for conservatives
who opposed the use of government spending to mute class differences at home, economic aid programs to Third World nations to stem the communist tide seemed ludicrous. As one conservative put it, "Communism is not a disease of the stomach,
it is a disease of the mind and soul."[107] Finally, conservatives'

belief in the superiority of Western Judeo-Christian traditions led them to dismiss the aspirations of Third World nations for liberation from colonial rule.

That a militant right-wing anticommunism formed a central component of many Orange Countians' worldview is, thus, not too surprising. The Right's messianic vision of the Soviet threat, its jealous regard for U.S. prerogative, and its conception of the proper role of the United States in the world provided the rationale for a foreign policy that relied almost exclusively on military solutions. While such an outlook was not purely instrumentalist, people usually do not embrace ideas that conflict with their economic interests. Militaristic anticommunism made sense to many Orange Countians who worked in military installations and defense-related industries or who indirectly benefited from the defense boom of the region. Here, conservative religious leaders, as well as Sunbelt politicians like Barry Goldwater, found fertile ground for their frightful scenarios of the Soviet Union's designs for world power and their calls for victory in the struggle against communism for, as Goldwater put it, "Victory is the key to the whole problem; the only alternative is—obviously—defeat."[108] *National Review* editor Frank Meyer asserted that "we are living in a world in which only victory over the Soviet enemy can preserve our nation and the civilized order for which it stands."[109] And California John Birch Society leader Granville Knight lamented in a similar vein that "there are too many who still laugh at the timetable of Communist world conquest, which has been advanced from 1975 to 1967. . . . They are the ignorant, the brainwashed or the timid, who spend their time playing golf, bridge or poker and watching television when they should be learning the facts of life."[110]

While such apocalyptic rhetoric provided a tool to galvanize middle-class conservatives into action, it also helped the conservative movement to earn the "extremist," "crackpot," and "loony" tag that haunted it in the 1960s. By the late 1960s, with a decline in Cold War tensions and the lessons learned from

the Goldwater campaign, conservative leaders and politicians—
Ronald Reagan foremost among them—were increasingly articulating a more cautious rhetoric.

This virulent anticommunism, combined with a call for
American military might, found an audience among conservative Southern Californians despite their hostility toward federal
power in other areas. For most Orange County conservatives,
antistatism stopped at the door of a strong defense, and they
willingly looked to the postwar Leviathan to protect America
against "subversion."[111] As one Santa Ana couple remarked,
"We will gladly pay taxes to keep our Navy and shipyards at
full capacity. We are, in fact, for every part of our armed forces
to be brought up-to-date and to full strength immediately."[112]
Another Orange Countian, a staunch libertarian, reflected back
on the foreign policy views he held in the 1960s. Some thirty
years later, he remarked,

> Back in 1964 with Goldwater, we had the Vietnam mess and
> Goldwater's position was basically, "okay, we're in it, we should
> get out fast and bomb them back to the Stone Age." . . . Not a
> real comfortable kind of situation to be in, but we were in the
> situation. . . . When I say we, I mean the United States govern-
> ment and the people we sent over there. If you're going to send
> the U.S. military to some other part of the world, you're going to
> have to squash the enemy hard and fast, with a minimum amount
> of killing to Americans and then get the hell out.[113]

The contradiction between conservatives' antistatist rhetoric and their embrace of a strong defense was easily elided in a
land whose prosperity was built on the military-industrial complex. Only the most hard-core antistatists dared suggest that the
United States had little to fear from an external military threat.
R. C. Hoiles, in an editorial in the *Register*, harking back to an
older isolationism, suggested that "the more we spend, the
harder the arms race grows, the more precarious does security
become." Instead, in a courageous but unpopular stance, he
called for "security through freedom."[114] Similarly, Robert Le-
Fevre, who moved his Freedom School from Colorado to Or-

ange County in the late 1960s and renamed it Rampart College, along with a small contingent of Orange County libertarians in the Young Americans for Freedom, condemned the Right's statist defense posture as simply another form of state coercion.[115] In this assessment, however, the *Register*, LeFevre, and the "radical-libertarians" in Young Americans for Freedom found themselves in a distinct minority.

While right-wing anticommunists in Orange County championed a militant defense posture in U.S. foreign policy, they were also concerned with a perceived domestic communist menace. Indeed, right-wing anticommunism often focused less on foreign military threats than on conquest by internal subversion. Robert Welch noted that "the real danger is not Russian rockets but internal Communist subversion." Dan Ferguson of Brea agreed, and sought to warn his fellow citizens about the "plague of communism" that, he believed, had infected all aspects of American society, from schools to politics. This sentiment was shared by Walter T. Allen of Stanton, who believed that even "Orange County is riddled with communist infiltration."[116] Just as conservatives' efforts to fight communism abroad led them to champion a strong defense, their concern with a domestic communist menace led easily to calls for the use of state power to protect against subversion because they believed, as May Trimbath from Garden Grove put it, that "communists should have none of the freedoms true Americans have."[117]

This concern with internal subversion and the fear of domestic "communism" evoked a broad set of concerns. After all, after the McCarthyite witch-hunting days of the 1950s and the Khrushchev-Stalin revelations, the Communist Party, U.S.A., was in shambles. Orange Countians' rhetoric about "communism," then, used a dominant and broadly shared discourse to express apprehensions that had as much to do with social, political, and cultural changes in American life during the 1960s as with the Cold War. One conservative activist, Cathy Sullivan, expressed this sentiment well when she explained, some thirty years later, that "anticommunism meant a lot of things. It didn't just mean, 'Let's go kill Russians.' That had nothing to do with it."[118] In unpacking the meaning of anticommunism, it becomes clear that it subsumed a host of concerns—concerns about the state's regulation of the economy and national life, changing cultural mores, and racial egalitarianism.

While anticommunism in the first half of the 1960s (building on the legacy of the 1950s) was the central concept employed in unifying right-wing opposition to New Deal liberalism, by the late 1960s, right-wing discourse had been refashioned. With the social turbulence of the decade, the seams that had held American liberalism together began to rip apart. At that time, conservative rhetoric about "morality," "intellectual elites," centralized power, and "liberal permissiveness" moved to the fore, and anticommunism, while still an important element of right-wing belief, receded to the background of conservative concerns.

For a moment, anticommunism became the primary symbol that Orange County conservatives evoked to legitimate themselves as the true upholders of American traditions and to articulate their broader vision of their world.[119] But "communism" was not the only villain conservatives had to stand against. Another symbol that had potent meaning for conservatives was the United Nations. This international body encompassed all they hated and feared. It represented a form of government centralization where decisions were made by distant powerful elites; it included among its members communist and socialist countries; and it celebrated cultural and moral relativism, with its emphasis on international understanding. In Orange County, the Right's hostility toward the United Nations had concrete consequences. Conservatives fought hard to limit the influence of the United Nations locally. In the Magnolia School District in the early 1960s, the United Nations was banned as an "unfit" topic for school discussion.[120] In Santa Ana and Garden Grove, city councils passed ordinances banning Halloween UNICEF (United Nations International Children's Emergency Fund) collections, and in Costa Mesa, a city council majority voted to strictly regulate collections, with a member of the board majority arguing that they represented "an insidious effort," with the ultimate aim of the United Nations being to take over the United States."[121]

For liberal Americans, participation in the United Nations brought hopes for world peace. They emphasized the importance of international bodies to resolve conflicts through compromise in a diverse world. While most liberals viewed the world in bipolar terms, seeing the United Nations as a means of maintaining U.S. hegemony, some liberals embraced a more idealistic vision of "one world."[122] A member of the ADA even went so far as to call for "universal total disarmament."[123] While pragmatic liberals may have dismissed such rhetoric as merely unrealistic, for conservatives it represented a betrayal of their notions of positive good in the world. Frequently and consistently, conservatives spoke of the grave danger the world organization posed to American national sovereignty, and above all, to the American "way of life." For a segment of the Right, the United Nations' power took on almost mythical proportions. The more extreme Right called for a complete withdrawal of the United States from the organization, while others sought to limit its prerogatives and called for reform.

The United Nations, in many conservatives' eyes, was the first step toward a "one-world government"—a government run by elites unaccountable to local communities and dominated by nations with very different concepts of property, different religious traditions, and different concepts of morality and values than the United States. Many conservative Orange Countians agreed with Reverend Bob Schuler, an old-time "hell-fire and damnation" fundamentalist preacher, who thought that the United Nations Educational, Scientific, and Cultural Organization (UNESCO) "means the complete destruction of the American way of life and the dethronement of true democratic freedom."[124] Congressman James B. Utt, who introduced a bill in 1962 to revoke membership of the United States in the United

Nations, held that "this nation cannot survive as a Republic as long as we are shackled to an organization by a treaty which supersedes the Constitution."[125]

Militant anticommunism contributed to fears of the United Nations. After all, since the Right opposed diplomatic overtures with the Soviet Union, summit talks, and treaties, it logically followed that it would oppose an organization in which the Soviet Union and representatives from other socialist nations had membership and contributed to negotiating solutions to world problems (even if the organizational structure may have favored Western interests). Bob Geier of Garden Grove took these fears to an extreme, asking, "What will protect us if the United Nations finds in its wisdom that for our own good we should be communist controlled?"[126] Such sentiments at times echoed older isolationist ideas that had a long tradition in the American heartland. R. J. Smith of Anaheim articulated this tradition explicitly when he asked, What would have happened "if this country had refused to associate or deal with one enemy? Suppose it hadn't recognized Russia, gone near Red China or joined the United Nations? Why wouldn't it now be stronger, safer and more respected?"[127]

Conservative opposition to participation in the United Nations and fears of "one-world government" went beyond Cold War concerns and beyond an older isolationism. They expressed fundamentally new concerns as well, especially about the emergence of new nations in Africa and Asia. The warnings about the loss of "United States sovereignty" were underpinned with racial preservationism—fears of the undermining of white Christian prerogatives in a multicultural organization. Some grassroots conservatives, for example, referred ominously to the "Afro-Asian bloc." John Stormer, in a book read in grassroots conservative circles, *None Dare Call It Treason*, warned, "Today, nearly one-third of the new nations of the world have no traditional concepts of law. Some have not completely rejected cannibalism." Even more frightening, he continued, "Only a handful of United Nations members have concepts of private property and freedom similar to those which made America strong."[128]

Concerns with U.S. participation in the United Nations were also deepened by the region's religious fundamentalists. Fundamentalist prophecy writers often pinpointed the United Nations as the forerunner of a "world state"—if not a proto–world government itself.[129] This world state heralded the world rule of the Antichrist—foretold in biblical prophecy—and represented absolute evil and the enemy of all believing Christians. For conservatives across the spectrum, from religious conservatives to libertarians, the United Nations was potentially dangerous to U.S. interests and sovereignty. While the organization was at the forefront of conservative apprehensions in the early 1960s, it continued to earn conservative hostility throughout the decade and afterward, even leading Ronald Reagan, for example, to withdraw the United States from UNESCO after he became president.

While the United Nations and communism were two powerful symbols evoked by conservatives to define a concrete enemy, these symbols subsumed a host of concerns that spurred conservatives to action throughout the 1960s: apprehensions over federal statism, over the loss of authority of the family and church, and over declining morals and values. These concerns were articulated not only by standing against powerful distant villains but also through concrete struggles much closer to home. One significant arena in which conservatives sought to assert their vision of the nation and the world was in education. This was a meaningful issue for conservatives because, as James Davison Hunter observed, "Together, the curriculum, the textbook literature, and even the social activities of the school convey powerful symbols about the meaning of American life."[130] Above and beyond that, he continued, "Schools are the primary institutional means of reproducing community and national identity for succeeding generations of Americans."[131] Not surprisingly, then, education was a critical arena in which grassroots Orange Countians sought to influence the shape of America's future.

Indeed, in no arena did apprehensions over morality and values play a more important role in defining conservative struggles in the 1960s than in the battle over how children should be educated in the nation's schools. Schooling reflected "the will and power of the state vis-a-vis the nation's public culture"; in conservatives' eyes, it was an arena in which the state threatened to undermine and thwart their beliefs through secularism, a commitment to scientific rationalism, and the liberal values many educators embraced.[132] Parents feared losing their authority over their children due to liberal schooling. Mrs. J. W. Netherton of Westminster warned: "Parents wake up, for goodness sake . . . there are so many things that we can and must do if our children are to remain ours. Otherwise, I am afraid they will become wards of the schools and we will be told what we can and cannot teach them."[133] Another woman, Beverly McDonald of Garden Grove, who fought against public school use of "sex knowledge tests," clearly expressed apprehensions over the distance between parents and children:

> I do feel the time has come when we must individually protect our children and our nation and BOLDLY speak out against the immoral, atheistic and un-American elements whose aims are to destroy us. . . . To those of you Christian parents, do you know your schools? Do you really know your own children?[134]

Apprehensions over values taught in schools were very likely exacerbated by the experience of living in Orange County itself. Migrants who moved from conservative Bible Belt townships and entered their children in California's school system were confronted with values far different from their own, values that they believed clearly undermined parental authority. Moreover, the new communities of Orange County may have indeed undercut internal familial cohesion: In these new suburbs, where Catholics and Protestants lived next to one another and where class and ethnic divisions were few, external forces did not promote internal familial and community cohesion. The children of the new migrants, moreover, grew up in a cultural environment very different from that of their parents and among a generation that questioned old assumptions and embraced alternative lifestyles. In this setting, parents' forebodings that they were "losing control" over their children had real meaning.

Social conservatives were extremely concerned with what they perceived to be the inculcation of morally relativist values by liberal educators.[135] The John Birch Society, for example, republished the nineteenth-century *McGuffey Readers*, the classic grammar school primers known to earlier generations of American schoolchildren, and heavily lobbied school boards for their adoption as textbooks. The readers, major influences not only in American education but also in American culture through the 1920s, had become the darling of conservatives, who believed their moral lessons and references to God and the Bible provided a sure antidote to liberal secular influences.[136]

As a result of clashing beliefs between parents and administrators, periodic conflicts flared up throughout the 1960s. In one of these incidents in 1961, Mrs. Ralph Tischler of Garden Grove gathered the signatures of 1,000 parents to demand that "schools adhere strictly to traditional treatments of morals, religion and patriotism in the classroom."[137] A group of parents formed Citizens for Fundamental Education to promote the teaching of fundamental values in schools.[138] Frequently, the hostility toward liberal influence in the schools was couched as a struggle against communism. As Ann Moore of Fullerton warned in 1961, "Corrupt the young, get them away from religion. Get them interested in SEX . . . destroy their ruggedness. This is the first list of the official Communist Party Rules for the Revolution."[139] The Right had viewed the struggle to remove Joel Dvorman as a school board trustee, the first spark that contributed to grassroots conservative mobilization in 1960, also as a fight against communism. By the late 1960s, however, concerns about "morality" and permissiveness would become the driving force behind a full-fledged battle over schools.

✧✧✧

Conservatives' ideological universe—their belief in the limits of state power, their distrust of federal solutions to social and economic ills, their hostility toward democratic "equalitarianism," and their belief in a natural organic order—had concrete and practical consequences not only in battles over schools but also in their responses to contemporary political and social issues. One issue of critical concern to conservatives was the expansion of civil rights for African-Americans. Grassroots conservatives' opposition to the liberal state's expansion of individual rights (although not property rights), their concern with growing federal government power, and their defense of custom and tradition (here understood as the traditions of the white majority) combined to create a strong opposition to federal support for civil rights. As the civil rights movement riveted public attention in the early years of the 1960s, and as the federal government responded by seeking to institute reforms that would breathe life into the Fourteenth and Fifteenth Amendments through the Civil Rights Act of 1964 and the Voting Rights Act of 1965, conservatives expressed serious misgivings about the civil rights movement and federal action in support of African-Americans. They blamed peaceful civil rights demonstrators for the violence white southerners rained down on them. And they branded Martin Luther King as a divisive influence, arguing that the civil rights movement was disrupting law and order.[140]

The attack on the civil rights movement was fueled by the deep-seated racial biases of many conservative Orange Countians and was expressed by prioritizing abstract states' rights over the concrete violation of the constitutional rights of African-Americans and in the active promotion of white community prerogatives. While most Orange County conservatives did not express the kind of harsh segregationist sentiments championed by southern leaders, making racism, in the words of one conservative, less "obvious [than] it was down South," since, as he remarked, "Orval Faubus and some of those people would come out and say things that offended individuals with more education," that did not change their bias.[141] Orange County conservatives were, by and large, opposed to using the state to empower disfranchised groups. They feared that such changes would impinge on their affluent white havens and would undermine their prosperity and, as they saw it, their way of life. Indeed, such concerns propelled, as one activist recalled, "almost like a hate group of people" among a segment of the conservative movement.[142]

The attack on the civil rights movement took many forms. A small segment of the Orange County Right expressed open segregationist and racist sentiments. For a brief period in the early 1960s, Garden Grove served as the organizational headquarters for the California chapter of the National States Rights Party under James P. Thornton.[143] One housewife, who lived in Santa Ana Canyon and whose husband worked as an engineer for a rubber company, argued that "morality is the key to white resistance to integration in the South. . . . I believe that integration depends considerably on the negro himself. If he will straighten up and live right he'll naturally be accepted."[144] And a few local right-wing leaders, such as Dr. Bob Wells of the Central Baptist Church of Orange County, championed segregation. Wells clothed his racist and segregationist arguments from the pulpit with biblical authority, arguing that integration was not in "God's plan."[145] Wells's racism was part of a broader militant white Christian identity that saw civil rights and Black Power as elements of a communist grand design. Behind this design, it was hinted, stood liberal Jews.

Indeed, this overt racism was linked to a virulent anti-Semitism. The tiny Anaheim-based Christian Anti-Defamation League, Wells's brainchild, claimed that "without a doubt the Anti-Defamation League of B'nai B'rith is probably the most powerful anti-Christ organization in America today."[146] Not only a number of Protestant fundamentalists but also a few Catholic conservatives evinced a belief in "Zionist" conspiracies.[147] Yet despite these manifestations of anti-Jewish bigotry, anti-Semitism was largely discredited within the broader grassroots movement. When anti-Semitic activity erupted in Newport Beach and Corona del Mar in July 1960, the *Register* strongly condemned the incidents.[148] While anti-Semitism was indeed present among a segment of the fundamentalist Right, and often hidden behind conspiracy theories, it did not play the same central role it had for the old Right.[149]

Opposition to civil rights was rarely voiced in overtly racist terms. Instead, civil rights were, in the first half of the decade, depicted by some conservatives as part of a communist plot to foster disorder. Sam Mitchell of Newport Beach, active in the American Legion's anticommunism work, observed that William Z. Foster, head of the Communist Party U.S.A. in 1932, had demanded "equal rights for the Negroes, and self-determination for the black belt." Creating a link between the civil rights movement and "communism" was a strong symbolic means of attempting to undermine the movement's legitimacy—and it was frequently reiterated in the literature of the John Birch Society, which set up the Task Force on Civil Disorder and painted the civil rights movement as part of a communist plot.

But while a segment of the Right explained civil rights in terms of a communist plot, the most prominent rationale for opposition to civil rights was based on arguments that these new federal laws overstepped the bounds of the Constitution and rode roughshod over states' rights. Conservatives' beliefs in the limits of federal power provided sufficient ground for opposing the assertion of federal over state power, an assertion that would, in their eyes, "undermine the Republic." Barry Goldwater, for example, placed his opposition to civil rights in these terms:

> Under present conditions, of course, there is a loud demand for additional anti-segregation laws. But I believe wisdom demands that we recognize there is a limit on how far we can go without upsetting the constitutional rights to freedom of association. For example, if the Congress acts hastily under the rope of urgency and enacts legislation to integrate department stores and restaurant facilities under the guise of regulating interstate commerce, we will have backed states rights clear out of the Constitution. Let me explain that I believe deeply in integration. But I believe that it must be brought about in accordance with our Constitution and the fundamental concepts of freedom.[150]

But it was not only the federal government's actions to end racial discrimination that many conservatives opposed. Much closer to home was the enactment of legislation at the state level to put an end to racial discrimination in housing. After liberal legislators succeeded in passing the 1963 Rumford Open Housing Act to prevent discrimination in housing, Orange Countians and Californians overwhelming voted for Proposition 14, a constitutional amendment that sought to repeal what conservatives termed the "Forced Housing Act." California property owners, they argued, should have the right to choose the people to whom they sold or rented their residential property—the "freedom to choose" without interference from government. "The philosophical fallacy of the Rumford Act," even the *Los Angeles Times* argued, "lies in seeking to correct such a social evil while simultaneously destroying what we deem a basic right in a free society." The proposition measure passed in Orange County by more than a two-to-one margin.[151]

Although "rights" were championed by the conservative movement, it was not civil rights that the conservatives supported, but individual property rights. The insistence on the untrammeled rights of property holders to control, utilize, sell, and profit from private property was at the heart of their thinking. And where civil rights—the right, for example, to purchase property without discrimination on the basis of color—interfered with property rights, they clearly sided with the property holder.[152]

After the Civil Rights Act was signed into law in 1964, the Right's hostility toward federal government remedies for racial discrimination focused on attacks against state fair housing legislation, affirmative action, and, in the late 1960s and 1970s, busing.[153] As the locus of civil rights struggles shifted simultaneously from the South to the North, white resistance to these demands broadened, providing the Right with new adherents.

While anticommunism remained the discursive bond that united antistatist libertarians and social conservatives until the mid-

1960s, as the decade progressed, concerns over "law and order" and "morality" and attacks on "sophisticated intellectuals" moved to center stage. As American liberalism began to unravel, the focus of the Right's discourse shifted away from communism toward a more direct attack on "liberal humanism" and the "open society." This shift in focus—which went hand in hand with the rise of the New Left, the student movement, the counterculture, the civil rights struggles in the North, and the Vietnam War—represented not fundamentally new concerns but rather new terrains of struggle on which conservative Orange Countians sought to articulate their vision of the world. These new conflicts gave conservative ideas a broader appeal among a wider constituency. Recognizing an opportunity, moreover, right-wing political leaders sought to refashion the conservative image, broadening its appeal by articulating a new conservative populism.[154] By end of the 1960s, conservatives' concerns with "law and order" as well as morality, and their critiques of "liberal elites" and "coddling criminals"—shorn of their apocalyptic, extremist tendencies—had become a part of the dominant political discourse. Building on the lessons learned from Goldwater's defeat and the new opportunities brought about by the social turbulence of the decade, conservatives moved increasingly into the respectable mainstream, while the mainstream moved toward them. Nowhere did these forces come together more powerfully than in the California gubernatorial campaign in 1966. The campaign was the first real triumph for the conservative movement, one that launched an aging actor on the path that would carry him, some fourteen years later, to the White House.

CHAPTER ✦ 5

THE BIRTH OF POPULIST CONSERVATISM

IF ORANGE COUNTY conservatives were disheartened
by the rejection of Barry Goldwater's message in November
1964, events in California only brought closer to home their
sense that American liberalism and Lyndon Johnson's Great Society threatened to undermine their prosperity and their way of
life. Just as they were assessing Goldwater's devastating loss, a
new and—to conservatives—frightening specter had arisen in
the northern part of the state. On September 30, 1964, a group
of Berkeley students, many of whom had recently returned from
a summer in Mississippi working for civil rights, staged a protest
against the university's new rules regarding political activity on
campus. After policemen arrested an activist for manning a Congress on Racial Equality (CORE) table on campus, students "sat
down" around a group of police officers in the car seeking to
carry him away. For thirty-two hours, students blocked the vehicle, marking the arrival of the student movement on the national
scene.[1]

The free speech movement was only a harbinger of what
was to come: With the escalation of the war in Southeast Asia
in 1965, the Vietnam Day Committee joined the fray, stopping
troop trains passing through Berkeley. Students staged innumer-
able demonstrations and sit-ins over the next years.[2] And it was
not just political radicalism that found its home in Berkeley. Students, following the example of the 1950s Beats, forged an alternative lifestyle that defiantly challenged older social norms. They
embraced new modes of dress, of relating, and of living, aban-

doning the pragmatic rationalism of their parents in search of a more meaningful world. By 1966, Berkeley was in ferment—a ferment that would eventually rip the fabric of American liberalism apart and play itself out to the advantage of conservatives. But at the time, conservatives simply saw a challenge to authority, to their values and social norms, and to the "American way of life" as they conceived of it.

Berkeley was not the only ominous portent for the future. Barry Goldwater had already emphasized the themes of "rising crime" and "law and order" in 1964—but in the summer of 1965, these issues had greater resonance for white Southern Californians when the Watts section of Los Angeles went up in flames. The rebellion was sparked when a white police officer arrested a young African-American, but its deeper roots lay in the community's anger and frustration over long-standing police abuses, poor living conditions, and the failure of the civil rights movement to improve the lives of the urban black poor.[3] After a week of upheaval, the despair and rage had resulted in thirty-four deaths, 1,032 injuries, almost 4,000 arrests, and the destruction of $40 million worth of property.[4] While liberals called for redress of the economic and social conditions that had fostered the riots, many white middle-class Orange Countians saw them as one more sign of "lawlessness," "immorality," and "social decay" brought about by liberal largesse and the "permissive society."

This liberal largesse seemed personified, moreover, in President Lyndon B. Johnson, who had returned to the White House in November 1964 with overwhelming popular support. Johnson believed strongly that American affluence would make it possible to eliminate poverty and fund an array of social programs. A thorough believer in the benevolence of big government, he pushed through a series of legislative programs to provide federal funds to support the arts, scientific research, racial equality, free health care for the aged and impoverished, and improvements in the lives of the poor. His rhetoric of social justice and equality went even further. Johnson declared in his January 1965 State of the Union message, "We're only at the beginning of the road to the Great Society. . . . Ahead now is a summit where freedom from the wants of the body can help fulfill the needs of the spirit."[5] While such rhetoric raised expectations among impoverished groups, it was anathema to conservatives. Yet with the Democrats thoroughly entrenched on the national political scene and California's governor, Edmund Brown, play-ing "Little Brother" to "Big Brother" in Washington, the pros-pects for conservatives seemed bleak.

One voice, however, offered hope that there might yet be life for the conservative agenda. Six months after the Goldwater debacle, Ronald Reagan stood before 1,200 members of the Santa Ana Young Republicans and called on conservatives to "rise from defeat" and begin the "second round to defend the Republic."[6] Berating what he termed a "misguided Democratic leadership," he warned that the Brown administration fostered "government by an intellectual elite" that would lead to "Wash-ington, D.C., controlling every facet of an individual's life."[7] The words of this man, introduced by Congressman James B. Utt as "one of the greatest Americans you have ever had before you," gave strong new voice to the concerns of Santa Ana Re-publican conservatives, lightening their hearts and rekindling their hopes.[8]

By 1965, Reagan was a prominent figure in California con-servative circles. A former liberal who had supported Democrat Helen Gahagan Douglas's 1950 campaign for the U.S. Senate and who had served as union president of the Hollywood Screen Actors Guild, he had moved increasingly to the right through the 1950s. By the decade's end, he was a full-fledged conservative ideologue, echoing many of the sentiments of right-wing Orange Countians.[9] In a 1959 letter to Richard Nixon, he spoke their hearts when he declared: "Shouldn't one tag Mr. Kennedy's *bold new imaginative* program with its proper age? Under the tousled boyish hair cut it is still old Karl Marx."[10] Reagan worked to spread the conservative free-enterprise message in speeches throughout the land. He railed against "Big Brother" and called for a return to local control and individual liberty.[11] For eight years, he served as a spokesperson for General Electric on "government encroachment" and made speeches for the National Association of Manufacturers (NAM) and other conservative business organizations.[12] His activities for the conservative cause included appearances before rallies of Fred Schwarz's Christian Anti-Communism Crusade.[13] Reagan became a familiar figure to Orange County conservatives. A woman from Anaheim, for example, first heard Reagan speak in 1958 and was then convinced that he was a crusader for "the . . . American Heritage our forefathers fought for and intended for us and our children to enjoy."[14]

But Reagan's work for the conservative cause was not limited to speeches on the "American heritage" to business and "patriotic" groups or as a spokesperson for General Electric. He also worked hard for Republican candidates, especially in California. In 1964, he served as state cochairman of the California Committee for Goldwater-Miller. In the eleventh hour of Goldwater's campaign, at a $1,000-a-plate fund-raising dinner in Los Angeles, Reagan presented a speech, "A Time for Choosing," that, in the words of one prominent conservative, "electrified the nation."[15] According to F. Clifton White, national director of Citizens for Goldwater-Miller, the response to Reagan's speech was so enthusiastic that "phones [have been] ringing around the clock here since your telecast."[16] Telegrams flooded Reagan, characterizing the speech as "outstanding," "magnificent," and, in the words of one supporter, "the greatest political speech we've heard."[17]

Indeed, the speech—a masterpiece of oration, according to some listeners—inspired tens of thousands, including thousands of Californians, to write to Reagan and urge him to run for office.[18] Shortly after the election, the volunteer who had run the Orange for Goldwater office during the 1964 campaign wrote to Reagan to compliment him on the "fine work you had performed . . . for Senator Goldwater" and to encourage him to run for the Senate or the governorship.[19] One year later, her enthusiasm undiminished, she remarked that those who had taken part in the Orange for Goldwater group were ready and willing to go to work for Reagan. She exuberantly noted that "there is a true 'grassroots' feeling in our city that you would be a great candidate and a fine Governor for the state of California."[20] And Mrs. Lucille Boston, past president of the Republican Women's Federation and president of the Young Republicans, observed that many Southern California grassroots Goldwater supporters were so inspired that over 100 efficient Goldwater precinct organizations in the Los Angeles area, rather than disbanding after the elections, reorganized under different names.[21] Indeed, some Southern California conservatives were so impressed with Reagan that they urged him to aspire not only to the governorship but also to the highest office in the land. One Anaheim supporter, for example, wrote to Reagan that he, along with many friends, were asking the question, "Do you suppose Mr. Reagan is going to run for President?" He encouraged him to do so because he was sure that Reagan was the "kind of man who may bring our nation back to the kind of Government it was mean't [sic] to be."[22]

With such grassroots support in place, a group of southland businessmen who had backed Barry Goldwater in 1964 decided to court Reagan as well, hoping he would run for governor.[23] This group of men—including Henry Salvatori, the head of the Los Angeles–based Western Geophysical Corporation; Holmes Tuttle, son of an Oklahoma cattle rancher and a highly successful entrepreneur; Cy Rubel, who had served as chairman of the Union Oil Company; and Ed Mills, former president of Van De Kamp's bakery—had the will and the wherewithal to groom a candidate for the highest office in what was soon to be the largest state in the Union.[24] In a series of meetings, they convinced Reagan to run. Soon afterward, in the spring of 1965, the group expanded to forty-one wealthy Friends of Reagan—a statewide executive committee that worked outside the formal party apparatus. The committee, with its members heavily drawn from the southland, included a number of prominent Orange Countians, like Walter Knott and Frank White, both of Knott's Berry Farm, along with J. S. Fluor of the Fluor Corporation.[25]

By the spring of 1965, Reagan had won the hearts and minds of both the leaders and the rank and file of southland conservatism. When he stood before an enthusiastic audience in late April 1965, in the heart of the region that would soon be dubbed "Reagan country," it was already evident that he had become the new conservative standard-bearer. The Orange County California Republican Assembly delegates led an effort at their statewide convention (nine months before Reagan officially announced his candidacy) to endorse him as a nominee for governor.[26] The Buena Park members of the conservative United Republicans of California named their chapter in his honor. And at the Orange County UROC convention in the spring of 1965, the 300 delegates unanimously adopted a resolution urging Reagan to run for governor.[27] As the news spread that Reagan would publicly announce his candidacy, more conservative Orange Countians entered the fray. The Rossmoor–Los Alamitos CRA passed a resolution in October 1965 pledging its resources to nominate and elect him the next governor of California.[28] And James Townsend, who had served as state chair of an organization that had worked to elect Goldwater, organized a private dinner in Orange County for Reagan with more than fifty "volunteer grass-roots leaders." According to Townsend, "only lack of space prevented another hundred" from attending.[29]

Reagan won the allegiance of the Orange County conservative Republican grass roots because he articulated, as Goldwater had before him, the principles these people hoped to bring into government: limiting the use of the state for purposes of more equitable economic distribution, reliance on private enterprise, a return to local control, and a simultaneous reinforcement of state power as enforcer of law and order and moral traditionalism. As one Orange County Reagan enthusiast put it, "We know that if our Nation is to survive, as a freedom loving Nation, we must pull those who seek to control us out of our seats of Government and put in those who have mind enough to understand that it is and was private enterprise which built this great Nation and that each person shall provide for themselves, and stop looking for this something for nothing bit and being a burden on their fellowmen."[30] A supporter from Tustin declared that he hoped Reagan would "knock hell out of the welfare concept of life at the Federal level and put control back in the hands of the local citizenry where it belongs."[31] Not to be outdone, the Rossmoor–Los Alamitos CRA proclaimed that it was "proud" of Reagan's "unparalleled contributions towards exposing the National Socialist menace facing the United States of America."[32]

But as the recent Goldwater debacle had made all too evident, the enthusiastic support of such conservative ideologues by no means translated into electoral victories. As soon as he made the decision to enter the race, Reagan worked with his financial backers to apply the lessons learned from the Goldwater campaign. Their first priority was to prevent the party factionalism that had proven so damaging to Goldwater. In March 1965, in an appearance before the CRA convention in San Diego, Reagan asserted that he objected to the use of labels resulting in "hyphenated Republicans." From now on, he remarked, he would prefer to be just a "republican Republican" rather than a conservative one, although, he reassured his audience, "I haven't changed my views."[33] He warned that he would forget any political plans if a bloody primary battle "seems inevitable."[34] The unity theme resonated among southland conservatives in the face of their resounding loss some months before. At the 1965 CRA convention, Nolan Frizzelle of Buena Park and Senator John Schmitz from Tustin stressed the importance of unity.[35] Gaylord Parkinson, a San Diego obstetrician and chair of the State Central Committee, moreover, invented the "Eleventh Commandment"—"Thou shall not speak ill of any fellow Republican"—to keep conservatives and moderate Republicans from attacking each other in the primary.[36]

A new awareness of the need to avoid the fratricidal wars within the party that had so weakened Goldwater spread not only among party leaders but also among the rank and file. Indeed, "the impulse for unity," according to Reagan, "sprang from the grass-roots." The "rank and file members of the party," he claimed, "were tired of fighting each other and . . . made it plain that they would settle for nothing less than a unified party supporting the ticket."[37] Some of these men and women, indeed, wrote to Reagan affirming their support for Parkinson's call for unity. One housewife from nearby Long Beach, whose husband worked for Douglas Aircraft, commended him "for keeping the eleventh commandment."[38] And another woman from Fullerton wished that Reagan's primary rival "would contribute unity in the party and abide by Dr. Parkinson's 11th Commandment."[39]

The call for party unity, as the letter from this Fullerton supporter suggests, did not convince moderate and centrist Republicans to join the Reagan camp. Instead, after U.S. Senator Thomas Kuchel decided not to enter the race for governor, centrist support fell to Reagan's one serious challenger, George Christopher, a multimillionaire dairyman who had served two terms as the mayor of San Francisco. Christopher gained the backing of prominent California Republicans like Caspar Weinberger, Leonard Firestone, and Justin Dart, but Reagan still had the support of a great deal of California money and, as important, the backing of the Republican grass roots.[40] Early in the campaign, a poll of Orange County showed that Republicans there preferred Reagan nearly two-and-a-half to one to Christopher.[41] The CRA, the largest volunteer preprimary endorsing body, moreover, easily endorsed Ronald Reagan at its March 1966 convention.[42] While moderate Christopher forces, aware of their weakness, sought to hold off a Reagan endorsement by calling on the 590 delegates not to endorse either candidate, the delegates overwhelmingly nominated Reagan.[43]

Reagan's trumpeting of unity was troubled not only by party moderates but also by a small group of staunch conservative southland leaders. Cyril Stevenson, who served as the CRA president in 1965 and, according to prominent CRA leaders, was a member of the John Birch Society, led a move to hinge support of Reagan's candidacy on the assurance of conservative appointments to his administration.[44] These efforts culminated at the statewide convention in the spring of 1966. They failed to dent Reagan's support, however, and he handily won the nomination.[45]

Besides easily winning the CRA primary, Reagan won the June 7 primaries hands down, driving home his popularity with the Republican grass roots. Reagan received 1,417,623 votes to Christopher's 675,683, with three minor candidates taking a total of 92,751.[46] By winning 65 percent of the total Republican vote, Reagan demonstrated that he could deliver the party unity that had eluded Goldwater, who had won his victory in the state's Republican primary in 1964 with only 52 percent.[47] Moreover, whereas Goldwater lost fifty-four of California's fifty-eight counties, Reagan won all but five.[48] "The Republican Party," as George Christopher conceded shortly after the election, "has conclusively shown its preference for the philosophy of Ronald Reagan."[49] Not surprisingly, no county made this preference more clearly known than Orange County, where voter turnout was especially heavy.[50] Orange County Republicans gave Reagan 81 percent of their votes.[51]

Even though Reagan's primary success boded well for November, he still had to overcome the close association in the public mind between himself and Goldwater—a link that left him vulnerable to charges of "extremism." This association was made evident by Bill Bagley, California Democratic assemblyman, who early in the campaign remarked, with a somewhat blind optimism, "Not one in ten thousand takes the Reagan movement seriously. . . . The Reagan movement is a remnant of the Goldwater movement. How in the Devil can a remnant expect to win an election?"[52] Although Bagley exaggerated, it was nonetheless precisely such associations with "Goldwaterism" that concerned Reagan's backers. They knew they would need to change that image if they were going to win.

The Friends of Reagan had snapped up the right campaign managers to do the job. In early 1965, they had already hired California's slickest political management team, Spencer-Roberts and Associates, which had headed Nelson Rockefeller's campaign for the California Republican Party presidential primary in 1964.[53] Spencer-Roberts announced in *Newsweek* in July 1965 that "our toughest job is going to be to prove [Reagan] isn't a right-winger" and worked hard to present "a reasonable picture of a candidate who is not the darling of the extremists, a sensible, reasonable guy who leans to the right but who doesn't spout all this nonsense about the Liberty Amendment and fluoridation."[54]

Armed with the strategic expertise of his handlers, Reagan not only heeded the advice himself but also sought to limit the fanaticism and militancy of his grassroots supporters. He urged conservatives "not to go on a witch hunt" in promulgating their philosophy.[55] He also declined to actively seek the endorsement of the United Republicans of California because of its extremist image.[56] When, during the general campaign, a booklet entitled "The Story of Ronald Reagan," put out by the Spirit of '76, a conservative and superpatriotic organization, was found for sale in a local Reagan headquarters, the Southern California cochairmen of the Reagan campaign sent out a memo to all county chairmen stating that "this material should not be in any Reagan headquarters."[57] From the start, Reagan set a different tone for his campaign than Goldwater had, working to build a new model of conservative respectability that would enable him and other conservatives after him to become viable electoral contenders.

While some conservatives were disappointed by Reagan's efforts to achieve respectability and especially by the distance he maintained from his most committed supporters, the lesson Reagan and his managers preached to conservatives fell, in general, on receptive ears.[58] After the debacle in 1964, these men and women appreciated the need to jettison the controversial rhetoric that had gotten Goldwater into trouble. In effect, they expounded a new brand of conservatism. One Laguna Hills supporter wrote to Reagan with advice on how to "help you over your two biggest hurdles: the cry of inexperience and Goldwater extremism."[59] A Westminster supporter urged Reagan not to become a "proverbial bird in Governor Brown's hand" by allowing Brown to link him to Goldwaterism.[60] And in a similar vein, a supporter from nearby Long Beach begged Reagan not to "let the mistakes which lost the election for Mr. Goldwater in '64, lose this election for you! Don't go out on the *extremism* limb."[61] These grassroots supporters, just like Reagan's handlers, were aware of the need to win broader popular support than Goldwater had been able to do, and they offered Reagan advice on how to accomplish the task. One Anaheim man wrote to the candidate early in the campaign that "a means must be found to explain to the man in the street what the abstract terms, welfare state, loss of freedom, etc., mean. The inability of the Goldwater people to get this across," he lamented, "contributed heavily to his defeat."[62]

With the primary in his pocket, it was to the man on the street that Reagan now turned. Reagan and his managers sought to broaden his message to win the votes of uncommitted, independent, and Democratic voters, essential for a Republican victory in California.[63] Their efforts to reach Democrats were greatly aided by fratricidal wars within the Democratic Party and the social and political turmoil sweeping the state. For while the California Republican Party had been busily trumpeting "unity," the state's Democratic Party was falling apart. Whereas in 1962 Brown had easily won a harmonious primary, by 1966 it was apparent that many Democrats were dissatisfied with his governorship. Controversies over issues such as race, fair housing, welfare, public spending, and taxes plagued the Brown administration and helped to split the party between its liberal and conservative wings.[64]

This tension between the conservative and liberal wings of the party was hardly new. The vast in-migration to the southland in the 1950s and 1960s had brought Democrats from diverse settings into Southern California. They settled in lower-middle-class and middle-class neighborhoods, such as Bellflower and Downey in Los Angeles, as well as in Garden Grove, Cypress, and the northwestern parts of Orange County. Some of these newcomers considered themselves liberal Democrats (some, like Joel Dvorman, even joined the ACLU), but many more thought of themselves as "Jeffersonian Democrats."[65] While their political loyalties led the number of Democratic registrants in Orange County to outpace registered Republicans for a brief period in 1960, they expressed their conservative tendencies by electing Democrats like Richard Hanna to Congress and William Dannemeyer to the State Assembly from 1962 to 1965. These men were hardly liberal champions; still Orange County Democrats' social conservative tendencies did not preclude them from giving strong support to Governor Edmund Brown. In 1962, for example, Brown carried the election in Buena Park, Cypress, Stanton, Westminster, and tiny Fountain Valley, and he came close in Garden Grove.[66]

But the tensions in the party rose to new heights with the social upheavals of the 1960s, especially the rise of a vocal liberal-Left contingent within the California Democratic Council (CDC), the party's volunteer organization. During the 1960s, the CDC became a grassroots forum of liberal dissent, challenging the policies of the party leadership and seeking to push the party to the left.[67] The strength of the liberal wing of the CDC made itself felt in 1965, when the volunteer organization approved resolutions on Vietnam calling for a cease-fire, an end to the bombing, and negotiations with the National Liberation Front.[68] In 1966, the CDC not only reaffirmed its support for these measures but also introduced resolutions calling for the establishment of local civilian police review boards, for admitting the People's Republic of China to the United Nations, and for lifting travel restrictions to Communist countries.[69] The progressive sentiments of the California Federation of Young Democrats, another volunteer organization, went even further, "support[ing] the basic idea of black power" and calling for the repeal of abortion and "morality laws" governing sexual behavior.[70] The liberal leadership of the CDC and the new radicalism that penetrated the party placed Brown in the awkward position of holding on to a pragmatic liberalism that satisfied neither the rank-and-file conservative Democrats nor the left wing of the party.

While newly minted Californians may have been unsettled by the party's liberalism for some time, the vocal Left within the

CDC and other volunteer organizations deeply disturbed them. To add insult to injury, the southland clubs were dominated, according to one prominent southland CDC leader, by men and women from the middle class and upper middle class.[71] The issues they championed were not the traditional economic majoritarian bread-and-butter New Deal ones that had ensured the loyalties of lower-middle-class white ethnic voters to the party, but a rights-based liberalism that championed the interests of African-Americans and the poor. Considering such a reorientation, it was hardly surprising that rank-and-file conservative Democrats felt more and more alienated from the party. One frustrated Democrat from nearby Whittier threatened, "I think it's time we Democrats rid ourselves of all the leftists and clean up our own party, or I won't be a Democrat much longer."[72] A man from Huntington Beach who had migrated from Iowa in the early 1960s remarked to Brown in 1965, "I . . . surely have been surprised at the number and strength of the far out groups here. . . . I suspect most of them are front organizations for the Communists and am quite sure the CDC can be put in this category."[73]

Brown's primary challenger, Samuel Yorty, drove these issues home. He blasted what he called the "leftist takeover of the Democratic Party."[74] Yorty, once a New Deal liberal Democrat who had cofounded California's own version of HUAC, had seesawed politically through the 1940s and 1950s, combining Red-baiting tactics with populist appeals against elites.[75] In 1960, he drew attention by backing Nixon, issuing a manifesto titled "I Cannot Take Kennedy."[76] In the 1961 campaign for mayor of Los Angeles, Yorty played on the race issue—an issue on which he further capitalized after the Watts riots and the repeal of Proposition 14. This conservative renegade spoke for the "average man" and attacked "left-wing Democrats," federal power, and centralized government, calling for local control with a populist, anti-elitist flare.[77]

Such a politics of resentment appealed to many lower-middle-class and middle-class white Orange County Democrats disillusioned with their party's liberalism. They formed a Yorty for Governor Committee and worked hard to get out the primary vote. George Rochester, who had been a member of the Democratic Party for decades, served as its campaign manager. Once a Brown supporter, he charged that Brown "sold the Democratic Party down the river. He turned it over to the California Democratic Council. . . . This small minority group represents the extreme left wing of the Democratic Party."[78]

Building on these resentments, Yorty did well in the primaries, winning 981,088 votes, compared with Brown's 1,355,262.[79] If it had been up to Orange County Democrats, Yorty would have won the primary election. They voted 57,176 to 47,564 in favor of the mayor from the City of Angels, making the county the only substantial one in the state to give Yorty a majority.[80] The heartland of right-wing Republicanism was thus also the home of the state's conservative Democrats. For them, it was only a small step to embrace those whose beliefs came much closer to their own: conservative Republicans. As one Anaheim Democrat put it, he was, by 1966, a "disenchanted Democrat" who "made a mistake in voting for LBJ" but now planned to "be out in the field drumming up votes" for Reagan and the Republican Party.[81] In a similar vein, a Democratic couple from nearby Bellflower remarked, "We may be Democrats, but find more and more the Conservative view is the American way."[82]

Sam Yorty had appealed to these sentiments. After his primary loss, however, his supporters regrouped to back Reagan. George Rochester, who had served as the campaign manager of the Yorty for Governor Committee for Orange County and who was chairman of the Democratic Associates of Orange County, forged ahead with a new organization: a statewide group called Californians for Reagan, which trumpeted Reagan's message to Democratic and independent voters.[83] The group's task was aided by Yorty himself, who refused to endorse Brown and instead courted Reagan, helping to bring these rank-and-file Democrats into the Reagan camp.[84]

Well aware of the splits within the Democratic Party and the popular discontent with Brown's administration, Reagan's managers infused his campaign with a populist message to attract the troubled Democratic voters who had so eluded Goldwater. Stuart Spencer, one member of the dynamic team that managed the campaign, boasted, "We did target other than Republicans. It was the first time we came up with the category 'white conservative Democrats' . . . we really went after them."[85] The managers designed some of their campaign media for this group and sent direct mail into areas that had gone heavily for Yorty in the primaries. And they sought to boost the efforts of independent Democrats by making Californians for Reagan an integral part of the Reagan organization.[86]

Reagan not only reached out to Democrats but also specifically sought to appeal to rank-and-file union voters, despite his close associations with manufacturers' organizations like the NAM.[87] On his visits to factories, he presented himself as a friend of the working man. At a campaign stop in San Bernardino, for example, standing amid the noise and dirt of a busy Kaiser steel mill, he made a plea for labor's support and sought to dispel Democratic charges that he was anti-union: "I spent twenty years as an officer and six terms as president of my union. . . . I don't know how in the hell . . . you can get an anti-labor position after that."[88] Reagan added that he had opposed right-to-work laws in the 1958 election and still opposed them.[89] Despite his close ties to anti-union forces, Reagan was able to convey a more populist image and to counter Democratic charges that he was "anti-labor."

Besides bringing a personal history to the campaign that made him potentially attractive to working-class voters, Reagan propagated a program that appealed to many of them. Affluent, homeowning, white blue-collar workers could be courted on issues of rising taxes and spending, since their own security came from private pensions and health insurance, not from public welfare benefits. High state spending did not seem to benefit them, particularly since conservative spokespersons blamed rising spending on welfare given to those "too lazy to work." These conservative populist appeals were even more effective when they were racially coded. Reagan played this card well: He stated that in his "Creative Society" there "will be no welfare benefits . . . for able-bodied persons who are too lazy to work," point-

edly adding that "many welfare recipients are members of minority groups."[90] Such statements appealed to white blue-collar
Democrats, one of whom wrote to Reagan from Long Beach
that "my husband is in strong agreement with you on all the
issues on which you have spoken out, i.e. welfare, taxes, stronger
laws, law enforcement, Supreme Court, the University of California investigation, etc."[91] She noted that her husband was not
alone among rank-and-file union members: "In spite of what
they are told from their San Francisco headquarters, there is . . .
strong feeling running in your favor and against the Brown Administration in its entirety, from top to bottom and in all
phases."[92] A factory worker's wife from Brea in Orange County
agreed, assuring Reagan that "you have many supporters among
us common people."[93]

Reagan, a man who knew how to package himself for his
public, was able to sustain a right-wing politics while also at-
tracting a broader group of constituents whose loyalties were up
for grabs. He was able to do so in part, as financial backer Henry
Salvatori put it some years later, because it was "the first time
the liberals saw a conservative . . . whom they couldn't depict as
a demon who was going to drop the bomb and destroy human-
ity."[94] Moreover, whereas Goldwater could be caught by his long
political record, Reagan was better known for his familiar and
friendly television face than for his statements on Social Security.

Yet it was not only his personal style and his populist rhetoric that made Reagan's task of winning Democratic voters easier.
In addition, the boiling cauldron of concerns over law and order,
race, and taxes generated in the two years between Goldwater's
and Reagan's campaigns played into conservative hands. First,
by the summer of 1966, developments at Berkeley had already
been in the public eye for some time. The New Left, Students
for a Democratic Society (SDS), and the counterculture had all
begun to make their marks. Many middle-aged men and women
who had lived through the Great Depression and war had
worked hard to achieve their piece of the American dream. Now,
they resented the young people who challenged the core meaning
of their lives. As one resident of South Laguna who himself had

graduated from the University of California seethed, "Our schools should be a place of learning and not a breeding ground of UnAmericans."[95] According to one of Reagan's campaign managers, "Every place that Ronald Reagan gave a speech, . . . somebody would get up and say, 'What are you going to do about those bastards at Berkeley,' . . . Mario Savio and that crowd."[96] Reagan, picking up on the issue, called for Brown to crack down on the "filthy speech movement."[97] With dissent on campus flaring up continuously throughout the campaign, Reagan gained an easy issue on which to capitalize. By the last week of the campaign, he declared to a Santa Rosa audience that "morality is the main issue of the campaign and the main focus of this issue is student conduct at Berkeley."[98] When asked by a student from Santa Cruz what he thought about a statement by Max Rafferty, state superintendent of public instruction, that the situation at Berkeley had developed into a "four year course in sex, drugs, and treason," Reagan grinned and said he respected Rafferty, adding that "sometimes he speaks in a flourishing manner."[99] As he did so often, Reagan handled the issue in a way that spoke to the concerns of hundreds of thousands of Californians but without employing the alarmist, conspiratorial tones associated with the Right.[100] By carefully pruning his rhetoric, he won the support of those like the Catholic Democrat from Covina, just to the north of Orange County, who declared that she had never voted Republican; as she explained, "I never thought I would but things have happened which had changed my mind." Most, important, she said, was the "stinking mess up at Berkeley."[101]

Campus upheaval and the rise of the New Left were not the only issues on which Reagan capitalized. The increasingly volatile race issue also helped to tear the liberal coalition apart.[102] While, in 1963, televisions across the nation had flashed pictures of white police officers clubbing black and white civil rights marchers in the South, in the summer of 1965, the nation's television screens carried images of enraged black youths in Watts looting businesses and neighborhoods in flames. Rising African-American militancy led to a growing white backlash, from which Reagan profited by playing to white racism. Calls for "law and order" and cries against "rising criminality" often served as a coded language that played to white suburban fears of the black masses of the inner cities. Reagan's own use of such language is evident in a document his administration wrote after he became governor:

> Charges of brutality are being raised by a small but disruptive segment of society, which is constantly challenging the authority of the law. . . . For the law abiding, the policeman is a friend. For all our science and sophistication, for all our justified pride in intellectual accomplishment, *the jungle is waiting to take over.* The man with the badge helps to hold it back. Too often the only thanks he gets is a charge of police brutality.[103]

Such language resonated with many white suburban middle-class Orange Countians, some of whom had moved from Los Angeles to escape the congestion, crime, and diversity of the city, and others who had settled in Orange County in part because of its very homogeneity. The riots made the dangers of the city seem all the more real, and many residents favored Reagan's calls for law and order, viewing Brown's response as inadequate. One Garden Grove woman wrote Brown accusingly, "Why protect the criminal and make us innocent people suffer?"[104] And another Orange County woman berated Brown for being too quick "to sympathize and take the side of groups pleading 'police brutality.'"[105]

Indeed, many Orange Countians saw their communities as "safe havens" from the problems they associated with economic and racial diversity. When this "world apart" was threatened by laws such as the California Fair Housing Act, they bitterly fought back. One opponent from the city of Orange spent over $200 of his own money and drove 3,000 miles campaigning against the Rumford Housing Act.[106] With the resounding success of Proposition 14, Orange Countians had bought themselves a reprieve from the "threat" of diversity. But when the California Supreme Court, in a five-to-two decision, repudiated Proposition 14 in 1966, the specter reared its head again, and

Ronald Reagan gained another issue he could use to mobilize support in the suburban white enclaves of the southland. In conservatives' eyes, open housing laws compromised absolute property rights in favor of civil rights and social justice, a compromise they were not willing to make. More concretely, these laws threatened to diversify homogeneous white enclaves by requiring landlords and property holders to rent or sell without discrimination on the basis of race. On the campaign trail, Reagan announced that all persons in a free society have a "basic and cherished right to do as they please with their property. If an individual wants to discriminate against Negroes or others in selling or renting his house he has a right to do so."[107] Reagan labeled fair housing laws and the Rumford Act as attempts "to give one segment of our population a right at the expense of the basic rights of all our citizens." Separating himself from blatant racists, however, he stressed the need for "voluntary action on the part of individuals" to put an end to "the cancer of racial discrimination."[108]

Civil rights issues, the riots, the protests in Berkeley, and rising state spending and taxes helped to rip suburban white constituents away from the Democratic Party—offering new opportunities for conservatives. As one Anaheim resident and registered Democrat remarked, "rising taxes" and "Commies in Government" were leading him to vote Republican.[109] Disillusionment ran so deep among some rank-and-file Democrats that one man from Seal Beach claimed, in exaggerated fashion, that concerns over "Taxes—Crime—Dope—Schools, etc." were leading "hundreds of thousands such as I that were registered life long Democrats [to change] our registrations to Republican."[110] Rhetoric about morality, freedom and responsibility, and "law and order"—long part of right-wing discourse—now resonated in new ways with increasing numbers of white and middle-class suburban Americans who were concerned with social and cultural changes and with the threat to their own privileges and entitlements posed by the radicalized demands for change, empowerment, and social justice put forth by other social groups.[111] Now the well-organized, well-financed, and artic-

Ronald Reagan speaks amid a sea of faces at a Garden Grove shopping center. (Reprinted by permission of the *Orange County Register.*)

ulate activists of Orange County met a more enthusiastic and less ambivalent reception when they made phone calls, walked precincts, and sought to get the vote out for their candidate. For the first time, they saw their standard-bearer not only win a Republican primary but also become a front-runner in the battle for a general election.

By the summer of 1966, Reagan was leading in the polls.[112] Brown sought to dampen Reagan's popularity by charging him with "extremism," the tag that had so damaged Goldwater only two years before: "My opponent," he railed, "is the captive of the radical right in California and . . . he will not, cannot, repudiate the John Birch Society because it would cost him the support of wealthy ultra-conservatives."[113] The CDC similarly attacked Reagan's close links to prominent right-wing ideologues.

Its campaign kit contained a report titled "Ronald Reagan, Extremist Collaborator," a thirteen-page document that connected the Reagan campaign to conservatives like Walter Knott, Patrick Frawley, Henry Salvatori, and others who were donors to conservative causes and who indeed now played important roles in Reagan's campaign.[114] But the charges proved ineffective. While Reagan refused to repudiate the John Birch Society, this refusal simply did not do to him the damage it had done to Goldwater only two years earlier. With students occupying campus buildings and militant African-Americans in the streets, it was the Left that became increasingly vulnerable to charges of "extremism." The world, it seemed, had turned upside down. Nixon, who only four years before had demanded the ouster of the John Birch members from the California Republican Party, now responded to Democratic charges of right-wing extremism by remarking that the only extremist issue "is Brown's refusal to repudiate the California Democratic Council which harbors the draft card burners, troop train blockers, and beatniks which brought the greatest university to its knees."[115]

Such attacks, not surprisingly, struck a chord with the conservative Republican grass roots. As one conservative, a deputy clerk of the municipal court in Whittier and a Reagan precinct worker, wrote, "Reagan should call the CDC 'the Communist leftist Dominated Council of California'—that is what it really stands for."[116] It was not only conservative Republicans who mocked Brown's "extremism" charges, however, but also many rank-and-file Democrats. As one Southern California Democrat asserted in a letter to Brown: Because "you have chosen to run most of your campaign against the John Birch Society we have chosen Ronald Reagan as our choice for governor." He continued, "The extremist CDC is worse than the JBS."[117] And one Santa Ana woman, who had received a copy of "Ronald Reagan, Extremist Collaborator" through her husband's union and who had voted for Brown in 1962, informed Reagan, "Even if you do believe as the Birch Society teaches, you still are better for California than the ADAs," the Americans for Democratic Action.[118]

Aware of his widespread support in the southland, Reagan spent time there in the last weeks of his campaign, working to get out the vote. One Orange County conservative activist remembered some thirty years later that "he was really truly grassroots. He was everywhere, he was out at Leisure World, he was over here, he was at so many places being with grassroots elements."[119] In the final week of the campaign, addressing a crowd of 5,000 supporters in Santa Ana, he blasted Brown on crime rates, taxes, the handling of Berkeley, welfare spending, the Rumford Act and "laxity of the courts in handling crime." And two days before the election, 4,000 supporters came to a Garden Grove shopping center to cheer him on to victory.[120]

Orange County had become "Reagan Country." The patriotic flags that adorned so many Orange County homes were now joined by Reagan posters. The cottage of one Birch member in Newport Beach, for example, which sported an American flag almost as large as the house itself and a plaque stating that "this nation under God shall have a new birth of freedom," was now adorned with a huge picture of Reagan on the front door.[121] For the committed conservative owner of this cottage, as well as many others, the campaign was "much more than a political campaign." It was a "great crusade."[122] Indeed, some conservatives went so far as to express the belief that Reagan was "God appointed."[123] As one staunch supporter from nearby Whittier put it, he would vote "six times" for Reagan "if it were legal."[124] Another, from the city of Orange, promised to "stump every soap box in your behalf."[125] One registered Democrat from Anaheim, indeed, presaged that Reagan was "a man who knows what the people of California, and subconsciously, the people of the United States want for the future."[126] Reagan himself, noting the strength of his support in Orange County, joked at a gathering of Los Angeles Young Republicans that if he did not win the election, "we'll all move down to Orange County and secede."[127]

But this was Orange County, and his strong support there, like that of Goldwater before him, would not necessarily reflect the sentiments of a majority of the state's voters. Yet when returns poured in on November 8, it was evident that Orange

County's politics had become the politics of a majority of California voters. Reagan, an unabashed conservative, won 58 percent of the vote, almost reversing the results of two years before: Whereas Goldwater had lost every county except five in the state's general election, Reagan won all but three California counties.[128]

In Orange County, not surprisingly, Reagan did even better than in the rest of the state: He won 72 percent of the vote, despite the fact that approximately half of all Orange Countians were still registered Democrats (only two years earlier, Johnson had won 44 percent of the local vote, and in 1962, Brown had still garnered 39 percent of the county's votes). Orange County's Democrats had already demonstrated their conservatism in earlier elections, but they now crossed party lines in larger numbers than ever before. While in 1962 Brown had managed to win the towns of Buena Park, Stanton, Fountain Valley, and Cypress and to come close in Garden Grove, in 1966, these towns all went for Reagan by an overwhelming majority.[129] But the swing vote was evident well beyond Orange County, with Reagan winning the endorsement of close to 1 million of the state's Democratic voters.[130]

Polling data revealed who these Democratic swing voters were: Brown had, according to political analyst Totton Anderson, suffered substantial losses among white working people and among lower income groups.[131] The ingredients for the conservative swing could be seen, Anderson observed, in a review of the issues found by the pollsters to be of public concern in mid-June 1966: Heading the list were crime, drugs, juvenile delinquency, racial problems, state taxes, and welfare programs.[132] Apparently, a majority of the state's voters found the conservatives' rhetoric on these issues appealing. Just as important, the high correlation between opposition to California's Fair Housing Act and support for Reagan lent credence to the supposition that Reagan's support could be attributed at least partially to "white backlash."[133] The Democratic swing voters, concerned with rising crime, "law and order," and white prerogative, swung to the conservatives who spoke to these issues.

Conservatives had come a long way. When Reagan began his campaign after Goldwater's tremendous defeat, many observers had given him little hope of winning. At that time, Assemblyman Bill Bagley had confidently asserted that "not one in ten thousand take the Reagan movement seriously." After all, he noted, "The Reagan movement is a remnant of the Goldwater movement."[134] And, indeed, Bagley was right in noting the continuity between the Goldwater and Reagan campaigns. Reagan embraced conservatives' ideology, their politics, and their agenda. Rather than being a "remnant on its way to disappearance," however, as liberals and the Left had fervently hoped and believed, the Right was part of a new and growing movement whose opportunities, due to national political, social, and economic changes in the United States in the 1960s and early 1970s, had only just begun to emerge. As Reagan put it in a letter to Goldwater shortly before his win, "You set the pattern and perhaps it was your fate to just be a little too soon, or maybe it required someone with the courage to do what you did with regard to campaigning on principles. I have tried to do the same and have found the people more receptive."[135]

In California, moreover, changes in apportionment, as a result of the 1965 reapportionment of legislative districts under the U.S. Supreme Court's "one man, one vote" decision (a decision, ironically enough, that conservatives had criticized), brought a permanent shift of political power to the southland, the most conservative region of the state. Eight southern counties, ranging from Santa Barbara in the north to San Diego in the south, now controlled more Senate and Assembly seats than the fifty remaining counties in the state. For the first time since California became a state, the balance of political power in the legislature shifted to the south.[136]

Events in California in 1966 presaged the rise of a majoritarian conservatism on the national scene. In the 1968 presidential election, Richard Nixon and George Wallace picked up on the discourse of "morality," "law and order," "welfare chiselers," and "liberal permissiveness" and rode a wave of popular middle-class and lower-middle-class resentment against the social changes of the decade. When the tide rolled in, it brought Nixon into the White House and provided George Wallace a whopping 13.5 percent of the national vote. While neither Nixon nor Wallace represented quintessential Sunbelt conservatism—Wallace with his harsh southern segregationist, anti-elitist rhetoric, and Nixon with his conservative pragmatism and his internationalist centrism tainted by his association with eastern Republicans—both put forward their own brands of conservative populist lingo that spoke to some, if not all, of right-wing Orange Countians' concerns.

By 1968, George Wallace's American Independent Party (AIP) showed its attractiveness to California voters by gaining 90,000 registrants in California, far more than the 70,000 who registered for the left-leaning American Peace and Freedom Party. Wallace drew in recruits from conservative Republican and conservative Democratic circles. Cyril Stevenson, for example, the prominent conservative Republican who had helped put through the Young Americans for Freedom's "Sharon Declaration" as the CRA's statement of principle, and who led the effort to link support for Reagan to conservative appointments, resigned his membership in the Republican Party in January 1968 to join the AIP.[137] In the Orinda-Lafayette Republican Assembly, moreover, thirteen of fifty-four members registered with the AIP.[138] And when Wallace, four years later, after being paralyzed by gunshot wounds, announced that he would not be a presidential candidate in 1972, John Schmitz, avowed Bircher and lame-duck congressman from Orange County, was nominated as the AIP candidate for president.[139] Conservative Republicans, however, joined the Wallace crusade only in small numbers. Wallace drew his main strength at the rank-and-file level from a broader socioeconomic base than that exemplified by the Republican adherents of the CRA. Rebecca Piggott, from Buena Park, highlighted this conservative populist appeal that drew its nourishment from the social turbulence of the decade:

I feel sure millions of other poor, hardworking, good, true American slaves don't like the way our law and order has not been enforced. Our tax money is wasted, our cities burned down, our schools invaded with dope—you name it, we have it on our streets, in our schools and in some of our public offices. We the people pay, pay, pay for all this. Quit making excuses in Washington. . . . I for one, am going to vote for Wallace, because he is a fighter for his country.[140]

But while some conservatives in Orange County and the southland found Wallace attractive, most remained loyal to the two-party system, a loyalty that ultimately benefited Nixon. Nixon won Orange County in the fall of 1968 by a large majority (314,905 votes to Democratic candidate Hubert Humphrey's 148,869), with fewer than 7 percent of votes going for the AIP. In the hotbed of conservatism, Wallace proved no more popular than in the rest of the state.[141] Wallace's populism built too much on working-class resentments to sustain an appeal with the mostly middle-class backers of the Right in Orange County. As George Shearer, a San Diego accountant who headed Wallace's California drive, later remarked, "When George Wallace closed his eyes and envisioned his audience, [he] saw people coming from every direction and walk of life, workers coming out of the factories and textile mills, farmers coming out of the fields and jumping off flat-bed cotton trucks, young people, little businessmen, . . . humble people, simple people."[142] Wallace's vision was too linked to a proletarian, blue-collar southern view of the world to attract the bulk of upper-middle-class and middle-class conservative Orange Countians. Reagan and Nixon's language of "middle America," without Wallace's hard edge, won their support more easily.[143]

Wallace's brawny southern politics failed to win broad appeal in Orange County not only because of its blue-collar edge but also because it drew on a font of ideas somewhat distinct from the conservative politics of the southland. Wallace tapped into a long tradition of populist racism in the South that championed white supremacy. This brand of politics flourished in the

Deep south, where race had been a determinant marker of populist politics through the twentieth century. In the 1950s and
1960s, these traditions helped to fuel the growth of the "racist
Right," championed at the elite and grassroots level by the
White Citizen's Councils, the Ku Klux Klan, and the National
States Rights Party.[144] While these organizations mirrored conservative Orange Countians' hostility toward federal control
and liberal elites, their strong racial emphasis did not resonate
in the Sunbelt West. Thus, while the John Birch Society, with
its staunch anticommunism, flourished in Orange County, the
Citizen's Councils, the Klan, and the National States Rights
Party gained few adherents. Some disillusioned southland Birchers did make common cause with the AIP, but by and large the
soil that nourished Birch growth did not prove as hospitable to
Wallace's brand of right-wing politics as did the southern soil
that nourished the politics of "massive resistance."[145]

If most right-wing Orange Countians remained aloof from
Wallace, they also had an ambivalent attitude toward Richard
Nixon. Even though Nixon was a native son and had been an
anticommunist hero in the 1950s, he had fallen out of conservative favor in 1960 as a result of his infamous "surrender of Fifth
Avenue."[146] In 1962, some southland grassroots conservatives
had even refused to work for Nixon's campaign for California
governor after he repudiated the support of the John Birch Society and sought to write its members out of the party.[147] But in
1964, Nixon had won the accolades of many conservatives by
championing Goldwater. He worked tirelessly for the Goldwater-Miller ticket, and after the election he castigated Rockefeller
and other "Eastern Republican dividers" as "spoilsports."[148]
Nixon, as historian David Reinhard has noted, "emerged from
the 1964 campaign as both an astute judge and a beneficiary of
Right Wing strength in the Republican Party."[149]

While hardly their "dream candidate," Nixon had nonetheless become the conservatives' choice for 1968.[150] Even though
many staunch right-wing ideologues were wary about his commitment to their politics, they saw him as the best hope in 1968.
Indeed, while Henry Salvatori brought F. Clifton White, Gold-

water's magic maker, onto a Reagan-for-president bandwagon for 1968, and southland conservatives backed Reagan as a "favorite son" candidate, Nixon had established strong conservative backing as early as 1965. Goldwater had announced in January 1965 that he would back Nixon in 1968. Patrick Buchanan, who had served a stint with YAF, had climbed aboard the Nixon bandwagon in 1966. Other conservatives followed: John Ashbrook; William F. Buckley; southerners such as John Tower, Peter O'Donnell, Bo Callaway, and Strom Thurmond; and influential conservative backers such as Roger Milliken and Jeremiah Milbank—all of whom had been key to Goldwater's primary win in 1964—now backed Nixon.[151] He even won over the "Arizona mafia" men such as Richard Kleindienst and conservative celebrities such as John Wayne. As Garry Wills noted shortly after Nixon's victory, "Reagan was not the heir to Goldwaterism in Miami, Nixon was."[152]

Nixon courted his conservative backers in 1968 by taking a hard line on "law and order," warning against the decline of national prestige and military might, attacking federal bureaucracy and "runaway government," and criticizing busing and affirmative action.[153] He also sought to respond to the resentments of those discontented Democrats, the lower-middle-class and middle-class whites who had been crucial to making Reagan's win possible. Indeed, building on the theme of a solid American "majority" fed up with protest, Nixon spoke—as Goldwater and Reagan had—of the "forgotten man," the middle-class American who paid his taxes, the productive American who resented his money being wasted on excessive government programs for the "lazy" and the "indolent." But while Goldwater's message had reached only a staunch ideological conservative core of voters, Nixon, like Reagan before him, was able to pick up a broader constituency in part because of more muted conservative stripes and in part because times had changed. Nixon played to those, as Garry Wills observed, "who succeeded but felt somehow cheated, forgotten, unrespected, mocked." He built, as Reagan had done in California before him, a new middle-class populism on the back of the turbulence and social changes of the decade.[154] As Kevin Phillips, Nixon's strategist on voter trends, astutely remarked, while "the clamor in the past has been from the urban or rural proletariat, . . . now 'populism' is of the middle class, which feels exploited by the Establishment."[155] The metaphor of "middle America" became, as Michael Kazin has noted, "the GOP's identity of choice."[156] The very looseness and breadth of this identity, evoking "an egalitarian social status most citizens either claimed or desired and a widespread feeling of being squeezed between penthouse and ghetto—between a condescending elite above and scruffy demonstrators and welfare recipients below," represented a new cast of populist conservatism.[157] It was, however, a populism without Wallace's southern, blue-collar edge.

In building his message, one that echoed some of the rhetoric of Reagan and Wallace, Nixon was creating a new politics that sought to build on the increasingly important voting blocs in America's burgeoning suburbs—middle-class Catholic voters and discontented Democrats shorn from their party by the volatile issues of the decade, those who, as Kevin Phillips observed, helped to form an "emerging Republican majority."[158] Vast middle-class suburban growth meant that, by 1969, large cities made up only 30 percent of the national population, compared with 35 percent in suburbs and 35 percent in rural areas and small towns. Demographic shifts, moreover, had made the South and West (the booming new areas of the Sunbelt and the new industrial frontiers of the South and the Southwest) increasingly more important—with the vote falling off in the older urban areas of the Northeast and the Midwest.[159] A core part of the emerging Republican majority, in Phillips's eyes, consisted of the new technocrats of Florida, Arizona, Texas, and Southern California (including Orange County), regions that had become, according to Phillips, "one of the most important voting blocs on the map."[160]

Those Southern Californians Phillips spoke about indeed heard Nixon's message and helped to carry him to victory. In 1968, Nixon lost the fifty counties of Northern California to Hubert

Humphrey by 144,000 votes, but his 367,000-vote plurality in the southland gave him the state and, with it, a majority in the nation's electoral college.[161] A new Republican majority was being built on the back of vast demographic shifts, the faltering of the liberal vision, and the rise of the Sunbelt (a term Phillips invented). And it was not the beneficent moderate Republicanism of the eastern establishment, with its noblesse oblige, but a western and southern half sister—of a far more conservative bent. By 1970, Orange County, with a population that now stood at close to 1.5 million inhabitants—that "far-out nut country," land of sun, fun, and Birchism—had played a role in making it happen.

CHAPTER 6

NEW SOCIAL ISSUES AND RESURGENT
EVANGELICALISM

By THE LATE 1960s, the Right had made important
political gains in both California and the nation. Ronald
Reagan, an unabashed conservative ideologue, had won a resounding victory in his run for governor. Richard Nixon, a centrist Republican who courted the Republican Right, had become
his party's presidential nominee and won the election through an
embrace of a new middle-class conservatism, even while George
Wallace, a law-and-order populist, had garnered 13.5 percent
of the national vote on a third-party ticket. Building on new
opportunities, the Right had refashioned itself, gaining new political respectability. As the late 1960s witnessed antiwar protests, a flourishing counterculture, and riots in the nation's inner
cities, the conservative critique of liberalism resonated with an
increasing number of Americans.

Increased political opportunities and the rise of new social
issues had an uneven impact on the decade-old conservative
movement in Orange County. Older organizations that had
been so critical to the mobilizations earlier in the decade declined, and new conservative initiatives sprang up—often led
by activists who had gotten their start in politics in the Goldwater movement. The center of grassroots activity moved away
from the anticommunist study groups and home meetings of the
early 1960s and toward new single-issue campaigns, as well
as to a conservative religious awakening. Moreover, while some

older recruits and activists dropped out, new participants joined the fray.

The John Birch Society, the organization that had played such an important role in channeling grassroots activity earlier in the decade, experienced the greatest decline. Orange County had proven fertile ground for the society's growth in the first half of the 1960s and, with the help of its southland neighbors, was responsible for making California the organization's "banner state." In the wake of Goldwater's defeat in November 1964, the society had picked up new recruits: By the end of 1965, its estimated membership in California stood at some 12,000 to 15,000, organized into as many as 1,200 chapters, a substantial gain from the estimated 700 chapters and 10,000 members the society could boast before Goldwater's loss.[1] Nineteen sixty-six seemed to be the dawn of a golden age for the John Birch Society. The society, recognizing the power and allure of issues such as campus upheaval, riots in inner cities, and a white backlash against civil rights, created the Task-Force on Civil Disorder and sponsored monthly agenda items such as "Support Your Local Police." New recruits were brought in through such campaigns, and they were as often concerned about the social changes happening around them as about the looming threat of communism. In the words of one former member, their motivations for becoming active were a "reaction to something."[2]

But even as it momentarily appeared to flourish, the society was running into trouble. Indeed, it had already started to experience difficulties directly after Goldwater's debacle. The "Birch" or "extremist" tag had hounded the conservative movement through middecade at a substantial cost of legitimacy. After the monumental defeat of 1964, prominent national conservatives like William F. Buckley, Jr., sought to forge a new image of respectability by redefining the movement's boundaries, with the society well outside them. In August 1965, Buckley issued statements that, for the first time, not only condemned the leadership of the society but also criticized the members for putting up with what he termed Robert Welch's "paranoid and unpatriotic drivel."[3] In October of the same year, *National Review* ran a special feature with numerous commentaries by prominent national conservatives in opposition to the Birch Society.[4]

It was Welch's neo-isolationist posture on Vietnam that earned him the most vociferous ire of the conservative movement leaders. In a convoluted, conspiratorial interpretation of events, Welch saw the war as a carefully managed fraud, designed to convince the U.S. public of President Johnson's anticommunist goals. In face of conservative attacks, Welch modified his position to the hawkish slogan "Victory in Vietnam Instead of Defeat," emphasizing the government's unwillingness to win the war.[5] This shift was more in tune with the positions of national movement leaders, such as Goldwater, who maintained a hawkish war position while remaining critical of the way the war was being fought. Still, throughout the war, the society not only remained critical of government conduct but also implied that an internal government conspiracy was responsible for the United States' failure to win. This posture was a serious bone of contention, damaging the society's reputation among movement leaders.[6]

The society encountered increasing hostility from once-friendly supporters, not only nationally, but also in California. In 1963, the California Fact-Finding Subcommittee on Un-American Activities had given the society a clean bill of health, declaring that the organization had attracted so many members because "it simply appeared to them to be the most effective, indeed, the only organization through which they could join in a national movement to learn the truth about the Communist menace and then take some positive action to prevent its spread."[7] In 1965, the same committee issued a second report with a very different tone, declaring that Robert Welch's organization "has attracted a lunatic fringe that is now assuming serious proportions" and had been beset by an influx of "emotionally unstable people."[8] In a letter to Barry Goldwater in 1965, Welch claimed that these attacks were affecting the operation of the organization. As he put it, "The results have made it more difficult for our field staff to get the kind of prospects we wanted to come to our presentation meetings. . . . The most serious effect of the unceasing smear has been the reluctance of Conservatives of national prominence to come to my . . . seminars."[9]

It was not only prominent national conservatives and regional elites who sought to distance themselves from the John Birch Society. Even grassroots conservatives, becoming more pragmatic, were aware of the damage inflicted by the organization's extremist tag. One Fullerton couple, pioneer members of the society in the early 1960s, dropped out by mid-decade because, as they put it, "We wanted to get into political action and we realized that the newspapers would kill us from that standpoint. . . . We dropped out so we could honestly say that we weren't members."[10] External pressures led this couple to withdraw from the society; other members were simply disillusioned with the organization. One of them was David Bergland, of Costa Mesa. A member of the society in the mid-1960s who moved into a leadership position, he was soon disenchanted with the conspiratorial elements of the society. As he explained it three decades later:

> It's just a process like anything else. You don't know everything, you have to learn it step by step. So you say, "Okay here is the John Birch Society and they're saying some stuff that sounds pretty good," so you go hang around with them for a while and see how things really fall out. The Illuminati and these centuries-old conspiracies and that sort of thing which don't have any evidence . . . that's not persuasive to me. I'm not sold by that. . . . So looking at some of the goofier John Birch theories, you start looking at that and say, "Gee, if I spend time with these people, I'm going to be spinning my wheels."[11]

Bergland's attitude was illustrative of a broader trend. Jean Crosby of the southland community of Pasadena, for example, who had founded five chapters of the John Birch Society in the early 1960s, was by 1972, in the words of her husband, "more and more disenchanted with the organization. . . . Birch Society members are inept, inexperienced and unbending in the field of politics. Their intransigence and insistence on adherence to conservative dogma prevent them from being politically effective."[12] At a time when their antiliberal rhetoric could have a potentially broader appeal, conservatives became increasingly aware that the conspiratorial and antidemocratic utterances of the society not only failed to gain them adherents but also threatened to leave them on the political margins of a shifting national discourse.

By the late 1960s, the society had also lost the strong financial backing necessary to sustain its large operations.[13] Welch conducted a hard-hitting fund-raising appeal, but to no avail.[14] The John Birch Society had to lay off its paid national field coordinators and then, as membership dwindled, resorted to "paid field coordinators," who were required to raise their own funds.[15] The society, according to the Anti-Defamation League's Pacific Southwest branch, "was increasingly trying to build the organization on the cheap."[16]

The society's top-down structure added to the problem of sustaining an appeal at the grass roots. By the end of the decade, the agenda items in the monthly bulletin appeared stale, despite the leadership's efforts to update them. A section leader in Orange County was especially critical, reportedly remarking in 1968 that "we are pussy-footing ourselves out of existence with nameless speakers, out-dated work, outmoded run-down agenda items and ancient boring bumper sticker clichés. We've said it all for years and years."[17] The national John Birch Society hierarchy made an effort to address the changing concerns at the grass roots, but it often simply followed the lead from below. For example, when grassroots conservatives in Orange County successfully organized opposition to sex education in Anaheim schools in 1968 and 1969 (a mobilization that gained national attention), the John Birch Society followed on their heels and established ad hoc committees to address the issue. In 1969, the society formed Movement to Restore Decency (MOTOREDE), recognizing the resonance of such "moral" issues, but despite these efforts, it was increasingly unable to gain new recruits.[18]

This impotence was due in no small part to the society's insistently virulent anticommunism. Communists, the Birch Society argued, were responsible for all social turmoil, ranging from the civil rights movement to the rise of the New Left. As the decade progressed, however, anticommunism had receded, while more salient domestic issues had come to the fore. The Birch Society's explanations for what was happening in America now seemed obsolete.[19] Even the journalists for that local champion of anticommunism, the *Register,* recognized the decreasing resonance of anticommunism when they declared in 1969 that "the days of the fiery Communist-hunting conservative are fading, to be replaced by a newer, younger conservative . . . [who] is a staunch opponent of Communist collectivism, but . . . [who] sees that threat as remote. More pressing in his mind is the threat of indoctrination of the young in the tax-supported system and court decisions that coddle criminals."[20]

Birch leaders responded to such critiques by trying to update their conspiracy theories.[21] Speaking before approximately 1,000 people at Santa Ana High School in 1969, Welch argued that communists were simply being used by a broader and larger conspiracy of "insiders" to advance their quest for power, and that Karl Marx himself was only a "hired hack." Liberals, from Robert and John Kennedy to George Romney and J. William Fulbright, were at the core of a mysterious group of "insiders."[22] Welch described his speech as a "new approach" to an old subject, but this too failed to bring in new recruits.[23] As the society became increasingly marginalized, it became more closely identified with the fringe Right. Indeed, as sociologist Sara Diamond has argued, this new approach, and the society's continued attacks on civil rights, increasingly moved it into an alliance with the Liberty Lobby, a populist right-wing organization that meshed nationalism, anti-Semitism, and biological racism.[24]

The society was simply too strongly identified with minoritarian utterances and outdated conspiracies to remain an important vehicle for channeling the new majoritarian conservatism. In the 1950s, the Birch Society had, for a moment, successfully linked an older Right, centered in the small-town Midwest that had backed McCarthyite anticommunism, with a newly emergent Right, located in the South and West. But at a time when right-wing ideals were being championed successfully through more powerful and less marginal channels, conservatives had fewer reasons to look toward the society.

The sentiments, grievances, and ideas the organization helped to define and mobilize, however, lived on and were championed by organizations and political leaders who thrust forth a new populist conservatism. Randall Smith, a conservative activist from Santa Ana who was never himself a member of the society, asserted in 1972: "You have to look at the Birch Society . . . as a sort of a boot camp. For every current member of the Birch Society, there are three or four former Birchers who still feel the same way. . . . They . . . got involved in other things or decided that it was too passive for them . . . but they are still in the same vein as far as thought goes."[25] Smith correctly pointed out that dropping out of the society by no means implied abandoning conservative politics. Another conservative reiterated this point. When asked what happened to the Birch Society in Southern California, Peggy Pearce emphasized the educational purpose of the organization: "I just think it branched out . . . into other organizations. When we originally organized, that was all we had; [a vehicle] to talk about what needed to be done. . . . Then we found avenues to do those things." For this activist, as well as many others, these avenues did not include continued membership in the society.[26]

Like the John Birch Society, the California Republican Assembly also experienced a decline in membership. The CRA had approximately 20,000 activists in its ranks in the spring of 1965; by late 1966, 6,000 of them had dropped out.[27] The missionary zeal that had driven thousands of conservative Californians into political activism during the exciting days of the Goldwater campaign had diminished. Moreover, with Reagan's election, some conservatives felt their work had been done; they had a man in the state's highest office who championed their interests. And by 1968, Nixon was echoing the conservatives' language and articulating at least some of their concerns directly from the White House. The less zealous activists, who had joined the conservative crusade in the heat of mobilization, now retreated from politics. One conservative, explaining the loss of membership in the CRA, remarked, "Once you win elections, the people think they can just take it easy. You're more inspired when you're the outs than when you're the ins."[28] Despite the decline in the number of adherents, however, the grassroots Right maintained its hold over the Republican Party volunteer organization, continuing to put forward the conservative agenda first established in 1964.

The decline of the John Birch Society in Southern California and the deflation of the ranks of the CRA did not signify that conservative activism had disappeared. Rather, the character of the grassroots movement had shifted. This reorientation was nowhere better illustrated than by the transfer of the resources of local right-wing businessmen to new arenas. Earlier in the decade, their infusion of money helped build local study groups and financed the dissemination of books and literature that had been critical to building a fervent anticommunist and free-enterprise revival. Their intent was to influence public opinion at a time when their ideas were marginalized and when they had little representation in high political office. Now the political landscape had shifted, and conservative regional businessmen could use their resources to more direct advantage by backing candidates for office and contributing to new single-issue campaigns. In 1966, for example, Walter Knott was a prominent supporter of the anti-obscenity proposition measure on the November ballot. In the same year, he served as the honorary chairman of a committee to elect conservative Robert Peterson as the superintendent of the Orange County schools.[29] Carl Karcher, of Carl Karcher Enterprises, served as the county chairman for Max Rafferty's Senate campaign in 1968; in the 1970s, according to a prominent activist, he backed the local pro-life movement.[30]

These businessmen-ideologues no longer sought to reshape opinion primarily through educational initiatives. Nothing better demonstrates this reorientation than the demise of the California Free Enterprise Association. Established by Walter Knott and local entrepreneurs in Orange County in 1960, it had played a critical role in spreading conservative ideology and building local mobilization; in 1973, it was phased out of existence.[31] Conservative resources now infused new initiatives—namely, single-issue campaigns and, more important, the institutional channels that might champion their interests. The southland businessmen who had backed Reagan, for example, set up a non-profit corporation—a committee for "government efficiency and cost control"—after his election. Some 250 representatives from business and professions around the state went to Sacramento to study government activities and find ways to cut spending. According to "Kitchen Cabinet" member Ed Mills, they formulated about 1,600 suggestions, many of which were implemented. Mills commented that Orange County's Walter Knott "contributed a man," paying him to go to Sacramento.[32]

This new influence of business leaders in shaping public policy made very clear the distinction between the two groups that made up the increasingly successful conservative coalition. The movement was split between conservative economic elites, the senior partners who now held not only economic power but also political leverage at the state level, and social conservatives, the junior partners who provided the conservative mass base but remained, by and large, outside the halls of power. While these groups' concerns overlapped, and while conservative elites often shared social conservatives' concerns and championed their interests, it became increasingly evident who held the reins of power and what their priorities were.

As conservative elites moved closer to the halls of power, the grassroots activists invigorated their movement by increasingly focusing on single-issue campaigns. These new issues expressed some of the same general concerns over moral corruption and traditional values that previously had been subsumed under the rubric of anticommunism. But these concerns now took on new dimensions, in large part in reaction to changes in family life, sexual liberation, a growing youth culture, and liberal Supreme Court decisions that expanded the scope of personal freedoms. As a result, various forms of "domestic corruption"—obscenity, sex education, abortion, and, by the late 1970s, an ever more assertive gay liberation movement—became the new targets of attack. And the enemy responsible for such ills was no longer an international, public, and political opponent, but the secular humanists in one's own community. These new issues drew in activists from among discontented Democrats who had previously been part of the liberal coalition.

Obscenity was one arena in which conservatives expressed growing dismay over the expansion of personal freedoms. Concerns over "filth" and "immorality" had preoccupied conservatives since early in the decade, after a Supreme Court decision of 1962 made prosecution of "obscenity" increasingly difficult. The Catholic newspaper the *Tidings*, among others, had warned southland Catholics of the dangers posed by pornography to the values and morals of the nation. When, in 1964, the Supreme Court, in *Jacobellis v. Ohio*, required that questionable material must be without "redeeming social importance" to be censored, making prosecution of obscenity even more difficult, conservatives feared that "decadence" and "moral decay" would destroy the moral fiber of the nation.

These concerns led southland right-wing forces to sponsor Proposition 16 for the November ballot in 1966. The measure was promoted by a group calling itself California League for Enlisting Action Now (CLEAN), whose advisory board included such future national Christian Right leaders as Timothy LaHaye (then pastor of Scott's Memorial Baptist Church in San Diego) and William Dannemeyer (then state assemblyman from Orange County).[33] The initiative gained the support of prominent businesspeople, such as Patrick Frawley of the Eversharp and Schick Razor Company, Joe Crail of the Coast Federal Savings and Loan Association, and Orange County's Walter Knott.[34] They and others were attracted to the measure because it promised to redefine pornography, disregarding the Supreme Court's exemption of works tinged with "redeeming social importance"—and it sought to put regulatory control in the hands of local communities. Reagan strongly endorsed the ballot initiative, gaining the accolades and gratitude of social conservatives.[35] It had sufficient backing in Orange County to win a majority at the polls.[36] While the measure did not convince the state's voters, conservative Orange Countians continued to mobilize around the issue within their local communities. In 1969, spurred on by a campaign led by the *Anaheim Bulletin* (part of libertarian R. C. Hoiles's "Freedom" newspaper chain), they shut down the Anaheim Chamber of Commerce for a day to display the "lewd and lascivious materials" that were available at local newsstands.[37] Local business boosters were central to the anti-obscenity crusade. The educational arm of the local Anaheim Chamber of Commerce, for example, eagerly worked to root out "smut".[38]

Following these campaigns, in the early 1970s, the county itself undertook the prosecution of obscenity when a Newport Beach restaurant owner complained to the police after receiving mail advertising illustrated books and films for adults. The incident eventually led to the influential 1973 Supreme Court decision in *Miller v. California*, which cheered anti-obscenity advocates while raising the hackles of civil libertarians.[39] In it, the Court favored respecting local sentiments in making decisions about what constituted obscenity and held that prurient, offensive depictions must have "serious literary, artistic, political, or scientific value" to merit First Amendment coverage. The decision, which historian Margaret Blanchard described as "another aspect of the conservative revolution being engineered by Richard Nixon," was, in her words, a "giant step backward" for the cause of free speech.[40]

The fight over sex education in the school systems was another arena where grassroots conservatives voiced concerns over "domestic corruption." In 1969, a band of dedicated Orange County conservatives made national headlines with their vigorous, and eventually successful, campaign to uproot a prominent and innovative sex education program.[41] The issue clearly marked the reorientation of the movement not only in its focus on explicit moral issues but also in its language and the cast of enemies it targeted. While earlier in the decade such a struggle would certainly have been blamed on a communist drive to undermine the morals of youth, now "secular humanists" were targeted as the force lurking behind the threat to morals, values, and the family.[42] In a similar vein, however, the accusations were tinged with conspiratorial utterances, demonstrating the linkages to an earlier discourse.[43]

The conflict was rooted in the development of a curriculum by Paul Cook, superintendent of the Anaheim Union School District. Under Cook's guidance, the district became one of the first large school districts in the country to establish a broad sex education program, with the help of the Sex Information and Education Council of the United States (SIECUS). The district encompassed more than 30,000 pupils in twenty-five schools.[44] In 1968, a year after the course had gone into full operation, it came under attack. Eleanor Howe, an Anaheim mother of four and a receptionist at Kwik-Set Lock Company, whose husband was a retired Marine Corps pilot, sparked the initiative when she wrote a letter to the *Anaheim Bulletin* condemning the program and calling for action against it.[45] Howe, a devout Catholic and a conservative who had cast her first Republican vote for Goldwater in 1964, gathered information about the program and sought to mobilize opposition. She and Jim Townsend, who had been active in local conservative circles since the Conservative Coordinating Council was born in 1961, spearheaded opposition under the rubric of the California Citizens' Committee, a grassroots organization he helped found that had strongly backed Goldwater. Later, they were joined by Jan Pippinger, a born-again Christian whose husband was the manager of a meat storage center for the Lucky Food Stores chain, along with other concerned parents, mostly women, many of them devoutly religious.[46] In the summer of 1968, they came before the school board to launch a formal complaint, demanding an end to the program. While the program had faced opposition before, in

1968 it came under full-scale attack as "godless, pornographic, and an affront to family privacy."[47]

The viciousness of the opposition to the sex education program was in some ways surprising because the curriculum itself was hardly radical. Developed with the support of local clergy and community organizations in response to changing sexual mores, it emphasized the negative consequences of premarital sex and was, according to its proponents, "designed to produce good family members."[48] Still, it represented a departure: Its broad and inclusive nature was an entirely new arena of "social engineering," usurping an area of authority that had previously been left to parents. Moreover, the Anaheim school administrators asserted that FLSE program discussion groups were intended to encourage students to make their own moral judgments about sexual and social behavior within the context of community norms.[49] Many religious conservatives resented this relativizing of moral absolutes, seeing in it a threat to Christian beliefs and values.[50]

Clearly, fears about the social changes of the decade underpinned support for the sex education struggle and for the right-wing conspiratorial utterances with which it was tinged. Conspiracy theories, embraced by the most zealous opponents, provided middle-class conservatives a safe explanation for young people's challenge to an older set of values. Eleanor Howe's remarks on the counterculture illustrate how young people's opposition to their parents' social values could be understood in this manner. Pointing to her discovery of the "conspiracy" underlying sex education, she remarked years later:

> It was so bad . . . all the rock groups, their music, . . . the movies, television. Everything was changing, the whole system of values that we treasured in this country. And it was all stemming from not having anything that is right or wrong. It was just, if it felt good do it. You know that Mario Savio thing from Berkeley, "If it feels good, do it." But it just doesn't happen, it has to be taught. Children don't know enough to change the value system of a country. So it wasn't the kids. So it had to be coming from somewhere. And that somewhere is what I uncovered.[51]

Conservative parents, such remarks suggest, feared a loss of control over the values and beliefs of their children. The sex education programs did promote more liberal values than those of staunch religious conservatives. This, opponents believed, undermined parental authority. As one pamphlet argued, "What the sex educators have in mind is simply this: Sex should be as easily discussed as any other subject in the curriculum, and any inhibitions, or moral and religious taboos should be eliminated. This obviously drives a wedge between the family, church and school, bolstering the authority of the school while casting doubts on the traditional moral teachings of the home or church."[52]

The battle occupied the Anaheim Union School Board for two years between 1968 and 1970.[53] By the fall of 1970, the program was, for all intents and purposes, dismantled. When the Citizens' Committee of California had launched the anti–sex education campaign, almost 99 percent of the district's more than 30,000 students in grades seven through twelve were enrolled in the course; by 1970, about 24 percent of students were enrolled at only three grade levels, and the film and text lists were drastically limited.[54] By that fall, Superintendent Paul Cook had resigned, and Sally Hansen, a SIECUS member and a program consultant, had been fired.[55]

The struggle, moreover, had ramifications beyond the local level. John Schmitz, state senator from Orange County, successfully led the passage of a law requiring parents' permission for their children to enter a sex education class and mandating that the curriculum material be open for inspection in advance.[56] The Republican conservatives also responded to the issue: In 1969, the CRA passed a resolution urging the dismantling of all sex education programs in the state.[57]

As with many other issues, this conflict caused some Democrats and former liberals to rethink their political allegiances. A Mrs. Burns of Cypress, a prominent sex education opponent and recent migrant to Orange County, remarked, "I was a Democrat. And I'm still a registered Democrat and I thought I was a liberal, but I really don't understand the meaning of the word."[58] Jan

Pippinger, a born-again Christian, demonstrated that religious conservatism did not always go hand in hand with a clear overall embrace of conservative economic ideology when she remarked to the school board: "Over a million dollars has been spent on this program and for what? More kids on dope than ever before, more young girls pregnant. . . . Kids walking out and leaving home. . . . Gentlemen, I am not satisfied with the answer that I received as to why our children cannot have a hot meal at noon in our schools because there is no money for that purpose. . . . I suggest you satisfy their stomachs, not their curiosity about sex."[59] Obviously, social conservatives' allegiance and votes were up for grabs, and conservative Republicans, rather than the liberal California Democratic Party, had something to offer them, responding to their concerns over "sexual liberation," the youth culture, and changes in family life.[60]

As liberalized pornography laws and sex education in schools provoked the ire of social conservatives, a third issue that demonstrated the shifting nature of conservative mobilization was the rising storm over abortion. By 1969, the women's liberation movement and abortion rights supporters had made important gains in liberalizing abortion laws. In California, Governor Reagan had signed the Therapeutic Abortion Act in 1967, a reform bill proposed after a group of physicians were indicted for performing abortions on women who had rubella. While the bill was intended to serve as a clarification of existing law, in practice, its stipulation that doctors could perform abortions if the birth of a child would "gravely impair the physical or mental health of the mother," or when the pregnancy was the result of rape or incest, led to a rapid sea change.[61] The number of legal abortions in the state rose dramatically, from 5,018 in 1968, the first year under the new law, to more than 100,000 by 1972.[62] At the same time, the debate that had been a reform argument among professionals was recast as a call by women's organizations for the repeal of all abortion laws. In 1969, the California Supreme Court became the first in the nation to strike down an abortion law. In *People v. Belous*, the court recognized that a woman possessed the constitutional right "to life and to choose whether to bear children." The court's decision struck down important provisions of the Therapeutic Abortion Act, passed only two years earlier. By 1972, the court had invalidated nearly all provisions of the 1967 law, providing for abortion on demand.[63]

Conservatives were profoundly dismayed by the growing sentiment in favor of abortion reform, which they saw as an attack by the state on their religious and family values. Concerns over abortion were driven, in part, by a belief in the sanctity of life. As one religious conservative from Orange wrote in 1971, "All lives have a right to live. . . . The Bible, God's word, says 'Thou shalt not kill.' And what are those doctors doing, they are breaking God's law, also killing a life."[64] Mrs. Thomas Tiernan, a Catholic from Santa Ana, put it just as starkly: "Who among us is so all-knowing as to say with certainty the exact moment that the life-giving principle joins the mass and becomes a human person?. . . Abortion is murder, period."[65]

But if concerns over abortion were driven by conservative religious beliefs, these beliefs encompassed a broader worldview in which God ordained natural roles for men and women.[66] Abortion posed a threat to women's traditional identities as wives and mothers by upsetting "natural roles" and enabling women to control their fertility.[67] In religious conservatives' eyes, it was part of a broader mentality that flouted the law of God by seeking to deny biological realities.[68] Not surprisingly, then, the women's rights movement was seen as responsible for promoting this "abortion mentality" and came under heavy attack. The interplay of antifeminism and pro-life issues was evident in the trajectories of activists who organized against both abortion and equal rights causes, and in joint "pro-family" and "pro-life" initiatives.[69]

As women's organizations won support for their call for legalized abortion, a small number of grassroots conservatives organized in response.[70] Cathy Sullivan, who had been a Goldwater supporter, a John Birch Society member, and a CRA activist in the 1960s, received a request in 1969 from two local priests asking her if she would head up the founding of the county's first antiabortion organization, the Citizens Action Committee. It was, in Sullivan's words, "an antipornography, pro-education, antiabortion grassroots organization comprised of both Democrats and Republicans."[71] The group symbolized the new alliance struck between Catholics and Protestant evangelicals at the grassroots level around abortion, as well as the early politicization of some churches around the issue.[72]

Not only was a new alliance struck between Protestants and Catholics, but the abortion issue also helped forge an alliance between registered Democrats and registered Republicans. In Orange County, according to Sullivan, "You had all these brand-new, former Democrats that were upset about this issue, some of them becoming Republican."[73] One of them was Beverly Cielnicky, who explained that for herself and her husband, their identities as conservative Republicans gradually emerged from their pro-life position. They had been Democrats in college, but "when we first got into pro-life, we said, well let's be one of each so we'll get all the information from both parties. Then we gradually learned that the Democratic Party had been taken over by the pro-abortionists."[74] The Cielnickys' strong pro-life stance and activities as part of the Protestant Church–based Crusade for Life eventually drew them into a broader conservative mobilization. Cielnicky, for example, opposed the Equal Rights Amendment.[75] She attended a rally at the University of Southern California where Phyllis Schlafly was a guest speaker, supported Schlafly's anti-ERA crusade, and joined "miniconventions" and rallies in San Diego led by Beverly LaHaye that eventually led to the founding of Concerned Women for America, the largest women's organization of the Christian Right during the 1980s and 1990s.[76] Further demonstrating Cielnicky's deepening conservative commitment, she left the mainline American Lutheran Church after years of unsuccessfully lobbying for it to take a pro-life stand. Eventually, she and her husband joined the Central Baptist church in Huntington Beach, which she described as "very, very pro-life."[77] Her pro-life stand remained at the core of her self-definition as a conservative for more than twenty-five years. While this might not be typical, the synthesis of social conservatism with the libertarian discourse on freedom and anti-statism bespoke a common impulse among grassroots conservatives. According to Cielnicky:

> Pro-life is number one. That's respect for all human life from the moment of conception until natural death. So that the human being in the image of God is the primary focus. . . . Secondly, to keep government from dictating, taking away freedoms. Some of it is pro-life and some of it is just basic, such as in the schools. The conservative position is that . . . parents, the family be the center.[78]

Although the pro-life movement remained small in the early 1970s, it created the institutional base and networks that would provide the foundation for its rapid growth after the Supreme Court, in *Roe v. Wade*, legalized abortion in 1973. Sullivan, for example, helped to found the Pro-Life Political Action Committee of Orange County, using as a model the bylaws of the California Republican Assembly: "We started it, then Californians for Life, the California Pro-Life Council, other organizations started to come about, bigger organizations." But Sullivan, true to her conservative leanings, sought to keep everything under local control: "I felt very strongly that we should never get any bigger than our little county, and we never have."[79]

Another early Orange County pro-life activist was Don Smith of La Habra, who had heard about Sullivan's Citizens Action Committee through a protest held in Anaheim on the occasion of the American Medical Association's annual convention. Smith contacted some of the organizers, who put him in touch with Sullivan, and he soon became active in pro-life circles.[80] He established Crusade for Life in 1971, a Protestant evangelical pro-life group that went on to become one of the largest pro-life organizations in the state. Smith also influenced the national abortion debate.[81] The Anaheim-based American Portrait Films he established in 1983 produced the controversial *Silent Scream*, depicting a suction abortion performed on a twelve-week fetus. The film was described by pro-life supporters

as "a weapon of battle for the right to life troops" and by opponents as a distorted propaganda piece.[82]

The continuities and discontinuities between the new social
issues mobilizations of the late 1960s and early 1970s and the
conservative initiatives ten years earlier are highlighted by the
front ranks of the early pro-life movement in Orange County.
In contrast to Sullivan, Smith, though a convert to rock-ribbed
conservatism already by the mid-1960s, did not become an activist until the early 1970s. The antiabortion struggle increasingly drew in new activists like Smith and Cielnicky.[83] Yet these
recruits often depended on the networks and initiatives established by earlier pioneers. More important, established activists
such as Sullivan or, in the sex education struggle, Jim Townsend,
played important roles in propelling the new issues to the forefront of the conservative movement's concerns.

Buffeted by the feminist movement, a vibrant youth culture, and
broader social change, religious conservatives lamented the decline of "traditional values" and changes in family life. These
concerns had emerged earlier in the 1960s, but issues such as
sex education and abortion pushed them to new heights in the
late 1960s and the 1970s. Yet while new social issues galvanized
the grassroots conservative movement and resonated with growing numbers of Americans, they would not prove to be the issues
that could sway the broader middle class to the conservative
agenda. Indeed, even those within conservative ranks did not
always agree on the centrality of social issues like abortion to
their cause. As Cathy Sullivan expressed it, "The conservatives
even at that time weren't looking at that as a big political
issue. . . . Finally . . . they saw it. I would say the biggest influence in getting them to see it would have been the evangelicals."[84] But even once conservatives adopted the issue, not all
agreed on the role the state should play in regulating abortion.
Edna Slocum, for example, a conservative CRA activist in the
1960s, asserted years later, "I think that it's too bad that it ever
became a national issue that's in the political arena. I could never

have an abortion because, to me, it is a religious belief. But my feeling is, if somebody else differs, if there is such a thing as a final judgment, they'll have to answer for it there, and I'm not going to concern myself with that issue. It's become so divisive."[85] Similarly, staunch libertarians believed that "the better way to deal with it and perhaps succeed in reducing the number of abortions are nongovernmental ways."[86] By no means, however, were all libertarians pro-choice; abortion had been a contentious issue with the Libertarian Party since its founding in 1972.[87] In Orange County, one activist noted, "There was a big movement of libertarians for life . . . they weren't an enemy . . . they were split."[88] The issue was a divisive one for the movement that has continued to haunt it into the twenty-first century.[89]

Aside from abortion, other social issues wrought divisions within the movement. Government regulation of pornography was one of them. While important to religious conservatives, it was not a priority to others. Libertarians such as David Bergland remembered being annoyed by conservative attempts to limit personal freedoms. Referring to efforts by United Republicans of California to get rid of pornography in the late 1960s, he remarked, "They did some things that I thought were just stupid, which were not tolerant. They wanted to shut down adult book-stores or something."[90] Social conservative issues divided the movement between those who prioritized libertarian issues and those who sought to build a godly world.

These divisions made themselves felt in conservative Orange County in 1972 when another anti-obscenity measure was placed on the ballot in California. In contrast to Proposition 16, which had won a majority in Orange County in 1966, Proposition 18 lost by a large margin. The different outcomes can be attributed, in part, to the far-reaching scope of Proposition 18, which went beyond the earlier measure in seeking to define obscenity, providing extremely detailed descriptions of "obscene acts."[91] The broad scope of Proposition 18 generated national opposition and must have appeared, even to many conservative voters, to be a threat to privacy. Just as important, Orange

County had, in the intervening years, continued its upward spiral of growth, bringing many new voters into the county.[92] The difference in outcomes hints that while Orange Countians continued to embrace a staunch law-and-order, limited-government, and pro-defense ethos, new residents were shifting the package of Orange County conservatism. Libertarian sentiments were taking hold among a broader group. Such changes, however, did not discourage social conservatives; in contrast, they encouraged them to become more vocal. Now they sought not only to limit but also to roll back cultural change.

While deepening concerns over expanded personal freedoms and their threats to the traditional family propelled social conservatives to action—and a segment of libertarians responded by championing privacy—they were by far not the only issues around which conservative Orange Countians now mobilized.[93] Other issues, indeed, unified the diverse strands of the movement, and none was more important than taxes. Critiques of rising taxes and state spending had long been a staple of right-wing beliefs, shared by both libertarians and social conservatives, and in 1968, resentment toward taxes was made manifest in an initiative for the November ballot. Proposition 9, or the "Watson amendment," proposed a five-year reduction in property taxes, which would eventually be limited to a maximum of 1 percent of a property's cash value. In Orange County, Virgil Elkins founded the Taxpayers Association to back the measure.[94] The initiative faced a good deal of opposition from the usual supporters of conservative causes, however, including the Orange County Chamber of Commerce, whose own anti-big-government rhetoric had helped legitimize the thinking behind the amendment.[95] Now, shifting gears, its members argued that Proposition 9 would result in "a general state of economic confusion." City and county officials and the region's large corporations also mobilized against it. Ironically, city boosters and companies like the Irvine Corporation and Standard Oil saw their own rhetoric of fiscal conservatism fueling a revolt by suburban homeowners and small businesses that threatened the base of the regional economic boom.[96]

Proposition 9 was defeated, failing not only because of the powerful interests stacked against it but also because high property taxes had not become a sufficiently pressing issue among suburban Orange Countians and across the state in 1968. Yet, during the next decade, this was to change radically. By 1978, a similar movement won overwhelming passage of Proposition 13, establishing a constitutional amendment limiting local property taxation to 1 percent of market value.[97] Proposition 13 tapped the frustrations of suburban homeowners over steeply rising property values and higher state taxes.[98] Howard Jarvis, one of the initiative's sponsors, had been prominent in Southern California conservative causes in the 1960s, speaking out against taxes as early as 1961, when he claimed that "the income tax is un-American and illegal" and voiced support for the Liberty Amendment, a proposal that would have amended the Constitution to repeal the federal income tax.[99] Jarvis "saw the day when taxes will have to end."[100] Despite fighting "one-worlders" and "government centralization" throughout the 1960s and early 1970s, Jarvis and his allies in the Orange County grassroots conservative community waited some two decades before scoring a huge success for the cause of limiting taxes.[101] It was only during the years of national economic crisis from the middle to late 1970s and soaring property taxes that Californians would heed the grassroots mobilization behind Proposition 13 and overwhelmingly vote for tax relief—a watershed event whose national repercussions, according to analysts, reversed the direction of domestic public policy.[102] Not only in California but also across the nation, the public—at a time of a national economic downturn—became receptive to conservative denunciations of "big government waste," "political fat cats," and "spenders."[103] As a result, tax rebels who had peppered the ranks of Orange County's Right in the 1960s became ever more vocal in the 1970s, forging organizations such as the Guardians of Freedom, the Tax Tyranny Resistance Committee of Orange

County, Taxpayers Anonymous, the Tax Action Council, Saddleback Homeowners Outraged Over Taxes (SHOOT), and the United Organization of Taxpayers. One militant rebel, for example, railed against "an un-constitutional enforcement of illegal statutes under which the IRS has been operating for all the years."[104]

At its most extreme, antitax and antiregulatory fervor spawned some rather bizarre projects. Morris Davis of Orange led a group of about twenty people in the early 1970s who sought to establish an independent republic where government would have almost only a secretarial function. Searching the world for unowned real estate, they found a coral outcropping in the middle of the Pacific and developed a plan to reclaim the land, to prove that, in the words of one supporter, "man can live in an almost libertarian society."[105] Backed by a group of conservative industrialists who sought to establish manufacturing there, the plan, not surprisingly, eventually came to naught because of opposition by Australia, New Zealand, and a nearby island whose leaders claimed that the outcropping was in their territorial waters. What is more amazing is that this group of eccentric antistatists went so far as to establish their own constitution, print money, and raise funds for their project.[106]

Another new concern among social conservatives and libertarians alike, one that drew on long-standing hostility to the use of the state to remedy racial discrimination, was busing. Since the passage of the Civil Rights Act of 1964 and the Voting Rights Act of 1965, conservatives had shifted the focus of their concerns on issues of race toward government mandates to remedy the effects of past discrimination. Now their discourse on the "controlled society" and tirades against "social planners" fell on a large, more receptive, audience.[107] Americans who had been willing to support basic equal opportunities for African-Americans turned against these efforts when they involved their own neighborhood schools and their own children. Cities from Boston to Los Angeles were the site of vociferous antibusing struggles in the early 1970s, drawing in large numbers of discontented lower-middle-class urban ethnics who were most often directly affected by busing.[108] These struggles were far removed from suburban Orange County, although residents there nonetheless feared the impingement of busing. As a result, in 1972, they backed an antibusing statute by a majority of two to one. In 1979, when a sweeping "Metropolitan Plan" threatened to expand mandatory school desegregation not only to Los Angeles but also into the broader Southern California region, including places like Orange County, their fears became more pressing. Orange County Busstop, and later Bus-Bloc, were forged. Led by Doris Allen, a social conservative who had been active earlier in antifeminist and pro-life circles, and Doris Enderle, the mobilization drew broad support in the county.[109] In 1979, a proposed state constitutional amendment against busing, propelled by groups like Bus-Bloc, carried the county by well over a three-to-one margin.[110]

The late 1960s and early 1970s witnessed the reorientation of the conservative movement away from its earlier focus on anticommunism. Seismic changes rocked the country; assertive liberalism, sexual liberation, the prominence of black and youth cultures, and changes in family life hit ever closer to home, promoting a cultural backlash. Even in the suburban enclaves of affluent Orange County, middle-class men and women could not shut out these changes; their children, influenced by the vibrant youth culture, literally brought them home. In the nearby seaside communities of Newport Beach and Laguna, a thriving hippie culture flourished. Orange County's burgeoning institutions of higher learning, including California State University, Fullerton, and the spanking new University of California, Irvine, became sites of protest, sprouting their own SDS chapters (as well as Young Americans for Freedom).[111] Even Disneyland, that sacred symbol of safety, certainty, and Americana, was, on August 6, 1970, taken over by an unruly group of about 300 yippies, who raised a Viet Cong flag on Tom Sawyer's Island.[112] Throughout the country, old certainties were giving way under pressure from newly assertive groups. As the women's and minority rights movements blossomed and gay liberationists became ever more assertive, religious and cultural conservatives became increasingly anxious. With the economic crisis of the 1970s, these concerns fused with a growing economic preservationism, the combination with which the Right would move into national political power in 1980.

This reaction to the social changes of the 1960s is vividly illustrated by the fantastic growth, in the late 1960s and 1970s, of born-again evangelical Christianity in Orange County and nationally.[113] While these developments came to national attention only in the late 1970s, when conservative Christians entered politics in a highly organized fashion, the religious awakening had been in the making for some ten years.[114]

The southland had a long history of conservative religious influence. It was the birthplace of the *Fundamentals*, the influential series of pamphlets published by the Stewart brothers of Union Oil from 1910 through 1915, which have become the symbolic reference point for identifying the beginnings of the fundamentalist movement.[115] In the 1920s, "Fighting" Bob Shuler spouted fire and damnation from his pulpit.[116] It was on Azusa Street in Los Angeles that twentieth-century Pentecostalism was born.[117] Sister Aimee Semple McPherson founded her Foursquare Bible Church in Los Angeles, drawing huge crowds.[118] And the Reverend Charles Fuller made his home in Placentia in Orange County, where he tended orange groves and leased land for drilling until he underwent a dramatic spiritual experience; then, from 1921, he worked as the president of Orange County Christian Endeavor. By 1942, his *Old-Fashioned Revival Hour* had become so popular that he reached more listeners than entertainer Bob Hope.[119]

Not only was the southland the birthplace of some of the most important figures and movements in twentieth-century evangelicalism; it also supported many small Pentecostal, evangelical, and fundamentalist churches.[120] In Orange County, these churches mushroomed with the in-migration of the 1950s and 1960s.[121] In a land where businessmen of all varieties made their starts and their fortunes, religious entrepreneurs had also come to build their kingdoms for God on earth. With rapid population growth, fueled by migrants from Bible Belt states, and the lack of an organic community in the newly built environment, they found plenty of recruits for God's army. Already during the early 1960s, the community provided by the conservative churches, the firm moorings they advocated, their simple doctrines of right living, and their apocalyptic messages had resonated among many Orange Countians and had established an institutional base for the county's conservative mobilization.[122] One religious conservative, Bee Gathright, argued that the "Christian movement" and the conservative movement "grew at the same time."[123] She herself became born again in the wake of the Goldwater campaign. But while the conservative religious influence was important earlier, it took on vastly new proportions in the late 1960s.[124] Fundamentalist and evangelical sects, associated in the public imagination with rural, poor, and backward folk of the Deep South, boomed in the new technocratic Sunbelt suburbs in regions like Cobb County, Georgia; Orange County; and Dallas, Texas.[125] These religious conservatives, in contrast to popular perceptions, were prosperous suburban middle-class men and women, both young and old.

The burgeoning counterculture of the late 1960s pointed to deep dissatisfaction among the nation's youth with the empty materialism, affluence, and pragmatic middle-class lifestyle of their parents. The growth of evangelical Christianity—which, at its heart, also represented a rejection of liberal secular pragmatism—suggested that these currents of discontent could be channeled in many directions, by very different social groups.[126] A search for authenticity and for meaning, along with dissatisfaction with the emptiness of modern consumer society no doubt contributed to the evangelical revival, just as it had to the counterculture.[127] But also at the heart of this movement's growth was an effort by middle-class men and women to assert their sense of a properly ordered world—one they felt was threatened by sexual liberation, the women's movement, the burgeoning Left, and the youth culture movements—by championing family values, authority, and tradition backed by the authority of the "word of God."[128]

A search for authenticity, the rejection of liberal rationality, a middle-class counterrevolution against 1960s "permissiveness," and a search for community created a cauldron mix that fueled the growth of evangelical Christianity. The "Jesus movement," born in Southern California in the late 1960s, best exhibits these linkages.[129] One of this movement's founders was the Reverend Chuck Smith, who had been pastor of a small fundamentalist congregation on Maple Street in Costa Mesa since December 1965. Smith built his church from its original twenty-five members into a multi-million-dollar religious corporation by 1978.[130]

Smith was a man with a vision. Initially repulsed by the lifestyle of the barefooted, long-haired youth drawn to a growing drug scene that had sprung up in Newport and Laguna Beach in the late 1960s (even Timothy Leary lived in Orange County for a time), he eventually saw an opportunity for an evangelical mission among the youth who had rejected both their parents' values and liberal rationalism in their search for a deeper, more fulfilling meaning of life. Having met some of the early converts to California's blossoming Jesus movement through his college-age daughter, Smith perceived, as he put it, "a spiritual hunger" among the youth, a hunger that he sought to fill:

> They had turned down the concept that materialism was the answer because they had seen their parents glutted with materialistic concepts, and yet their parents were not at all satisfied or happy or well adjusted, as far as the kids were concerned. . . . Their experimentation with drugs was almost a gospel, almost a religion. . . . So as we began to communicate with these young people we discovered that they were very open. They weren't, of course, eager to become involved in a structured organized church as such, but were willing to talk about Jesus Christ.[131]

Recognizing an opportunity to bring the youth "to Christ," Smith built a mission where young Orange Countians could feel comfortable. He began his work with informal Bible studies and set up his first communal house in May 1968, inviting uprooted youth to live together in an atmosphere, Smith said, "where Jesus Christ was the common denominator." More such houses were later established in Santa Ana, Garden Grove, Huntington Beach, Newport Beach, Buena Park, and Whittier, as well as in Corona, Fontana, and Phoenix.[132] To build his mission, Smith adopted countercultural symbols and motifs, called himself and his followers "radical Christians," and built his church in an informal style that welcomed the barefooted youth to worship Christ.[133] He also pioneered a brand of evangelical Christian folk music that appealed to young adults—later transforming this branch into a multi-million-dollar business "for the Lord." And he conducted mass ocean baptisms in Corona del Mar, where scores of young hippies, in jeans and barefoot, plunged into the ocean—into the new life of Christ under the ministrations of Pastor Chuck.[134]

Beyond counterculture teenagers, however, Smith was able to attract thousands of adult and middle-class Orange Countians who embraced his redemptive mission. The redemption of hippie youth (the ultimate symbol of liberal permissiveness) was the cornerstone for the growth of his church and remains central to the church's narration of its own history.[135] Even as the church expanded to take in a more traditional constituency, however, it remained open to diverse audiences and kept an informal Southern Californian style.

The church grew rapidly. When a new Calvary Chapel was built in south Santa Ana, the congregation had outgrown the new building before it even opened its doors. Two years and three months later, the church had to double its seating capacity by moving the walls out. Even this did not suffice to meet the church's growth, and by July 1972, it had bought eleven acres of property a few blocks away in Costa Mesa and moved into a large tent that held 2,000 people.[136] The church spread to Brea, Downey, Buena Park, Dana Point, Huntington Beach, El Toro,

Fundamentalist preacher Chuck Smith baptizing hundreds of new converts in Corona del Mar. Such services were held regularly in the early 1970s. (© *Orange County Illustrated*, 1972.)

Yorba Linda, and Westminster. By 1978, the mother church alone reached 25,000 members; today it is one of the largest single churches in the country.[137]

The church's success was based, in part, on its informal Southern California style, combining large services with intimate Bible studies and folk music. Smith adopted hip, modern trappings, but his message was a far cry from the anti-authoritarian, individualist, countercultural message "If it feels good, do it." He offered an apocalyptic, emotive, communal, and utopian vision, based on fundamentalist Christianity. Smith believed in the literal interpretation of the Scriptures and saw his church as the middle ground between the fundamentalist and Pentecostal traditions.[138]

The rapid growth of his church made Smith a central figure among the nation's prophecy thinkers. His books and tracts, in the best tradition of premillennialist fundamentalist belief, warned of disintegration, threats to family cohesion, wick-

Chuck Smith baptizing a young born-again Christian. (© *Orange County Illustrated*, 1972.)

edness, and the rise of a "standardized" global order.[139] His apocalyptic and conspiratorial messages echoed fears of a "one world order."[140] In 1973, presaging a post–Cold War turn, Smith warned that "the decline of the economy and government of the United States will open the doors to the rise of the anti-Christ to world power as head of the [European] common market countries."[141] His writings alerted those who would not be "raptured" with the church (the moment when all believers will rise to meet Christ in the air, an event for which all Christians must ready themselves) that they must "refuse to take any mark upon you either on your forehead or your hand. If you accept the mark of the world ruler known in the Bible as the Beast or Anti-Christ you shall be ETERNALLY LOST and will forever separate yourself from God's grace."[142]

These apocalyptic—and pessimistic—beliefs, lying at the heart of premillennial American fundamentalist ideology, suggested a

Calvary Chapel's meshing of "old-time religion" with a new folksy style succeeded in bringing together born-again countercultural youth and older middle-class Christian conservatives in the late 1960s and 1970s. (© *Orange
County Illustrated*, 1972.)

profound sense of apprehension about the world. They challenged, according to historian Paul Boyer, "modernity to the
core."[143] Seeing the world as doomed would also seem, in
eschatological tendency, to lead adherents to social inactivism.
Yet although the primary concern of Pastor Chuck and his conservative Christian ministers was to harvest souls for "the
Lord," their beliefs also laid the ideological base for a thoroughly conservative politics. The emphasis on patriarchal family
values, concern with "evil"—crime, abortion, pornography—
and the critique of "centralized power" all went along with conservative ideas.[144]

Smith's apocalyptic message was part of a long tradition of
prophetic thinking in post–World War II fundamentalist Christianity, far more common in popular culture than most scholars
have yet acknowledged.[145] That such thinkers held an appeal in
high-tech Orange County is at first surprising. But on closer ex-

amination, it is precisely such a new and hypermodern environment that created ambivalence about the consequences of modernity. Indeed, Boyer has noted a strong correlation between apocalyptic writing and technology: A good number of prophecy writers were engineers, scientists, and military men.[146] Their metaphors of the "end times," linked to a technocratic, consolidated, and standardized world order, made their imagery evocative and real for middle-class Orange Countians, who lived and worked in a high-tech environment.

Furthermore, the church's promise for community resonated with Orange Countians. The church was a place where an intensive community could flourish, tailored to meet a variety of needs, eventually ranging through bereavement support groups, "singles fellowships," men's and women's breakfasts, Bible studies, "young married men's prayer fellowships," "new believers fellowships," summer art classes, camping clubs, weekly movies, retreats, and high school and junior high school fellowships.[147]

The Church's success was also aided by its unique combination of a rejection of many elements of "modernity"—namely, rationalism, secularism, a faith in scientific progress—and the simultaneous embrace of thoroughly modern trappings.[148] Calvary Chapel not only became a multi-million-dollar venture in its own right, but it also founded large business enterprises, like Maranatha, a thriving tax-exempt concern selling crosses, records, and music tapes. By 1978, Maranatha had become a well-established record company, selling more than 500,000 records and cassettes in that year alone.[149] A devoted Calvary member, moreover, with Pastor Chuck's blessing, built Maranatha Village, a Christian shopping center, offering wares ranging from pottery to jewelry to the John-One-Ten line of clothing. Picking up on this successful combination of Christianity and consumption, "born-again businesses" sprang up in Orange County, such as Maranatha Tire Company and Maranatha Plastering.[150] The growth of Christian-identified businesses meant that, by 1976, Orange County evangelicals did not need to look in the Yellow Pages when seeking to buy furniture or have their floors redone or their sewers unclogged. If they so chose, they could instead pick up the Orange County edition of *The Christian Business and Professional Directory* and deal only with fellow Christians.[151] Similar directories were available in nearby Glendale, Pomona Valley, Covina, San Bernardino, Hollywood, and San Diego.[152]

Calvary Chapel was not alone in spreading a conservative Christian message that reveled in "Christian" consumer culture. Robert Schuller's Garden Grove Community Church also symbolized this odd mix, with Schuller calling his church a "shopping center for God."[153] Bob Schuller, a pastor affiliated with the Reform Church of America, established the world's first drive-in church in Garden Grove, California, in 1958, holding services on top of a snack bar in a drive-in theater.[154] In the early 1960s, he had participated in right-wing anticommunist mobilizations, serving as the religious sponsor for Fred Schwarz's School of Anti-Communism and joining Californians' Committee to Combat Communism.[155] His activities and preaching attracted conservatives to his church. Indeed, according to one Garden Grove activist, "Many, many of the active people went out there to church."[156] By the late 1960s, however, Schuller's growing success led him to abandon controversial political activities and concentrate on ministering to his flock, which, by 1969, had reached 5,000.[157] Marking his rising success, in 1968, Schuller built the thirteen-story Tower of Hope, a large church topped with a ninety-foot neon cross.[158]

His desire to build a mission that would bring the unchurched to God did not end with the Tower of Hope. Schuller, ever the entrepreneur, expanded his activities to television evangelism, inspired by Billy Graham's visit to Anaheim in 1969.[159] First broadcast on KTLA Los Angeles in February 1970, his show, *The Hour of Power*, taped during church services and combining media spectacle with Christian worship, catapulted him to national fame.[160] By 1976, he had 8,000 members in his home congregation in Garden Grove, and 3 million people per week viewed his broadcasts.[161] By 1978, he was ranked as one of the twenty most influential religious figures in the nation.[162]

Robert Schuller's drive-in church in the late 1950s. Schuller
adopted modern methods and a positive therapeutic variant
of evangelical Christianity to reach new audiences. (Courtesy
of Robert Schuller Ministries.)

His phenomenal success led him to ever-larger plans.
Schuller hired professional fund-raisers as well as the famed architect Phillip Johnson, and, with the help of a million-dollar
gift from Orange County mobile home manufacturers John and
Donna Crean, laid plans for the Crystal Cathedral. This spectacular project, which eventually cost $19.5 million, opened for
service in the heart of Orange County in 1980.[163] Its design,
based on the four-point star of Bethlehem, consisted of a steel
structure with 10,600 glass windows and two built-in doors,
each more than ninety feet tall, that opened up so that people
sitting outside in their cars could still attend church. The church

Schuller's success prompted his move to new properties, where he built the world's first walk-in/drive-in church in Garden Grove in 1961. By 1968, his success led to the church's expansion and, eventually, the creation of the Crystal Cathedral. This photograph depicts a meeting of congregants in the late 1960s. (Courtesy of Robert Schuller Ministries.)

itself seated 3,000, contained elaborate fountains, and housed one of the largest organs in the world, with more than 16,000 pipes.[164] *Newsweek* declared it "one of the most spectacular religious edifices in the world."[165]

What was the message that sold so well to Orange Countians and eventually to the nation? Schuller preached the necessity of accepting Christ into one's life. But in contrast to old-time evangelism that had centered on damnation and sin, he emphasized self-help. This worldly message talked of discontent rather than sin—turning toward and accepting Christ was the first step toward self-fulfillment. After accepting Christ, Schuller's message suggested, one must pursue success in personal and mundane ways.[166]

At the same time that Schuller justified Orange Countians' search for profits (a message that appealed to them by validating their own lives), he also provided spiritual nourishment by in-

The new Crystal Cathedral, established in 1980, linked Christian evangelical religion with consumer spectacle. (Courtesy of Robert Schuller Ministries.)

voking the language of their everyday consumer lives.[167] Speaking of the "good life" that many Orange Countians had come to search for, he advised, "If you want to have a life of joy and peace and a sense of fulfillment, you will not find this in material things." Using the analogy of shopping for a carpet to describe the emptiness of materialism, he pointed out to his faithful:

> We get a certain amount of excitement shopping for it, looking for it, waiting for it to be delivered, putting it just in the right place, then suddenly, days, weeks, months, pass and we haven't even been conscious of this thing. . . . To break our boredom then, we must get on a new kick, a new car kick, or a new carpet kick, we break the boredom, we have a new interest, but things in themselves bore us. . . . Love is the fulfillment of life; for man is born to love! And we are empty inside until we are able to give our love away.[168]

Schuller sought to give meaning to lives filled with material-ism, while not challenging the grounding of those lives. "God loves you," he would tell his audiences, and to prove that one loved him back, one needed only to acknowledge Christ—and succeed in life—because "God wants you to succeed." It was this "very positive message" that drew conservative activists like Jan Averill to his church in the late 1960s. As she later put it, "He kind of gave you a boost."[169] Dissatisfied with the increas-ingly liberal Presbyterian church she had attended previously, whose new minister "was talking about Cesar Chavez and the grape boycott, you just don't want to go to church and hear that instead of the gospel. . . . We started looking for another church."[170] Together, her family and her parents began attending Schuller's church, where they remained for the next twenty years.[171]

But perhaps as important as Schuller's message was his me-dium. His presentations resembled a religious consumer specta-cle. In Schuller's church, according to one observer, "The distinc-tion between medium and message, public relations image and religious substance, was banished."[172] And, like those of other evangelists, Schuller's church provided community services, linking his large congregation to smaller groups. Here was a city of God and a community where one could come together with like-minded folk.

Schuller's evangelism, though different from that of Pastor Chuck or other fundamentalists, also spread a social conserva-tism that meshed well with conservative Republican Party poli-tics. Schuller did so, however, without being labeled as a member of the Religious Right, which haunted more controversial tele-vangelists.[173] He avoided, for example, taking stands on homo-sexuality or abortion, staples of fundamentalist concerns. In-stead, he promoted a theologically and socially conservative message and a positive pro-family, pro-Christian ethos. Above all, Schuller emphasized the possibilities of individual success—a message that suggested a critique of social and governmental solutions to social inequality, class divisions, and discrimination. Failure, he preached, rested solely on one's own shoulders:

"Now let me tell you why you fail," he explained to readers of *Reach Out for New Life*. "You fail because you deliberately, knowingly, and willingly choose to fail."[174] Echoing the conservative Republican ethos, Schuller declared that "we are not allowed to blame our failures on the circumstances of race, sex, education, class or financial resources. People must stop playing the game of Let's Pick Out the Villain."[175]

Smith's folksy fundamentalism and Schuller's inspirational evangelical message were only two varieties of the broad spectrum of evangelical Christianity. Another evangelical style that had a long presence in Orange County was Pentecostalism. With the rising tide of evangelical Christianity, charismatic faith healers were also boosted to new prominence. The appeal of this Holy Roller religion in the southland was evident in the story of the birth of Melodyland Christian Center, "an improbable conglomerate of fundamentalist believers set in the midst of one of Southern California's largest concentrations of hotels, bars and amusement and sports facilities"—across the street from Disneyland.[176]

Ralph Wilkerson, a traveling minister, got his humble start in Anaheim, holding services in 1960 at the Anaheim Assistance League for his twenty-seven followers. By 1969, however, the 900-seat building he had rented was too small for his growing congregation. Inspired by a "vision from God," who, he believed, told him to purchase Melodyland, a theater spot that had run into community opposition for its topless shows, Wilkerson took out loans for his new church.[177] Keeping the name and also, for a time, the Celebrity Lounge, the largest bar in Orange County, his church grew by leaps and bounds. By 1978, Melodyland had 12,000 members, although it was estimated that 17,000 to 18,000 faithful attended services each week, drawn by the marquee that announced Wilkerson's sermons, much like that of a movie theater. Wilkerson brought to his parishioners "God's healing power," with his charismatic faith healing that was at the heart of his services combining his fire-and-brimstone sermons and a pro-America message with the right-wing tracts available at his Melodyland book center.[178] A preacher who believed that God had designed America for a special destiny, he invited to his church religious leaders such as Glendale pastor W. S. McBirnie, whose radio program, *Voice of America*, confined its message mainly to political issues of interest to "right-thinking Americans."

Orange County preachers and evangelists not only built churches but also developed other innovative means to spread "God's word." Charles Taylor set up headquarters for his show, *Today in Bible Prophecy*, in Huntington Beach—broadcasting on more than twenty stations nationally and globally. Taylor, a premillennial fundamentalist, who spoke of the approaching chaos of the "end times," advised Californians who missed the "rapture" to move east of the San Andreas Fault. He added, "If you have a gun, take it with you, plus a good supply of ammunition."[179] Orange County became home not only to TV preachers but also to a prominent Christian broadcasting network. Paul Crouch, a migrant from Missouri who had worked as a country-and-western disc jockey and served as an associate pastor at a local Assembly of God church, first worked as the general manager of a Christian radio and then founded the Trinity Broadcasting Network in 1972.[180] Setting up home in the Irvine Industrial Complex, the church distinguished itself from its neighboring office buildings only by its white dove-and-cross logo and the content of its programs.[181] TBN's twenty-four-hour-a-day operation made it one of the most active of all religious stations in the nation.[182] Along with Pat Robertson's Christian Broadcasting Network, it brought born-again prophecy shows to homes across the nation.[183]

These religious entrepreneurs formed part of a shoal of Pentecostal, evangelical, and fundamentalist churches that flourished in the southland during the late 1960s and 1970s. While some rose quickly and subsequently declined, new churches were born to take their place.[184] Orange County was home to some of the most important "megachurches," prophecy thinkers, and televangelists of the day.[185] By the 1990s, the Southern

California region had the highest concentration of "mega-churches"—large, mostly conservative theological churches—in the nation.[186] The strength of the evangelical community was such that it could support three different editions of a regional evangelical paper, the *Southern California Times*, one each for San Diego, Orange County, and Los Angeles.[187]

The variety of churches represented a hodgepodge of the evangelical, fundamentalist, and Pentecostal spectrum—and a consumer haven of "praising the Lord." But all these religious entrepreneurs provided a message of the inerrancy of the Bible, preached the need to accept Christ into one's life, and promoted a social conservative ethos of God, family, and strict morality. All contributed—in their own ways—to making the southland part of the national resurgence of born-again Christianity that would so deeply affect the politics of the nation.[188] While some of those attending the new churches had deep roots in the anti-communist mobilizations of the earlier 1960s (even Fred Schwarz, the leader of the Christian Anti-Communism Crusade, for example, eventually ended up attending the large and growing Saddleback Community Church, a southern Baptist mega-church in South Orange County), the phenomenal growth of these churches suggests that their appeal ranged well beyond those who had fought against communism and for Goldwater during the 1960s.[189]

The appeal of what has often been considered arcane, rural patterns of thought in one of the most modern communities in America, and among a suburban, middle-class population, strongly suggests that, in contrast to the belief that conservative Christianity would fade with modernity, it has, in fact, deepened its hold.[190] Sociologist Martin Marty has asserted that evangelicalism is the "most adaptive and inventive new ('Modern') faith."[191] Moderns, he asserted, "want their religion to be 'hot.' . . . It must be accessible and instantly open to experience and interpretation by common people."[192] Certainly, the new churches in Orange County fit the bill. At the same time, religious conservative churches provided moral certainties in a time of change.[193] They provided utopian narratives that echoed with real-world events, frequently referring to the disorder, crime, depravity, and violence that were, and still are, a real part of the United States. But rather than seeking solutions to these problems through social change, religious conservatives found solace in a message that decried these evils and told them, in no uncertain terms, that they were not responsible for them if they stood right with Christ. If the rest of the nation came to Christ, they, too, would "be saved." These beliefs provided comfort in a harsh world without challenging the underpinnings of middle-class Orange Countians' lives. They won adherents exactly because they failed to account for the material causes for the social breakdown of families, for drugs, and for social violence, namely, the free market and the deep class divisions it generated.

What were the implications of the growth of conservative religious Christianity for the national political Right? Mark Hertel, the manager of Maranatha Village in Costa Mesa, made clear the profoundly political, as well as social, meaning of these beliefs in 1978, when he said:

> ... This country is in serious trouble right now. ... I can't see God left with any other choice than to bring judgment on the United States. ... The only thing holding back God's hand right now is the body of believers in this country. ... United, we could have a tremendous effect on this government ... we could fill Congress with Christians. We could pass legislation that would get the smut out of every store you walk into, that would clean up dope.[194]

And organize they did, joining the Religious Right's political crusade for a more "Godly nation."[195] The opening salvo was fired against the growing gay rights movement. Rather than seeing homosexuality as an alternative lifestyle, born-again Christians saw it as a challenge to biblical precepts of right and wrong, a threat to the traditional family, and one more sign of the moral corruption of American society. Following on the heels of Anita Bryant's successful 1977 campaign to overturn Miami–Dade County's inclusion of gays in the local antidiscrimination laws, John Briggs, the state senator from Orange County and a self-proclaimed born-again Christian, placed on his state's 1978 ballot a referendum that would have allowed public school boards to ban teachers "who publicly admit being homosexual or who promote homosexuality as a life-style."[196] He became the first politician to tap the region's growing evangelical movement, claiming the support of about 500, mostly fundamentalist, churches.[197] Hymn-singing rallies in the southland in support of the amendment, according to the *Los Angeles Times*, "resembled revival meetings more than political assemblies."[198] Symbolizing the national networks of the newly politicized evangelicals, the Reverend Jerry Falwell, of the 16,000-strong Thomas Road Baptist Church in Virginia, attended a rally held at the San Diego Convention Center in favor of the measure, thundering that Proposition 6 was needed to save California's children "from homosexuals." Falwell urged born-again Christians to political involvement. "The government calls this political," he railed, "we call it moral."[199]

Christian conservatives lost their crusade; the initiative went down to defeat, even in Orange County. Although more Orange County voters approved of the measure than the rest of the state's voters (46 percent, compared to 42 percent), it was still not a majority. Prominent conservatives like Ronald Reagan and Howard Jarvis, moreover, came out against the initiative. Reagan asserted that, while he did not approve of teaching "a so-called gay life-style in our schools . . . Proposition 6 has the potential of infringing on basic rights of privacy and perhaps even constitutional rights."[200] Opposition by such prominent conservatives damaged the initiative's chances and showed once again the dividing lines between economic conservatives, like Jarvis and Reagan, and their social conservative brethren.[201] While religious conservatives were a significant force, they by no means represented the whole of Orange County's conservatism. More libertarian measures, such as the Jarvis-Gann initiative and antibusing movements, proved far more popular with voters.

The defeat, however, did not lead to retreat. In the wake of the loss, Briggs joined with a Pomona minister to form Citizens for Decency and Morality, a statewide network of fundamentalist pastors and their congregations.[202] The campaign also consolidated "an activist network opposed to gay rights."[203] A strong backer of the crusade, the Reverend Louis Sheldon of Anaheim, for example, became more immersed in national politics to oppose homosexuality, eventually leading him, three years after the defeat, to establish the Traditional Values Coalition, which has since become a prominent national organization in the Christian Right's crusade against gay rights, claiming some 31,000 churches as members.[204]

Out of the evangelical churches' deepening concerns over new social issues came an ever more organized voice in politics. The southland was the site of the first national Christian Right organization, the Christian Voice.[205] It circulated Christian morality scorecards on the voting records of legislators and actively raised funds and advertised for Ronald Reagan's presidential campaign.[206] By 1981, the organization boasted 200,000 members, tens of thousands of them ministers, and it remained a "major Christian Right electoral vehicle" in the 1980s.[207] In Orange County, Jim Willems, owner of Maranatha Village, moreover, established a newspaper, Contemporary Christian Acts, a publication for and about the fundamentalist community that offered its followers advice on "the caliber of men Christians should vote for."[208]

These newly politicized Christian voters helped elect Ronald Reagan in 1980. In Orange County, the votes they cast, along with those of conservatives of other stripes, brought Reagan 68 percent of the county's vote, nearly three times as many as Jimmy Carter received. In no other large county in the nation was Reagan's victory as overwhelming.[209] But while Orange County's vote, just like that fourteen years earlier, made it the heart of "Reagan Country," Reagan appealed broadly across the nation. The conservative stalwart, who had gotten his political start in the southland's conservative movement, had not only made it onto the national stage, but American voters, hearing his message of freedom from government, firm nationalism, and the support of "traditional values," had also chosen, in a landslide vote, to make him their national leader.[210]

With Reagan's election came a new seat at the table of national power not only for conservative economic elites who had established a growing number of think tanks in the 1970s to assert their cause, but also for the mass of religious Christians who had provided the social base for the movement and who now descended on Washington, lobbying to make their voices heard.[211] Conservatism, refashioned and newly respectable, had emerged from its days of communist-hunting fervency and arrived in the halls of power. The sense of elation and triumph conservatives felt in their victory was expressed by Reagan himself, in the wake of his inauguration: "Fellow citizens, fellow conservatives . . . our time has come . . . our moment has arrived."[212]

This moment had been more than twenty years in the making. The seeds of Reagan's victory were planted with the organizational networks, ideas, and strategies of the conservative movement of the 1960s. That movement, which first mobilized middle-class men and women to action against the communist menace, had reconstructed itself, earning a new political respectability. The Right had not strayed from its long-standing core concerns over "social planners" and government waste, but with new opportunities, it had abandoned the conspiratorial, apocalyptic language in which these concerns had been couched earlier. While "moral" issues had long been part of a broader conservative package, these concerns gained a new prominence. At the same time, anticommunism receded to the background, no longer providing the glue uniting economic and religious conservatives. Gone were the educational meetings and "Freedom" study groups, and in their place stood Bible study groups, evangelical tent meetings, pro-life and "pro-family" organizations, along with a more organized and separate libertarian movement, symbolized best by the Libertarian Party.

The reworked conservative package, voiced ever more in the language of the "people," resonated with growing numbers of Americans, bringing conservatives to a position of power that they had previously enjoyed only prior to the New Deal. With their new power, conservatives began to dismantle what they had long perceived as the nightmarish collectivism of the "New Deal order." In so doing, they hoped to bring late twentieth-century Americans into a world with parallels to an earlier time in American life, when government responsibilities in the lives of citizens were minimal and a staunch moral Protestantism reigned supreme. Yet, as this book suggests, conservatives were not seeking a wholesale return to a rural life of simpler times. They reveled in the world of consumer culture, and were part of the bureaucratized, skilled, and technological modern America. They found the principles of an earlier time, a staunch laissez-faire capitalism often linked with a belief in absolute moral values, relevant to their very modern lives and communities. The economic and social settings that have fostered thriving conservative cultures, like that in Orange County, suggest not only that "it is possible to live in the modern world and enjoy its largess without absorbing modern values" but also, and even more, that modernity itself may foster values often considered incompatible with it: a militant religiosity, an unbending belief in the fundamental truth of the "rock of ages," and a strident laissez-faire individualism.[213] If this is the case, then we can expect the Right to have a vibrant place in American life in the years to come.

EPILOGUE

THE CONSERVATIVE MOVEMENT that this book chronicles came a long way between 1960 and 1980 in Orange County and elsewhere. Its transformation earned it new respectability and a well-organized constituency of supporters, many of whom were evangelicals. Just as the movement changed, so too, a new cast of characters became active in conservative politics. There were then discontinuities between the movement in the 1960s and the more recent mobilizations of the 1970s and afterward.

As we have seen, the movement was reshaped in numerous ways. Part of this change was the result of new recruits filling the ranks of conservative organizations by the late 1970s. In Orange County, some of these new activists had moved there only in the late 1960s or afterward, and had not participated in earlier mobilizations. As before, Orange County continued to grow rapidly, bringing in many new residents, some of whom joined the movement's ranks.[1] The population, which had been 703,925 in 1960, doubled between 1960 and 1970, and reached almost 2 million by 1980. Equally important, the new prominence of evangelical churches and their calling on Christians to make their voices heard in politics no doubt drew people to conservative causes. While the new leadership of the mobilizations of the 1970s shared the socioeconomic background of an earlier generation of activists (they were solidly middle-class), evidence suggests that the Right had broadened its class appeal.[2]

Just as important to understanding the changing composition of the grassroots conservative movement were the men and women who, by the 1970s, had dropped out of political activism. Unsurprisingly, the nature of the commitments of many former activists shifted over the years; age, family and job issues, and occasional disillusionment with party politics sometimes led them to abandon active participation. A Goldwater activist from the city of Orange, Armstrong Dowell, for instance, explained that serious health problems in his family constrained his later involvement in politics.[3] After Richard Nixon's election in 1968, another activist from Tustin went back to full-time teaching, which left her little time for politics. And Estrid Kielsmeier, from Garden Grove, who had campaigned hard for Goldwater, abandoned involvement in party politics but remained immersed in "issues that . . . I chose to be involved in," such as the sex education struggle.[4] Despite a diminishing activism among some of the people interviewed for this book, not one of these men and women strayed from their conservative leanings. Armstrong Dowell emphasized, for example, that he remained a "dyed-in-the-wool conservative," and Kielsmeier (now Kieffer) asserted that she now feels "even stronger" about conservative concerns.[5] These activists formed the rank-and-file constituency of the New Right, even if they left the leafleting and organizing to others.

The path Bee Gathright followed illustrates this trajectory. Gathright had attended anticommunist study groups and offered her home as a neighborhood Goldwater headquarters during her active years in the 1960s, but by the early 1970s, she was immersed in "Christian work rather than political work. . . . We would go door to door asking if you were saved."[6] She has remained an unbending conservative Christian, but she no longer walks precincts or stuffs envelopes. Indeed, when she moved from Garden Grove to Placentia in the early 1970s, she lost touch with many of those with whom she had been involved. At the same time, she began a new career in real estate that took up much of her time. Yet despite these commitments, newly created organizations such as the Christian Voice and the Moral Majority received her support in the late 1970s. Twenty years later, in the late 1990s, she said she kept up on "how our elected leaders are doing" through literature by the Reverend Lou Sheldon of the Traditional Values Coalition. As she remarked, "I'm on everybody's mailing list . . . politically I support them. They are all good causes."[7] She considers herself a member of the "Christian

Right" and listens avidly to right-wing radio commentator Rush Limbaugh. In a comment that elicits the links and shifts in the movement over time, she declared, "The thing I appreciate about him [is that] back when we were reading the same things he believes and thinking the same way he does nobody wanted to hear it . . . so I appreciate that he has a large audience because people are still being educated."[8]

Gathright was one of the hundreds of thousands of grass-roots men and women who made their lives in the rich evangelical subcultures that have thrived in the South and West. Men and women like her forged the social base of the Christian Right, a social base that explains the movement's endurance and political strength.[9] Yet listening to a national radio commentator or having one's name on a set of mailing lists is a very different commitment from pounding the pavement for candidates and organizing community meetings, all of which defined Gathright's earlier activism. Gathright became one individual making up the mass constituency of the national New Right, but she did little to strengthen the conservative movement at the local level.

While Gathright's story illustrates one tendency among earlier activists, other conservatives deepened their political commitments after the turbulent 1960s had come and gone. Thus, while there were discontinuities between the new social issues activism of the late 1960s and 1970s and the earlier crusades, the degree of continuity of ideas and people is even more striking. Many of the pioneers of the conservative movement worked long and hard through the 1970s and beyond, and a few of them left national marks. Some remained active in conservative Republican Party circles; others moved in different directions. The political trajectories of some of the activists who propelled the anticommunist and Goldwater mobilization in the 1960s illustrate the many directions that the grassroots women and men of Huntington Beach, Fullerton, Anaheim, and Newport Beach took their commitments.

One tendency of the activists was to move into more institutional channels, not only campaigning but also becoming candidates for local or state political office. Nolan Frizzelle, for example, who had been a key mover in the conservative takeover of the California Republican Assembly, remained active in Republican circles through the 1970s. Riding the wave of conservative enthusiasm that brought Reagan into office in 1980, Frizzelle won a California State Assembly seat as a staunch conservative from Fullerton, an office he held for twelve years. In a somewhat different vein, Jan Averill of La Habra, who had participated in Fred Schwarz's Schools of Anti-Communism in the early 1960s and belonged to a conservative study club for much of the decade, became more involved in local education issues in the 1970s. Offended by the liberal educational philosophy of their local school district, a number of concerned parents urged her to run for the school board in 1972, in a heated campaign. Her prior involvement in conservative initiatives served her well:

> I don't think I ever would have done it had I not had the background of the Tuesday morning study club. . . . I mean it just gave me the confidence that really, the way they were going was not going to pay off in the long run. So I got on the board. I took our own school and made a plan and we called it Academics Plus . . . copied from a model of a fundamental school in Pasadena. . . . Gradually we got more on the board, one at a time, that had conservative ideas. We got three people on the board and we finally got it through. The whole district started to take on the characteristics of the traditional . . . curriculum—they all got grades, they all took on phonics.[10]

Since that time Averill has remained active in the Republican Party and in local and national educational issues.[11]

Like Frizzelle and Averill, David Bergland of Costa Mesa also ran for political office, but he was drawn increasingly into third-party politics. An objectivist follower of Ayn Rand in the 1960s, as well as a Goldwater and Reagan supporter, by the

early 1970s, Bergland had become immersed in national libertarian circles. In 1973, a year after the founding of the national
Libertarian Party, he attended the founding meeting of the Orange County chapter of the new Libertarian Party of California.[12] Elected an officer, he soon became prominent, both statewide and nationally, promoting the libertarian cause. By 1976,
Bergland ran as the party's vice presidential candidate; in 1980,
he was its presidential candidate.

While Bergland was exceptional (although not unique)
among local activists in moving into a national leadership position in conservative and libertarian circles, his deepening
involvement illustrates a broader trend. In Bergland's case, it led
him to an abandonment of the Republican Party. For others, it
led to an embrace of more militant tactics. Cathy Sullivan, for
example, who had been a rank-and-file Goldwater supporter
and CRA activist, became deeply involved in pro-life circles in
the 1970s. After she founded the Orange County Pro-Life Political Action Committee in 1973, most of her efforts were spent
running the committee. Her commitment to this "single issue"
led her into civil disobedience; borrowing tactics from the left,
she "sat-in" at an Orange County abortion clinic in the mid-
1970s.[13] At the same time, despite her support of pro-life Democrats over pro-choice Republicans, Sullivan did not abandon her
activism within conservative Republican Party circles. She campaigned heavily for Ronald Reagan in 1980. Only after his election did her activities slow down; a downward turn in her husband's business forced her return to full-time work. In a
statement that illustrates some of the paradoxes of the role of
conservative women and their prominent place in grassroots activism, she later noted, "I had to go to work, to leave a family
at home and it was hard. . . . I would be much happier and
would still choose to be a homemaker at home. . . . Why? First
of all, I could do more volunteer political activity."[14]

Sullivan was not the only activist from the 1960s who dedicated herself to pro-life issues, but the depth of her commitment
was exceptional. Probably more typical was the sporadic activ-

ism of someone like Mary Haller, although her self-described "extremism" placed her on the fringe of the Right and was hardly typical. Haller had gotten her start in politics during the battle to unseat liberal school board trustee Joel Dvorman in 1961, an issue focused on concerns over communist influence in the schools. She joined the Cardinal Mindszenty Foundation, a Catholic anticommunist organization, in the early 1960s. Some thirty years later, she still embraced the conspiratorial worldview of the extremist fringe of the Right that she had adopted in the early 1960s, although the conspiracy seems to have shifted from a communist cabal to a hodgepodge of distant "enemies," drawn from various conspiracy writers. Haller's concerns moved away from anticommunism, and the pro-life movement became central to her later involvement. She attended numerous pro-life rallies and even, in 1992, joined a pro-life contingent that went to the Republican Party convention in Houston, where the strong showing of conservatives succeeded in pulling the party firmly to the right. She recalled: "We went to Houston in August for the week, and that's all we did; rallies, . . . bumping around in an old school bus, picketing Planned Parenthood. We stayed at a Christian Camp . . . went to a couple of Rescues."[15] Her hero and standard-bearer, moreover, now was Catholic conservative Patrick Buchanan.[16]

In contrast, for Rufus and Peggy Pearce, Ronald Reagan remained a conservative inspiration well after his decline from the national limelight. They, like many of the other grassroots Goldwater activists, had worked in Republican Party circles for Reagan's candidacy in 1966. Through the 1970s, Peggy Pearce remained active in the CRA and the local chapter of the Republican Federated Women. She served as an alternate delegate to the Republican National Convention in 1976, hoping to win Reagan the nomination over Gerald Ford, and did not slow her activities until Reagan moved into the White House. Afterward, she, like Sullivan, did retreat, feeling that it was time to "let someone else do the work for a while."[17] Still, the number of conservative journals to which she and her husband subscribed at the time they were interviewed, close to twenty years later, suggests that conservative politics still played a very important role in their lives.

In a more unusual twist, Tom Rogers of San Juan Capistrano also remained active in conservative circles, but his activism drew him in a different direction, symbolizing the evolving concerns of Orange County's affluent conservative homeowners. Rogers, a strong Goldwater supporter, had been active in the campaign against Proposition 14 and had served as the finance chairman for John Birch Society member John Schmitz's assembly run in 1964. Rogers continued his activism in Republican Party circles, serving as chair of the Orange County Republican Central Committee from 1969 to 1973. In addition, from the midsixties through the midseventies, he served as an associate editor of the *Wanderer*, a national Catholic traditionalist paper. His concerns over moral corruption led him to support the evangelical Reverend Lou Sheldon of the Traditional Values Coalition after he came on the Orange County scene in the late 1970s. But in the 1980s, although he still considered himself a "hardcore right-winger," Rogers became a leader in the county's "slow-growth movement."[18]

Spiraling growth in Orange County led earlier and affluent homeowners, particularly in the southern portion of the county, where Rogers lived, to seek to protect the open spaces and beauty that had made their towns and cities, in their eyes, such pleasant places to live in. They fought huge corporations like the Irvine Corporation, Rancho Mission Viejo, and Mission Viejo Company, which sought to reduce open space with their large-scale developments.[19] A rancher, Rogers ran into confrontations with developers seeking to pave over a creek to develop land close to where he lived.[20] His hostility to corporate developers, whom he labeled "the whores of the twentieth century," led him to associations with unlikely bedfellows, such as progressive environmentalist Larry Agran.[21] Demonstrating the limits of Orange Countians' belief in unrestrained property rights, he later asserted:

Being a rancher, you can't help but be an environmentalist, when I see what they do. . . . I see them tearing down hills and stuff like that . . . where they didn't have to make more money. Well, they've got bankers to deal with, and they have to deal in density, so if they've got to get twenty-two units per acre, they're going to get twenty-two units per acre no matter what happened.[22]

Seeking to preserve their "utopias," Rogers and many conservative homeowners, in an assertion of their own affluence and in protest against the urbanization of suburbia, came "to embrace a structural reform implying massive regulation of one of the most sacred marketplaces (land development)."[23] They did so in the somewhat unconvincing language of the "people" against the heartless corporations.

By the time Reagan was elected, not only were the commitments of these activists changing, but Orange County itself, as the slow-growth movement suggests, was also rapidly becoming a different place. Like much of the Sunbelt and West, it remained an area of dynamic growth, although in Orange County the pace of growth slowed from the astronomical rates of the 1960s. Defense remained an important part of the county's economic base, but the economy was diversifying. In the 1960s, as Spencer Olin observed, "Manufacturing, largely in aerospace-defense, was the key to Orange County's transformation . . . from an agricultural to industrial economy."[24] In the 1970s, gains in the aerospace industry were matched, and even surpassed, by growth in other areas. In 1973, for example, the main employment growth sectors were finance, insurance, real estate, trade, and services.[25] After the mid-1970s, Orange Countians labored primarily in the information sector, and international trade assumed major importance.[26] At the same time, the county was becoming far more racially diverse than it had been in the 1960s. The county's minority population doubled to more than 20 percent between 1970 and 1980, a trend that has continued ever since.[27] The growing Hispanic population engaged in a series of grassroots protests of their own in the late 1970s and 1980s, in an attempt to force local government to address their concerns.[28] Yet even with these changes and the many challenges they have brought to the county's conservatives, Orange County has remained a "right-wing node," although within it, libertarian ideas have become ever more prominent, reshaping the package of Orange County conservatism.[29] Not only in 1980, but also in 1984, the county voted more heavily for Ronald Reagan than did any other large county in the country.[30] Indeed, in 1984, Orange Countians voted for Reagan over Walter Mondale by more than 400,000 votes: 615,099 to 200,477. And since the 1970s, Republicans and independents have been surpassing Democrats in terms of growth.[31] In 1987, there were 591,395 registered Republicans, 387,041 Democrats, as well as 110,000 independents and minor party registrants. In a survey conducted in 1987, 69 percent of county residents agreed that Orange County has "very conservative political attitudes."[32]

These staunch beliefs, including, not least, a firm belief in the inefficiency and wastefulness of government, forced local government to operate under tight fiscal conditions, especially after the Proposition 13 tax rebellion crippled county revenue. As a result, Orange County government officials sought creative ways to increase revenues to provide the services still demanded by county residents; they embraced a faith in the magic of the private market and adopted risky investment strategies to increase public funds without having to face the painful task of raising taxes. The mixture of conservative ideology, the very real demands placed on local and state government, and Orange Countians' firm faith in the market proved explosive, leading, in 1994, to the biggest municipal bankruptcy in U.S. history. Orange County's bankruptcy was especially shocking, given that it occurred in a growing suburban region rather than a declining city, and that the county, only months before, had one of the highest credit ratings in the country. While it took the county only eighteen months to emerge from bankruptcy, the legacy of the fiscal crisis remains, as scholar Mark Baldassare has noted, "in tight local fiscal budgets, large debt payments to recover from the crisis, and service cuts for the poor."[33]

Orange County, this utopia of mid-twentieth-century America, was one of the nation's most important centers of economic and social conservatism. But Orange County was not unique. It was, instead, an important part of broader developments that have reshaped American politics in the recent past. Orange County was at the leading edge of economic and social changes that have propelled a deep-rooted and ever more powerful conservative political culture in significant areas of the Sunbelt and West. An older set of cultural and political traditions—linked with the particular trajectory of Orange County's economic development, its decentralized spatial organization, its in-migrants, and its powerful entrepreneurs—made it a fertile ground for many manifestations of conservatism, from libertarianism to evangelical Christianity. Similar forces have underwritten the growth of more recent boom regions in the South and West, such as the middle-class communities of Cobb County, Georgia; Scottsdale and the suburbs north of Phoenix, Arizona, in Maricopa County; Fort Worth, Texas, and the suburbs northeast of Dallas; the affluent suburbs of Jefferson Parish, Louisiana; and Colorado Springs, Colorado, to name just a few.[34] The population, size, affluence, and economic importance of these places have enabled them to help shape the political direction of the nation.

But if conservatives have flourished in these regions and won growing political prominence, they have done so by building on older evangelical and antistatist ideological inheritances deeply rooted in American life. While the Right's political fortunes nationally have ebbed and flowed over the course of the century, conservative traditions and beliefs among a segment of the population have long given the Right a strong regional base of support. Conservative forces have had remarkable staying power in American life. Indeed, they have thrived, as this book has shown, in the last half of the century in settings considered least conducive to them: modern, suburban regions.

272 ✦ E P I L O G U E

The Right has thrived because it has addressed concerns and issues relevant to many people who inhabit these communities. In the face of social and cultural change, conservatives have spoken to concerns over the autonomy of communities, the erosion of individualism, the authority of the family, and the place of religion in national life. Just as important, they have provided a total set of explanations for what they believe is wrong with America, focusing specifically on the dangers of federal power and control along with liberal efforts to distribute power more equitably in society. These ideas resonated with many middle-class and lower-middle-class men and women not only because they were familiar but also because at their core they seemed to safeguard these people's way of life and a set of power relations in American society they wished to preserve.

Yet conservatism has not been unchanging or inflexible. Grassroots conservatism has taken on vastly different expressions across the century: In the 1920s, the Ku Klux Klan, with its "100 percent Americanism," attacked Catholics, Jews, and African-Americans as threats to righteousness and a godly nation. During the Great Depression, right-wing organizing evinced a corporatist, even protofascist, ethos distinct from past and future mobilizations and brought in a broadened constituency through the Catholic conservative populist appeals of Father Charles Coughlin. From the 1950s until the mid-1960s, the Right's attacks focused on the threat of communism in driving America to the brink of moral bankruptcy and to "collectivism." With the fading of anticommunism and the rise of new social issues by the late 1960s and 1970s, big-government liberals, feminists, and gay rights advocates were targeted as obstacles to making America a more God-centered nation. Through the decades, conservatives have championed staunch nationalism, moral absolutes, and a belief in limited government, yet they have also adapted themselves to new circumstances and reconfigured the package of conservative enemies and targets. In the post–World War II period, this has meant abandoning older essentialist racial ideas (as well as anti-Catholicism and anti-Semitism) that once propelled earlier initiatives. And among religious conservatives, it has meant an embrace of modern consumer trappings and often a therapeutic ethos to forward the message of "old-time religion" to new audiences. It is the combination of preservationism and adaptation that helps explain the Right's staying power and that promises the Right a place in American life in years to come.

It is in the story of the making of suburban Orange County— and, with it, the making of the Sunbelt and modern West—that we uncover the forging of the New Right and, in a larger sense, the reconfiguration of twentieth-century American politics. Sub-urbanization and modernization in the boom regions in the South and West have only deepened an already established con-servative political culture (while at the same time reshaping it) and given it vast new political power—a combination that has had dramatic results for the shape of American politics in the late twentieth century.[35]

NOTES

INTRODUCTION

1. Theodore H. White, *The Making of the President, 1964* (New York: Atheneum, 1965), 118.

2. Nelson Rockefeller, in stark contrast, paid for signature collecting and required weeks to get 44,000 signatures. Estrid Kieffer (formerly Kielsmeier), interview with author, 3 October 1998; see also White, *The Making of the President, 1964*, 118; "Goldwater for President" campaign newsletter, 16 March 1964, Box 29, KM Papers.

3. Kieffer (formerly Kielsmeier), interview.

4. Garden Grove was one of the twenty-four incorporated cities of Orange County in 1964. See Orange County Planning Department, Population Research Committee, *Quarterly Population Report*, 31 December 1964, 31 December 1965.

5. Tellingly, in the popular imagination, the county erroneously earned the reputation as the national home of the John Birch Society, although the actual headquarters of the society were in Belmont, Massachusetts. See Barbara Shell Stone, "The John Birch Society of California" (Ph.D. diss., University of Southern California, 1968), 1; Larry Peterson, "Stereotype: Orange County's Image as Bastion of Conservatism Dies Hard," *Orange County Register*, 29 June 1987; Sheldon Zalznick, "The Double Life of Orange County," *Fortune*, October 1968; James Q. Wilson, "A Guide to Reagan Country: The Political Culture of Southern California," *Commentary* 43 (May 1967): 37–45. See also Michael Paul Rogin and John L. Shover, *Political Change in California: Critical Elections and Social Movements, 1890–1966* (Westport, Conn.: Greenwood, 1970), 153–212.

6. On the increasingly Republican politics of the New South and New West, see Bruce J. Schulman, *From Cotton Belt to Sunbelt: Federal Policy, Economic Development, and the Transformation of the South, 1938–1980* (New York: Oxford University Press, 1991), 206–21; Peter Applebome, *Dixie Rising: How the South Is Shaping American Values, Politics, and Culture* (New York: Times Books, 1996), 4–55, 90–114; Richard White, *"It's Your Misfortune and None of My Own": A New History of the American West* (Norman: University of Oklahoma Press, 1991), 541–77. See also Paul Kleppner, "Politics without Parties: The Western States, 1900–1984," in *The Twentieth-Century West: Historical Interpretations*, ed. Gerald D. Nash and Richard Etulain (Albuquerque: University of New Mexico Press, 1989), especially 330–31. It is important to note, however, that the Sunbelt and the West are extremely diverse regions that also contain strong Democratic constituencies, large numbers of minorities, and persistent poverty amid wealth. For a discussion of the "shadows" of Sunbelt development, see Schulman, *From Cotton Belt to Sunbelt*, 174–205. On the diversity of the West, see also White, *"It's Your Misfortune,"* 574–612.

7. Kevin P. Phillips, *The Emerging Republican Majority* (New Rochelle, N.Y.: Arlington House, 1969), 435. For discussions of the political traditions of Southern California, see also Wilson, "A Guide to Reagan Country," 37–45; Rogin and Shover, *Political Change in California*, 153–212; and Karl A. Lamb, *As Orange Goes: Twelve California Families and the Future of American Politics* (New York: Norton, 1974). Michael Paul Rogin's evocative analy-

sis of right-wing voting behavior in Southern California seeks to explain the strength of the Right there through attention to the southland's cultural patterns. In a very different vein, Karl Lamb seeks to demolish the myth that Orange County is a monolithic landscape of rabid conservative ideologues. While Lamb refutes the notion of Orange County as a "stereotype," the evidence of most voting statistics and the story this book tells point to the strength of conservatism among many of the region's inhabitants. Important as it is to see the complexities and ambivalences of Orange Countians' thinking, what is to be explained is why the region generated such a staunch conservative politics—a question Lamb does not address.

8. The shift in politics in the West was evident earlier than that in the South. The change from a Democratic to a Republican West was apparent by 1960, according to Richard White. As he writes, "The liberal majority evaporated; western political opinion had shifted." The Republican penetration in the solid Democratic South began only in the 1960s and deepened through the 1970s. See White, "*It's Your Misfortune*," 576; Schulman, *From Cotton Belt to Sunbelt*, 214–19.

9. Catherine Sullivan, interview with author, 1 December 1992.

10. For the successes and failures of the progressive mobilizations of the 1960s, see Michael Kazin and Maurice Isserman, "The Failure and Success of the New Radicalism," in *The Rise and Fall of the New Deal Order, 1930–1980*, ed. Steve Fraser and Gary Gerstle (Princeton, N.J.: Princeton University Press, 1989), 212–42.

11. Zalznick, "The Double Life of Orange County." Other examples of these labels include *Newsweek*'s labeling of Southern California as "Cuckoo Land"—"headquarters of the state's estimated 500,000 extreme right-wingers." See "Can Anyone Stop Goldwater Now?" *Newsweek*, 15 June 1964, 23. The *Nation* went even further, labeling conservative Republican efforts to remake the party as a "putsch in the GOP" and remarking on these men's and women's "pathological lust for power, . . . commando-like tactics, . . . and Mein Kampf program." See Donovan Bess, "Putsch in the GOP," *Nation*, 11 May 1964, 474–76. The exception to the rule of characterizing Southern California as "nut country" is James Q. Wilson's insightful essay, "A Guide to Reagan Country."

12. See Robert Welch, *The Politician* (Belmont, Mass.: Belmont, 1963), 66, 83; Howard Seelye and Don Smith, "A Century of Politics in Orange County," reprint edition, *Los Angeles Times*, 21 March 1976; Peterson, "Stereotype: Orange County's Image as Bastion of Conservatism Dies Hard." See also Ir-

278 ❖ Notes to Introduction

ving G. McCann, *Case History of the Smear by CBS of Conservatives* (Washington, D.C.: McCann Press, 1966), 89.

13. See Daniel Bell, "The Dispossessed," in *The Radical Right*, ed. Daniel Bell (Garden City, N.Y.: Doubleday, 1963), 1–38; Seymour Martin Lipset and Earl Raab, *The Politics of Unreason: Right-Wing Extremism in America, 1790–1977* (New York: Harper and Row, 1978). See also Richard Hofstadter, *The Paranoid Style in American Politics, and Other Essays* (Chicago: University of Chicago Press, 1979). For useful discussions of liberal consensus scholars' perceptions of the Right, see William B. Hixson, *The Search for the American Right Wing: An Analysis of the Social Science Record, 1955–1987* (Princeton, N.J.: Princeton University Press, 1992), 51–56, 3–26.

14. "What the right wing is fighting in the shadow of Communism is, essentially, 'modernity,'" wrote Bell. See Bell, "The Dispossessed," 12.

15. Other historians who have recently revisited the history of right-wing mobilization earlier in the twentieth century have also rejected the dismissive explanations of consensus-school scholars that tended to explain much of conservatism as a kind of pathology. See, for example, Leonard J. Moore's *Citizen Klansmen: The Ku Klux Klan in Indiana, 1921–1928* (Chapel Hill: University of North Carolina Press, 1991); Kathleen M. Blee, *Women of the Klan: Racism and Gender in the 1920s* (Berkeley: University of California Press, 1991); Nancy MacLean, *Behind the Mask of Chivalry: The Making of the Second Ku Klux Klan* (New York: Oxford University Press, 1994); Alan Brinkley, *Voices of Protest: Huey Long, Father Coughlin and the Great Depression* (New York: Vintage, 1982). The proliferating literature on the post–World War II Right has also jettisoned this frame, sometimes explicitly, other times implicitly. See, for example, Sara Diamond, *Roads to Dominion: Right-Wing Movements and Political Power in the United States* (New York: Guilford Press, 1994); George H. Nash, *The Conservative Intellectual Movement in America since 1945* (New York: Basic Books, 1976); Jerome L. Himmelstein, *To the Right: The Transformation of American Conservatism* (Berkeley: University of California Press, 1990).

16. Alan Brinkley points out that recent scholarship has begun to support such findings for religious conservatives more broadly. See Brinkley, "The Problem of American Conservatism," *American Historical Review* 99 (April 1994): 427–28.

17. I borrow here from Michael Kazin's use of the Gramscian term "common sense" to denote a received "conception of the world which is uncritically absorbed by the various social and cultural environments in which the moral individuality of the average man is developed." Walter L. Adamson, *Hegemony and Revolution: A Study of Antonio Gramsci's Political and Cultural The-*

ory (Berkeley: University of California Press, 1980), 123, quoted in Michael Kazin, "The Grass-Roots Right: New Histories of U.S. Conservatism in the Twentieth Century," *American Historical Review* 97 (February 1992): 149.

18. S. Engeloff, "Tongue-in-Cheek Candidate," *Life*, 17 September 1965, 49–50. Barry Goldwater was often portrayed as psychologically maladjusted and unstable. See, for example, Ralph Ginzburg, "Goldwater: The Man and the Menace," *Fact*, September–October 1964. Referring to Barry Goldwater, moreover, Richard Hofstadter asked, "When, in all our history, has anyone with ideas so bizarre, so archaic, so self-confounding, so remote from the basic American consensus, ever got so far?" See Hofstadter, "A Long View: Goldwater in History," *New York Review of Books*, October 1964, 17–20, quoted in Brinkley, "The Problem of American Conservatism," 411–12.

19. Relative to the John Birch Society nationally, Sara Diamond also rejects the term "radical" in reference to the organization. Instead, she characterizes its politics as both oppositional and system-supportive. See Diamond, *Roads to Dominion*, 53–55.

20. *Register*, 9 April 1962.

21. Here I draw on Jerome Himmelstein's formulation of the content of conservative ideology. See Himmelstein, *To the Right*, 14. See also Nash, *The Conservative Intellectual Movement*, 84–153.

22. These studies complement an already large literature on McCarthyism. The second "Red Scare" has received a good deal of scholarly attention. Studies of the anticommunist crusades of the post–World War II period include Ellen Schrecker, *Many Are the Crimes: McCarthyism in America* (Princeton, N.J.: Princeton University Press, 1998); Richard Gid Powers, *Not Without Honor: The History of American Anticommunism* (New York: Free Press, 1995); Richard M. Fried, *Nightmare in Red: The McCarthy Era in Perspective* (New York: Oxford University Press, 1990); David M. Oshinsky, *A Conspiracy So Immense: The World of Joe McCarthy* (New York: Free Press, 1983); M. J. Heale, *American Anticommunism: Combating the Enemy Within, 1830–1970* (Baltimore: Johns Hopkins University Press, 1990), 145–90; David Caute, *The Great Fear: The Anti-Communist Purge under Truman and Eisenhower* (New York: Simon and Schuster, 1978); Robert Griffith, *The Politics of Fear: Joseph R. McCarthy and the Senate* (Lexington: University Press of Kentucky, 1970); *The Specter: Original Essays on the Cold War and the Origins of McCarthyism*. Athan Theoharis and Robert Griffith, eds. (New York: New Viewpoints, 1974). But as much as we know about Joe McCarthy and the damage McCarthyism did to liberal and progressive reform movements in the 1950s, we still know remarkably little about the anticommunist movement itself. We have few studies that chart the popular base of McCarthyism, uncov-

ering who the mobilizers and followers were, and their continuities and discontinuities with earlier generations of conservative activists.

23. An attenuated list of some of these studies includes Nash, *The Conservative Intellectual Movement*; Patrick Allitt, *Catholic Intellectuals and Conservative Politics in America, 1950–1985* (Ithaca, N.Y.: Cornell University Press, 1993); Mary C. Brennan, *Turning Right in the Sixties: The Conservative Capture of the GOP* (Chapel Hill: University of North Carolina Press, 1995); John A. Andrew, *The Other Side of the Sixties: The Young Americans for Freedom and the Rise of Conservative Politics* (New Brunswick, N.J.: Rutgers University Press, 1997); and Gregory L. Schneider, *Cadres for Conservatism: Young Americans for Freedom and the Rise of the Contemporary Right* (New York: New York University Press, 1999). On biographical treatments of conservative leaders, see Robert Alan Goldberg, *Barry Goldwater* (New Haven, Conn.: Yale University Press, 1995), and Dan T. Carter, *The Politics of Rage: George Wallace, the Origins of the New Conservatism, and the Transformation of American Politics* (New York: Simon and Schuster, 1995). Overviews of the Right since 1945 include Michael W. Miles, *The Odyssey of the American Right* (New York: Oxford University Press, 1980); David Reinhard, *The Republican Right since 1945* (Lexington: University Press of Kentucky, 1983); and journalist Godfrey Hodgson's *The World Turned Right Side Up: A History of the Conservative Ascendancy in America* (Boston: Houghton Mifflin, 1996). E. J. Dionne Jr. and Thomas Byrne Edsall and Mary D. Edsall provide insights into the issues that offered conservatives new opportunities. See Dionne, *Why Americans Hate Politics* (New York: Simon and Schuster, 1991); and Edsall with Edsall, *Chain Reaction: The Impact of Race, Rights, and Taxes on American Politics* (New York: Norton, 1991). In addition, two recent studies of the decade of the 1960s have paid significant attention to the conservative side of the period. See Maurice Isserman and Michael Kazin, *America Divided: The Civil War of the 1960s* (New York: Oxford University Press, 2000); and Rebecca Klatch, *A Generation Divided: The New Left, the New Right and the 1960s* (Berkeley: University of California Press, 1999).

24. Sociologist Sara Diamond has written an ambitious study tracing the trajectory of distinctive variants of the Right from 1945 in *Roads to Dominion*. Jerome Himmelstein has looked at the shifting fortunes of the conservative movement over time in *To the Right*. Political scientist Michael Lienesch has reviewed the manner in which scholars have studied social movements in the twentieth century and its applications to the modern Christian Right. See Michael Lienesch, "Right-Wing Religion: Christian Conservatism as a Political Movement," *Political Science Quarterly* 97 (fall 1982), 403–26. For a review of the manner in which social scientists have viewed the Right using models of

collective behavior to social movement theory, see Hixson, *The Search for the American Right Wing.*

25. They have, moreover, contributed to debunking the dismissive paradigms of the consensus school scholars. Some scholars, such as Diamond, have done so explicitly; see *Roads to Dominion,* 5–6. For other examples, see Nash, *The Conservative Intellectual Movement,* and Himmelstein, *To the Right.*

26. There is one recently published statewide study of the Right. See Kurt Schuparra, *Triumph of the Right: The Rise of the California Conservative Movement, 1945–1966* (Armonk, N.Y.: M. E. Sharpe, 1998). His focus on the state-level movement, however, once again fails to explore the grassroots social movement base of the Right.

27. Several historians have remarked on this significant gap in our understanding of twentieth-century conservatism. See Leonard Moore, "Good Old-Fashioned New Social History and the Twentieth-Century American Right," *Reviews in American History* 24 (1996): 555–73; Brinkley, "The Problem of American Conservatism," 409–29; Kazin, "The Grass-Roots Right," 136–55.

28. See Ronald P. Formisano, *Boston against Busing: Race, Class, and Ethnicity in the 1960s and 1970s* (Chapel Hill: University of North Carolina Press, 1991); Jonathon Rieder, *Canarsie: The Jews and Italians of Brooklyn against Liberalism* (Cambridge, Mass.: Harvard University Press, 1985); and Thomas Sugrue, *The Origins of the Urban Crisis: Race and Inequality in Postwar Detroit* (Princeton, N.J.: Princeton University Press, 1996).

29. While this study is informed largely by historical methods and interpretative questions, I have drawn on social movement and resource mobilization theory to understand how and when social movements occur. For a survey of this useful literature, see J. Craig Jenkins, "Resource Mobilization and the Study of Social Movements," *Annual Review of Sociology* 9 (1983): 527–53. See also Aldon D. Morris and Carol McClurg Mueller, eds., *Frontiers in Social Movement Theory* (New Haven, Conn.: Yale University Press, 1992).

30. In doing so, this study suggests that one-sided theories of resource mobilization or traditional discontent hypotheses are inadequate to explain complex historical processes. Any serious study of social movements must provide a multifaceted explanation that includes both an exploration of movement resources and attention to the social networks, ideas, values, and grievances of movement actors. Here, I draw on social movement theory. See Morris and McClurg Mueller, *Frontiers in Social Movement Theory.*

31. A number of scholars of the new western history have noted the importance of libertarianism and Republicanism in the West, but few have linked this analysis to a broader study of the Right in the United States and its rise to

power. See White, "*It's Your Misfortune*," 601–11. See also Kleppner, "Politics without Parties," especially 354–55.

32. In telling the story of conservatism's rise through this western locale, I do not wish to deny the significance of race in the reconfiguration of national politics over the past forty years. Rather, I hope to point to the broader patterns of socioeconomic change that have contributed to conservative Republican fortunes in the West and the South. The South's Republican gains, after all, have far outlived the racial strife of the 1960s. Indeed, in some states, Republican registration has deepened once racial strife abated. See Schulman, *From Cotton Belt to Sunbelt*, 214–15.

Chapter 1

1. *Los Angeles Times*, 18 July 1955.

2. White, "*It's Your Misfortune*," 550; see also Alan Bryman, *Disney and His Worlds* (New York: Routledge, 1995), 63–80.

3. Lois Lundberg, interview with author, 25 August 1994.

4. Rob Kling, Spencer Olin, and Mark Poster, "The Emergence of Postsuburbia: An Introduction," in *Postsuburban California: The Transformation of Orange County since World War II*, ed. Rob Kling, Spencer Olin, and Mark Poster (Berkeley: University of California Press, 1991), 1–3.

5. Orange County Planning Department, Population Research Committee, *Quarterly Population Report* 30, September 1961.

6. Pamela Hallan-Gibson, *The Golden Promise: An Illustrated History of Orange County* (Northridge, Calif.: Windsor, 1986), 209–12.

7. Martin J. Schiesl, "Designing the Model Community: The Irvine Company and Suburban Development, 1950–1988," in *Postsuburban California: The Transformation of Orange County since World War II*, ed. Rob Kling, Spencer Olin, and Mark Poster (Berkeley: University of California Press, 1991), 55–56.

8. Orange County Planning Department, Population Research Committee, *Quarterly Population Report*, 30 June 1963.

9. Stanford Research Institute, *Orange County: Its Economic Growth, 1940–1980* (Pasadena: Southern California Laboratories, 1959), 22; Security First National Bank, Economic Research Division, *The Growth and Economic Stature of Orange County*, November 1961, 10.

10. In nullifying the land titles, they broke the Treaty of Guadalupe Hidalgo. Hallan-Gibson, *The Golden Promise*, 47–62.

11. Gilbert G. Gonzalez, *Labor and Community: Mexican Citrus Worker Villages in a Southern California County, 1900–1950* (Urbana: University of Illinois Press, 1994), 44.

12. Hallan-Gibson, *The Golden Promise*, 135; Richard Dale Batman, "Anaheim Was an Oasis in the Wilderness," *Journal of the West* 4 (January 1965): 3–15.

13. Batman, "Anaheim Was an Oasis," 17.

14. Stanford Research Institute, *Orange County: Its Economic Growth*, 108.

15. Security First National Bank, Economic Research Division, *The Growth and Economic Stature of Orange County*, May 1967, 15; Stanford Research Institute, *Orange County: Its Economic Growth*, 9; Associated Chambers of Commerce of Orange County, *The Majestic Empire of Orange County, California* (1953).

16. Richard Dale Batman, "Gospel Swamp . . . The Land of Hog and Hominy," *Journal of the West* 4 (1965): 239.

17. For discussions of the monumental impact of World War II on the West, see Gerald D. Nash, *World War II and the West: Reshaping the Economy* (Lincoln: University of Nebraska Press, 1990); and Nash, *The American West Transformed: The Impact of the Second World War* (Bloomington: Indiana University Press, 1985).

18. Leo Friis, *Orange County through Four Centuries* (Santa Ana, Calif.: Pioneer Press, 1965), 152; Hallan-Gibson, *The Golden Promise*, 219–21.

19. Friis, *Orange County through Four Centuries*, 156; Hallan-Gibson, *The Golden Promise*, 219–21.

20. Security First National Bank, *The Growth and Economic Stature of Orange County*, May 1967, 20–22.

21. Hallan-Gibson, *The Golden Promise*, 236.

22. Ann Markusen, Peter Hall, Scott Campbell, and Sabina Deitrick, *The Rise of the Gunbelt: The Military Remapping of Industrial America* (New York: Oxford University Press, 1991), 3.

23. James L. Clayton, "Defense Spending: Key to California's Growth," *Western Political Quarterly* 15 (June 1962): 280. The number refers to all defense contracts in the United States.

24. Ibid.; James L. Clayton, "The Impact of the Cold War on the Economies of California and Utah, 1946–1965," *Pacific Historical Review* 36 (November 1967): 449.

25. Nash, *The American West Transformed*, 25.

26. Clayton, "Defense Spending," 283.

27. Clayton, "The Impact of the Cold War," 459.

28. Ibid., 460.

29. Spencer C. Olin, "Globalization and the Politics of Locality: Orange County, California, in the Cold War Era," *Western Historical Quarterly* 22 (May 1991): 148.

30. Clayton, "Defense Spending," 286.

31. Security First National Bank, *The Growth and Economic Stature of Orange County*, May 1967, 4.

32. Ibid., 4.

33. *Orange County Industrial News*, 1959–64.

34. Olin, "Globalization and the Politics of Locality," 146; Markusen et al., *The Rise of the Gunbelt*, 104–5.

35. Security First National Bank, *The Growth and Economic Stature of Orange County*, November 1961.

36. *Orange County Industrial News*, September 1959, 21.

37. Olin, "Globalization and the Politics of Locality," 148–49.

38. On the seeds of the decline of the cities of the urban North, see Sugrue, *The Origins of the Urban Crisis*.

39. Richard Dale Batman, "Great Cities Grow on Citrus Lands," *Journal of the West* 4 (October 1965): 573.

40. Security First National Bank, *The Growth and Economic Stature of Orange County*, November 1961.

41. John M. Findlay, *Magic Lands: Western Cityscapes and American Culture after 1940* (Berkeley: University of California Press, 1992), 57–60.

42. Ibid., 57–63.

43. Security First National Bank, *The Growth and Economic Stature of Orange County*, May 1967, 15.

44. *Orange County Industrial News*, September 1960; Security First National Bank, *The Growth and Economic Stature of Orange County*, November 1961, 12–14.

45. M. Gottdiener and George Kephart, "The Multinucleated Metropolitan Region: A Comparative Analysis," in *Postsuburban California: The Transformation of Orange County since World War II*, ed. Rob Kling, Spencer Olin, and Mark Poster (Berkeley: University of California Press, 1991), 40.

46. Kevin Starr, *Material Dreams: Southern California through the 1920s* (New York: Oxford University Press, 1990), 131.

47. Stephen Gould, *An Annotated Bibliography of Orange County Sources* (Tustin, Calif.: Western Association for the Advancement of Local History, 1988).

48. Starr, *Material Dreams*, 135.

49. Ibid.

50. Ernest Robert Sandeen, *The Roots of Fundamentalism: British and American Millenarianism, 1800–1930* (Chicago: University of Chicago Press, 1970), 195. See also George M. Marsden, *Fundamentalism and American Culture: The Shaping of Twentieth-Century Evangelicalism, 1870–1925* (New York: Oxford University Press, 1980), 118–19.

51. Vinson Synan, *The Holiness-Pentecostal Tradition: Charismatic Movements in the Twentieth Century* (Grand Rapids, Mich.: William B. Eerdmans, 1997), 84–106.

52. Starr, *Material Dreams*, 137.

53. L. David Lewis, "Charles Fuller," in *Twentieth-Century Shapers of American Popular Religion*, ed. Charles H. Lippy (New York: Greenwood Press, 1989), 148–55.

54. *Register*, 2 October 1963.

55. Richard Melching, "The Activities of the Ku Klux Klan in Anaheim, California, 1923–1925," *Southern California Quarterly* 56 (summer 1974), 176; Roger Morris, *Richard Milhous Nixon: The Rise of an American Politician* (New York: Henry Holt, 1990), 71. See also Christopher N. Cocoltchos, "The Invisible Government and the Viable Community: The Ku Klux Klan in Orange County, California, during the 1920s" (Ph.D. diss., University of California, Los Angeles, 1979), 20–21, 118–45. Cocoltchos notes that prior to the successful Anaheim Klavern led by Pastor Leon Myer, a klavern had briefly existed in Santa Ana.

56. Cocoltchos, "The Invisible Government and the Viable Community," 631–33.

57. Republicans won elections in Orange County even though party registration was relatively equal between the two parties, and between 1936 and 1944, Democrats held a slight majority. Despite the conservative flavor of the farming region, however, Republican politics assumed a nonpartisan flavor as a result of the cross-filing system, particularly in the 1940s and 1950s. Gordon Richmond, who served as the GOP Central Committee chairman from Orange County from 1940 to 1948, was Earl Warren's county campaign manager in 1942 and managed Warren's vice presidential campaign in 1948. But Richmond, who completely dropped out of politics by the early 1960s, argued that conservative sentiment grew strong in Orange County in the late 1950s and early 1960s: "Radicals or ultraconservatives . . . that mentality, just grew and grew in the Republican Party to the point where I became very glad that I had not chosen to stay in politics professionally." See interview with Gordon Richmond in Charles L. Beaman and Michael A. Jones, *Turmoil and Change: An Interim Report on the Politics of Orange County, California,*

1945–1979, 1980, Oral History Program, California State University, Fullerton, 18, 34–35.

58. Howard Seelye and Don Smith, "A Century of Politics in Orange County," *Los Angeles Times*, 21 March 1976.

59. Robert L. Pritchard, "Orange County during the Depressed Thirties: A Study in Twentieth-Century California Local History," *Southern California Quarterly* 50 (June 1968): 197–98.

60. Ibid., 201.

61. Mike Davis, *City of Quartz: Excavating the Future in Los Angeles* (New York: Verso, 1992), 37; Carey McWilliams, *Southern California: An Island on the Land* (Salt Lake City, Utah: Peregrine Smith Books, 1983), 294–308; Friis, *Orange County through Four Centuries*, 144–45.

62. Alan Brinkley, *Voices of Protest: Huey Long, Father Coughlin, and the Great Depression* (New York: Vintage, 1983), 226.

63. The vote on the 1938 ballot initiative suggests that many Orange Countians backed the plan: 22,506 voted for "Ham and Eggs," while 31,443 opposed it. Friis, *Orange County through Four Centuries*, 144–45. For a statewide discussion of this California pension plan, see Kevin Starr, *Endangered Dreams: The Great Depression in California* (New York: Oxford University Press, 1996), 205–7.

64. McWilliams, *Southern California*, 305.

65. Davis, *City of Quartz*, 37. For a detailed history of social and political conditions in California during the 1930s, see Starr, *Endangered Dreams*.

66. Judith Neuman, "Orange County: Through the Looking Glass," *Orange County Register*, 25 April 1982.

67. Ibid. It is important to note, however, that while Utt showed the more extreme edge of local conservatism, because of the weak party structure in California and cross-filing, state politics through the 1940s and much of the 1950s were dominated by nonpartisan candidates, such as Earl Warren and Goodwyn Knight.

68. Pritchard, "Orange County during the Depressed Thirties," 193–95.

69. Notes from Foundation for Economic Education (FEE), 21 May 1956; Nash, *The Conservative Intellectual Movement in America since 1945*, 24.

70. Eckard V. Toy, "Spiritual Mobilization: The Failure of an Ultra-Conservative Ideal," *Pacific Northwest Quarterly* 61 (April 1970): 77–86; Toy, "The Conservative Connection: The Chairman of the Board Took LSD before Timothy Leary," *American Studies* 21 (fall 1980): 68, 72–73.

71. *Southern California Business*, 29 February 1960, 1.

72. Starr, *Endangered Dreams*, 156–194; see also Clarke A. Chambers, *California Farm Organizations: A Historical Study of the Grange, the Farm*

Bureau, and the Associated Farmers, 1929–1941 (Berkeley: University of California Press, 1952), 162, 185, 196–202; Gilbert Gonzalez, *Labor and Community: Mexican Citrus Worker Villages in a Southern California County, 1900–1950* (Urbana: University of Illinois Press, 1984), 135–82.

73. For battles between the Right and the Left in this period, see Starr, *Endangered Dreams.*

74. Confidential Memorandum, Better America Federation, 19 September 1950, box 1, Margaret Kerr Papers, Secretary of the Board and Manager, Better America Federation, HIWRP. See also Starr, *Endangered Dreams*, 156–157.

75. Lists were broken down according to industry and included, for example, oil, aircraft, and maritime. See "CPUSA members," box 1, Margaret Kerr Papers, HIWRP.

76. Confidential Memorandum, Better America Federation, 19 September 1950; letter from James E. Davis to California Oil & Gas Association, 18 January 1936, box 1, Margaret Kerr Papers, HIWRP.

77. M. J. Heale, "Red Scare Politics: California's Campaign against Un-American Activities, 1940–1970," *Journal of American Studies* 20 (1986): 13–14.

78. Ibid.

79. Senator Jack B. Tenney, "The Fight to Save America," acceptance speech, Christian Nationalist Party, 14 September 1952, Biltmore Hotel, Los Angeles, box 6, Radical Right Collection, HIWRP.

80. Morris, *Richard Milhous Nixon*, 321–29.

81. Ibid., 580–81; see also Greg Mitchell, *Tricky Dick and the Pink Lady: Richard Nixon vs. Helen Gahagan Douglas—Sexual Politics and the Red Scare, 1950* (New York: Random House, 1998).

82. The newspaper went through a series of name changes. The *Santa Ana Register* became simply the *Register* on 12 November 1952, and on 19 May 1985, it was changed to the *Orange County Register.*

83. *The Copley Press* (Aurora, Ill.: Copley Press, 1953), 161; Robert Gottlieb and Irene Wolt, *Thinking Big: The Story of the Los Angeles Times, Its Publishers, and Their Influence on Southern California* (New York: Putnam, 1977), 366–72.

84. Kleppner, "Politics without Parties," 328–31; Nash, *World War II and the West*, 215–16.

85. The resentment that regional entrepreneurs harbored toward Washington was mirrored by county and city boosters. In a speech to the Santa Ana service clubs, Mayor Bowron of Los Angeles—who had commissioned a study of the official register of the Washington government and found that of 3,800 people in the federal administration, only 27 had a connection to the south-

land—complained that, of these, "not a single person . . . from all of Southern California, is in any position where he has any part in governmental policy making. . . . Show me one, just one, from Southern California who helps make policy at Washington." Roger W. Lotchin, *Fortress California, 1910–1961: From Warfare to Welfare* (New York: Oxford University Press, 1992), 153.

86. Pritchard, "Orange County during the Depressed Thirties," 194.

87. Brinkley, "The Problem of American Conservatism," 418.

88. Federal ownership of the Tidelands was one hot political issue in California that led to an antifederal control ethos among regional elites. In Orange County itself, developer Ross Cortese serves as an illustration of the conflicts that occurred time and again between new western entrepreneurs and the federal government, and of their contribution to an antifederal regional ethos. The government presence in the county presented a formidable obstacle to Cortese's dream of retirement communities. The El Toro Marine Corps Air Base, the largest and most important base in the county, sought to prevent the construction of Leisure World on land adjacent to the base, arguing that the planned development would interfere with the base's mission. Opposition by the Marine Corps led to denied financing applications and problems gaining zoning, as well as to restrictions on how Cortese could develop his land and to suits and countersuits between Cortese and the Marine Corps over the next twenty-five years. See Tracy E. Strevey and associates, *Fulfilling Retirement Dreams: The First Twenty-five Years of Leisure World, Laguna Hills* (Laguna Hills, Calif.: Leisure World Historical Society of Laguna Hills, 1989), 10.

89. *Register*, 17 April 1948.

90. Pritchard, "Orange County during the Depressed Thirties," 194–98.

91. *Orange County Industrial News*, September 1960, 10.

92. Ibid., November 1961, 19.

93. Ibid., 18.

94. Edna Slocum, interview with author, 26 August 1994. In addition, another activist commented on the meaning conservative politics provided her life in Orange County, remarking, "I was interested in politics, even before I came to Orange County. But in Orange County, it was a way of life. It was my social life, my hobby; it wasn't my job, but it was everything else." Lundberg, interview.

95. This concept is borrowed from M. Gottdiener, who asserts that Orange County, like other suburban regions, underwent this form of development. See "Orange County's Built Environment: An Interview with M. Gottdiener," *Orange County Studies* 2 (spring 1989): 4; see also M. Gottdiener, *Planned Sprawl: Private and Public Interests in Suburbia* (Beverly Hills, Calif.: Sage, 1977).

96. M. Gottdiener makes the same argument with reference to Suffolk County, Long Island. See *Planned Sprawl*, 9–12.

97. Marcida Dodson, "Anaheim: The Little Town That Had Big Plans," *Los Angeles Times*, 6 July 1982.

98. Schiesl, "Designing the Model Community," 62–63.

99. Strevey and associates, *Fulfilling Retirement Dreams*, 4.

100. Ibid., 6.

101. Ibid., 5

102. Michael M. Hertel, "Community Associations and Their Politics: An Evaluation of Twelve Community Associations on the Irvine Ranch" (Ph.D. diss., Claremont Graduate School, 1972), 19–30.

103. Schiesl, "Designing the Model Community," 62–63.

104. Ibid., 68–69.

105. Hertel, "Community Association and Their Politics," x.

106. Schiesl, "Designing the Model Community," 62–63.

107. Ibid., 65–68.

108. Ibid., 65.

109. Cultural geographers and urban studies scholars have argued that spatial distinctiveness and the built environment have important social consequences and contain ideological meaning that can and should be "read." See M. Gottdiener, *The Social Production of Urban Space* (Austin: University of Texas Press, 1985), 1–24. For a critical review of the arguments on the malformations of the western urban space, see Findlay, *Magic Lands*, 47–51.

110. *Register*, 19 June 1961.

111. Ibid.

112. More than 14 percent of the workforce were professionals and semi-professionals; 10 percent were managers, officials, and proprietors; 22 percent were in sales or clerical work. Skilled workers made up just under 15 percent, and unskilled operatives and laborers under 19 percent of the workforce. Military personnel made up just over 4 percent of the population. Stanford Research Institute, *Orange County: Its Economic Growth, 1940–1980*, supplement (Pasadena: Stanford Research Institute, 1962), A-11.

113. The amount is equivalent to $33,000–$49,000 in 1998 dollars. Orange County Planning Department, Population Research Committee, *Quarterly Population Report*, 30 June 1963.

114. Orange County Planning Department, Population Research Committee, *Quarterly Population Report*, 30 September 1963.

115. Davis, *City of Quartz*, 153–218.

116. Security First National Bank, *The Growth and Economic Stature of Orange County*, November 1961.

117. James Q. Wilson has also noted the importance of these forces in contributing to the conservative political ethos of the region. See Wilson, "A Guide to Reagan Country," 39–45.

118. *Register*, 5 August 1969.

119. U.S. Department of Commerce, Bureau of the Census, *United States Census of the Population, 1960*, 6, Characteristics of the Population, part 6, California, 6–186.

120. The population of individuals of Hispanic origin stood at 52,575 in 1960. See U.S. Department of Commerce, Bureau of the Census, *United States Census of Population, 1960*, Subject Reports, Persons of Spanish Surnames, 185.

121. C. Wollenberg, "*Mendez v. Westminster*: Race, Nationality, and Segregation in California Schools," *California Historical Quarterly* 53 (winter 1974): 317–33; Wollenberg, "All Deliberate Speed" (Ph.D. diss., University of California, Irvine, 1976). Orange County, in fact, became the site of one of the first important challenges to school segregation in the Supreme Court decision *Mendez v. Westminster*. Gonzalo Mendez, a popular café owner, and some 5,000 similarly affected persons had brought suit because their children were forced into schools designated for "Mexicans."

122. Galal Kernahan, "Racism in Suburbia: A Constructive Answer," reprinted from *Christian Century*, 10 April 1957; Robert Bland, "Report on Garden Grove," issued by the Los Angeles County Conference on Community Relations, document 217.2, SC-ACLU Papers.

123. Kernahan, "Racism in Suburbia"; Bland, "Report on Garden Grove," SC-ACLU Papers.

124. *Register*, 30 June 1961.

125. Joshua White, interview by Lillie King and Chris Kirby, 1975, in "Harvest," Oral History Program, California State University, Fullerton.

126. Robert Bernhagen, "The Magnolia School District: A Case Study in Neo-McCarthyism" (Master's thesis, California State College, Fullerton, 1966), 15.

127. U.S. Department of Commerce, Bureau of the Census, *United States Census of the Population, 1960*, part 6, California.

128. Southern California Research Council, *Migration and the Southern California Economy*, report 12 (Los Angeles: Occidental College, 1964), 12.

129. Additionally, of 164,804 married couples in the county, 104,758 included husbands under forty-five years of age. Robert Seng-Pui Wong, "A Study of Population Growth and Its Impact in Orange County, California" (Ph.D. diss., University of California, Irvine, 1974), 104–7.

130. Kling, Olin, and Poster, "The Emergence of Postsuburbia," 3.

131. Most had seen service in World War II and Korea. In the nation as a whole, only 37 percent of men over age fourteen had been members of the armed forces. U.S. Department of Commerce, Bureau of the Census, "Estimated Number of Veterans in Civil Life, 1865–1970," *Historical Statistics of the United States*, vol. 2 (White Plains, N.Y.: Kraus International, 1989), 1145; U.S. Department of Commerce, Bureau of the Census, "Marital Status of Population by Age and Sex, 1890–1970," *Historical Statistics of the United States*, vol. 1 (White Plains, N.Y.: Kraus International, 1989), 20; U.S. Department of Commerce, Bureau of the Census, *United States Census of the Population, 1960*, part 6, Characteristics of the Population, California. The large number of veterans reinforced a sense of commitment to defending America against perceived threats from within and without. According to at least one conservative activist, it was the large number of ex-servicemen that explained the strong conservative ethos in the county. As she put it some thirty years later: "The men having come back from the service, they got roots and they had time for politics. They knew what they didn't like . . . and they knew how they thought." While her explanation is incomplete (especially since veterans were often strong unionists and staunch defenders of New Deal entitlements), she correctly perceived that the large number of veterans reinforced the region's strong drive for God, country, and the "American way." Lois Lundberg, interview with author.

132. Kling, Olin, and Poster, "The Emergence of Postsuburbia," 3.

133. California Department of Motor Vehicles, *Migration to California: A Sample of 31,358 Families Registering an Out of State Vehicle, January–April 1962* 13 (March 1963), 13–15.

134. Ibid.

135. *Los Angeles Times*, 21 March 1976.

136. Ibid.

137. Leland D. Hine, *Baptists in Southern California* (Valley Forge, Pa.: Judson Press, 1966), 168–69.

138. *Orange County Telephone Directory*, March 1950 (Pacific Telephone and Telegraph, 1950); *Telephone Directory, Orange County*, November 1960 (Pacific Telephone and Telegraph, 1960).

139. *Orange County Telephone Directory*, March 1950; *Telephone Directory, Orange County*, November 1960.

140. *Official Catholic Directory*, Anno Domini 1951 (New York: Kennedy, 1951); *Official Catholic Directory*, Anno Domini 1961 (New York: Kennedy, 1961).

141. R. I. Morris, ed., *Orange County Progress Report* 2 (March 1962), 12.

142. Orange County Planning Department, Population Research Committee, *Quarterly Population Report*, 30 June 1962.

143. *Orange County Industrial News*, November 1961, 37, 48.

144. Orange County Research Institute, *Orange County Newsletter*, reprinted in *Orange County Industrial News*, October 1961.

Chapter 2

1. Letter from William Brashears to educators, n.d., Orange County School of Anti-Communism folder, FCC; *Register*, 5 March 1961, 8 March 1961, 9 March 1961, 7 September 1961; Bernhagen, "The Magnolia School District," 37.

2. *Los Angeles Times*, 9 March 1961.

3. *Register*, 5 March 1961.

4. Ibid., 23 June 1961.

5. Ibid., 25 June 1961, 5 November 1962; undated leaflet by the Californians' Committee to Combat Communism, Californians' Committee to Combat Communism folder, Freedom Forum Bookstore folder, FCC; *Freedom Newsletter* 5, July–August 1961, Freedom Forum Bookstore folder, FCC.

6. See, for example, Joe R. Feagin, *Free Enterprise City: Houston in Political-Economic Perspective* (New Brunswick, N.J.: Rutgers University Press, 1988); Kirkpatrick Sale, *Power Shift: The Rise of the Southern Rim and Its Challenge to the Eastern Establishment* (New York: Random House, 1975); Schulman, *From Cotton Belt to Sunbelt*, 135–231; Gerald D. Nash and Richard W. Etulain, eds., *The Twentieth-Century West: Historical Interpretations* (Albuquerque: University of New Mexico Press, 1989).

7. The strength of the movement there gained Orange County the reputation as the national home of the John Birch Society. (The actual headquarters was in Belmont, Massachusetts.) Although stereotypes exaggerated the county's right-wing character, even earning it the dubious distinction, according to a 1968 article in *Fortune*, as "America's nut country," the county did indeed witness an exceptionally vigorous conservative movement. See, for example, Stone, "The John Birch Society of California," 1; Sheldon Zalznick, "The Double Life of Orange County," *Fortune*, October 1968; Larry Peterson, "Stereotype: OC's Image as Bastion of Conservatism Dies Hard," *Register*, 29 June 1987; Wilson, "A Guide to Reagan Country," 37–42.

8. Jerold Simmons, "The Origins of the Campaign to Abolish HUAC, 1956–1961: The California Connection," *Southern California Quarterly* 64 (summer 1982): 141–57.

9. *Garden Grove News,* 8 January 1962; *Anaheim Bulletin,* 5 November 1960.

10. "Notes on facts in Dvorman case," box 910, SC-ACLU Papers; regular minutes of meetings, Board of Trustees, Magnolia School District, Anaheim California, 1 August 1960, 6 September 1960.

11. "Notes on facts in Dvorman case," box 910, SC-ACLU Papers.

12. Simmons, "The Origins of the Campaign to Abolish HUAC," 143; Douglas T. Miller, *On Our Own: Americans in the Sixties* (Lexington, Mass.: D. C. Heath, 1996), 182.

13. "Notes on facts in Dvorman case," box 910, SC-ACLU Papers; Simmons, "The Origins of the Campaign to Abolish HUAC," 151.

14. California Legislature, Senate Fact-Finding Subcommittee on Un-American Activities, *Eighth Report of the Senate Fact-Finding Subcommittee on Un-American Activities,* 1943, 107; see also California Legislature, Senate Investigating Committee on Education, *The 1951 Hearings: Tenth Report,* 1951, 83. A later report exonerated the national ACLU but still found that the Southern California chapter "devoted an unusually large part of its time and energies to the protection and defense of Communist Party members and to the support of Communist organizations and fronts." See California Legislature, Senate Fact-Finding Subcommittee on Un-American Activities in California, *Tenth Report of the Senate Fact-Finding Committee on Un-American Activities,* 1959, quoted in *Garden Grove News,* 25 October 1960.

15. Heale, "Red Scare Politics," 18.

16. Simmons, "The Origins of the Campaign to Abolish HUAC," 141–57; Heale, "Red Scare Politics," 5–37; M. J. Heale, *American Anticommunism: Combating the Enemy Within, 1830–1970* (Baltimore: Johns Hopkins University Press, 1990), 196.

17. *Register,* 13 April 1961.

18. Bernhagen, "The Magnolia School District," 19–20.

19. Regular minutes of meetings, Board of Trustees, Magnolia School District, Anaheim California, 1 August 1960, 6 September 1960.

20. "Notes on facts in Dvorman case," box 910, SC-ACLU Papers.

21. "Four Reasons Why Joel Dvorman Must Be Recalled from the Magnolia School District Board of Trustees," leaflet, box 910, SC-ACLU Papers.

22. *Register,* 4 November 1960.

23. Marilyn Ryan, interview with author, 6 October 1998.

24. *Register,* 13 April 1961, 18 April 1961.

25. Ibid., 18 April 1961.

26. *Los Angeles Times,* 8 January 1961, 15 January 1961; *Register,* 3 April 1961.

27. *Freedom Newsletter* 5 (July–August 1961), FCC.

28. *Register*, 22 June 1961; letter from William Brashears to educators, n.d., Orange County School of Anti-Communism folder, FCC.

29. Raymond E. Wolfinger, Barbara Kaye Wolfinger, Kenneth Prewitt, and Sheilah Rosenhack, "America's Radical Right: Politics and Ideology," in *The American Right Wing: Readings in Political Behavior*, ed. Robert A. Schoen-berger (New York: Holt, Rinehart and Winston, 1969), 9–47.

30. Leo P. Ribuffo, *The Old Christian Right: The Protestant Far Right from the Great Depression to the Cold War* (Philadelphia: Temple University Press, 1983), 259; Clyde Wilcox, *God's Warriors: The Christian Right in Twentieth-Century America* (Baltimore: Johns Hopkins University Press, 1992), 74.

31. Wilcox, *God's Warriors*, 74.

32. *Christian Anti-Communism Crusade Newsletter*, 1 December 1966, box 32, KM Papers.

33. *Time*, 9 February 1962, 19.

34. Letter from William Brashears to educators, n.d., Orange County School of Anti-Communism folder, FCC.

35. Ibid.

36. Sullivan, interview; Peggy and Rufus Pearce and Shirley and Harold Muckenthaler, interviews with author, 4 October 1998.

37. *Register*, 18 June 1961, 6 April 1961.

38. Ibid., 26 November 1961.

39. Ibid., 2 March 1961, 3 March 1961.

40. *Freedom Newsletter* 5 (July–August 1961), FCC.

41. *Freedom Newsletter* 6 (March–April 1962), FCC.

42. Pearce and Muckenthaler, interviews; *Freedom Newsletter* 5 (July–August 1961), FCC.

43. Sullivan, interview.

44. Letter from Michael Owalube to Senator Thomas Kuchel, 10 May 1961, carton 8, TK Papers.

45. "Memorandum Re: a New Magazine," n.d., box 10, James Burnham Papers, HIWRP; Russell Kirk, "The Principles of a Monthly Journal," n.d., box 39, Henry Regnery Papers, HIWRP.

46. Arnold Forster and Benjamin R. Epstein, *Danger on the Right* (New York: Random House, 1964), 188.

47. California Legislature, Senate Fact-Finding Subcommittee on Un-American Activities in California, *Twelfth Report of the Senate Fact-Finding Subcommittee on Un-American Activities*, 1963, 20; Anti-Defamation League of B'nai B'rith, "The John Birch Society, A Pre-publication Summary," January

1963, folder 4, box 17, Leonard Finder Papers, Dwight D. Eisenhower Presidential Library, Abilene, Kansas.

48. "The Sharon Statement," *New Guard*, March 1969.

49. Popularity is here measured in terms of receipts received. See Wilcox, *God's Warriors*, 71; Wolfinger et al., "America's Radical Right."

50. Attention to the right-wing resurgence ranged from journalistic articles and books to academic scholarship. See, for example, P. Horton, "Revivalism on the Far Right," *Reporter*, 20 July 1961, 25–29; A. Gottfried and S. Davidson, "New Right in Action," *Nation*, 29 July 1961, 48–51; "Rightist Revival: Who's on the Far Right," *Look*, 13 March 1962, 21–28; Forster and Epstein, *Danger on the Right*; Irwin Suall, *The American Ultras: The Extreme Right and the Military-Industrial Complex* (New York: New America, 1962); Daniel Bell, ed., *The Radical Right* (Garden City, N.Y.: Doubleday, 1963).

51. Forster and Epstein, *Danger on the Right*; Bell, "The Dispossessed," 2, 33. One author, so enchanted with the notion of the pluralist consensus, went so far as to characterize any deviation from pluralism, from either the Left or the Right, as pathological. See, for example, Franklin Hamlin Littell, *Wild Tongues: A Handbook of Social Pathology* (New York: Macmillan, 1969).

52. See Bell, "The Dispossessed," 1–38; and Richard Hofstadter, "Pseudo-Conservatism Revisited: A Postscript," in *The Radical Right*, ed. Daniel Bell (Garden City, N.Y.: Doubleday, 1963), 81–86.

53. The characterization of the Right in this period as waging a "rearguard" battle against "modernity" was made by Bell in "The Dispossessed," and by Hofstadter in "Pseudo-Conservatism Revisited."

54. Miles, *The Odyssey of the American Right*; George Mayer, *The Republican Party, 1854–1966*, 2d ed. (New York: Oxford University Press, 1967), 475–527; Reinhard, *The Republican Right since 1945*, 97–137.

55. Allen J. Matusow, *The Unraveling of America: A History of Liberalism in the 1960s* (New York: Harper and Row, 1984), 3; Heale, *American Anticommunism*, 195–96.

56. *Los Angeles Times*, 6 November 1958; *Oakland Tribune*, 16 January 1959; Jeff Broadwater, *Adlai Stevenson and American Politics: The Odyssey of a Cold War Liberal* (New York: Twayne, 1994), 172.

57. Broadwater, *Adlai Stevenson and American Politics*, 172.

58. *Los Angeles Times*, 21 March 1976.

59. Friedrich A. Hayek, *The Road to Serfdom* (Chicago: University of Chicago Press, 1944).

60. James Townsend, interview with author, 2 October 1998.

61. Tom Anderson, column, *Register*, 2 April 1962.

62. National Council of Churches, *Highlights of 1963* (New York: National Council of Churches, 1964); on the social action of the National Council of Churches, see also James F. Findlay, *Church People in the Struggle: The National Council of Churches and the Black Freedom Movement, 1950–1970* (New York: Oxford University Press, 1993); Henry J. Pratt, *The Liberalization of American Protestantism: A Case Study in Complex Organizations* (Detroit: Wayne State University Press, 1972); K. L[loyd]. Billingsley, *From Mainline to Sideline: The Social Witness of the National Council of Churches* (Washington, D.C.: Ethics and Public Policy Center, 1990).

63. Diane Ravitch, *The Troubled Crusade: American Education, 1945–1980* (New York: Basic Books, 1983), 233; David B. Tyack, ed., *Turning Points in American Educational History* (Waltham, Mass.: Blaisdell, 1967); Clarence Karier, *The Individual, Society, and Education: A History of American Educational Ideas* (Urbana: University of Illinois Press, 1986).

64. "Our Traditional Christmas Must Be Preserved," *Magnolia Way*, December 1963, in author's possession.

65. *Register*, 24 November 1961.

66. Thomas G. Paterson, *Contesting Castro: The United States and the Triumph of the Cuban Revolution* (New York: Oxford University Press, 1994).

67. Pearce and Muckenthaler, interviews.

68. Nash, *The Conservative Intellectual Movement in America since 1945*, 1–3.

69. This new optimism and drive for reform among liberals are outlined by Matusow, *The Unraveling of America*, 3–29.

70. Bernhagen, "The Magnolia School District," 41.

71. *Anaheim Star*, 27 October 1960.

72. *Register*, 5 December 1960, 8 April 1961; *Los Angeles Times*, 2 April 1961.

73. *Register*, 8 April 1961; *Los Angeles Times*, 2 April 1961; various newspaper clippings, Dvorman folder, box 910, SC-ACLU Papers.

74. Bernhagen, "The Magnolia School District," 39.

75. *Register*, 9 April 1961.

76. Ibid.

77. *Los Angeles Times*, 8 January 1964; *Register*, 10 January 1964; "The American Heritage Program in the Lampasas Schools," n.d.; regular minutes of meetings, Board of Trustees, Magnolia School District, Anaheim, California, 1959–64.

78. "Our Traditional Christmas Must Be Preserved."

79. "Materials, Methods, and Morals," *Magnolia Way*, n.d; regular minutes of meetings, Board of Trustees, Magnolia School District, Anaheim, Cali-

fornia, 1961–64; Joseph N. Bell, "I Fought Against Hatred among My Neighbors," *Good Housekeeping*, September 1965, reprint, FCC.

80. *Christian Science Monitor*, 4 May 1964; *Los Angeles Times*, 4 February 1964.

81. *Los Angeles Times*, 11 March 1964; *Register*, 23 January 1964, 29 April 1964, 30 April 1964.

82. *Register*, 24 November 1961.

83. Ibid., 6 June 1961.

84. Ibid., 8 March 1961, 5 June 1961.

85. Ibid., 19 November 1961.

86. Ibid., 25 November 1960.

87. "Four Reasons Why Joel Dvorman Must Be Recalled from the Magnolia School District Board of Trustees," leaflet, box 910, SC-ACLU Papers.

88. Nolan Frizzelle, interview with author, 23 November 1992.

89. Ibid.

90. Benjamin R. Epstein and Arnold Forster, *Report on the John Birch Society, 1966* (New York: Vintage, 1966), 3.

91. California Legislature, Senate Fact-Finding Subcommittee on Un-American Activities, *Twelfth Report of the Senate Fact-Finding Committee on Un-American Activities*, 1963, 3, 58–59; *Los Angeles Times*, 5 March 1961; *Register*, 9 April 1961.

92. Robert Welch, *The Blue Book of the John Birch Society* (Belmont, Mass.: Western Islands, 1961).

93. Epstein and Forster, *Report on the John Birch Society, 1966*, 1–2. In 1965, SDS claimed 10,000 members, approximately one-tenth of John Birch Society membership during the same period. See James Miller, *"Democracy Is in the Streets": From Port Huron to the Siege of Chicago* (New York: Simon and Schuster, 1985), 255.

94. *Register*, 2 April 1961; Lipset and Raab, *The Politics of Unreason*, 304–5.

95. *Boston Herald*, 12 December 1961.

96. Memorandum from Marvin Liebman regarding the John Birch Society, 16 January 1962, Marvin Liebman Papers, HIWRP.

97. *The Register*, 8 April, 1961, 16 April 1961.

98. John B. Judis, *William F. Buckley, Jr., Patron Saint of the Conservatives* (New York: Simon and Schuster, 1988), 196–97.

99. Pearce and Muckenthaler, interviews.

100. Letter to Federal Bureau of Investigation, 7 November 1960, name withheld, Federal Bureau of Investigation, John Birch Society, California files, file no. 100–59001–67.

101. *Freedom Newsletter* 6 (March–April 1962), FCC.

102. Letters from Patricia Hitt to Thomas Kuchel, 21 February 1961, 31 January 1961, TK Papers.

103. California Legislature, Senate Fact-Finding Subcommittee on Un-American Activities in California, *Twelfth Report of the Senate Fact-Finding Committee on Un-American Activities*, 1963, 58–59.

104. This number has been derived from the California legislative estimates for the state. The senate committee investigating the society estimated 20 members for each chapter. Since it counted thirty-eight chapters for Orange County, this would make 760 members. See California Legislature, Senate Fact-Finding Subcommittee on Un-American Activities in California, *Twelfth Report of the Senate Fact-Finding Committee on Un-American Activities*, 1963, 58–59. Additionally, it is highly likely that some members did not belong to individual chapters but were members of the home office. Barbara Shell Stone has found a good many of the members in her study of the California John Birch Society. See Stone, "The John Birch Society of California," 43–44.

105. *Los Angeles Times*, 21 March 1976; Hallan-Gibson, *The Golden Promise*, 244.

106. Stone, "The John Birch Society of California," 43–44.

107. Jan Averill, interview with author, 3 October 1998.

108. Sullivan, interview.

109. Stone, "The John Birch Society of California," 53–54.

110. Letter from Mr. and Mrs. Nelson to Edmund G. Brown, 22 September 1966, carton 878, EGB Papers.

111. Report on John Birch Society meeting, 8 May 1963, San Francisco, California, in author's possession.

112. *Bulletin*, September 1963.

113. Alan F. Westin, "The John Birch Society: 'Radical Right' and 'Extreme Left' in the Political Context of Post World War II–1962," in *The Radical Right*, ed. Daniel Bell (Garden City, N.Y.: Doubleday, 1963), 208–9.

114. Undated leaflet, Californians' Committee to Combat Communism folder, FCC.

115. *New York Times*, 8 November 1962, 18; 27 October 1962, 24; 25 October 1962, 10; 8 July 1962, 24.

116. Ibid., 8 November 1962, 18.

117. Ibid., 27 October 1962, 24.

118. Ibid., 8 July 1962, 24.

119. Ibid., 25 October 1962, 10.

120. California Secretary of State, *Statement of Vote*, General Election, 6 November 1962.

121. *New York Times*, 8 July 1962, 24; *Register*, 8 July 1962.

122. *Register*, 8 July 1962.

123. Ibid., 20 April 1962, 8 July 1962, 25 April 1962.

124. Ibid., 8 July 1962; undated solicitation letter from D. W. Kirkpatrick for *Liberty Bell*, in author's possession.

125. Townsend, interview.

126. Bee Gathright, interview with author, 5 October 1998.

127. Ibid.

128. Quakers in Iowa abandoned many of the precepts associated with strict Quakerism in favor of a Protestant evangelistic style. Influenced by settlers from the South, the dominant Quaker style in Indiana and Iowa became little different from other strict Protestant evangelical sects, complete with pastor, hymns, and sermons. See, for example, Louis Thomas Jones, *The Quakers of Iowa* (Iowa City: State Historical Society of Iowa, 1914), 95–117.

129. Gathright, interview.

130. Lundberg, interview.

131. Leaders' names were traced back in city directories to determine the year in which they originally appeared. I was able to determine how long these leaders had been residents within their communities. This sample suggests only their length of time at their present address or within the immediate city of residence, since names were traced back within their local city directories. They may have migrated from other areas within the county or from nearby Los Angeles.

132. Leaders' names from four local right-wing initiatives were culled from newspaper articles and organizational literature. The names were then traced through local city directories in order to identify occupations. The few women who were listed among the leadership were identified by their husbands' occupations.

133. I have drawn this conclusion from a perusal of letters by right-wing adherents to the "Clearing House" section of the *Register* in the first years of the 1960s. They often quote long passages from books or recommend particular government reports or national right-wing journals. They are, moreover, well versed in foreign policy issues. My findings regarding the class status of activists also affirm the conclusions of social science studies of the John Birch Society and the Christian Anti-Communism Crusade conducted during the 1960s, which found that members of these organizations were better educated and wealthier than the average American. See, for example, Lipset and Raab, *The Politics of Unreason*, 295; Stone, "The John Birch Society of California"; Frederick W. Grupp Jr., "Social Correlates of Political Activists: The John Birch Society and the ADA" (Ph.D. diss., University of Pennsylvania, 1968); Wol-

finger et al., "America's Radical Right," 17–19; Seymour Martin Lipset, "Three Decades of the Radical Right," in *The Radical Right*, ed. Daniel Bell (Garden City, N.Y.: Doubleday, 1963), 354; Hixson, *The Search for the American Right Wing*, 77.

134. *Register*, 8 March 1961, 13 April 1961.

135. Letter from Acting Secretary, Doctors for America, to members, 21 September 1962, in author's possession.

136. "Celebrate! Orange County's First One Hundred Years," *Los Angeles Times*, 22 May 1988.

137. Names of the recall committee are listed in an anti-Dvorman leaflet. I traced these individuals within telephone books and city directories to determine their occupations. See "Four Reasons Why Joel Dvorman Must Be Recalled from the Magnolia School District Board of Trustees," leaflet, box 910, SC-ACLU Papers.

138. In 1962, 12,103 military personnel were stationed in the county, making up 4.8 percent of the employed population. See Stanford Research Institute, *Orange County: Its Economic Growth, 1940–1980*, supplement, 7.

139. *Los Angeles Times*, 21 March 1976.

140. Lundberg, interview. While her husband "loved Goldwater," Lundberg was a friend of Richard Nixon and campaigned hard for him in 1960 and 1962, placing her closer to mainline Republicanism than many of the right-wing activists in Orange County, who worked only reluctantly (or not at all) for Nixon. Still, she considered herself a staunch conservative.

141. Eleanor Howe, interview with author, 21 August 1994.

142. Slocum, interview.

143. *Los Angeles Times*, 21 March 1976; *Register* 18 April 1961.

144. This sample was randomly drawn from letters over the six-year period 1960–66, with the bulk of the letters drawn from the first three years of the 1960s. I included religious conservatives libertarians and virulent anticommunists in my definition of "right-wing." Letters often included an address or, at the very least, the city in which the writer resided, which made precise identification possible. These names were then traced through city directories. If there were too many individuals with the same name to make precise identification possible, or if the name was not listed, these names were dropped from the sample. Of a sample of more than 200 randomly drawn letter writers, I was able to identify 110 through city directories. Their occupations were traced through these directories. When no occupation was listed in a particular directory, I checked prior years and listed the occupation given in previous years. Female letter writers, if married, were ranked by their husbands' occupa-

tions in order to determine family class standing. Since directories listed only the husband's occupation as the head of the family, it is difficult to know if these women held jobs. Certainly, it is clear from my oral history interviews that some did, although even these women saw their primary occupation as housewife.

145. Seventy-seven of 110 letter writers were from the middle and upper-middle classes.

146. This was true within the constituency of the John Birch Society of Southern California, according to a study by Barbara Shell Stone. See Stone, "The John Birch Society of California." Certainly, within my own work I have found that women did a good deal of the letter stuffing and precinct walking among the grass roots.

147. Stone, "The John Birch Society of California," 87–88.

148. Sullivan, interview.

149. Lundberg, interview.

150. Pearce and Muckenthaler, interviews; Gathright, interview.

151. Averill, interview.

152. Kieffer (formerly Kielsmeier), interview; Gathright, Averill, Lundberg, and Sullivan, interviews.

153. *Register*, 4 June 1961.

154. Gathright, interview.

155. *Luskey's Official Anaheim Criss-Cross City Directory* (Anaheim, Calif.: Luskey Brothers, 1957–58, 1960, 1963, 1964).

156. Ibid.

157. Sullivan, interview.

158. *Los Angeles Times*, 6 July 1982.

159. Townsend, interview.

160. Ibid.

161. Ibid.

162. Tom Rogers, interview with author, 2 October 1998.

163. Pearce and Muckenthaler, interviews.

164. Daniel Bell so labeled the social base of the Right in this period. See Bell, "The Dispossessed," 1–38.

165. Armstrong Dowell, interview with author, 6 October 1998.

166. David Bergland, interview with author, 5 October 1998.

167. Slocum, interview.

168. Sullivan, interview.

169. James Penner, *Goliath: The Life of Robert Schuller* (New York: HarperCollins, 1992), 33–51.

170. Gathright, interview.

171. Ibid.

172. Lundberg, interview.

173. *Los Angeles Times*, 6 July 1982.

174. The characterization of the Right in this period as waging a "rear-guard" battle against "modernity" was made by Bell in "The Dispossessed," 1–38, and by Hofstadter in "Pseudo-Conservatism Revisited," 81–86.

175. Kieffer (formerly Kielsmeier), interview.

176. Conservatives called for a reinvigoration of the family, but their strong emphasis on the nuclear family, I argue, represented a departure from the past. Calls for strengthening the family meant shoring up parental (and particularly patriarchal) authority within this smaller family unit and did not encompass a vision of larger, extended networks that had been the cornerstone of earlier understandings of the family. Such an atomized (and modern) meaning of the family helped to mute potential conflicts inherent in a simultaneous emphasis on family values and an embrace of the free market. Seemingly, the migration and mobility so many Orange Countians experienced, while uprooting them from older generations and extended kin networks, did not threaten this more limited family with disintegration.

177. Slocum, interview.

178. J. Edgar Hoover, *Masters of Deceit: The Story of Communism in America and How to Fight It* (New York: Henry Holt, 1958), 319.

179. Ibid., 320.

180. Fred Schwarz, *You Can Trust the Communists (to Be Communists)* (Englewood Cliffs, N.J.: Prentice-Hall, 1960), 8.

181. Ibid., 168, 182.

182. I draw here on Lawrence Goodwyn's formulations of the stages of "movement building." See Lawrence Goodwyn, *The Populist Moment: A Short History of the Agrarian Revolt in America* (New York: Oxford University Press, 1978), xviii–xix.

183. Sullivan, interview.

184. Slocum, interview.

185. Gathright, interview.

186. Letter to educators from R. D. Peterson, n. d. Orange County School of Anti-Communism folder, FCC.

187. Norman E. Nygaard, *Walter Knott: Twentieth Century Pioneer* (Grand Rapids, Mich.: Zondervan, 1965), 18–19.

188. Ibid., 15–22.

189. Walter Knott, "The Enterprises of Walter Knott," interview conducted by Donald J. Schippers, 1965, Oral History Program, University of California, Los Angeles.

190. Ibid., 116.

191. Robert L. Coate, Chairman, Democratic State Central Committee, "Ronald Reagan, Extremist Collaborator, An Expose," 8, in author's possesion; also in EGB papers.

192. Californians' Committee to Combat Communism folder, FCC; CFEA folder, FCC.

193. Knott, "The Enterprises of Walter Knott," interview, 112–14.

194. Ibid.; "San Francisco Riot," undated leaflet, CFEA folder, FCC.

195. Knott, "The Enterprises of Walter Knott," interview, 112–14.

196. Ibid.

197. Freedom Center leaflet, n.d., CFEA folder, FCC.

198. CFEA catalog, CFEA folder, FCC.

199. CFEA pamphlet 17, CFEA folder, FCC.

200. CFEA pamphlet 45, CFEA folder, FCC.

201. CFEA, "Freedom Study Clubs—A Guide" (CFEA, Ghost Town Station, Buena Park, n.d.), CFEA folder, FCC.

202. Ibid.

203. Letter from Walter Knott to Howard E. Kershner, Christian Freedom Foundation, 25 November 1961, Howard Kershner Papers, University of Oregon, Eugene.

204. *Orange County Industrial News*, August 1961, 19; "You Can Have Your Choice—Freedom under the U.S. Constitution, Peace at Any Price," printed in *Fullerton News-Tribune*, 27 February 1962.

205. *Orange County Industrial News*, September 1961, 22.

206. For coverage of the school, see *Los Angeles Times*, 28 August–1 September 1961.

207. David Shaw, "Knott: Tourist Mecca Developer, Conservative and Ardent Patriot," *Register*, 4 December 1981; Nygaard, *Walter Knott*.

208. Carolyn B. Knight, *Making It Happen: The Story of Carl Karcher Enterprises* (Anaheim, Calif.: Karcher Enterprises, 1981), 64–70, 85–96.

209. Ribuffo, *The Old Christian Right*, 260–61.

210. Starr, *Material Dreams*, 131–44; Synan, *The Holiness-Pentecostal Tradition*, 84–106; Frank Bartleman, *How Pentecost Came to Los Angeles* (Los Angeles: Privately printed, 1925); A. C. Valdez with James F. Scheer, *Fire on Azusa Street* (Costa Mesa, Calif.: Gift Publications, 1980).

211. Hine, *Baptists in Southern California*, 168–69.

212. This number was drawn from newspaper sources listing churches that sponsored right-wing speakers or film showings.

213. *Register*, 17 April 1961.

214. Ibid., 22 April 1961.

215. Ibid., 7 October 1962.

216. See chapter 4.

217. "Who Are the Traitors in Our Pulpits?" transcript of a sermon delivered by Dr. Bob Wells to the congregation of the Central Baptist Church of Orange County, n.d., Voice of Truth and Freedom folder, FCC; *Voice of Truth and Freedom*, January 1968, Voice of Truth and Freedom folder, FCC.

218. *Register*, 20 April 1962.

219. *Voice of Truth and Freedom*, January 1968, Voice of Truth and Freedom folder, FCC.

220. *Register*, 7 April 1962.

221. Ibid.

222. "Who Are the Traitors in Our Pulpits?" Voice of Truth and Freedom folder, FCC.

223. *Register*, 7 April 1962.

224. Ibid.; various leaflets, 1961, Voice of Truth and Freedom folder, FCC.

225. See Welch, *The Blue Book of the John Birch Society*, 48; Stone, "The John Birch Society of California," 91–92.

226. *Los Angeles Times*, 5 March 1961.

227. Wilcox, *God's Warriors*, 87–89.

228. *Register*, 23 April 1963.

229. Penner, *Goliath*, 108.

230. Dennis Voskuil, *Mountains into Goldmines: Robert Schuller and the Gospel of Success* (Grand Rapids, Mich.: William B. Eerdmans, 1983), 113–14.

231. Robert Schuller, *God's Way to the Good Life* (Grand Rapids, Mich.: William B. Eerdmans, 1963), 84, quoted in Voskuil, *Mountains into Goldmines*, 158.

232. Letter from D. W. Kirkpatrick to fellow Californians, n.d., Californians' Committee to Combat Communism folder, FCC.

233. Regular minutes of meetings, Board of Trustees, Magnolia School District, 16 December 1963.

234. Pearce and Muckenthaler, interviews.

235. Gathright, interview.

236. Westin, "The John Birch Society," 218–19; Lipset and Raab, *The Politics of Unreason*, 262–63.

237. See Francis J. Weber, *His Eminence of Los Angeles: James Francis Cardinal McIntyre* (Mission Hills, Calif.: Saint Francis Historical Society, 1997), especially 625–40. These volumes present a sympathetic biographical portrait of McIntyre. They also, however, are a good source of information on McIntyre's leadership of the Los Angeles diocese. His stance on controversial issues like Proposition 14 and his views on "patriotism and communism" are outlined.

238. Davis, *City of Quartz*, 332.

239. Ibid. See also Weber, *His Eminence of Los Angeles*, especially 625–40.

240. Davis, *City of Quartz*, 332–33; Westin, "The John Birch Society," 218–19.

241. Among those few activists whose religion I have been able to determine, a large number (though by no means a majority) were Catholic: Jim Wallace, Cathy Sullivan, Loretta Tambourine, Nolan Frizzelle, John and Mary Schmitz, Eleanor Howe, Mary Haller, Harold Muckenthaler, Tom Rogers, and Carl Karcher were local leaders and rank-and-file activists, and all were staunch Catholics. Robert Welch maintained, moreover, that 40 percent of John Birch Society members were Catholics. While studies have placed this number a good deal lower, the Right, as Seymour Martin Lipset has argued and this study confirms, held a strong appeal for the Catholics. See Lipset and Raab, *The Politics of Unreason*, 262.

242. See *Register*, 4 March 1962.

243. St. Boniface Parish bulletin, 19 November 1961, cited in *Register*, 28 November 1961.

244. Mary Breasted, *Oh! Sex Education!* (New York: Praeger, 1970), 47. Breasted asserted that two leaders of the anti–sex education struggles were St. Boniface parishioners. One of them, however, James Townsend, attended church at the behest of his wife, an active parishioner. He himself was not a Catholic.

245. *Register*, 20 April 1961.

246. Ministers of local churches were, for example, prominent in the struggle against the passage of Proposition 14. See Proposition 14 box, FCC.

247. Averill, interview.

248. *Register*, 3 March 1962, 28 November 1961.

249. Ibid., 28 April 1962.

250. Michael McFadden, "Raymond Cyrus Hoiles," *Orange County Illustrated*, September 1964, 22–23. The name of the newspaper changed from the *Santa Ana Register* to the *Register* in 1952. It since became the *Orange County Register* in 1985.

251. Orange County Planning Department, *Orange County Progress Report* 2 (March 1961), 27.

252. *Register*, 26 November 1961.

253. Ibid.

254. Slocum, interview.

255. *Register*, 20 April 1962, 26 November 1961.

256. By 1962, Orange County had two "Freedom Newspapers," the *Register* and the *Anaheim Bulletin*, with a total circulation of just under 100,000. Orange County Planning Department, *Orange County Progress Report* 2 (March 1961); Bernhagen, "The Magnolia School District," 76.

CHAPTER 3

1. *Los Angeles Times*, 6 November 1958.

2. *New York Times*, 3 May 1964; Minutes of the Meeting of the Board of Directors of the California Republican Assembly, 4–6 December 1964, box 1, CRA Papers. Estimates of membership at this time range from 14,000 to 15,000.

3. Proceedings of the Thirtieth Annual Convention of the California Republican Assembly, Fresno, California, 13–15 March 1964, box 50, CRA Papers.

4. *CRA Enterprise*, May 1964, box 11, CRA Papers.

5. Letter to Ms. Louise Leigh from William Nelligan, 9 April 1964, box 50, CRA Papers.

6. See, for example, Donovan Bess, "Putsch in the GOP," *Nation*, 11 May 1964; Jim Wood, "California Republicans: Are the Birchers Taking Over?" *Reporter*, 7 May 1964; "Right Wing Gains in Coast G.O.P. Organizations," *New York Times*, 3 May 1964, 64; and CRA clippings, box 121, CRA Papers.

7. *Nation*, 11 May 1964.

8. Nicol C. Rae, *The Decline and Fall of the Liberal Republicans: From 1952 to the Present* (New York: Oxford University Press, 1989), 57.

9. Ibid., 56–58; John Howard Kessel, *The Goldwater Coalition: Republican Strategies in 1964* (Indianapolis: Bobbs-Merrill, 1968), 87–89; White, *The Making of the President, 1964*, 112.

10. *First National Directory of "Rightist" Groups, Publications and Some Individuals in the United States and Some Foreign Countries* (San Francisco, 1957); *First National Directory of "Rightist" Groups, Publications and Some Individuals in the United States and Some Foreign Countries*, 5th. ed. (Los Angeles, 1965).

11. Knott, "The Enterprises of Walter Knott."

12. Charles Armour, district governor of the West Coast regional office of the John Birch Society, pointed out that the society wanted to "exert influence on the average congressional district. We like to have one book store, about

fifty John Birch chapters and about 1,000 members in each district." *Orange County Illustrated*, October 1973, 43. See also Epstein and Forster, *Report on the John Birch Society, 1966*, 67.

13. Epstein and Forster, *Report on the John Birch Society, 1966*, 67.

14. Letter from Howard Jarvis to the editor, *Register*, 14 April 1964.

15. Ibid.

16. Ibid.

17. See *Congressional Quarterly's Guide to U.S. Elections* (Washington, D.C.: Congressional Quarterly, Inc., 1993), 462.

18. In 1968, Wallace gained less than 7 percent of the vote in conservative Orange County, significantly less than his national strength of 13.5 percent. See California Secretary of State, *Statement of Vote*, General Election, 5 November 1968.

19. John R. Owens, Edmond Costantini, and Louis F. Weschler, *California Politics and Parties* (New York: Macmillan, 1970), 42.

20. Ibid., 47; Totton J. Anderson, "The 1958 Election in California," *Western Political Quarterly* 20 (March 1959): 276–300.

21. Rogin and Shover, *Political Change in California*, 142; Owens, Costantini, and Weschler, *California Politics and Parties*, 42–46.

22. Howard Seelye and Don Smith, "A Century of Politics in Orange County," reprint edition, *Los Angeles Times*, 21 March 1976; Beaman and Jones, *Turmoil and Change*, 15–18.

23. One of the major monuments to antipartyism in the state, cross-filing permitted a candidate for a partisan public office to seek and to gain the nomination of more than one party. The system was in operation from 1913 to 1959. In 1952, the electorate approved a change in the Elections Code that served to reduce the incidence of successful cross-filing, and in 1959, the system was fully abolished. Owens, Costantini, and Weschler, *California Politics and Parties*, 90–92; Rae, *The Decline and Fall of the Liberal Republicans*, 48; see also James Q. Wilson, "Party Organization: The Search for Power," in *The Challenge of California*, ed. Eugene C. Lee and Willis D. Hawley (Boston: Little, Brown, 1970), 55–61.

24. Letter from Glenn M. Jackson, president, Conservative Coordinating Council, to members, 30 May 1962, FCC.

25. Conservative Coordinating Council of Orange County, Statement of Objectives and Principles, 23 August 1961, FCC.

26. Frizzelle, interview.

27. Rae, *The Decline and Fall of the Liberal Republicans*, 49; Kurt Schuparra, "Barry Goldwater and Southern California Conservatism: Ideology,

Image and Myth in the 1964 California Republican Presidential Primary," *Southern California Quarterly* 74 (fall 1992): 281.

28. Minutes of the Meeting of the Board of Directors of the California Republican Assembly, 6–7 June 1959, folder 1959–65, box 1, CRA Papers; Dick Darling, "Republican Activism: The California Republican Assembly and Ronald Reagan," 1981, Oral History Program, UCLA.

29. The party system in California does not resemble the parties within the eastern states. Due to Progressive Era reforms, the parties are quite weak. They are not, for example, able to endorse before a primary. The CRA was chartered in order to bypass the state election code and give the Republican Party a way to endorse nominees. The party itself is divided on several levels: county, state, and finance committee, and the volunteer organizations. The structural weaknesses of the parties is one reason why campaign management teams and independent candidate organizations, along with the volunteer organizations, have played such an important role. As James Q. Wilson has noted: "The absence of a hierarchical party, with authority clearly distributed in some regularized pattern, means that men with ability but little seniority can rise rapidly." This was, of course, the hope of grassroots conservatives. Eric Christopher Larson, "The Issue of Birchism in the 1962 California Republican Gubernatorial Primary" (master's thesis, California State University, Fullerton, 1975); Gladwin Hill, *Dancing Bear: An Inside Look at California Politics* (Cleveland: World, 1968), 118–19; Wilson, "Party Organization," 55–61.

30. *CRA Newsletter*, November 1967, box 14, CRA Papers.

31. Minutes of the Meeting of the Board of Directors of the California Republican Assembly, 26–27 September 1959, 15 September 1963, 6–7 June 1959, box 1, CRA Papers. By 1964, the Orange County CRA had eighteen chapters with close to 3,000 members. Activists described their activities in interviews: Frizzelle, interview; Sullivan, interview; Slocum, interview.

32. *CRA Enterprise*, May 1964.

33. Ibid., September 1964.

34. Frizzelle, interview.

35. Slocum, interview.

36. Frizzelle, interview.

37. Pearce and Muckenthaler, interviews.

38. The organizations' membership lists overlap.

39. Memorandum on the *Liberty Bell* by D. W. Kirkpatrick, in author's possession; Frizzelle, interview.

40. Slocum, interview.

41. Nixon did, however, succeed in getting through a compromise resolution that condemned Robert Welch's labeling of Eisenhower as a "dedicated

conscious agent of the Communist conspiracy." See Larson, "The Issue of Birchism in the 1962 California Republican Gubernatorial Primary," 181–202.

42. *New York Times*, 31 March 1962; see also Totton Anderson, "The 1962 Election in California," *Western Political Quarterly* 14 (March 1963): 393–414.

43. Kieffer (formerly Kielsmeier), interview.

44. Rae, *The Decline and Fall of the Liberal Republicans*, 52; *New York Times*, 31 March 1962, 10; Larson, "The Issue of Birchism in the 1962 California Republican Gubernatorial Primary," 181–202.

45. Letter from Walter Knott to Richard Nixon, 11 June 1962, box 421, General Correspondence file, RN Papers.

46. Memorandum to Richard Nixon from Al Moscow, 18 April 1962, box 621, General Correspondence file, RN Papers.

47. *New York Times*, 31 March 1962.

48. Ibid., 7 June 1962, 1; for conservative hostility to Nixon nationally in 1960, see also Goldberg, *Barry Goldwater*, 145.

49. Letter from James Utt to Richard Nixon, 20 February 1962, box 778, General Correspondence file, RN Papers.

50. Letter from Walter Knott to Richard Nixon, 11 June 1962, box 421, General Correspondence file, RN Papers.

51. *New York Times*, 7 June 1962, 1.

52. Kieffer (formerly Kielsmeier), interview.

53. Gaylord B. Parkinson, "Issues and Innovations in the 1966 Republican Party Campaign," 1980, Bancroft Regional Oral History Program, University of California, Berkeley, 13.

54. With the 78 percent voter turnout, Nixon got virtually all the Republican vote in November, along with about 400,000 Democratic votes. Hill, *Dancing Bear*, 176.

55. This record, for example, enabled him to retain the support of even some staunch right-wingers like Patrick Frawley. Note from Patrick Frawley to Richard Nixon, n.d., box 272, General Correspondence file, RN Papers; letter from Richard Nixon to Patrick J. Frawley, 22 June 1962, box 272, General Correspondence file, RN Papers.

56. Pearce and Muckenthalter, interviews; Kieffer (formerly Kielsmeier), interview.

57. *Newsweek*, 11 March 1963; *CRA Enterprise*, May 1964.

58. *Newsweek*, 11 March 1963.

59. *Human Events*, 19 December 1964.

60. *CRA Enterprise*, May 1964.

61. See Goldberg, *Barry Goldwater,* 142–43.

62. Letter from Paul Talbert to all members, 17 June 1960, Goldwater Clubs, Freedom Center, California State University, Fullerton, in Larson, "The Issue of Birchism in the 1962 California Republican Gubernatorial Primary."

63. Goldberg, *Barry Goldwater,* 142–45.

64. Jonathan Martin Kolkey, *The New Right, 1960–1968, with Epilogue, 1969–1980* (Washington, D.C.: University Press of America, 1983), 177; Brennan, *Turning Right in the Sixties,* 19–38.

65. *Newsweek,* 10 April 1961; *Time,* 23 June 1961.

66. See, for example, J. Bell, "Mr. Conservative: Barry Goldwater," *Christian Century* 1 (August 1962): 939. See also Goldberg, *Barry Goldwater,* for Goldwater's position as the conservative standard-bearer in the early 1960s.

67. Quoted in Kolkey, *The New Right,* 181.

68. Goldberg, *Barry Goldwater,* 145.

69. Ibid., 145–46.

70. White, *The Making of the President, 1964,* 92. See also Brennan, *Turning Right,* for a sketch of these developments, and Goldberg, *Barry Goldwater,* 161–65.

71. White, *The Making of the President, 1964,* 91–94; F. Clifton White with William Gill, *Suite 3505: The Story of the Draft Goldwater Movement* (New Rochelle, N.Y.: Arlington House, 1967).

72. Rae, *The Decline and Fall of the Liberal Republicans,* 46–58.

73. White, *The Making of the President, 1964,* 132.

74. Kessel, *The Goldwater Coalition,* 59–90; White, *The Making of the President, 1964,* 98–129; Rae, *The Decline and Fall of the Liberal Republicans,* 46–56.

75. *Time,* 22 May 1964.

76. *New York Times,* 27 May 1964, 4 June 1964, 21; White, *The Making of the President, 1964,* 139–40; Kessel, *The Goldwater Coalition.*

77. Kieffer (formerly Kielsmeier), interview. Follow-up telephone interview, 15 August 1999.

78. Estimates on the number of signatures gathered before noon range from 36,000 to 70,000. White, *The Making of the President, 1964,* 118; "Goldwater for President," campaign newsletter, 16 March 1964, box 29, KM Papers.

79. Sullivan, interview; Lundberg, interview; Pearce and Muckenthaler, interviews.

80. Minutes of the Meeting of the Board of Directors of the California Republican Assembly, 4–6 December 1964, box 1, CRA Papers; Frizzelle, interview; *Register,* 30 March 1965.

81. *Newsweek,* 11 March 1963.

82. Kieffer (formerly Kielsmeier) interview.

83. Orange Countians dominated the conservative leadership. They were Ronald Rankin, publisher of a local conservative newsletter, Nolan Frizzelle, and John Schmitz, a marine reserve pilot and instructor who taught a popular class at Santa Ana College called "History of Communist Aggression."

84. *Nation*, 11 May 1964.

85. *Newsweek*, 16 March 1964, 33.

86. *CRA Enterprise*, May 1964; *New York Times*, 3 May 1964.

87. *CRA Enterprise*, May 1964.

88. *Sacramento Bee*, 13 March 1964, CRA clippings, box 121, CRA Papers.

89. *Nation*, 11 May 1964, 477.

90. *Newsweek*, 4 March 1963.

91. *Reporter*, 7 May 1962, 25; *Newsweek*, 4 March 1963.

92. *Newsweek*, 16 March 1964, 33.

93. *Nation*, 11 May 1964, 474.

94. In the CRA, five of the sixteen leaders of the statewide organization were John Birch Society members by the end of 1965. Denison Kitchel, Goldwater's campaign manager, had been a John Birch Society member but dropped his membership in 1960 because of Welch's remarks in *The Politician* on Dwight D. Eisenhower. F. Clifton White and William Gill, moreover, have noted that many important participants in the Goldwater coalition were Birch members, although the Draft Goldwater Movement specifically sought to ensure that they did not take publicly visible leadership positions or publicly display Birch support. See Rae, *The Decline and Fall of the Liberal Republicans*, 53; letter from Denison Kitchel to Robert Welch, 8 June 1960, box 4, Denison Kitchel Papers, HIWRP; White with Gill, *Suite 3505*, 159.

95. Armstrong Dowell, interview.

96. *CRA Enterprise*, 5 September 1964.

97. *Register*, 1 May 1962.

98. Ibid., 21 April 1961. Utt argued that the John Birch Society had a "terrific message," but he opposed the domination of the society by Robert Welch and hoped the society would divorce itself from Welch. See also James B. Utt, "Is the John Birch Society a Menace?" *Congressional Record*, 1 May 1961.

99. Judis, *William F. Buckley, Jr.*, 196. Ronald Reagan would not repudiate John Birch Society support in his 1966 gubernatorial campaign, claiming that if members backed him, they were supporting his philosophy, not vice versa. James B. Utt, for example, while having criticized Welch's statements on Eisenhower, claimed that to repudiate the John Birch Society on these grounds was "ridiculous." See letter from James B. Utt to Richard Nixon, 20 February

1962, box 778, General Correspondence File, RN Papers. See also Goldberg, *Barry Goldwater*, 158–60.

100. Memorandum to "All Concerned" from Marvin Liebman, 16 January 1962, Marvin Liebman Papers, HIWRP.

101. See, for example, S.E.D. Brown, "The Anatomy of Liberalism," *American Opinion*, October 1961.

102. *CRA Newsletter* 1 (1965), folder 1, box 11, CRA Papers; "The Sharon Statement," reprinted in the *New Guard*, March 1969. For a discussion of the adoption of the "Sharon Statement" and its principles, see Schneider, *Cadres for Conservatism*, 34–36.

103. Minutes of the Meeting of the Board of Directors of the California Republican Assembly, 4–6 December 1964, box 1, CRA Papers.

104. Brown, "The Anatomy of Liberalism," 42.

105. Minutes of the Meeting of the Board of Directors of the California Republican Assembly, 4–6 December 1964, box 1, CRA Papers.

106. Ibid.

107. *Human Events*, 4 July 1964.

108. Kolkey, *The New Right*, 181.

109. Ibid., 183.

110. Letter to Assemblyman William T. Bagley from Southern California Republican Women's organization member, Los Angeles, n.n., n.d., Leonard Finder Papers, Dwight D. Eisenhower Presidential Library, Abilene, Kansas.

111. California primary election, "A Choice Not an Echo! Goldwater for President," campaign literature, box 23, CRA Papers; nationwide TV address on Soviet shift and U.S. policy, 21 October 1964, box 19, 1964 Presidential Campaign, BG Papers.

112. See chapter 1.

113. Kolkey, *The New Right*, 188–93.

114. For Goldwater's increasing emphasis on moral issues, see Goldberg, *Barry Goldwater*, 155.

115. Raymond E. Wolfinger and Fred I. Greenstein, "The Repeal of Fair Housing in California: An Analysis of Referendum Voting," *American Political Science Review* 62 (September 1968): 753.

116. Rogers, interview.

117. See, for example, "Senator Goldwater Speaks Out on the Issues," 1964, pp. 16–17, box 2, folder 24, CRA Papers; "A Choice Not an Echo! Goldwater for President," box 23, CRA Papers; nationwide TV address on "The Free Society," 22 October 1964, box 19, 1964 Presidential Campaign, BG Papers. See also White, *The Making of the President, 1964*, 332.

118. In his campaign speeches, Goldwater referred to the lack of leadership that had "turned our streets into jungles" and "brought our public and private morals into the lowest state of our history." See campaign speech at Minneapolis, Minnesota, 10 September 1964, box 19, 1964 Presidential Campaign, BG Papers.

119. Wolfinger and Greenstein, "The Repeal of Fair Housing in California," 753.

120. Areas that were heavily for Goldwater, such as Orange County, also strongly backed Proposition 14. Not surprisingly, areas that had voted more strongly for Johnson, such as the Bay Area, were not as strongly in favor of the measure. See ibid., 753–69.

121. Speech at Minneapolis, Minnesota, 10 September 1964, box 19, BG Papers.

122. White, *The Making of the President, 1964*, 337.

123. Rae, *The Decline and Fall of the Liberal Republicans*; 49; Mike Davis, *Prisoners of the American Dream: Politics and Economy in the History of the U.S. Working Class* (New York: Verso, 1986), 171–74.

124. Out of $5.5 million raised for Goldwater's nomination, $2 million came from California alone. Rockefeller, in contrast, while having "all the money in the world," according to his campaign managers, received only $25,000 from inside the state. Although some business leaders, such as Leonard Firestone and Justin Dart, backed his candidacy, "all of the money for his campaign came from New York." See Rae, *The Decline and Fall of the Liberal Republicans*, 58; Stuart Spencer, "Issues and Innovations in the 1966 Republican Gubernatorial Campaign," 1980, Bancroft Regional Oral History Program, University of California, Berkeley, 5, 22.

125. Telegram from Barry Goldwater to William Knowland, 15 January 1964, box 32, folder 19, CRA Papers.

126. California Goldwater for President Committee letterhead, letter to Worth Brown from William Knowland, 14 February 1964, box 32, CRA Papers; Robert L. Coate, Chairman, Democratic State Central Committee, "Ronald Reagan Extremist Collaborator, An Expose."

127. Letter from Paul H. Talbert to Senator Barry Goldwater, 29 February 1960, Goldwater, Unprocessed Papers, w–7, Finance Committee folder, BG Papers.

128. Regnery, referring to the possible sponsorship and very large distribution of Russell Kirk's, *The American Cause, by Constructive Action*, stated that they had "distributed something like 500,000 copies of *None Dare Call It Treason*." See *Orange County Sun*, September 1965; letter to Russell Kirk

from Henry Regnery, 13 May 1966, box 40, Henry Regnery Collection, HIWRP.

129. Schuparra, "Barry Goldwater and Southern California Conservatism," 279.

130. Dowell, interview.

131. I share here Lawrence Goodwyn's belief in the importance of an autonomous "movement culture" in creating a social movement, and I draw on his formulations. See Goodwyn, *The Populist Moment*, 17–21.

132. Sullivan, interview.

133. *Newsweek*, 15 June 1964.

134. "Clergymen for Social and Political Conservatism: A Declaration of Political Faith," Proposition 14 box, FCC.

135. Ibid.

136. See, for example, Erik von Kuehnelt-Leddihn, "Democracy Is a Failure in Much of the World," *Tidings*, 15 May 1964, and "Democratic Government Not Article of Faith," *Tidings*, 8 May 1964. See also "Reds Need Violence in Revolution," *Tidings*, 24 April 1964; Frank Meyer, "Dean Rusk and J. W. Wage Umbrella War," *Tidings*, 22 May 1964; and "Cardinal Speaks to Students on Natural Law," *Tidings*, 8 May 1964.

137. *Register*, 28 July 1964, 23 July 1964.

138. *Human Events*, 30 November 1963.

139. California Goldwater for President Committee, Letter to Mr. Bale from Mrs. John D. Bowler, Jr., Los Angeles County Co-Chairman, 28 February 1964, box 29, CRA Papers.

140. *Time*, 12 June 1964.

141. Kessel, *The Goldwater Coalition*, 88; Rae, *The Decline and Fall of the Liberal Republicans*, 44–58.

142. California Secretary of State, *Statement of Vote*, Consolidated Primary Election, 2 June 1964. See also Totton J. Anderson and Eugene C. Lee, "The 1964 Election in California," *Western Political Quarterly* 18 (June 1965): 451–74.

143. *New York Times*, 27 May 1964, 4 June 1964, 21; Kessel, *The Goldwater Coalition*, 84–86.

144. Kessel, *The Goldwater Coalition*, 88.

145. *New York Times*, 4 June 1964, 4; 7 June 1964.

146. Quoted in Rae, *The Decline and Fall of the Liberal Republicans*, 74; emphasis added. See also White, *Suite 3505*, 443.

147. Ibid.; White, *The Making of the President, 1964*, 217; Kolkey, *The New Right*, 183.

148. Republican Platform 1964, "For the People," presented to the Republican National Convention, 14 July 1964, San Francisco, California, box 33, folder 26, CRA Papers.

149. Republican Platform 1964, "For the People," box 33, folder 26, CRA Papers.

150. Ibid.

151. White, *The Making of the President, 1964*, 195–97.

152. Letter to John Anson Ford from Edmund G. Brown, 21 August 1964, carton 742, EGB Papers; letter to Stephen F. Switzer from Edmund G. Brown, 18 September 1964, carton 742, EGB Papers.

153. Text of 12 July letter from Scranton to Goldwater, box 20, 1964 Presidential Campaign, BG Papers; *Los Angeles Times*, 14 July 1964. See also Goldberg, *Barry Goldwater*, 200.

154. White, *The Making of the President, 1964*, 321.

155. See "Business and Financial Leaders Form Independent Committee to Support President Johnson and Senator Humphrey," press release, 3 September 1964, 1964 Campaign file, box 2, RN Papers.

156. Richard Hofstadter, "A Long View: Goldwater in History," *New York Review of Books*, October 1964, 17–20, quoted in Brinkley, "The Problem of American Conservatism," 409–29.

157. White, *The Making of the President, 1964*, 337.

158. There were only two small counties with a higher vote for Goldwater. Tiny rural Alpine, with a population of 397, voted 57 percent Republican, and Mono voted 56.1 percent Republican. California Secretary of State, *Statement of Vote*, General Election, 3 November 1964. See also Anderson and Lee, "The 1964 Election in California," 451–74.

159. Governmental Affairs Institute, *America at the Polls: A Handbook of American Presidential Election Statistics, 1920–1964* (New York: Arno Press, 1976). A large metropolitan region was considered to have a population above 400,000 according to the U.S. Census Bureau in 1960. No major metropolitan area outside of the Deep South outdid Orange County in its support for Goldwater. However, two counties with approximately half the population of Orange County came close, and two surpassed Orange County in the percentage of the vote given to Goldwater: Du Page, Illinois, population 313,459, voted 59.9 percent Republican; Douglas, Nebraska, population 343,490, voted 56.8 percent; Broward County, Florida, a fast-growing region with a population of 333,946, voted 55.5 percent; and Tulsa, Oklahoma, population 346,038, voted 55.6 percent. Finally, many counties with populations of under 100,000 surpassed Orange County in the strength of their support for Goldwater.

160. John Schmitz managed to capture the Republican primary nomination from political stalwart Bruce Sumner, who served in the California Assembly for many years, in a run for the California Senate. See Seelye and Smith, "A Century of Politics in Orange County"; Beaman and Jones, *Turmoil and Change*, 15–18.

161. White, *The Making of the President, 1964*, 380.

162. See, for example, *Register*, 18 November 1964.

163. Slocum, interview.

164. Some weeks after the election, Goldwater wrote to Raymond Moley that, "had the Rockefellers and the Romneys, et al., pulled just a bit on the oar, it is highly possible that the results would have been much closer. I would never predict victory, because I never believed that a Republican could defeat Johnson in this year of plenty, and a very phony peace." See letter from Barry Goldwater to Raymond Moley, 30 November 1964, box 19, Raymond Moley Papers, HIWRP.

165. ECP Meeting Report, 1 December 1964, Barry Goldwater Post-election Correspondence, Cornell University, Ithaca, New York, microfilm.

166. Letter from Gordon Greb, Johnson County Chair for Citizens for Goldwater-Miller, Kansas, to Barry Goldwater, 25 November 1964, Barry Goldwater Post-election Correspondence, Cornell University, Ithaca, New York, microfilm.

167. Letter from Margaret Minek of Fairfield, California, to Barry Goldwater, 7 February 1965, Barry Goldwater Post-election Correspondence, Cornell University, Ithaca, New York, microfilm.

168. Epstein and Forster, *Report on the John Birch Society, 1966*, 83.

169. Hallan-Gibson, *The Golden Promise*, 235.

170. James Toft, interview with Duff Witman Griffith, 18 August 1972, in Duff Witman Griffith, "Before the Deluge: An Oral History Examination of Pre-Watergate Conservative Thought in Orange County, California" (master's thesis, California State University, Fullerton, 1976).

171. Epstein and Forster, *Report on the John Birch Society, 1966*, 83.

172. Letter from Robert Welch to Barry Goldwater, 4 November 1965, Denison Kitchel Papers, HIWRP.

173. Epstein and Forster, *Report on the John Birch Society, 1966*, 74.

174. Ibid., 64–69; Harry Harvey, "Whatever Happened to the John Birch Society?" *Orange County Illustrated*, October 1973, 38–44.

175. *Christian Science Monitor*, 11 January 1965; "List of ACU Contributors of $500 or More," 1965, box 57, Marvin Liebman Papers, HIWRP.

176. Minutes of the Meeting of the Board of Directors of the ACU, 18–19 December 1964, box 57, Marvin Liebman Papers, HIWRP.

177. *New York World-Telegram and Sun*, 12 April 1966.

178. Letter from Joseph Lally to Henry Regnery, 29 October 1964, box 43, Henry Regnery Papers, HIWRP.

CHAPTER 4

1. See, for example, P. Horton, "Revivalism on the Far Right," *Reporter*, 20 July 1961, 25–29; A. Gottfried and S. Davidson, "New Right in Action," *Nation*, 29 July 1961, 48–51; "Rightist Revival: Who's on the Far Right," *Look*, 13 March 1962, 21–28; Forster and Epstein, *Danger on the Right*; Suall, *The American Ultras*; Bell, *The Radical Right*.

2. Bell, "The Dispossessed," 2, 33. See also Dionne, *Why Americans Hate Politics*, 67.

3. Westin, "The John Birch Society," 225; Dionne, *Why Americans Hate Politics*, 67.

4. Leo P. Ribuffo, "Why Is There So Much Conservatism in the United States and Why Do So Few Historians Know Anything about It?" *American Historical Review* 99 (April 1994): 439–41.

5. Lionel Trilling, *The Liberal Imagination: Essays on Literature and Society* (Garden City, N.Y.: Doubleday, 1953).

6. I use the term "ideology" here as defined by Eric Foner, who calls it "the system of beliefs, values, fears, prejudices, reflexes and commitments—in sum, the social consciousness—of a social group, be it a class, a party, or a section." See Eric Foner, *Free Soil, Free Labor, Free Men: The Ideology of the Republican Party before the Civil War* (New York: Oxford University Press, 1970), 4.

7. Eric Hobsbawm, *The Age of Extremes: A History of the World, 1914–1991* (New York: Pantheon, 1994).

8. For a good discussion of post–World War II American liberalism, see Steven M. Gillon, *Politics and Vision: The ADA and American Liberalism, 1947–1985* (New York: Oxford University Press, 1987), 83–155. See also Alonzo L. Hamby, *Liberalism and Its Challengers: FDR to Reagan* (New York: Oxford University Press, 1985), 52–230; Nathan Liebowitz, *Daniel Bell and the Agony of Modern Liberalism* (Westport, Conn.: Greenwood Press, 1985); Stephen P. Depoe, *Arthur M. Schlesinger, Jr., and the Ideological History of American Liberalism* (Tuscaloosa: University of Alabama Press, 1994).

9. Gillon, *Politics and Vision*, 129, 133.

10. For a discussion of Kennedy's cautious liberalism, see ibid., 131–54. See also Hamby, *Liberalism and Its Challengers*, 204–5; David Burner and Thomas R. West, *The Torch Is Passed: The Kennedy Brothers and American Liberalism* (New York: Atheneum, 1984), 63–192.

11. Hobsbawm, *The Age of Extremes*.

12. Depoe, *Arthur M. Schlesinger, Jr., and the Ideological History of American Liberalism*, 10–12.

13. Edsall with Edsall, *Chain Reaction*, 44–49.

14. Himmelstein, *To the Right*, 14.

15. Ibid.

16. Nash, *The Conservative Intellectual Movement in America Since 1945*; Allitt, *Catholic Intellectuals and Conservative Politics in America*; Brinkley, "The Problem of American Conservatism," 409–29; Himmelstein, *To the Right*, 45–62.

17. Himmelstein, *To the Right*, 46.

18. *American Mercury*, September 1961, 25–26.

19. Quoted in Dionne, *Why Americans Hate Politics*, 152–153.

20. *Register*, 7 June 1961.

21. Kolkey, *The New Right, 87*.

22. Ibid.

23. *Register*, 1 October 1964.

24. Ibid., 7 June 1961.

25. Morris Davis, interview with Duff Witman Griffith, 19 October 1972, in Griffith, "Before the Deluge," 6.

26. Lundberg, interview.

27. Sara Diamond makes this point in her very definition of what it means to be right-wing. See Diamond, *Roads to Dominion*, 9.

28. *Register*, 23 April 1962.

29. Ibid., 8 April 1963.

30. Brinkley, "The Problem of American Conservatism," 418.

31. Ibid., 418. See also *Register*, 20 November 1962.

32. *Register*, 27 November 1960.

33. Ibid., 27 November 1960.

34. Ibid., 20 November 1962.

35. Brinkley, "The Problem of American Conservatism," 419.

36. *Anaheim Gazette*, 8 August 1963.

37. *Register*, 1 November 1961.

38. Frizzelle, interview.

39. Averill, interview.

40. James Davison Hunter, *Culture Wars: The Struggle to Define America* (New York: Basic Books, 1991), 110–16.

41. Ibid.

42. Ibid.

43. Ibid., 111–12.

44. John Stormer, *None Dare Call It Treason* (Florrissant, Mo.: Liberty Bell Press, 1964), 124.

45. *Tidings*, 8 May 1964.

46. See Edsall with Edsall, *Chain Reaction*, 43–47. Decisions included protection against illegally obtained evidence (*Mapp v. Ohio*) and against self-incrimination (*Malloy v. Hogan, Miranda v. Arizona*); and granted defendants the right to counsel (*Gideon v. Wainwright, Escobedo v. Illinois*), to silence (*Miranda*), to due process (*Pointer v. Texas*), and to a speedy trial (*Mallory v. United States*).

47. Ralph De Toledano, "Why Crime Rates Continue to Rise," *Human Events*, 4 July 1964, 12.

48. Claude Bunzel, interview with Duff Witman Griffith, 13 January 1972, in Griffith, "Before the Deluge," 4, 13.

49. *Register*, 3 January 1961.

50. Frizzelle, interview.

51. *Register*, 8 July 1962.

52. Slocum, interview.

53. *American Standard*, March–April 1963, Right-Wing Collection of the University of Iowa, 1918–77, University of Iowa, microfilm, reel 8.

54. Kolkey, *The New Right*, 57.

55. Ibid., 60.

56. *Human Events*, 18 July 1964. See also Max Rafferty, *What They Are Doing to Your Children* (New York: New American Library, 1964); Rafferty, *Suffer, Little Children* (New York: Devin-Adair, 1962); Rafferty, *Max Rafferty on Education* (New York: Devin-Adair, 1968).

57. In a 1972 interview, Robert LeFevre, president of Rampart College in Santa Ana, articulated well this distinction between libertarians and social conservatives when asked about conspiratorial thinking on the Right: "I think the conservative has a tendency—this is not the libertarian—to create a monstrous bugbear and then to run frightened from the product of their creation. I think they did it with the Communists. They helped to build the Communists into something that was absolutely omniscient and omnipotent. . . . to imagine that they have engineered everything that has happened in the world is really superstition. It's witchcraft. And of course, the same is true of setting up a particular group of people of any kind, blacks, whites or Catholics, Jews, the Council of Foreign Relations, the Illuminati . . . or whatever, this is equivalent to the kind of stuff we had two hundred years ago, when people believed in witches. It doesn't have any real bearing on a reasonable mind." See Robert LeFevre, interview, in Griffith, "Before the Deluge," 16.

58. Sam Campbell, a staunch fundamentalist Christian, for example, believed in "a moneyed conspiracy." See Sam Campbell, interview with Duff Witman Griffith, 7 September 1972, in Griffith, "Before the Deluge," 4.

59. *American Mercury*, September 1961, 25–26.

60. *Calvary Chapel Movement* (Twin Peaks, Calif.: Calvary Chapel Bible College, 1994), 2; Charles B. Strozier, *Apocalypse: On the Psychology of Fundamentalism in America* (Boston: Beacon Press, 1994), 193; Paul S. Boyer, *When Time Shall Be No More: Prophecy Belief in Modern American Culture* (Cambridge, Mass.: Harvard University Press, 1992); Marsden, *Fundamentalism and American Culture.*

61. See chapter 1 for an expansion of this argument.

62. Charles Forcey, "Robert A. Nisbet: Architect of Postwar American Traditionalism" (paper delivered at conference "From Redemption to Reaganism," Princeton University, Princeton, N.J., 4 May 1996); Forcey, "From the Quest for Community to the Quest for Authority, Robert A. Nisbet and the Traditionalist Response to the 1960s" (paper delivered at the Organization of American Historians, 1996 annual conference); Nash, *The Conservative Intellectual Movement in America since 1945*, 86–87.

63. Forcey, "Robert A. Nisbet: Architect of Postwar American Traditionalism"; Forcey, "From the Quest for Community to the Quest for Authority"; Nash, *The Conservative Intellectual Movement in America since 1945*, 53–54.

64. Forcey, "Robert A. Nisbet: Architect of Postwar American Traditionalism"; Nash, *The Conservative Intellectual Movement in America since 1945*, 53–54.

65. *Register*, 19 June 1961.

66. Ibid., 7 April 1961. See LeFevre, interview, in Griffith, "Before the Deluge," 10.

67. *Register*, 7 April 1961, 30 June 1962. See also Davis, interview, in Griffith, "Before the Deluge," 22–27.

68. *Register*, 8 July 1962, 10 July 1962.

69. Bergland, interview.

70. Hunter, *Culture Wars*, 44–45.

71. Ibid. For libertarians' staunch belief in natural law and their distinction between this and "artificial law," see *Register*, 1 April 1962.

72. See, for example, LeFevre, interview, in Griffith, "Before the Deluge," 7.

73. Kolkey, *The New Right*, 53.

74. *Register*, 20 April 1965.

75. See, for example, LeFevre, interview, in Griffith, "Before the Deluge," 1–19.

76. *American Mercury*, September 1961.

77. For a general discussion of the significance of narratives about the past among both "progressive" and "orthodox" communities, see Hunter, *Culture Wars*, 108–10.

78. *Register*, 10 July 1962.

79. Hunter, *Culture Wars*, 108–10.

80. *Register*, 5 October 1962.

81. See, for example, interviews with Sam Campbell and John Schmitz, 7 September 1972, in Griffith, "Before the Deluge."

82. Kieffer (formerly Kielsmeier), interview.

83. The religious roots of his belief only came through when he later asserted that "there are only two powers. There is the governmental power, which I think is essentially Satanic because it is coercive, or there is the power of God, which is the spirit of liberty." Campbell, interview, in Griffith, "Before the Deluge," 7.

84. Pearce and Muckenthaler, interviews.

85. Nash, *The Conservative Intellectual Movement in American since 1945*, 174–81.

86. Allitt, *Catholic Intellectuals and Conservative Politics in America*, 60–110.

87. Boyer, *When Time Shall Be No More*, 157–66.

88. *Register*, 1 November 1961.

89. Kolkey, *The New Right*, 75–79.

90. *Human Events*, 21 July 1961, quoted in Kolkey, *The New Right*, 77.

91. *Register*, 10 July 1960.

92. Letter from Mr. and Mrs. A. J. Delphino to Lyndon B. Johnson, 19 January 1964, carton 195, EGB Papers.

93. Gillon, *Politics and Vision*, 116.

94. Stephen E. Ambrose, *Rise to Globalism: American Foreign Policy since 1938*, 5th ed. (New York: Penguin, 1988), 181–200; Burner and West, *The Torch Is Passed*, 98–149; Hamby, *Liberalism and Its Challengers*, 195, 213–21; Paul Y. Hammond, *Cold War and Detente: The American Foreign Policy Process since 1945* (New York: Harcourt Brace Jovanovich, 1975), 148–203.

95. Gillon, *Politics and Vision*, 116.

96. Ibid., 118.

97. Ambrose, *Rise to Globalism*, 182.

98. Gillon, *Politics and Vision*, 122.

99. Ibid.

100. Ambrose, *Rise to Globalism*, 182.

101. Hammond, *Cold War and Detente*, 156.

102. Letter from C. L. Gutzeit to Thomas H. Kuchel, 30 April 1961, carton 140, TK Papers.

103. *New York Times Magazine*, 17 September 1961, quoted in Kolkey, *The New Right*, 188.

104. For a full discussion of the conservative abandonment of isolationism for a new reformulated anticommunist interventionism, see Himmelstein, *To the Right*, 31–45.

105. Ibid., 42–43.

106. For discussions of the isolationist tradition in the United States, see Ronald E. Powaski, *Toward an Entangling Alliance: American Isolationism, Internationalism, and Europe, 1901–1950* (New York: Greenwood Press, 1991); Thomas N. Guinsburg, *The Pursuit of Isolationism in the United States Senate from Versailles to Pearl Harbor* (New York: Garland Press, 1982); Gordon Martel, ed., *American Foreign Relations Reconsidered, 1890–1993* (New York: Routledge, 1994). For an overview of the transformation of anticommunist isolationism to anticommunist interventionism among conservatives, see Himmelstein, *To the Right*, 31–43.

107. Kolkey, *The New Right*, 126–27.

108. Ibid., 75–79, 113–14.

109. *Register*, 10 July 1960.

110. *American Mercury*, September 1961, 25–26.

111. *Register*, 8 May 1961.

112. Letter from Mr. and Mrs. A. J. Delphino to Lyndon B. Johnson, 19 January 1964, carton 195, EGB Papers.

113. Bergland, interview.

114. *Register*, 2 January 1960.

115. *RAP*, fall–winter 1970, Right-Wing Collection of the University of Iowa, University of Iowa, microfilm, reel 92. California had a strong libertarian contingent in YAF, whose deepening opposition to traditionalism, as well as right-wing militarism, led to a purge of California leaders and a split in YAF nationally. The Orange County YAF chairman, Dana Rohrabacher, and Orange County leader John Schureman were two of those libertarian leaders purged by the national office. Jonathan Schoenwald, "The Other Counterculture: Young Americans for Freedom, 1960–1969" (unpublished conference paper, "Towards a History of the 1960s," State Historical Society of Wisconsin, Madison, 28 April–1 May 1993). On Orange County YAF, see also letter from Patrick Dowd to Dana Rohrabacher, 3 April 1969, box 1, PD Papers; letter from Patrick Dowd to Wayne Thorburn, 23 October 1969, box 1, PD Papers; letter from Patrick Dowd to John Schureman, Seal Beach, 17 March

1969, PD Papers; letter from Patrick Dowd to Mr. Rick Barry, Fullerton, California, 17 March 1969, PD Papers; letter from Patrick Dowd to Randal C. Teague, 22 August 1969, PD Papers; letter from John Schureman, executive Director, YAF Orange County, to Patrick Dowd, 17 May 1969, box 1, PD Papers. For broader discussions of the YAF split nationally, see Schneider, *Cadre for Conservatism*, 127–41.

116. *Register*, 26 November 1961, 18 June 1961, 2 November 1961.

117. Ibid., 8 March 1961.

118. Sullivan, interview.

119. Hunter, *Culture Wars*, 136.

120. Joseph N. Bell, "I Fought Hatred among My Neighbors," *Good Housekeeping*, September 1965.

121. *Register*, 4 October 1962, 19 October 1962, 2 October 1962, 28 November 1961, 30 June 1961, 20 November 1961, 24 November 1961.

122. Gillon, *Politics and Vision*, 150–53.

123. Ibid., 151.

124. *Register*, 21 April 1961.

125. *Congressional Record*, 87th Cong., 2d sess., 15 January 1962.

126. *Register*, 20 April 1962.

127. Ibid., 9 April 1961.

128. Stormer, *None Dare Call It Treason*, 120.

129. Boyer, *When Time Shall Be No More*; Strozier, *Apocalypse*.

130. For an insightful discussion of the significance of educational issues in contemporary cultural conflict between liberals and conservatives, see Hunter, *Culture Wars*, 197–224.

131. Ibid., 174.

132. Ibid., 109, 174.

133. *Register*, 25 November 1960.

134. Ibid., 1 January 1961.

135. Conservatives opposed liberal and experimental educational methods, which they lumped under the rubric of "progressive education." They despised what they saw as progressive education's moral relativism, its psychological orientation and focus on personality formation as well as its encouragement of an inwardly conscious individualism, which they believed challenged parental authority and moral absolutes. The foremost proponent of traditional educational methods, California's school superintendent, Max Rafferty, articulated their criticisms: "The progressive educationalist holds the only eternal verity to be that of constant change and flux. . . . So the only thing worth teaching to youngsters is the ability to react to an ever-shifting environmental kaleidoscope. It is a way of thinking and of teaching with which American democracy

324 ◆ NOTES TO CHAPTER 4

cannot coexist. Within it lies the seeds of the rumbles and the riots, the frantic search for 'kicks,' the newsstand filth and the cinematic garbage which mark the last descent into the cloying, clinging sickness of ultimate decay by every civilization which has ever permitted this infection to overcome its resistance." See *Human Events*, 26 December 1964. Barry Goldwater also criticized progressive education, arguing that "in our attempt to make education fun we have neglected the academic disciplines that develop sound minds and are conducive to sound character." For the ideas of progressivists themselves, see, for example, Lester Dix, *A Charter for Progressive Education* (New York: Columbia University Teachers College, 1939); see also Gilbert G. Gonzalez, *Progressive Education: A Marxist Interpretation* (Minneapolis, Minn.: Marxist Educational Press, 1982), 90–94.

136. See William Holmes McGuffey, *McGuffey's Fifth Eclectic Reader* (1879; New York: New American Library, 1962).

137. *Register*, 5 June 1961.

138. Ibid., 25 November 1960.

139. Ibid., 3 January 1961.

140. Muckenthaler and Pearce, interviews; Sullivan, Frizzelle, and Rogers, interviews; Mary Haller, interview with author, 1 December 1992.

141. Rogers, interview.

142. Pearce and Muckenthaler, interviews.

143. *Register*, 13 April 1963.

144. Ibid., 20 April 1965, 9 April 1965.

145. "The Bible and the Race Question," sermon by Dr. Bob Wells to the congregation of the Central Baptist Church of Orange County, 18 August 1963, Voice of Truth and Freedom Folder, FCC.

146. Christian Anti-Defamation League, Anaheim California, n.d., Voice of Truth and Freedom Folder, FCC. See also Olsen, interview, in Griffith, "Before the Deluge," 15–17. Olsen evinces the mix of anti-Semitic stereotypes that permeate right-wing thought.

147. Haller, interview.

148. When swastikas were painted on the door of a Corona del Mar coffee shop and when the Coast highway billboards were defaced with swastikas, the *Register* published an editorial, speaking to a supposed Jewish audience, lamenting, "Heaven forbid you thought that expression of a few sick people actually expressed the conviction of all the people in this wonderful land of ours and all of you started to pack your bags. . . . If you ever have to leave love goes with you, our Republic goes with you, everything I and all my buddies fought for in World War II goes with you. God goes with you, I'm going with

you too." *Register*, 19 January 1960. See interview with LeFevre, in Griffith, "Before the Deluge," 16.

149. See interviews, in Griffith, "Before the Deluge."

150. *Human Events*, 21 September 1963.

151. *Los Angeles Times*, 2 February 1964; Wolfinger and Greenstein, "The Repeal of Fair Housing in California," 753–69.

152. W. S. McBirnie, "That Rumford Act," carton 78, EGB Papers.

153. Orange County, for example, twice voted strongly against busing. In 1972, it supported an antibusing statute more than two to one; in 1979, a state constitutional amendment against busing carried the county 241,427 to 67,898. See *Register*, 26 April 1982.

154. Even in 1965, *Life* magazine referred to William Buckley as "the enfant terrible of the far right." As this reference shows, contemporary characterizations of the "extreme" or far right was often a rubric encompassing the entire spectrum of the conservative movement. That such characterizations would later shift in itself exemplifies conservatism's increasing legitimacy. See S. Engeloff, "Tongue-in-Cheek Candidate," *Life*, 17 September 1965, 49–50.

CHAPTER 5

1. W. J. Rorabaugh, *Berkeley at War: The 1960s* (New York: Oxford University Press, 1989), 21.

2. Ibid., 124–45.

3. David Farber, *The Age of Great Dreams: America in the 1960s* (New York: Hill and Wang, 1994), 111–16; Matusow, *The Unraveling of America*, 361–62.

4. Theodore H. White, *The Making of the President, 1968* (New York: Atheneum, 1969), 28.

5. Douglas T. Miller, *On Our Own: Americans in the Sixties* (Lexington, Mass.: D. C. Heath, 1996), 131.

6. *Register*, 21 April 1965.

7. Ibid.

8. Ibid.

9. For Reagan's early career, see Anne Edwards, *Early Reagan* (New York: Morrow, 1987). For his California campaign, see Bill Boyarsky, *The Rise of Ronald Reagan* (New York: Random House, 1968); Lou Cannon, *Ronnie and Jesse: A Political Odyssey* (Garden City, N.Y.: Doubleday, 1969).

10. Letter from Ronald Reagan to Richard Nixon, 15 July 1959, box 621, General Correspondence, RN Papers.

11. Transcript of televised appearance by Ronald Reagan, 4 November 1962, RN Papers. See also Ronald Reagan, "Encroaching Government Controls," *Human Events*, 21 July 1961.

12. *Register*, 13 November 1966; *New York Times Magazine*, 14 November 1965, 174–75.

13. *New York Times*, 23 January 1965.

14. Letter from Ruth P. Smith to Edmund G. Brown, 28 October 1966, carton 921, EGB Papers.

15. Henry Salvatori, "Kitchen Cabinet: Four Citizen Advisors to Ronald Reagan," 1983, Oral History Program, California State University, Fullerton (herein abbreviated as CSUF), 15.

16. Telegram from F. Clifton White to Ronald Reagan, box 38, RR Papers.

17. Telegrams to Ronald Reagan, box 38, RR Papers.

18. William E. Roberts, "Issues and Innovations in the 1966 Republican Gubernatorial Campaign," 1980, Bancroft Regional Oral History Program, University of California, Berkeley, 10.

19. Letter from Frances Dowell to Ronald Reagan, n.d., box 22, RR Papers.

20. Ibid.

21. *Ramparts*, November 1965, 35.

22. Letter from Raymond R. Woolsey to Ronald Reagan, 9 June 1965, box 22, RR Papers.

23. Lou Cannon, *Reagan* (New York: Putnam, 1982), 102–7. Some of these men had already approached Reagan to run in 1962 for the U.S. Senate. See Edward Mills, "Kitchen Cabinet: Four Citizen Advisors to Ronald Reagan," 1983, Oral History Program, CSUF.

24. See interviews with Salvatori, Mills, and Holmes Tuttle in "Kitchen Cabinet: Four Citizen Advisors of Ronald Reagan," 1983, Oral History Program, CSUF.

25. Dick Darling, "Republican Activism: The California Republican Assembly and Ronald Reagan," 1981, Oral History Program, University of California, Los Angeles, 4.

26. *Register*, 30 March 1965.

27. Ibid., 21 April 1965.

28. Letter from Robert A. Bernard, President of the Rossmoor–Los Alamitos California Republican Assembly, to Ronald Reagan, 12 November 1965, with attached resolution of the Rossmoor–Los Alamitos California Republican Assembly, 22 October 1965, box 2, RR Papers.

29. Letter from James Townsend to Ronald Reagan, 29 January 1967, box 159, RR Papers.

30. Letter from Raymond Woolsey to Ronald Reagan, 9 June 1965, box 22, RR Papers.

31. Letter from Charles E. Brown to Ronald Reagan, 8 March 1966, box 2, RR Papers.

32. Letter from Robert A. Bernard to Ronald Reagan, 12 November 1965, box 2, RR Papers.

33. *Register,* 28 March 1965.

34. Ibid.

35. Ibid.

36. Lyn Nofziger, "Issues and Innovations in the 1966 Republican Gubernatorial Campaign," 1980, Bancroft Regional Oral History Program, University of California, Berkeley, 11–12.

37. Letter to Mr. William B. Covert from Ronald Reagan, 11 July 1966, box 2, RR Papers.

38. Letter from Mrs. Jack Bickle to Ronald Reagan, n.d., box 2, RR Papers.

39. Letter from Fran Bouton to Ronald Reagan, 15 March 1966, box 2, RR Papers.

40. Nofziger, "Issues and Innovations in the 1966 Republican Gubernatorial Campaign," 35.

41. Opinion Research of California, "A Public Opinion Issue and Attitude Survey Concerning the Republican Gubernatorial Primary Election in the State of California," 12–13 March 1966, box 35, RR Papers.

42. *New York Times,* 13 April 1966, 44, 63.

43. Darling, "Republican Activism," 41.

44. Frizzelle, interview; Dick Darling, interview with author, 23 August 1996.

45. Letter from Ronald Reagan to Helen Kirk, 10 September 1965, box 35, RR Papers; letter from Ronald Reagan to Robert A. Bernard, 16 September 1965, box 2, RR Papers; letter from Helen Kirk to Ronald Reagan, 10 April 1966, box 7, RR Papers; Darling, interview.

46. Cannon, *Reagan,* 112.

47. Ibid.; California Secretary of State, *Statement of Vote,* Consolidated Primary Election, 2 June 1964.

48. California Secretary of State, *Statement of Vote,* Direct Primary Election, 7 June 1966.

49. *New York Times,* 8 June 1966.

50. Ibid.

51. California Secretary of State, *Statement of Vote,* Direct Primary Election, 7 June 1966.

52. *Ramparts,* November 1965, 35.

53. *Newsweek*, 5 July 1965, 18–19.

54. Ibid.

55. *Register*, 21 April 1965.

56. Reagan was willing to accept the endorsement if offered, but he announced that he would not bid for it. See *Register*, 30 April 1966.

57. Inter-Office Communication to All County and Regional Chairmen from Thomas Pike and Dirk Eldredge, Southern California Co-Chairmen, 1 August 1966, box 36, RR Papers.

58. Indeed, the respectable distance Reagan maintained from his grassroots supporters during the general election led some southland volunteer leaders to complain of the "wall" that Spencer and Roberts built around him. Letter from George Cheesley to Ronald Reagan, 20 April 1966, box 2, RR Papers. After receiving complaints from the San Diego CRA about its inability to get him as a speaker, Reagan responded, "I can understand all the people in your group thinking they've been abandoned. . . . the situation now, however, is that we must count on our friends while we turn our attention to getting those Democrats who voted for Yorty." Letter from John T. Schall, San Diego CRA President, to Ronald Reagan, 11 August 1966, box 13, RR Papers; letter from Ronald Reagan to John T. Schall, 18 August 1966, box 13, RR Papers.

59. Letter from Lawrence Bartlett to Ronald Reagan, 2 May 1966, box 2, RR Papers.

60. Letter from Reginald Crozier to Ronald Reagan, 13 June 1966, box 2, RR Papers.

61. Letter from Marguerite Lynn to Ronald Reagan, 12 September 1966, box 7, RR Papers.

62. Letter from William Best to Ronald Reagan, 17 February 1966, box 2, RR Papers.

63. *New York Times*, 10 March 1966. Republicans were outnumbered by Democrats in California by about 1.3 million, although party regularity was unpredictable.

64. Peter Wiley and Robert Gottlieb, *Empires in the Sun: The Rise of the New American West* (New York: Putnam, 1982), 112; Hill, *Dancing Bear*, 254–55; Owens, Costantini, and Weschler, *California Politics and Parties*, 50–51.

65. Edna Slocum used this term to describe herself and her husband, who had been Democrats before moving to California. Slocum, interview.

66. California Secretary of State, *Supplement to Statement of Vote*, General Election, 6 November 1962, 51.

67. For a history of the California Democratic Council, see Larry N. Gerston, "The California Democratic Council and Political Reform: Promise and Performance" (Ph.D. diss, University of California, Davis, 1975).

68. Ibid., 221.

69. *New York Times*, 21 February 1966, 19; *Los Angeles Herald-Examiner*, 21 February 1966, A-11; draft of press release, Democrats for Reagan, box 36, RR Papers.

70. "Power Backed by Young Demos," news clipping, attached to letter from Clara Lynch to Edmund G. Brown, 20 September 1966, carton 928, EGB Papers.

71. Charles B. Gant, "The California Democratic Council and Grass-Roots Politics," interview by Sandra B. Taylor, 1970, Oral History Program, University of California, Los Angeles, 1972.

72. Letter from Gary S. Niles to Edmund G. Brown, n.d., carton 667, EGB Papers.

73. Letter from Earl E. Glassburner to Edmund G. Brown, 9 April 1965, carton 840, EGB Papers.

74. *Examiner*, 17 August 1966, news clipping, carton 201, EGB Papers.

75. Wiley and Gottlieb, *Empires in the Sun*, 112; Hill, *Dancing Bear*, 254–55; Owens, Costantini, and Weschler, *California Politics and Parties*, 50–51; Rogin and Shover, *Political Change in California*.

76. Samuel Yorty, "I Cannot Take Kennedy," RN Papers; Hill, *Dancing Bear*, 254.

77. Letter from Samuel Yorty to Richard Nixon, 27 February 1958, RN Papers; Hill, *Dancing Bear*, 254.

78. *George Rochester*, draft of speech for Californians for Reagan, 10 September 1966, box 36, RR Papers.

79. Hill, *Dancing Bear*, 254.

80. California Secretary of State, *Statement of Vote*, Direct Primary Election, 7 June 1966.

81. Letter from Don Collins to Ronald Reagan, 9 June 1966, box 2, RR Papers.

82. Letter from Mr. and Mrs. Ronald Chronister to Edmund G. Brown, n.d., carton 921, EGB Papers.

83. Letter from George Rochester to Edmund G. Brown, 9 June 1966, carton 928, EGB Papers; draft of press release for Californians for Reagan, 10 September 1966, box 36, RR Papers; minutes of first steering committee meeting, Statler Hotel, 15 July 1966, box 36, RR Papers.

84. Hill, *Dancing Bear*, 254.

85. Spencer, "Issues and Innovations in the 1966 Republican Gubernatorial Campaign," 34–36.

86. Minutes of first steering committee meeting, Statler Hotel, 15 July 1966, box 36, RR Papers; inter-office communication, 1 August 1966, RR Papers.

87. *Register*, 13 October 1966. See also "Where Does Ronald Reagan Stand on Right-to-Work?" campaign leaflet, CRA Papers; "Rank-and-File Union Members Present Reagan Rally," Labor for Reagan Committee campaign leaflet, CRA Papers.

88. *Register*, 13 October 1966. See also "Where Does Ronald Reagan Stand on Right-to-Work?" CRA Papers; "Rank-and-File Union Members Present Reagan Rally," CRA Papers.

89. *Register*, 13 October 1966.

90. Ibid., 25 November 1966.

91. Letter from Jean Kerr to Ronald Reagan, 31 July 1966, box 7, RR Papers.

92. Ibid.

93. Letter from Shirlee Coling to Ronald Reagan, n.d., box 2, RR Papers.

94. Salvatori, "Kitchen Cabinet: Four Citizen Advisors to Ronald Reagan," 15.

95. Letter to Ronald Reagan, n.n., n.d., box 17, RR Papers.

96. Spencer, "Issues and Innovations in the 1966 Republican Gubernatorial Campaign," 31.

97. Roberts, "Issues and Innovations in the 1966 Republican Gubernatorial Campaign," 21.

98. *Register*, 9 October 1966.

99. Ibid.

100. In response to John Barry Knorp of Hollywood, for example, who had written that "the Free Speech Movement . . . was . . . a dress rehearsal for a revolution in which future cadres received on-the-job-training," Reagan wrote that while he agreed with him "about the conspiracy behind the disturbances," he cautioned that this could not be explained enough as part of the campaign: "It just may be one of those things you don't talk about now, but do something about if you can get elected." Letter from John Barry Knorp to Ronald Reagan, 27 December 1965, box 7, RR Papers; letter from Ronald Reagan to John Barry Knorp, 3 January 1966, box 7, RR Papers.

101. Letter from Mr. and Mrs. F. A. McBride to Edmund G. Brown, 25 October 1966, carton 921, EGB Papers.

102. Farber, *The Age of Great Dreams*, 90–117.

103. See "To Keep Our People Safe and Free: One of a Series of Creative Studies by the Reagan Administration," n.d., box 3, folder 4, CRA Papers; emphasis added.

104. Letter from Kathleen Stone to Edmund G. Brown, 1 November 1966, carton 921, EGB Papers.

105. Letter from Kathleen Stone to Edmund G. Brown, 1 November 1966, carton 921, EGB Papers; letter from Ruth P. Smith to Edmund G. Brown, 28 October 1966, carton 921, EGB Papers.

106. Letter from A. W. Nissley to Edmund G. Brown, 8 January 1965, carton 928, EGB Papers.

107. *Register*, 29 November 1966.

108. Ibid.

109. Letter from E. J. Stidham to Edmund G. Brown, 17 May 1966, carton 928, EGB Papers.

110. Letter from Victor A. MacFarlane to Edmund G. Brown, n.d., carton 928, EGB Papers.

111. *CRA Newsletter*, August 1966, box 3, CRA Papers.

112. *New York Times*, 26 June 1966.

113. *Register*, 13 October 1966.

114. *New York Times*, 12 August 1966, 15; Robert. L. Coate, Chairman, Democratic State Central Committee, "Ronald Reagan, Extremist Collaborator, An Expose."

115. *CRA Newsletter*, August 1966.

116. Letter from Edward Anderson to Ronald Reagan, 28 October 1966, box 1, RR Papers.

117. Letter from Mr. and Mrs. Ronald Chronister to Edmund G. Brown, n.d., carton 921, EGB Papers.

118. Letter from Kathryn W. Johnson to Ronald Reagan, 13 September 1966, box 7, RR Papers.

119. Sullivan, interview.

120. *Register*, 6 November 1966.

121. Letter from Marjorie Carnes to Ronald Reagan, n.d., box 2, RR Papers.

122. Letter from Barbara Adams to Ronald Reagan, 8 October 1966, box 1, RR Papers.

123. Ibid.

124. Letter from Edward Anderson to Ronald Reagan, 28 October 1966, box 1, RR Papers.

125. Letter from W. L. Coddington to Ronald Reagan, 23 March 1966, box 2, RR Papers.

126. Letter from Don Collins to Ronald Reagan, 9 June 1966, box 2, RR Papers.

127. Downey Young Republican Meeting, Transcript of questions and answers, 25 August 1965, box 36, RR Papers.

128. Eugene C. Lee and Bruce E. Keith, eds., *California Votes, 1960–1972: A Review and Analysis of Registration and Voting* (Berkeley: Institute of Governmental Studies, University of California, 1974).

129. Totton J. Anderson and Eugene C. Lee, "The 1966 Election in California," *Western Political Quarterly* 20 (June 1967): 547.

130. Hill, *Dancing Bear*, 218–21; Anderson and Lee, "The 1966 Election in California," 547.

131. Anderson and Lee, "The 1966 Election in California," 549; see also Phillips, *The Emerging Republican Majority*, 441.

132. Anderson and Lee, "The 1966 Election in California," 549.

133. Ibid.

134. *Ramparts*, November 1965, 35.

135. Letter from Ronald Reagan to Barry Goldwater, 11 June 1966, box 23, RR Papers.

136. Anderson and Lee, "The 1966 Election in California," 535.

137. Letter from Cyril Stevenson to Frank P. Adams, 10 January 1968, box 14, CRA Papers. See also *San Francisco Examiner*, 28 December 1967. Stevenson's decision to join the American Independent Party had as much to do with his disillusionment with Reagan's failure to cut taxes and spending as with any attraction to Wallace's populist appeal. Referring to the Republican platform in 1966, he said, "We promised to hold the line and shift taxes. We promised to repeal or amend the Rumford Forced Housing Act. The elected Republicans did not keep their promises. . . . It seems to me the CRA has deserted its principles and lost its positive spirit, all to the bleat of unity and the Republican Party's leftward drift. . . . At last California voters now have an alternative to Socialist Party A and Socialist Party B, the unshackled American Independent Party."

138. Letter from Ted H. Lefever to V. Adm. Albert E. Jarrel, 15 January 1968, box 14, CRA Papers.

139. Schmitz was defeated in the primary run of the heavily Republican Fortieth District in Orange County. His defeat was largely attributed to his bitter opposition to Richard Nixon (one of Schmitz's constituents). Two months later, after becoming the new standard-bearer for the AIP, Schmitz abandoned the Republican Party. See *Los Angeles Times*, 5 August 1972, 10; 8 June 1972.

140. *Register*, 23 October 1968.

141. Phillips, *The Emerging Republican Majority*, 450–51.

142. *California Statesman*, April 1973, John Schmitz Collection, University of California, Irvine.

143. How conservatives successfully harnessed the metaphor of "middle America" and the way in which it helped to steer populism in their direction is discussed by Michael Kazin in *The Populist Persuasion*, 253.

144. For a discussion of the mobilization of white racist sentiment and its political implications, see Diamond, *Roads to Dominion*, 67–90, 142–59.

145. The National States Rights Party, American Nazi Party, and Citizen's Councils did exist in the southland, but their following was "very small in membership and influence," according to a report by the attorney general. See *New York Times*, 13 April 1965, 15.

146. Reinhard, *The Republican Right since 1945*, 153–54. Staunch conservatives were angered by Nixon's pact with Nelson Rockefeller that offered Rockefeller's support (and thus that of the eastern Republican wing of the party) for Nixon's candidacy in return for compromises on national and foreign policy.

147. Larson, "The Issue of Birchism in the 1962 California Republican Gubernatorial Primary," 181–202; *New York Times*, 7 June 1962, 1.

148. See, for example, editorial, "Nixon on Target," *Indianapolis News*, 9 November 1964; and "The Need for Unifiers," *Charleston News and Courier*, 7 November 1964.

149. Reinhard, *The Republican Right since 1945*, 218.

150. Kazin, *The Populist Persuasion*, 248.

151. Reinhard, *The Republican Right since 1945*, 219; Garry Wills, *Nixon Agonistes: The Crisis of the Self-Made Man* (Boston: Houghton Mifflin, 1970), 9–11, 256.

152. Wills, *Nixon Agonistes*, 257.

153. Reinhard, *The Republican Right since 1945*, 219. See also "The Nixon Stand," campaign leaflet, box 3, folder 4, CRA Papers; Kazin, *The Populist Persuasion*, 250.

154. Wills, *Nixon Agonistes*, 312. See also Jonathan Rieder, "The Rise of the 'Silent Majority,'" in *The Rise and Fall of the New Deal Order, 1930–1980*, ed. Steve Fraser and Gary Gerstle (Princeton, N.J.: Princeton University Press, 1989), 243–68.

155. See Wills, *Nixon Agonistes*, 266. See also Michael Kazin's discussion of Nixon's creation of a populism of "middle America," in *The Populist Persuasion*, 248–55.

156. Kazin, *The Populist Persuasion*, 253.

157. Ibid.

158. See Phillips, *The Emerging Republican Majority*; Reinhard, *The Republican Right since 1945*, 220; Wills, *Nixon Agonistes*, 265–68.

159. Wills, *Nixon Agonistes*, 266.

160. Ibid.

161. Rogin and Shover, *Political Change in California*, 154.

CHAPTER 6

1. Epstein and Forster, *Report on the John Birch Society, 1966*, 83; George Thayer, *The Farther Shores of Politics: The American Political Fringe Today* (New York: Simon and Schuster, 1967), 194.

2. Sullivan, interview.

3. *National Review*, 19 October 1965, 913–28.

4. Ibid. In early 1965, moreover, the newly born American Conservative Union went on record as "distinguishing their membership as wholly separate from the John Birch Society." See Minutes of the Meeting of the Board of Directors of the American Conservative Union, 18–19 December 1964, box 57, Marvin Liebman Papers, HIWRP.

5. Diamond, *Roads to Dominion*, 147–48.

6. Ibid.

7. California Legislature, Senate Fact-Finding Subcommittee on Un-American Activities in California, *Twelfth Report of the Senate Fact-Finding Subcommittee on Un-American Activities*, 1963, 61.

8. Epstein and Forster, *Report on the John Birch Society, 1966*, 6.

9. Letter from Robert Welch to Barry Goldwater, 4 November 1965, Denison Kitchel Papers, HIWRP.

10. Pearce and Muckenthaler, interviews.

11. Bergland, interview.

12. *Register*, 10 May 1972.

13. Epstein and Forster, *Report on the John Birch Society, 1966*, 64–69. Although Epstein and Forster read Robert Welch's hard-hitting 1965 fundraising appeal as part of the society's continued drive to influence national politics, their evidence points to serious financial problems for the organization. See also Harry Harvey, "Whatever Happened to the John Birch Society?" *Orange County Illustrated*, October 1973, 38–44.

14. Thayer, *The Farther Shores of Politics*, 193.

15. See Harvey, "Whatever Happened to the John Birch Society?" 38–44; "Report on the John Birch Society, Western States," 14 April 1969, Anti-Defamation League Pacific Southwest Regional Office.

16. "Report on the John Birch Society, Western States," 14 April 1969, Anti-Defamation League Pacific Southwest Regional Office.

17. Ibid.

18. *New York Times*, 17 January 1969, 17; Breasted, *Oh! Sex Education!* 75; Joseph N. Bell, "Why the Revolt against Sex Education?" *Good Housekeeping*, November 1969, 93.

19. As late as 1969, when the Birch Society entered the sex education struggle, it still could not entirely abandon its focus on communist conspirators. See Breasted, *Oh! Sex Education!*, 224.

20. *Register*, 5 August 1969, 4 August 1969.

21. This new conspiracy, first suggested in an article in the society's magazine in 1962, was picked up by Welch in a speech in Chicago in 1964 and articulated in greater detail in *American Opinion* in November 1966. Lipset and Raab, *The Politics of Unreason*, 252.

22. *Register*, 13 November 1969.

23. Ibid.

24. Diamond, *Roads to Dominion*, 148. Diamond also notes that activists from these organizations supported the Wallace campaign and future American Party campaigns. My thanks to Jerome Himmelstein for pointing out this shift.

25. Randall Smith, interview with Duff Witman Griffith, 10 October 1972, in Griffith, "Before the Deluge," 5–6.

26. Pearce and Muckenthaler, interviews.

27. Minutes of the Meeting of the Board of Directors of the California Republican Assembly, 4–6 December 1964, box 1, CRA Papers; Frizzelle, interview; *Register*, 30 March 1965, 2 May 1965; *CRA Newsletter*, August 1966, box 3, CRA Papers; *Orange County Observer*, January 1971, 21.

28. Slocum, interview.

29. *Register*, 6 June 1966.

30. See Hill, *Dancing Bear*, 215–17; Sullivan, interview.

31. Letter from W. W. Toy, California State University, Fullerton, to California Free Enterprise Association, 28 March 1975, returned with the notation that the "California Free Enterprise Association was phased out of existence two years ago." California Free Enterprise Association folder, FCC.

32. Edward Mills, "Kitchen Cabinet: Four Citizen Advisors to Ronald Reagan," 1983, Oral History Program, California State University, Fullerton, 78–80.

33. Timothy LaHaye, close to two decades later, founded the influential Washington-based American Coalition for Traditional Values, and William Dannemeyer's career in Congress in the 1980s earned him the reputation as

one of the most outspoken and controversial spokespersons for the Religious Right on Capitol Hill. Letter to Ronald Reagan from California League Enlisting Action Now, 18 July 1966, box 3, RR Papers; William Dannemeyer, interview with author, 7 October 1998.

34. *CRA Newsletter*, August 1966, box 3, CRA Papers; Hill, *Dancing Bear*, 215–17.

35. *CRA Newsletter*, August 1966, box 3, CRA Papers; Hill, *Dancing Bear*, 215–17.

36. The results were 189,676 to 185,742. California Secretary of State, *Statement of Vote*, supplement, General Election, 8 November 1966.

37. Breasted, *Oh! Sex Education!*, 24–25; transcript of special meeting on FLSE, 21 August 1969, 17, minutes, Board of Trustees, Anaheim Union High School District, Anaheim, California, 1968–70.

38. Letter from Ronald H. Lincoln and Pat Patterson to Congressman James B. Utt, 21 January 1970, box 40, JS Papers.

39. *Miller v. California*, Supreme Court Report 93A 411–413 U.S., October Term 1973, 2610–2611.

40. Richard F. Hixson, *Pornography and the Justices: The Supreme Court and the Intractable Obscenity Problem* (Carbondale: Southern Illinois University Press, 1996), 113–15; Margaret A. Blanchard, *Revolutionary Sparks: Freedom of Expression in Modern America* (New York: Oxford University Press, 1992), 388.

41. William Martin devoted a chapter in his book on the rise of the Christian Right nationally to the Anaheim struggle over sex education. See William C. Martin, *With God on Our Side: The Rise of the Religious Right in America* (New York: Broadway Books, 1996), 100–116.

42. Breasted, *Oh! Sex Education!*, 31–33.

43. Ibid.

44. Begun as a pilot program in 1965 called Family Life and Sex Education (FLSE), the curriculum was expanded into a full-fledged program with the help of the Sex Information and Education Council of the United States (SIECUS). By 1967, the four-and-one-half-week courses were taught in grades seven through twelve, serving as a model for districts looking to establish such programs. *Los Angeles Times*, 24 October 1969.

45. Howe, interview; Bell, "Why the Revolt Against Sex Education?"

46. Breasted, *Oh! Sex Education!*, 62.

47. *Los Angeles Times* (Orange County edition), 29 March 1970.

48. Breasted, *Oh! Sex Education!*, 34.

49. Ibid., 35.

50. Transcript of special meeting on FLSE, 21 August 1969, 25, minutes, Board of Trustees, Anaheim Union High School District, Anaheim, California, 1968–70.

51. Howe, interview.

52. See Gordon Drake, "Is the Schoolhouse the Proper Place to Teach Raw Sex?"; quoted in Breasted, *Oh! Sex Education!*, 224.

53. Minutes, Board of Trustees, Anaheim Union High School District, Anaheim, California, 1968–70.

54. *Los Angeles Times*, 11 April 1970.

55. Ibid., 24 October 1969.

56. *Register*, 1 May 1970.

57. Minutes of the meeting of the Board of Directors of the California Republican Assembly, 26–28 September 1969, box 1, CRA Papers.

58. Breasted, *Oh! Sex Education!*, 58.

59. Transcript of special meeting on FLSE, 21 August 1969, 25, minutes, Board of Trustees, Anaheim Union High School District, Anaheim, California, 1968–70.

60. These new concerns formed a central part of the creation of what has come to be called the New Right. Rather than seeing it as something completely "new," however, I see it as a conservative reorientation. For a discussion of the New Right, see Allen Hunter, "In the Wings: New Right Ideology and Organization," *Radical America* 15 (spring 1981): 113–38.

61. Kristen Luker, *Abortion and the Politics of Motherhood* (Berkeley: University of California Press, 1984), 134; Mary C. Segers and Timothy A. Byrnes, eds., *Abortion Politics in American States* (Armonk, N.Y.: M. E. Sharpe, 1995), 171–73; Dallas A. Blanchard, *The Anti-abortion Movement and the Rise of the Religious Right: From Polite to Fiery Protest* (New York: Twayne, 1994), 25–26.

62. Segers and Byrnes, *Abortion Politics in American States*, 171–73.

63. Luker, *Abortion and the Politics of Motherhood*, 134; Segers and Byrnes, *Abortion Politics in American States*, 171–73.

64. Letter from Cora Carney to Congressman John Schmitz, 16 June 1971, box 1, JS Papers.

65. *Register*, 30 June 1970.

66. For an excellent discussion of the worldview of pro-life activists, see Luker, *Abortion and the Politics of Motherhood*, 158–91.

67. Ibid., 161–63.

68. Ibid.

69. Such was the case, for example, with Barbara Dallenegra, president of Christian Women in Action in 1979, and Beverly Cielnicky. For the meshing

of these concerns organizationally, see Christian Women in Action Newsletter, Anaheim, California, January 1977, FCC.

70. Sullivan, interview.

71. Ibid.

72. Reverend Daily of the Pentecostal Assembly of God Church in Santa Ana, Reverend Ray Chappell of the Bethel Baptist Church of Santa Ana, Reverend Tandema of the Community Christian Reformed Church, and Reverend Ramsey of the Shiloh Baptist Church, together with a number of medical doctors and priests from Saint Barbara's parish, joined the mobilization. Letter from Inek Vifinkle, Secretary, Citizens Action Committee, to Congressman John Schmitz, 9 March 1971, box 1, folder 6, JS Papers; letter from Cathy Sullivan, Co-Chairman, Citizens Action Committee, to Congressman John Schmitz, 20 December 1971, box 64, JS Papers.

73. Sullivan, interview.

74. Beverly Cielnicky, interview with author, 9 October 1998.

75. Ibid.

76. Ibid. For a brief history of the origins of Concerned Women for America, see Janna Hansen, "The Role for Which God Created Them: Women in the United States Religious Right" (bachelor's thesis, Harvard University, 1997), 39–40.

77. Cielnicky, interview.

78. Ibid.

79. Sullivan, interview.

80. Don Smith, interview with author, 16 August 1999.

81. See pamphlet "What Is Crusade for Life?" n.d., in author's possession; and Don Tanner, ed., *The Silent Scream: The Complete Text of the Documentary Film with an Authoritative Response to the Critics*, comp. by Donald S. Smith (Anaheim, Calif.: American Portrait Films, 1985), 91–93.

82. Tanner, *The Silent Scream*.

83. Smith, interview.

84. Sullivan, interview.

85. Slocum, interview.

86. Bergland, interview.

87. Ibid.

88. Sullivan, interview.

89. Indeed, the divisiveness of the issue had led even some staunch conservatives who opposed abortion to hope to shelve it to solidify conservative ranks. Pearce and Muckenthaler, interviews.

90. Bergland, interview.

91. Voters who went to the polls read that the initiative would define "nudity, obscenities, sadomasochistic abuse, sexual conduct, sexual excitement and other related terms." California Secretary of State, *Statement of Vote and Supplement*, General Election, November 1972. See also California Secretary of State, *California Voters Pamphlet*, General Election, November 1972.

92. The number of registered voters in the years between 1966 and 1972 increased by 53 percent (from 518,004 to 794,174).

93. The dividing line between "pure" libertarians and religious conservatives deepened, moreover, as social issues took a front seat in propelling grassroots conservatives to action, and a small number of libertarians responded by championing personal freedom. These divisions were most evident in the ranks of the Young Americans for Freedom, which had an active contingent in Orange County. California YAF was at the forefront of the battle that split the conservative student organization ranks between its radical libertarian and traditionalist wings in 1969. Responding to the growing "anarcho-libertarian" contingent that stressed personal freedoms, hostility toward traditionalist moralism, and increasing opposition to the Vietnam war, the national office purged most of the California state board from its ranks. The Orange County YAF chairman, Dana Rohrabacher, was one of the libertarian leaders purged by the national office. Jonathan Schoenwald, "The Other Counterculture: Young Americans for Freedom, 1960–1969 (unpublished conference paper, Towards a History of the 1960s, State Historical Society of Wisconsin, Madison, 28 April–1 May 1993). On Orange County YAF, see Letter from Patrick Dowd to Dana Rohrabacher, 3 April 1969, box 1, PD Papers; letter from Patrick Dowd to John Schureman, Seal Beach, 17 March 1969, box 1, PD Papers; letter from Patrick Dowd to Mr. Rick Barry, Fullerton, California, box 1, PD Papers; letter from Patrick Dowd to Randal C. Teague, box 1, PD Papers; letter from John Schureman, Executive Director, YAF Orange County, to Patrick Dowd, 17 May 1969, box 1, PD Papers. For broader discussions of the YAF split nationally, see Schneider, *Cadre for Conservatism*. John Andrews is also useful for the early history of YAF. Andrews, *The Other Side of the Sixties*.

94. *Register*, 20 October 1968.

95. Ibid., 24 October 1968.

96. Ibid., 23 October 1968, 9 October 1968.

97. Proposition 9 and an alternative measure, Proposition 1, both went down to defeat. California Secretary of State, *Statement of Vote*, General Election, 5 November 1968. For discussions of the implications of Proposition 13 on county and state finances, see David O. Sears and Jack Citrin, *Tax Revolt: Something for Nothing in California* (Cambridge, Mass.: Harvard University Press, 1982); and Mark Baldassare, *When Government Fails: The Orange*

County Bankruptcy (Berkeley: University of California Press, 1998), 21–28, 61–67. Baldassare argues that Proposition 13 was one of a set of factors that explained the conditions contributing to the bankruptcy of Orange County in 1994.

98. For local expressions of such outrage in Orange County, see *Register,* 30 November 1976, C10; 12 August 1976, A4; 29 August 1976, A6.

99. Ibid., 29 June 1961, 13 January 1961; Diamond, *Roads to Dominion,* 51–52.

100. Ibid.

101. *Riverside Enterprise,* 13 January 1962.

102. Sears and Citrin, *Tax Revolt,* 26, 89–90, 95, 235.

103. Ibid., 44; *California Journal,* October 1979, 332–33.

104. *Register,* 20 June 1973, 22 January 1973, 12 August 1973, 21 August 1976. See also Marvin Olsen, interview with Duff Witman Griffith, 17 October 1972, in Griffith, "Before the Deluge."

105. Marvin Olsen, interview with Duff Witman Griffith, 17 October 1972.

106. Ibid., 17–18.

107. This language permeated antibusing mobilization. Orange County Bus-Bloc, 4 January 1979, leaflet, FCC.

108. For a detailed history of this struggle in Boston, see Formisano, *Boston against Busing.*

109. Orange County Bus-Bloc, 4 January 1979, leaflet, FCC; Christian Women in Action Newsletter, January 1977; Christian Women in Action, leaflet, 18 January 1978, FCC; Sullivan, interview.

110. Orange County Bus-Bloc, 4 January 1979, leaflet, FCC; California against Forced Busing, FCC; *Register,* 26 April 1982.

111. *Register,* 8 August 1970, 6 June 1970.

112. *Los Angeles Times,* 6 August 1970.

113. Jeffrey K. Hadden, "Religious Broadcasting and the Mobilization of the New Christian Right," in *Fundamentalism and Evangelicalism,* ed. Martin E. Marty (Munich: K. G. Saur, 1993), 295; James Davison Hunter, *American Evangelicalism: Conservative Religion and the Quandary of Modernity* (New Brunswick, N.J.: Rutgers University Press, 1983); Steve Bruce, *The Rise and Fall of the New Christian Right: Conservative Protestant Politics in America, 1978–1988* (Oxford: Clarendon Press, 1988); Bruce B. Lawrence, *Defenders of God: The Fundamentalist Revolt against the Modern Age* (San Francisco: Harper and Row, 1989). See also Nancy T. Ammerman, "North American Protestant Fundamentalism," in *Fundamentalisms Observed,* vol. 1, ed. Martin E. Marty and R. Scott Appleby (Chicago: University of Chicago Press, 1991), 37–47; Martin E. Marty and R. Scott Appleby, *The Glory and the*

Power: The Fundamentalist Challenge to the Modern World (Boston: Beacon Press, 1992); Wilcox, *God's Warriors.*

114. See, for example, Dean M. Kelley, *Why Conservative Churches Are Growing: A Study in Sociology of Religion* (New York: Harper and Row, 1972), an early discussion by a liberal Protestant leader seeking to explain the growth of evangelical Christianity; Reginald Bibby, "Why Conservative Churches Really Are Growing," *Journal for the Scientific Study of Religion* 17 (June 1978): 129–37. In addition, Robert Wuthnow notes the fantastic growth of evangelical denominations in the 1970s, which far outpaced that of more liberal denominations. See Wuthnow, *The Restructuring of American Religion: Society and Faith since World War II* (Princeton, N.J.: Princeton University Press, 1988), 192–93. Mark Shibley has studied data showing that between 1971 and 1990, evangelical churches added more than 6 million new members, while the mainline moderate Protestant churches lost about 2.6 million. See Shibley, *Resurgent Evangelicalism in the United States: Mapping Cultural Change since 1970* (Columbia: University of South Carolina Press, 1996), 27. See also David A. Roozen and C. Kirk Hadaway, "Denominations Grow as Individuals Join Congregations," in *Church and Denominational Growth*, ed. David A. Roozen and C. Kirk Hadaway (Nashville, Tenn.: Abingdon Press, 1993), 15–45.

115. Sandeen, *The Roots of Fundamentalism*, 195. See also Marsden, *Fundamentalism and American Culture*, 118–19.

116. Starr, *Material Dreams*, 136–37.

117. Synan, *The Holiness-Pentecostal Tradition*, 84–106.

118. For biographical information on McPherson and her church, see Edith Waldvogel Blumhofer, *Aimee Semple McPherson: Everybody's Sister* (Grand Rapids, Mich.: William B. Eerdmans, 1993).

119. Lewis, "Charles E. Fuller," 148–54.

120. For the conservative religious influence in Los Angeles, see Starr, *Material Dreams*, 133–44. James Gregory has successfully charted the conservative religious influence and the vibrant evangelical subculture created among dust bowl migrants and their children in the 1930s and 1940s upon migrating to California (particularly the Central Valley region). See Gregory, *American Exodus: The Dust Bowl Migration and Okie Culture in California* (New York: Oxford University Press, 1989). For further evidence of the strong evangelical influence in Southern California, see Robert Durrenberger, *California, the Last Frontier* (New York: Van Nostrand Reinhold, 1969); F. Patrick Nichelson, "Non-Protestants in Southern California," in *The American West and the Religious Experience*, ed. William Kramer (Los Angeles: Will Kramer, 1975), 74–75; Eldon G. Ernst with Douglas Firth Anderson, *Pilgrim Progression: The*

Protestant Experience in California (Santa Barbara, Calif.: Fithian Press, 1993), especially 83–100.

121. See chapter 1.

122. See chapter 2.

123. Gathright, interview.

124. By 1975, according to a survey conducted by the Orange County Human Relations Commission, 17 percent of Orange County churches belonged to the theologically and socially conservative National Association of Evangelicals. Only 33 percent of churches were affiliated with the liberal National Council of Churches. See Orange County Human Relations Commission, "Churches of Orange County: A Profile of Services, Concerns and Priorities," 1975, Mother Colony History Room, Anaheim Public Library. In response to a question the commission posed regarding the "social concerns" of clergy and parishioners, by far of greatest importance for Orange County churchgoers were concerns over "problems of family relations," "widespread immorality," and "lack of spiritual and moral commitment." Ranked lowest on the list were concerns over unemployment, lack of available housing for low-income and minority groups, and inadequate public health facilities. Clearly, many Orange County churchgoers did not embrace the "social gospel" of mainline Protestantism.

125. "Megachurches," huge congregations sharing a conservative theology, have mushroomed in these suburban regions. See *New York Times*, 16 April 1995. Additionally, Mark Shibley has found that evangelical churches have grown at a faster rate in the West than in the traditional southern Bible Belt. See Shibley, *Resurgent Evangelicalism in the United States*, 27.

126. Dionne, *Why Americans Hate Politics*, 219–21.

127. Donald Miller, who has closely examined the draw of what he terms "new paradigm churches," offers support for this argument. He contends that they are successful in part because of their emphasis on emotional expressiveness, authenticity, and immediacy, as well as picking up on the anti-establishment themes of the counterculture. See Donald E. Miller, *Reinventing American Protestantism: Christianity in the New Millennium* (Berkeley: University of California Press, 1997), 1–20. Martin Marty also contends that the new secularism of the 1960s "did not satisfy the religious needs and interest of people as they faced a period of diffusion, of confusion over social location, of bewilderment over the questions, 'Who am I?' and 'To whom do I belong?' " Evangelicalism, by forming a new community rooted in clear, authoritative answers, "helped provide boundaries for the psyche," he says. See Marty, "The Revival of Evangelicalism and Southern Religion," in *Varieties of Southern*

Evangelicalism, ed. David Edwin Harrell Jr. (Macon, Ga.: Mercer University Press, 1981), 17–19.

128. Leonard I. Sweet, "The 1960s: The Crisis of Liberal Christianity and the Public Emergence of Evangelicalism," in *Evangelicalism and Modern America*, ed. George Marsden (Grand Rapids, Mich.: William B. Eerdmans, 1984), 29–45.

129. The movement had gained national attention by 1971. See Brian Vachon, "The Jesus Movement Is Upon Us," *Look*, 9 February 1971, 15–20; "The New Rebel Cry: Jesus Is Coming," *Time*, 21 June 1971, 56–63; James Nolan, "Hogwash and Holy Water," *Ramparts*, August 1971, 20–26.

130. For an overview of the history of Calvary Chapel and its success in planting new churches, see Miller, *Reinventing American Protestantism*, 27–52. See also *Los Angeles Times*, 5 July 1971.

131. Harry Harvey, "The Jesus Movement: National Religious Awakening among Young People Began in Orange County," *Orange County Illustrated*, July 1972, 47; *Register*, 29 November 1966.

132. Harvey, "The Jesus Movement," 47; *Register*, 29 November 1966.

133. "Jesus Lives," *Maranatha Goodnews Paper*, 1 (2) 1973, Maranatha folder, FCC.

134. Harvey, "The Jesus Movement," 44–48; *Register*, 26 March 1978; Michael S. Smith, "Apocalypse Now," *New West*, 12 March 1979, SC-2–SC-3.

135. Chuck Smith and Tal Brooke, *Harvest* (Old Tappan, N.J.: Chosen Books, 1989). Even today, the church continues to build on this founding legacy: The cover of *Harvest*, a brief history of the Calvary Chapel, announces, "Gang members, drug addicts, mental patients, society's rejects . . . Chuck Smith's amazing story of Calvary Chapel and the unlikely leaders God called."

136. Harvey, "The Jesus Movement," 44–48; Miller, *Reinventing American Protestantism*, 34.

137. Smith, "Apocalypse Now," SC-3; *Register*, 26 March 1978; Larry Taylor, *What Calvary Chapel Teaches: A Brief Explanation of the Doctrine of the Calvary Chapel Movement* (Twin Peaks, Calif.: Calvary Chapel Bible College, 1994). See also "Modest Pastor Sees Costa Mesa Flock Grow," *Los Angeles Times*, 12 October 1990.

138. Taylor, *What Calvary Chapel Teaches*, 2.

139. Boyer, *When Time Shall Be No More*, 160. Boyer, in his discussion of prophecy thinkers in post–World War II America, draws on the writings of Chuck Smith along with several other major writers. Boyer, *When Time Shall Be No More*, 269–70.

140. "Jesus Lives," *Maranatha Goodnews Paper*, 1 (2) 1973, Maranatha folder, FCC. See also Chuck Smith, *What the World Is Coming To* (Costa

Mesa, Calif.: Word for Today, 1980); Smith *Future Survival* (Costa Mesa, Calif.: Word for Today, 1978).

141. "Jesus Lives," *Maranatha Goodnews Paper*, 1 (2) 1973, Maranatha folder, FCC.

142. Ibid.

143. Boyer, *When Time Shall Be No More*, 269–70; Strozier, *Apocalypse*, 193.

144. Robert G. Clouse, "The New Christian Right, America, and the Kingdom of God," in *Fundamentalism and Evangelicalism*, ed. Martin E. Marty (Munich: K. G. Saur, 1993), 281–94. For an analysis of the conservative beliefs of pastors and members of new paradigm churches like Calvary Chapel in surveys conducted in the 1990s, see Miller, *Reinventing American Protestantism*, 133.

145. Boyer, *When Time Shall Be No More*, 5–18.

146. Ibid., 305.

147. Charles B. Strozier has emphasized that "what defines the fundamentalist church is the intensity of its group interaction and the way it draws the individual into its rituals in an active way. Participation is never casual. This creates, in his words, "a strong cohesive community." See Strozier, *Apocalypse*, 16; "This Week at Calvary Chapel," weekly schedule of events for 14 August 1994, in author's possession.

148. For a broader discussion of the way in which the Protestant evangelical community has made its peace with commercial culture by deciding to become a "bigger roadside attraction," see R. Laurence Moore, *Selling God: American Religion in the Marketplace of Culture* (New York: Oxford University Press, 1994), 238–65.

149. *Register*, 26 March 1978.

150. Smith, "Apocalypse Now," SC-3.

151. The directory was intended to "encourage" Christians to patronize other Christians. *The Christian Business and Professional Directory*, Orange County Edition, 1976–77 (Santa Ana, Calif.: California Christian Business Service). See also Moore, *Selling God*, 255.

152. *San Diego Church News*, August 1976.

153. T. D. Allman, "Jesus in Tomorrowland," *New Republic*, 27 November 1976, 8.

154. Penner, *Goliath*, 108.

155. See also chapter 2.

156. Gathright, interview.

157. Voskuil, *Mountains into Goldmines*, 26; Penner, *Goliath*, 182.

158. Voskuil, *Mountains into Goldmines*, 25; Penner, *Goliath*, 179, 165.

159. Penner, *Goliath*, 182.

160. Ibid., 217.

161. Allman, "Jesus in Tomorrowland," 6–9; *Register*, 5 March 1978.

162. This ranking came out of a poll by *Christian Century*. Voskuil, *Mountains into Goldmines*, 55.

163. Penner, *Goliath*, 228.

164. Ibid., 284–85.

165. *Newsweek*, 6 October 1980, 97; Voskuil, *Mountains into Goldmines*, 35. Schuller, however, did not escape criticism. Many observers saw the cathedral as a massive symbol of materialism and self-indulgence. Voskuil, *Mountains into Goldmines*, 31.

166. Voskuil, *Mountains into Goldmines*, 131.

167. Ibid., 158.

168. *Register*, 8 April 1962.

169. Averill, interview.

170. Ibid.

171. Ibid.

172. Allman, "Jesus in Tomorrowland," 6–9; *Register*, 5 March 1978.

173. Voskuil, *Mountains into Goldmines*, 67.

174. Ibid., 67.

175. Ibid., 77–78.

176. *Register*, 12 March 1978.

177. Breasted, *Oh! Sex Education!*, 25.

178. *Register*, 12 March 1978.

179. Boyer, *When Time Shall Be No More*, 257.

180. For the growth of "televangelism," see Jeffrey K. Hadden and Charles E. Swann, *Prime-Time Preachers: The Rising Power of Televangelism* (Reading, Mass.: Addison-Wesley, 1981).

181. *Register*, 19 March 1978.

182. Ibid.

183. Boyer, *When Time Shall Be No More*, 5.

184. Melodyland, for example, entered visible decline by the 1990s. At the same time, large churches like Calvary Chapel have spawned independent offshoot congregations that have become successful in their own right. The Vineyard, for example, a charismatic evangelical church located in Anaheim Hills, was founded by a close follower of Chuck Smith in the mid-1980s. It has since spawned hundreds of little Vineyard missions throughout the southland and the West.

185. Boyer, *When Time Shall Be No More*, 5; *New York Times*, 16 April 1995.

186. *New York Times*, 16 April 1995.

187. Sara Diamond, *Not by Politics Alone: The Enduring Influence of the Christian Right* (New York: Guilford Press, 1998), 47.

188. Not all theologically conservative churches were necessarily politically conservative. Some scholars have thus argued for the significance of political diversity among evangelicals. However, while evangelical commitments sometimes led to progressive and liberal politics, a great deal more evidence points to a politically conservative direction of evangelical commitments. See, for example, Richard V. Pierard, *The Unequal Yoke: Evangelical Christianity and Political Conservatism* (Philadelphia: Lippincott, 1970); Lienesch, "Right-Wing Religion," 403–25; James L. Guth, "The New Christian Right," in *The New Christian Right: Mobilization and Legitimation*, ed. Robert C. Liebman and Robert Wuthnow (Hawthorne, N.Y.: Aldine, 1983), 31–45; Guth et al., eds., *The Bully Pulpit: The Politics of Protestant Clergy* (Lawrence: University Press of Kansas, 1997); Perry Deane Young, *God's Bullies: Native Reflections on Preachers and Politics* (New York: Holt, Rinehart and Winston, 1982); Robert Zwier, *Born-Again Politics: The New Christian Right in America* (Downers Grove, Ill.: InterVarsity Press, 1982); Richard John Neuhaus and Michael Cromartie, eds., *Piety and Politics: Evangelicals and Fundamentalists Confront the World* (Washington, D.C.: Ethics and Public Policy Center, 1987).

189. Fred Schwarz, interview with author, 21 August 1996.

190. Hunter, *American Evangelicalism*; Bruce, *The Rise and Fall of the New Christian Right*; Lawrence, *Defenders of God*. See also Ammerman, "North American Protestant Fundamentalism"; Wilcox, *God's Warriors*.

191. Marty, "The Revival of Evangelicalism and Southern Religion," 11.

192. Ibid., 15.

193. Dionne, *Why Americans Hate Politics*, 223–24.

194. Hertel was converted to fundamentalist Christianity by a fellow officer while serving in the Marine Corps; Smith, "Apocalypse Now."

195. Lienesch, "Right-Wing Religion," 403–26; Guth, "The New Christian Right," 31–45; Young, *God's Bullies*; Zwier, *Born-Again Politics*.

196. *Los Angeles Times*, 6 October 1978, 1. See also Diamond, *Roads to Dominion*, 171.

197. *Christianity Today*, 1 December 1978, 40; *Los Angeles Times*, 2 March 1979.

198. *Los Angeles Times*, 31 October 1978.

199. Ibid.

200. *Los Angeles Times*, 23 September 1978, 9 November 1978, 6 October 1978, 24.

201. Ibid.

202. *Los Angeles Times*, 2 March 1979.

203. Diamond, *Roads to Dominion*, 171.

204. *New York Times*, 19 December 1994.

205. Young, *God's Bullies*. And in nearby San Diego, Timothy LaHaye, an important prophecy writer and head of the influential Scott Memorial Baptist Church, sat on the Moral Majority's first board of directors. See Himmelstein, *To the Right*, 117. Christian Cause leaflet, 1977, by the Reverend Robert Grant, in author's possession. See also Diamond, *Roads to Dominion*, 171.

206. Hunter, "In the Wings," 124–25; Young, *God's Bullies*, 101–6.

207. Diamond, *Roads to Dominion*, 171.

208. Smith, "Apocalypse Now."

209. California Secretary of State, *Statement of Vote*, General Election, 4 November 1980. "Large" is defined here as a county of more than 250,000 residents. Many small counties surpassed Orange County.

210. In the general election in November, Reagan won handily, with 51 percent of the popular vote to Carter's 41 percent. The Republican landslide also gave that party control of the Senate for the first time since 1954.

211. On the strengthening of older think tanks and the establishment of new ones, see Diamond, *Roads to Dominion*, 199–205. See also Sanford M. Jacoby, *Modern Manors: Welfare Capitalism since the New Deal* (Princeton, N.J.: Princeton University Press, 1997). On the Christian Right's focus on Washington lobbying and its relationship to the Reagan administration, see Diamond, *Roads to Dominion*, 234–36.

212. *Conservative Digest*, 26 April 1981, quoted in Jerome Himmelstein, *To the Right*.

213. Alan Brinkley has made this argument, but I would take it one step further and argue that there is a causal link between modern cultures and staunch fundamentalist morality. Brinkley, "The Problem of American Conservatism," 427.

EPILOGUE

1. Some examples of the prominence of relatively recent migrants among social issues activists are Lou Sheldon, who moved to Orange County to pastor a church in 1969, and Barbara Dallenegra, president of Christian Women to Action in 1978, who had lived in the county for a decade. Additionally, Beverly Cielnicky, who became involved in the pro-life movement, and Mrs. Burns, who was involved in the sex education struggle, both moved to the county in the late 1960s.

2. I draw this conclusion from an examination of the socioeconomic status of the key leaders of the later mobilization that closely paralleled the middle-class movement in the 1960s. Yet given the participation of Democrats and "former liberals" in, for example, the sex education struggle, it seems that these newer social issues drew in a broader base that included conservative lower-middle-class and even working-class elements. While my evidence is only suggestive here, other studies on the rank-and-file base of New Right struggles confirm a broadened class appeal. See, for example, Martin, *With God on Our Side*, 117–43; Kazin, *The Populist Persuasion*, 255–60; Rieder, *Canarsie*; Formisano, *Boston against Busing*; and Lienesch, "Right-Wing Religion," 413–14.

3. Dowell, interview.

4. Kieffer (formerly Kielsmeier), interview.

5. Dowell, interview; Kieffer (formerly Kielsmeier), interview.

6. Gathright, interview.

7. Ibid.

8. Ibid.

9. It is possible that more activists were "disillusioned" with conservative politics than is evident from the oral history interviews conducted for this book. One could argue that those individuals who were more likely to agree to be interviewed were those who remained dedicated to the movement. In a similar vein, one could argue that those who dropped out or altered their worldviews may have seen their activities in the 1960s as overzealous and were less likely to want to be associated with them. While I am aware of this argument, preinterview discussions made it quite evident that those who did not wish to be interviewed were most often motivated by a distrust of sharing their stories with an East Coast historian from an Ivy League university, rather than by any disillusionment or change of views.

10. Averill, interview.

11. She has, for example, been involved in the recent controversy over national history standards. Averill, interview.

12. Bergland, interview. For the formation of the national Libertarian Party, see Nash, *The Conservative Intellectual Movement in America since 1945*, 314; Diamond, *Roads to Dominion*, 123–27.

13. Sullivan, interview; follow-up interview, 24 August 1994.

14. Ibid.

15. Diamond, *Roads to Dominion*, 1; Haller, interview.

16. Haller, interview.

17. Pearce and Muckenthaler, interviews.

18. For a history of this movement in Southern California and some of its successes, see Spencer Olin, "Intraclass Conflict and the Politics of a Fragmented Region," *Postsuburban California: The Transformation of Orange County since World War II*, ed. Rob Kling, Spencer Olin, and Mark Poster (Berkeley: University of California Press, 1991), 238–41. See also Davis, *City of Quartz*, 151–221; *New York Times*, 19 August 1987. See also Larry Agran, "Orange County Populism and the Politics of Growth," *Journal of Orange County Studies* 1 (fall 1998): 6–8.

19. Rogers, interview.

20. Ibid.

21. Ibid.

22. Ibid.

23. Davis, *City of Quartz*, 188.

24. Olin, "Globalization and the Politics of Locality," 153.

25. Ibid.

26. Ibid., 152.

27. William Gayk, "The Changing Demography of Orange County," *Journal of Orange County Studies* 3–4 (spring 1990): 13–18; Baldassare, *When Government Fails*, 35–36; *Register*, 29 June 1987.

28. Lisbeth Haas, "Grass-Roots Protest and the Politics of Planning: Santa Ana, 1976–1988," in *Postsuburban California: The Transformation of Orange County since World War II*, ed. Rob Kling, Spencer Olin, and Mark Poster (Berkeley: University of California Press, 1991), 254–80.

29. Peter Applebome, "A Suburban Eden Where the Right Rules," *New York Times*, 1 August 1994; Judith Neuman, "Defining Orange County Conservatism," *Register*, 26 April 1982; *Register*, 29 June 1987. See also Baldassare, *When Government Fails*, 43–46; and Mark Baldassare, *Trouble in Paradise: The Suburban Transformation of America* (New York: Columbia University Press, 1986), 133–34.

30. *Register*, 29 June 1987.

31. Baldassare, *When Government Fails*, 42.

32. *Register*, 29 June 1987.

33. Baldassare, *When Government Fails*, 5–10. Baldassare's book provides an insightful analysis of the crisis.

34. For a broad survey of some of the conditions fostering the growth of Sunbelt Republicanism, see Schulman, *From Cotton Belt to Sunbelt*, 135–73, 206–22. For a brief survey of the socioeconomic and political character of the communities mentioned here, see Philip D. Duncan and Christine C. Lawrence, *Congressional Quarterly's Politics in America: 1998, the 105th Congress* (Washington, D.C.: CQ Press, 1997). Relative to Cobb County, Peter

Applebome observed in 1994 that it "is in some ways less Southern than it is purely suburban, with politics not much different from that of Orange County, California, which also has an aerospace economy and conservative politics." See Applebome, "A Suburban Eden Where the Right Rules." See also Dean Foust, "Welcome to Newt's Neighborhood," *Business Week*, 28 November 1994. "The district's culture," noted *Business Week*, "combines rugged individualism born of an agrarian past, old-fashioned religious values, and a visceral disdain for Washington."

35. For the prominence of the New South in recent politics, see Applebome, *Dixie Rising*. It is important to note that Orange County, as a dynamic, fast-growing region, has undergone tremendous change in the past twenty years. Most important, it has become quite ethnically diverse, with its minority populations rising to almost one-third of its residents. This, of course, has had an impact on the course of politics. Other changes in the economy are evident in the county's declaration of bankruptcy in 1994. For a recent study on the political economy of Orange County, see Baldassare, *When Government Fails*. For the reshaping of Orange County since the 1970s, see also the essays in Rob Kling, Spencer Olin, and Mark Poster, eds., *Postsuburban California: The Transformation of Orange County since World War II* (Berkeley: University of California Press, 1991).

BIBLIOGRAPHY

ARCHIVAL SOURCES

American Civil Liberties Union of Southern California Papers, University of California, Los Angeles.

American Conservative Union Papers, Brigham Young University, Provo, Utah.

Edmund G. Brown Papers, University of California, Berkeley.

William F. Buckley Jr. Papers, Yale University, New Haven, Connecticut.

James Burnham Papers, Hoover Institution on War, Revolution, and Peace, Stanford, California.

California Republican Assembly Papers, University of California, Los Angeles.

Patrick Dowd Papers, Hoover Institution on War, Revolution, and Peace, Stanford, California.

Leonard Finder Papers, Dwight D. Eisenhower Presidential Library, Abilene, Kansas.

Freedom Center Collection, Archives and Special Collections, California State University, Fullerton.

Barry Goldwater Papers, Arizona State University, Tempe, Arizona.

Barry Goldwater Post-election Correspondence, Cornell University, Ithaca, New York.

Friedrich Hayek Papers, Hoover Institution on War, Revolution, and Peace, Stanford, California.

Margaret Kerr Papers, Hoover Institution on War, Revolution, and Peace, Stanford, California.

Howard Kershner Papers, Libertarian Collection, University of Oregon, Eugene.

Denison Kitchel Papers, Hoover Institution on War, Revolution, and Peace, Stanford, California.

Thomas Kuchel Papers, University of California, Berkeley.

Marvin Liebman Papers, Hoover Institution on War, Revolution, and Peace, Stanford, California.

Knox Mellon, Collection of Materials about the John Birch Society, 1959–67, University of California, Los Angeles.

Richard Milhous Nixon, Pre-presidential Papers, National Archives, Pacific South-West Region.

Radical Right Collection, Hoover Institution on War, Revolution, and Peace, Stanford, California.

Ronald Reagan Papers, Hoover Institution on War, Revolution, and Peace, Stanford, California.

Henry Regnery Papers, Hoover Institution on War, Revolution, and Peace, Stanford, California.

Right-Wing Collection of the University of Iowa Libraries, 1918–77 (Microfilm Corporation of America, 1977).

John Schmitz Papers, Wichita State University, Wichita, Kansas.

F. Clifton White Papers, 1952–70, Cornell University, Ithaca, New York.

Periodicals

American Mercury
American Opinion
American Standard
Anaheim Bulletin
Anaheim Gazette
Anaheim Star
Boston Herald
Business Week
California Journal
California Statesman
Charleston News and Courier
Christian Anti-Communism Crusade Newsletter
Christian Century
Christian Science Monitor
Christianity Today
Commentary
CRA Enterprise
CRA Newsletter
Fortune
Freedom Newsletter
Fresno Bee
Fullerton News-Tribune
Garden Grove News
Good Housekeeping
Herald Express
Human Events
Indianapolis News

Life
Look
Los Angeles Times
Magnolia Way
Maranatha Goodnews Paper
Nation
National Review
New Guard
New Republic
New West
New York Times
New York World-Telegram and Sun
Newsweek
Notes from FEE
Oakland Tribune
Orange County Illustrated
Orange County Industrial News
Orange County Life, Business and Industry
Orange County Observer
Orange County Studies
Orange County Sun
Ramparts
Register
Reporter
Riverside Enterprise
Sacramento Bee
San Diego Church News
San Francisco Examiner
Saturday Evening Post
Southern California Business
Santa Ana Register (1 April 1911–12 Nov. 1952; *Register*, 13 Nov. 1952–18
    May 1985; *Orange County Register*, 19 May 1985–present)
Tidings
Time

ORAL HISTORY INTERVIEWS

Interviews with Author

Jan Averill, 3 October 1998.
David Bergland, 5 October 1998.
Beverly Cielnicky, 9 October 1998.

William Dannemeyer, 7 October 1998.

Dick Darling, 23 August 1996.

Armstrong Dowell, 6 October 1998.

Jacqueline Dvorman, 8 October 1998.

Nolan Frizzelle, 23 November 1992.

Bee Gathright, 5 October 1998.

Mary Haller, 1 December 1992.

Eleanor Howe, 21 August 1994.

Estrid Kieffer (formerly Kielsmeier), 3 October 1998.

Lois Lundberg, 25 August 1994.

Vern Martin, 20 November 1992.

Shirley and Harold Muckenthaler, 4 October 1998.

Peggy and Rufus Pearce, 4 October 1998.

Tom Rogers, 2 October 1998.

Marilyn Ryan, 6 October 1998.

Fred Schwarz, 21 August 1996.

Edna Slocum, 26 August 1994.

Don Smith, 16 August 1999.

Catherine Sullivan, 1 December 1992.

James Townsend, 2 October 1998.

Oral History Program, California State University, Fullerton

Beaman, Charles L., and Michael A. Jones. *Turmoil and Change: An Interim Report on the Politics of Orange County, California, 1945–1979.* 1980.

Mills, Edward. "Kitchen Cabinet: Four Citizen Advisers of Ronald Reagan: Interviews." 1983.

Salvatori, Henry. "Kitchen Cabinet: Four Citizen Advisers of Ronald Reagan: Interviews." 1983.

Tuttle, Holmes. "Kitchen Cabinet: Four Citizen Advisers of Ronald Reagan: Interviews." 1983.

White, Joshua. "Harvest." 1975.

Regional Oral History Program, Bancroft Library, University of California, Berkley

Nofziger, Lyn. "Issues and Innovations in the 1966 Republican Gubernatorial Campaign: Interviews." 1980.

Parkinson, Gaylord B. "Issues and Innovations in the 1966 Republican Party Campaign: Interviews." 1980.

Plog, Stanley. "More Than Just an Actor: The Early Campaigns of Ronald Reagan." 1981.

Robets, William E. "Issues and Innovations in the 1966 Republican Gubernatorial Campaign: Interviews." 1980.

Spencer, Stuart. "Issues and Innovations in the 1966 Republican Gubernatorial
Campaign: Interviews." 1980.

Weinberger, Caspar. "San Francisco Republicans." 1980.

Oral History Program, University of California, Los Angeles

Darling, Dick. "Republican Activism: The California Republican Assembly
and Ronald Reagan." 1982.

Gant, Charles B. "The California Democratic Council and Grass-Roots Politics." 1972.

Knott, Walter. "The Enterprises of Walter Knott." 1965.

GOVERMENT DOCUMENTS

Anaheim, California. Anaheim Union High School District, Board of Trustees.
Regular Minutes of Meetings. 1968–70.

Anaheim, California. Magnolia School District, Board of Trustees. Regular
Minutes of Meetings. 1959–1964.

California Department of Motor Vehicles. *Migration to California: A Sample
of 31,358 Families Registering an Out of State Vehicle, January–April 1962.*
March 1963.

California Legislature. Senate. Fact-Finding Subcommittee on Un-American
Activities in California. *Eighth Report of the Senate Fact-Finding Subcommittee on Un-American Activities.* 1943.

California Legislature. Senate. Fact-Finding Subcommittee on Un-American
Activities in California. *Tenth Report of the Senate Fact-Finding Subcommittee on Un-American Activities.* 1959.

California Legislature. Senate. Fact-Finding Subcommittee on Un-American
Activities in California. *Twelfth Report of the Senate Fact-Finding Subcommittee on Un-American Activities.* 1963.

California Legislature. Senate. Investigating Committee on Education. *(The
1951 Hearings: Tenth Report).* 1951.

California Secretary of State. *California Voters Pamphlet.* General Election.
November 1972.

California Secretary of State. *Statement of Vote.* Consolidated Direct Primary
Election and Special Statewide Election. 5 June 1962.

California Secretary of State. *Statement of Vote.* Consolidated Primary Election. 2 June 1964.

California Secretary of State. *Statement of Vote*. Direct Primary Election. 7 June 1966.

California Secretary of State. *Statement of Vote*. General Election. 6 November 1962.

California Secretary of State. *Statement of Vote*. General Election. 3 November 1964.

California Secretary of State. *Statement of Vote*. General Election. 8 November 1966.

California Secretary of State. *Statement of Vote*. General Election. 5 November 1968.

California Secretary of State. *Statement of Vote*. General Election. 4 November 1980.

California Secretary of State. *Statement of Vote and Supplement*. General Election. November 1972.

California Secretary of State. *Supplement to Statement of Vote*. General Election. 6 November 1962.

Orange County Planning Department. (*Orange County Progress Reports*). 1958–65.

Orange County Planning Department. Population Research Committee. *Quarterly Population Report*. 30 September 1961

Orange County Planning Department, Population Research Committee. *Quarterly Population Report*. 30 June 1962.

Orange County Planning Department, Population Research Committee. *Quarterly Population Report*. 30 June 1963.

Orange County Planning Department, Population Research Committee. *Quarterly Population Report*. 30 September 1963.

Orange County Planning Department, Population Research Committee. *Quarterly Population Report*. 31 December 1964.

Orange County Planning Department, Population Research Committee. *Quarterly Population Report*. 31 December 1965.

U.S. Department of Commerce, Bureau of the Census. "Estimated Number of Veterans in Civil Life, 1865–1970," *Historical Statistics of the United States*. Vol. 2. White Plains, N.Y.: Kraus International, 1989.

U.S. Department of Commerce, Bureau of the Census. "Marital Status of Population by Age and Sex, 1890–1970," *Historical Statistics of the United States*. Vol. 1. White Plains, N.Y.: Kraus International, 1989.

U.S. Department of Commerce, Bureau of the Census. *United States Census of the Population, 1960*. Characteristics of the Population. Part 6. California.

U.S. Department of Commerce, Bureau of the Census. *United States Census of the Population, 1960*. Subject Reports. Persons of Spanish Surnames.

U.S. Federal Bureau of Investigation. John Birch Society, California Files. File number LA 59001.

REPORTS

Associated Chambers of Commerce of Orange County. *The Majestic Empire of Orange County, California.* Huntington Beach, Calif.: Associated Chambers of Commerce. 1953.
Security First National Bank of Los Angeles, Economic Research Division. *The Growth and Economic Stature of Orange County.* Los Angeles, May 1967.
Security First National Bank of Los Angeles, Economic Research Division. *The Growth and Economic Stature of Orange County.* Los Angeles, November 1961.
Southern California Research Council. *Migration and the Southern California Economy* 12. Los Angeles: Occidental College, 1964.
Stanford Research Institute, *Orange County: Its Economic Growth, 1940–1980.* Pasadena, Calif.: Southern California Laboratories, 1959.
Stanford Research Institute. *Orange County: Its Economic Growth, 1940–1980.* Supplement. Pasadena, Calif.: Stanford Research Institute, 1962.

DIRECTORIES

The Christian Business and Professional Directory. Orange County Edition. 1976–77. Santa Ana, Calif.: California Christian Business Service.
First National Directory of "Rightist" Groups, Publications and Some Individuals in the United States and Some Foreign Countries. San Francisco, 1957.
First National Directory of "Rightist" Groups, Publications and Some Individuals in the United States and Some Foreign Countries. 5th ed. Los Angeles, 1965.
Luskey's Fullerton-Brea, Placentia and Yorba Linda Criss-Cross Directory. 1965.
Luskey's 1955–1966 Official Anaheim Criss-Cross City Directory. 1955.
Luskey's 1957–1958 Official Anaheim Criss-Cross City Directory. 1957.
Luskey's 1961 Anaheim Yellowbook Criss-Cross City Directory. 1961.
Luskey's 1963 Anaheim Criss-Cross City Directory and Blue Book Home Edition. 1963.
Luskey's 1964 Anaheim Criss-Cross City Directory and Blue Book Edition. 1964.
Luskey's Official Anaheim Criss-Cross City Directory. 1959.

Luskey's Official Northern Orange County City Directory. 1950.
Luskey's Official Santa Ana, Orange, Tustin and Central Orange County Criss-Cross City Directory, 1952.
Luskey's Official Southern Orange County City Directory. 1951.
Official Catholic Directory. New York: Kennedy. 1951–61.
Orange County Telephone Directory. Pacific Telephone and Telegraph. 1950–65.

BOOKS

Adamson, Walter L. *Hegemony and Revolution: A Study of Antonio Gramsci's Political and Cultural Theory.* Berkeley: University of California Press, 1980.
Adorno, T. W., Else Frenkel-Brinswik, Daniel J. Levinson, and R. Nevitt Sanford. *The Authoritarian Personality.* New York: Harper and Row, 1950.
Allitt, Patrick. *Catholic Intellectuals and Conservative Politics in America, 1950–1985.* Ithaca, N.Y.: Cornell University Press, 1993.
Ambrose, Stephen E. *Rise to Globalism: American Foreign Policy since 1938.* 5th ed. New York: Penguin, 1988.
Andrew, John A. *The Other Side of the Sixties: Young Americans for Freedom and the Rise of Conservative Politics.* New Brunswick, N.J.: Rutgers University Press, 1997.
Applebome, Peter. *Dixie Rising: How the South Is Shaping American Values, Politics, and Culture.* New York: Times Books, 1996.
Apter, David Ernest. *Ideology and Discontent.* New York: Free Press of Glencoe, 1964.
Baldassare, Mark. *Trouble in Paradise: The Suburban Transformation of America.* New York: Columbia University Press, 1986.
———. *When Government Fails: The Orange County Bankruptcy.* Berkeley: University of California Press, 1998.
Bartleman, Frank. *How Pentecost Came to Los Angeles.* Los Angeles: privately printed, 1925.
Bell, Daniel, ed. *The Radical Right.* Garden City, N.Y.: Doubleday, 1963.
Bennett, David H. *The Party of Fear: From Nativist Movements to the New Right in American History.* Chapel Hill: University of North Carolina Press, 1988.
Billingsley, K. L[loyd]. *From Mainline to Sideline: The Social Witness of the National Council of Churches.* Washington, D.C.: Ethics and Public Policy Center, 1990.
Blanchard, Dallas A. *The Anti-abortion Movement and the Rise of the Religious Right: From Polite to Fiery Protest.* New York: Twayne, 1994.

Blanchard, Margaret A. *Revolutionary Sparks: Freedom of Expression in Modern America.* New York: Oxford University Press, 1992.

Blee, Kathleen M. *Women of the Klan: Racism and Gender in the 1920s.* Berkeley: University of California Press, 1991.

Blumenthal, Sidney. *The Rise of the Counter-establishment: From Conservative Ideology to Political Power.* New York: Times Books, 1986.

Blumhofer, Edith Waldvogel. *Aimee Semple McPherson: Everybody's Sister.* Grand Rapids, Mich.: William B. Eerdmans, 1993.

Boyarsky, Bill. *The Rise of Ronald Reagan.* New York: Random House, 1968.

Boyer, Paul S. *When Time Shall Be No More: Prophecy Belief in Modern American Culture.* Cambridge, Mass.: Harvard University Press, 1992.

Branch, Taylor. *Parting the Waters: America in the King Years, 1954–1963.* New York: Simon and Schuster, 1988.

Breasted, Mary. *Oh! Sex Education!* New York: Praeger, 1970.

Brennan, Mary C. *Turning Right in the Sixties: The Conservative Capture of the GOP.* Chapel Hill: University of North Carolina Press, 1995.

Brinkley, Alan. *Voices of Protest: Huey Long, Father Coughlin, and the Great Depression.* New York: Vintage, 1983.

Broadwater, Jeff. *Adlai Stevenson and American Politics: The Odyssey of a Cold War Liberal.* New York: Twayne, 1994.

Broyles, J. Allen. *The John Birch Society: Anatomy of a Protest.* Boston: Beacon Press, 1964.

Bruce, Steve. *The Rise and Fall of the New Christian Right: Conservative Protestant Politics in America, 1978–1988.* Oxford: Clarendon Press, 1988.

Bryman, Alan. *Disney and His Worlds.* New York: Routledge, 1995.

Buchanan, Patrick J. *Right from the Beginning.* Boston: Little, Brown, 1988.

Buckley, William F., Jr. *Up from Liberalism.* New York: McDowell, Obolensky, 1959.

Burner, David, and Thomas R. West. *The Torch Is Passed: The Kennedy Brothers and American Liberalism.* New York: Atheneum, 1984.

Cain, Edward. *They'd Rather Be Right: Youth and the Conservative Movement.* New York: Macmillan, 1963.

[Calvary Chapel]. *Calvary Chapel Movement.* Twin Peaks, Calif.: Calvary Chapel Bible College, 1994.

Cannon, Lou. *Ronnie and Jesse: A Political Odyssey.* Garden City, N.Y.: Doubleday, 1969.

———. *Reagan.* New York: Putnam, 1982.

Carmines, Edward G., and James A. Stimson. *Issue Evolution, Race and the Transformation of American Politics.* Princeton, N.J.: Princeton University Press, 1989.

Carson, Clayborne. *In Struggle: SNCC and the Black Awakening of the 1960s.* Cambridge, Mass.: Harvard University Press, 1981.

Carter, Dan T. *The Politics of Rage: George Wallace, the Origins of the New Conservatism, and the Transformation of American Politics.* New York: Simon and Schuster, 1995.

Chafe, William H. *Civilities and Civil Rights: Greensboro, North Carolina, and the Black Struggle for Freedom.* New York: Oxford University Press, 1980.

Chambers, Clarke A. *California Farm Organizations: A Historical Study of the Grange, the Farm Bureau, and the Associated Farmers, 1929–1941.* Berkeley: University of California Press, 1952.

Cook, Fred J. *Barry Goldwater: Extremist of the Right.* New York: Grove Press, 1964.

[Copley Press]. *The Copley Press.* Aurora, Ill.: Copley Press, 1953.

Cosman, Bernard. *Five States for Goldwater: Continuity and Change in Southern Presidential Voting Patterns.* Tuscaloosa: University of Alabama Press, 1966.

————, ed. *Republican Politics: The 1964 Campaign and Its Aftermath for the Party.* New York: Praeger, 1968.

Crawford, Alan. *Thunder on the Right: The "New Right" and the Politics of Resentment.* New York: Pantheon, 1980.

Cronon, William, George Miles, and Jay Gitlin, eds. *Under an Open Sky: Rethinking America's Western Past.* New York: Norton, 1992.

Cummings, Milton C., ed. *The National Election of 1964.* Washington, D.C.: Brookings Institute, 1966.

Davis, Mike. *Prisoners of the American Dream: Politics and Economy in the History of the U.S. Working Class.* New York: Verso, 1986.

————. *City of Quartz: Excavating the Future in Los Angeles.* New York: Verso, 1990.

Depoe, Stephen P. *Arthur M. Schlesinger, Jr., and the Ideological History of American Liberalism.* Tuscaloosa: University of Alabama Press, 1994.

Diamond, Sara. *Roads to Dominion: Right-Wing Movements and Political Power in the United States.* New York: Guilford Press, 1995.

————. *Not by Politics Alone: The Enduring Influence of the Christian Right.* New York: Guilford Press, 1998.

Dionne, E. J., *Why Americans Hate Politics.* New York: Simon and Schuster, 1991.

Dix, Lester. *A Charter for Progressive Education.* New York: Columbia University Teachers College, 1939.

Dudman, Richard. *Men of the Far Right.* New York: Pyramid Books, 1962.

Duncan, Philip D., and Christine C. Lawrence. *Congressional Quarterly's Politics in America: 1998, the 105th Congress.* Washington, D.C.: CQ Press, 1997.

Durrenberger, Robert. *California, the Last Frontier.* New York: Van Nostrand Reinhold, 1969.

Eatwell, Roger, and Noël O'Sullivan. *The Nature of the Right: American and European Politics and Political Thought since 1789.* Boston: Twayne, 1990.

Echols, Alice. *Daring to Be Bad: Radical Feminism in America, 1967–1975.* Minneapolis: University of Minnesota Press, 1989.

Edsall, Thomas Byrne. *The New Politics of Inequality.* New York: Norton, 1984.

Edsall, Thomas Byrne, with Mary D. Edsall. *Chain Reaction: The Impact of Race, Rights, and Taxes on American Politics.* New York: Norton, 1991.

Edwards, Anne. *Early Reagan.* New York: Morrow, 1987.

Epstein, Benjamin R., and Arnold Forster. *Report on the John Birch Society, 1966.* New York: Vintage, 1966.

———. *The Radical Right: Report on the John Birch Society and Its Allies.* New York: Random House, 1967.

Ernst, Eldon G., with Douglas Firth Anderson. *Pilgrim Progression: The Protestant Experience in California.* Santa Barbara, Calif.: Fithian Press, 1993.

Evans, M. Stanton. *The Future of Conservatism: From Taft to Reagan and Beyond.* New York: Holt, Rinehart and Winston, 1968.

Farber, David. *Chicago '68.* Chicago: University of Chicago Press, 1988.

———. *The Age of Great Dreams: America in the 1960s.* New York: Hill and Wang, 1994.

———, ed. *The Sixties: From Memory to History.* Chapel Hill: University of North Carolina Press, 1994.

Feagin, Joe R. *Free Enterprise City: Houston in Political-Economic Perspective.* New Brunswick, N.J.: Rutgers University Press, 1988.

Findlay, James F. *Church People in the Struggle: The National Council of Churches and the Black Freedom Movement, 1950–1970.* New York: Oxford University Press, 1993.

Findlay, John M. *Magic Lands: Western Cityscapes and American Culture after 1940.* Berkeley: University of California Press, 1992.

Foner, Eric. *Free Soil, Free Labor, Free Men: The Ideology of the Republican Party before the Civil War.* New York: Oxford University Press, 1970.

Formisano, Ronald P. *Boston against Busing: Race, Class, and Ethnicity in the 1960s and 1970s.* Chapel Hill: University of North Carolina Press, 1991.

Forster, Arnold, and Benjamin R. Epstein. *Danger on the Right.* New York: Random House, 1964.

Fraser, Steve, and Gary Gerstle, eds. *The Rise and Fall of the New Deal Order, 1930–1980*. Princeton, N.J.: Princeton University Press, 1989.

Fried, Richard M. *Nightmare in Red: The McCarthy Era in Perspective*. New York: Oxford University Press, 1990.

Friis, Leo J. *Orange County through Four Centuries*. Santa Ana, Calif.: Pioneer Press, 1965.

Gillon, Steven M. *Politics and Vision: The ADA and American Liberalism, 1947–1985*. New York: Oxford University Press, 1987.

Goldberg, Robert Alan. *Barry Goldwater*. New Haven, Conn.: Yale University Press, 1995.

Goldwater, Barry. *The Conscience of a Conservative*. Shepherdsville, Ky.: Victor Publishing House, 1960.

———. *The Conscience of a Majority*. Englewood Cliffs, N.J.: Prentice-Hall, 1970.

Gonzalez, Gilbert G. *Progressive Education: A Marxist Interpretation*. Minneapolis, Minn.: Marxist Educational Press, 1982.

———. *Labor and Community: Mexican Citrus Worker Villages in a Southern California County, 1900–1950*. Urbana: University of Illinois Press, 1994.

Goodwyn, Lawrence. *The Populist Moment: A Short History of the Agrarian Revolt in America*. New York: Oxford University Press, 1978.

Gottdiener, Mark. *Planned Sprawl: Private and Public Interests in Suburbia*. Beverly Hills, Calif.: Sage, 1977.

———. *The Social Production of Urban Space*. Austin: University of Texas Press, 1985.

Gottlieb, Robert, and Irene Wolt. *Thinking Big: The Story of the Los Angeles Times, Its Publishers, and Their Influence on Southern California*. New York: Putnam, 1977.

Gould, Stephen. *An Annotated Bibliography of Orange County Sources*. Tustin, Calif.: Western Association for the Advancement of Local History, 1988.

Governmental Affairs Institute, *America at the Polls: A Handbook of American Presidential Election Statistics, 1920–1964*. New York: Arno Press, 1976.

Gregory, James N. *American Exodus: The Dust Bowl Migration and Okie Culture in California*. New York: Oxford University Press, 1989.

Griffith, Robert. *The Politics of Fear: Joseph R. McCarthy and the Senate*. Lexington: University Press of Kentucky, 1970.

Griffith, Robert, and Athan Theoharis, eds. *The Specter: Original Essays on the Cold War and the Origins of McCarthyism*. New York: New Viewpoints, 1974.

Guinsburg, Thomas N. *The Pursuit of Isolationism in the United States Senate from Versailles to Pearl Harbor.* New York: Garland Press, 1982.

Guth, James L., John C. Green, Corwin E. Smidt, Lyman A. Kellstedt, and Margaret M. Poloma, eds. *The Bully Pulpit: The Politics of Protestant Clergy.* Lawrence: University Press of Kansas, 1997.

Hadden, Jeffrey K., and Charles E. Swann. *Prime-Time Preachers: The Rising Power of Televangelism.* Reading, Mass.: Addison-Wesley, 1981.

Hallan-Gibson, Pamela. *The Golden Promise: An Illustrated History of Orange County.* Northridge, Calif.: Windsor, 1986.

Hamby, Alonzo L. *Liberalism and Its Challengers: FDR to Reagan.* New York: Oxford University Press, 1985.

Hammond, Paul Y. *Cold War and Detente: The American Foreign Policy Process since 1945.* New York: Harcourt Brace Jovanovich, 1975.

Harrell, David Edwin, Jr. *Varieties of Southern Evangelicalism.* Macon, Ga.: Mercer University Press, 1981.

Hartz, Louis. *The Liberal Tradition in America: An Interpretation of American Political Thought since the Revolution.* New York: Harcourt and Brace, 1955.

———. *The Founding of New Societies: Studies in the History of the United States, Latin America, South Africa, Canada, and Australia.* New York: Harcourt, Brace, and World, 1964.

Hayek, Friedrich A. *The Road to Serfdom.* Chicago: University of Chicago Press, 1944.

Heale, M. J. *American Anticommunism: Combating the Enemy Within, 1830–1970.* Baltimore: Johns Hopkins University Press, 1990.

Hess, Stephen, and David S. Broder. *The Republican Establishment: The Present and Future of the GOP.* New York: Harper and Row, 1967.

Hill, Gladwin. *Dancing Bear: An Inside Look at California Politics.* Cleveland: World, 1968.

Himmelstein, Jerome L. *To the Right: The Transformation of American Conservatism.* Berkeley: University of California Press, 1990.

Hine, Leland D. *Baptists in Southern California.* Valley Forge, Pa.: Judson Press, 1966.

Hixson, Richard F. *Pornography and the Justices: The Supreme Court and the Intractable Obscenity Problem.* Carbondale: Southern Illinois University Press, 1996.

Hixson, William B. *The Search for the American Right Wing: An Analysis of the Social Science Record, 1955–1987.* Princeton, N.J.: Princeton University Press, 1992.

Hobsbawm, Eric. *The Age of Extremes: A History of the World, 1914–1991*. New York: Pantheon, 1994.

Hodgson, Godfrey. *The World Turned Right Side Up: A History of the Conservative Ascendancy in America*. Boston: Houghton Mifflin, 1996.

Hoeveler, J. David. *Watch on the Right: Conservative Intellectuals in the Reagan Era*. Madison: University of Wisconsin Press, 1991.

Hofstadter, Richard. *The Paranoid Style in American Politics, and Other Essays*. Chicago: University of Chicago Press, 1979.

Hoover, J. Edgar. *Masters of Deceit: The Story of Communism in America and How to Fight It*. New York: Henry Holt, 1958.

———. *Communist Target Youth: Communist Infiltration and Agitation Tactics, A Report*. Washington, D.C.: U.S. Government Printing Office, 1960.

Hunter, James Davison. *American Evangelicalism: Conservative Religion and the Quandary of Modernity*. New Brunswick, N.J.: Rutgers University Press, 1983.

———. *Culture Wars: The Struggle to Define America*. New York: Basic Books, 1991.

Hutchins, Lavern C. *The John Birch Society and United States Foreign Policy*. New York: Pageant Press, 1968.

Isserman, Maurice, and Michael Kazin, *America Divided: The Civil War of the 1960s*. New York: Oxford University Press, 2000.

Jackson, Kenneth T. *Crabgrass Frontier: The Suburbanization of the United States*. New York: Oxford University Press, 1985.

Jacoby, Sanford. *Modern Manors: Welfare Capitalism since the New Deal*. Princeton, N.J.: Princeton University Press, 1997.

Jones, Louis Thomas. *The Quakers of Iowa*. Iowa City: State Historical Society of Iowa, 1914.

Judis, John B. *William F. Buckley, Jr., Patron Saint of the Conservatives*. New York: Simon and Schuster, 1988.

Karier, Clarence. *The Individual, Society, and Education: A History of American Educational Ideas*. Urbana: University of Illinois Press, 1986.

Kazin, Michael. *The Populist Persuasion: An American History*. New York: Basic Books, 1995.

Kelley, Dean M. *Why Conservative Churches Are Growing: A Study in Sociology of Religion*. New York: Harper and Row, 1972.

Kendall, Willmoore. *The Conservative Affirmation*. Chicago: Henry Regnery, 1963.

Kessel, John Howard. *The Goldwater Coalition: Republican Strategies in 1964*. Indianapolis: Bobbs-Merrill, 1968.

Kirk, Russell. *A Program for Conservatives*. Chicago: Henry Regnery, 1954.

Kirk, Russell, and James McClellan. *The Political Principles of Robert A. Taft.* New York: Fleet Press, 1967.

Klatch, Rebecca E. *Women of the New Right.* Philadelphia: Temple University Press, 1987.

———. *A Generation Divided: The New Left, the New Right and the 1960s.* Berkeley: University of California Press, 1999.

Kling, Rob, Spencer Olin, and Mark Poster, eds. *Postsuburban California: The Transformation of Orange County since World War II.* Berkeley: University of California Press, 1991.

Knight, Carolyn B. *Making It Happen: The Story of Carl Karcher Enterprises.* Anaheim, Calif.: Karcher Enterprises, 1981.

Kolkey, Jonathan Martin. *The New Right, 1960–1968, with Epilogue, 1969–1980.* Washington, D.C.: University Press of America, 1983.

Kramer, William, ed. *The American West and the Religious Experience.* Los Angeles: Will Kramer, 1975.

Lamb, Karl A. *As Orange Goes: Twelve California Families and the Future of American Politics.* New York: Norton, 1974.

Lawrence, Bruce B. *Defenders of God: The Fundamentalist Revolt against the Modern Age.* San Francisco: Harper and Row, 1989.

Lee, Eugene C., and Willis D. Hawley, eds. *The Challenge of California.* Boston: Little, Brown, 1970.

Lee, Eugene C., and Bruce E. Keith, eds. *California Votes, 1960–1972: A Review and Analysis of Registration and Voting.* Berkeley: Institute of Governmental Studies, University of California, 1974.

Levitas, Ruth, ed. *The Ideology of the New Right.* Cambridge, Mass.: Polity Press, 1986.

Liebman, Robert C., and Robert Wuthnow, eds. *The New Christian Right: Mobilization and Legitimation.* Hawthorne, N.Y.: Aldine, 1983.

Liebowitz, Nathan. *Daniel Bell and the Agony of Modern Liberalism.* Westport, Conn.: Greenwood Press, 1985.

Lippy, Charles H., ed. *Twentieth-Century Shapers of American Popular Religion.* New York: Greenwood Press, 1989.

Lipset, Seymour Martin, and Earl Raab. *The Politics of Unreason: Right-Wing Extremism in America, 1790–1977.* New York: Harper and Row, 1978.

Littell, Franklin Hamlin. *Wild Tongues: A Handbook of Social Pathology.* New York: Macmillan, 1969.

Lotchin, Roger W. *Fortress California, 1910–1961: From Warfare to Welfare.* New York: Oxford University Press, 1992.

Luker, Kristin. *Abortion and the Politics of Motherhood.* Berkeley: University of California Press, 1984.

MacLean, Nancy. *Behind the Mask of Chivalry: The Making of the Second Ku Klux Klan.* New York: Oxford University Press, 1994.

Markusen, Ann, Peter Hall, Scott Campbell, and Sabina Deitrick. *The Rise of the Gunbelt: The Military Remapping of Industrial America.* New York: Oxford University Press, 1991.

Marsden, George, M. *Fundamentalism and American Culture: The Shaping of Twentieth-Century Evangelicalism, 1870–1925.* New York: Oxford University Press, 1980.

———, ed. *Evangelicalism and Modern America.* Grand Rapids, Mich.: William B. Eerdmans, 1984.

Martel, Gordon, ed. *American Foreign Relations Reconsidered, 1890–1993.* New York: Routledge, 1994.

Martin, William C. *With God on Our Side: The Rise of the Religious Right in America.* New York: Broadway Books, 1996.

Marty, Martin E., ed. *Fundamentalism and Evangelicalism.* Munich: K. G. Sauer, 1993.

Marty, Martin E., and R. Scott Appleby. *The Glory and the Power: The Fundamentalist Challenge to the Modern World.* Boston: Beacon Press, 1992.

———, eds. *Fundamentalisms Observed*, Vol. 1. Chicago: University of Chicago Press, 1991.

———. *Fundamentalisms and Society: Reclaiming the Sciences, Family, and Education.* Chicago: University of Chicago Press, 1993.

Mathews, Donald G., and Jane Sherron DeHart. *Sex, Gender, and the Politics of ERA: A State and the Nation.* New York: Oxford University Press, 1990.

Matusow, Allen J. *The Unraveling of America: A History of Liberalism in the 1960s.* New York: Harper and Row, 1984.

Mayer, George. *The Republican Party, 1854–1966.* 2d ed. New York: Oxford University Press, 1967.

McAdam, Doug. *Political Process and the Development of Black Insurgency, 1930–1970.* Chicago: University of Chicago Press, 1982.

McCann, Irving G. *Case History of the Smear by CBS of Conservatives.* Washington, D.C.: McCann Press, 1966.

McCormick, Thomas J. *America's Half-Century: United States Foreign Policy in the Cold War.* Baltimore: Johns Hopkins University Press, 1989.

McGuffey, William Holmes. *McGuffey's Fifth Eclectic Reader.* 1879. New York: New American Library, 1962.

McWilliams, Carey. *Southern California: An Island on the Land.* Salt Lake City, Utah: Peregrine Smith Books, 1983.

Miles, Michael W. *The Odyssey of the American Right.* New York: Oxford University Press, 1980.

Miller, Donald E. *Reinventing American Protestantism: Christianity in the New Millennium.* Berkeley: University of California Press, 1997.

Miller, Douglas T. *On Our Own: Americans in the Sixties.* Lexington, Mass.: D. C. Heath, 1996.

Miller, James. *"Democracy Is in the Streets": From Port Huron to the Siege of Chicago.* New York: Simon and Schuster, 1985.

Mitchell, Greg. *Tricky Dick and the Pink Lady: Richard Nixon vs. Helen Gahagan Douglas—Sexual Politics and the Red Scare, 1950.* New York: Random House, 1998.

Moore, Leonard J. *Citizen Klansmen: The Ku Klux Klan in Indiana, 1921–1928.* Chapel Hill: University of North Carolina Press, 1991.

Moore, R. Laurence. *Selling God: American Religion in the Marketplace of Culture.* New York: Oxford University Press, 1994.

Morris, Aldon D. *The Origins of the Civil Rights Movement: Black Communities Organizing for Change.* New York: Free Press, 1984.

Morris, Aldon D., and Carol McClurg Mueller, eds. *Frontiers in Social Movement Theory.* New Haven, Conn.: Yale University Press, 1992.

Morris, Roger. *Richard Milhous Nixon: The Rise of an American Politician.* New York: Henry Holt, 1990.

Nash, George H. *The Conservative Intellectual Movement in America since 1945.* New York: Basic Books, 1976.

Nash, Gerald D. *The American West Transformed: The Impact of the Second World War.* Bloomington: Indiana University Press, 1985.

———. *World War II and the West: Reshaping the Economy.* Lincoln: University of Nebraska Press, 1990.

Nash, Gerald D., and Richard W. Etulain, eds. *The Twentieth-Century West: Historical Interpretations.* Albuquerque: University of New Mexico Press, 1989.

National Council of Churches. *Highlights of 1963.* New York: National Council of Churches, 1964.

Neuhaus, Richard John, and Michael Cromartie, eds. *Piety and Politics: Evangelicals and Fundamentalists Confront the World.* Washington, D.C.: Ethics and Public Policy Center, 1987.

Novak, Robert D. *The Agony of the GOP, 1964.* New York: Macmillan, 1965.

Nygaard, Norman E. *Walter Knott: Twentieth Century Pioneer.* Grand Rapids, Mich.: Zondervan, 1965.

O'Brien, Michael. *McCarthy and McCarthyism in Wisconsin.* Columbia: University of Missouri Press, 1980.

Osborne, David, and Ted Gaebler. *Reinventing Government: How the Entrepreneurial Spirit Is Transforming the Public Sector.* Reading, Mass.: Addison-Wesley, 1992.

Oshinsky, David M. *A Conspiracy So Immense: The World of Joe McCarthy.* New York: Free Press, 1984.

Owens, John R., Edmond Costantini, and Louis F. Weschler. *California Politics and Parties.* New York: Macmillan, 1970.

Paterson, Thomas G. *Contesting Castro: The United States and the Triumph of the Cuban Revolution.* New York: Oxford University Press, 1994.

Peele, Gillian. *Revival and Reaction: The Right in Contemporary America.* Oxford: Clarendon Press, 1984.

Penner, James. *Goliath: The Life of Robert Schuller.* New York: HarperCollins, 1992.

Perry, David C., and Alfred J. Watkins, eds. *The Rise of the Sunbelt Cities.* Beverly Hills, Calif.: Sage, 1977.

Phillips, Kevin P. *The Emerging Republican Majority.* New Rochelle, N.Y.: Arlington House, 1969.

———. *Post-conservative America: People, Politics, and Ideology in a Time of Crisis.* New York: Random House, 1982.

Pierard, Richard V. *The Unequal Yoke: Evangelical Christianity and Political Conservatism.* Philadelphia: Lippincott, 1970.

Powaski, Ronald E. *Toward an Entangling Alliance: American Isolationism, Internationalism, and Europe, 1901–1950.* New York: Greenwood Press, 1991.

Powers, Richard Gid. *Not Without Honor: The History of American Anticommunism.* New York: Free Press, 1995.

Pratt, Henry J. *The Liberalization of American Protestantism: A Case Study in Complex Organizations.* Detroit: Wayne State University Press, 1972.

Rae, Nicol C. *The Decline and Fall of the Liberal Republicans: From 1952 to the Present.* New York: Oxford University Press, 1989.

Rafferty, Max. *Suffer, Little Children.* New York: Devin-Adair, 1962.

———. *What They Are Doing to Your Children.* New York: New American Library, 1964.

———. *Max Rafferty on Education.* New York: Devin-Adair, 1968.

Ravitch, Diane. *The Troubled Crusade: American Education, 1945–1980.* New York: Basic Books, 1983.

Reinhard, David W. *The Republican Right since 1945.* Lexington: University Press of Kentucky, 1983.

Ribuffo, Leo P. *The Old Christian Right: The Protestant Far Right from the Great Depression to the Cold War.* Philadelphia: Temple University Press, 1983.

Rieder, Jonathan. *Canarsie: The Jews and Italians of Brooklyn against Liberalism.* Cambridge, Mass.: Harvard University Press, 1985.

Rogin, Michael Paul. *The Intellectuals and McCarthy: The Radical Specter.* Cambridge, Mass.: MIT Press, 1967.

Rogin, Michael Paul, and John L. Shover. *Political Change in California: Critical Elections and Social Movements, 1890–1966.* Westport, Conn.: Greenwood, 1970.

Roozen, David A., and C. Kirk Hadaway, eds. *Church and Denominational Growth.* Nashville, Tenn.: Abingdon Press, 1993.

Rorabaugh, W. J. *Berkeley at War: The 1960s.* New York: Oxford University Press, 1989.

Rovere, Richard H. *The Goldwater Caper.* London: Methuen, 1966.

Rusher, William A. *The Rise of the Right.* New York: Morrow, 1984.

Sale, Kirkpatrick. *Power Shift: The Rise of the Southern Rim and Its Challenge to the Eastern Establishment.* New York: Random House, 1975.

Saloma, John S., III. *Ominous Politics: The New Conservative Labyrinth.* New York: Hill and Wang, 1984.

Sandeen, Ernest Robert. *The Roots of Fundamentalism: British and American Millenarianism, 1800–1930.* Chicago: University of Chicago Press, 1970.

Schlafly, Phyllis. *A Choice, Not an Echo: "The Inside Story on How American Presidents Are Chosen."* Alton, Ill.: Pere Marquette Press, 1964.

Schneider, Gregory L. *Cadres for Conservatism: Young Americans for Freedom and the Rise of the Contemporary Right.* New York: New York University Press, 1999.

Schoenberger, Robert A., ed. *The American Right Wing: Readings in Political Behavior.* New York: Holt, Rinehart and Winston, 1969.

Schrecker, Ellen. *Many Are the Crimes: McCarthyism in America.* Princeton, N.J.: Princeton University Press, 1998

Schuller, Robert. *Let's Feel Good about Ourselves: God's Way to the Good Life.* Grand Rapids, Mich.: William B. Eerdmans, 1963.

Schulman, Bruce J. *From Cotton Belt to Sunbelt: Federal Policy, Economic Development, and the Transformation of the South, 1938–1980.* New York: Oxford University Press, 1991.

Schuparra, Kurt. *Triumph of the Right: The Rise of the California Conservative Movement, 1945–1966.* Armonk, N.Y.: M. E. Sharpe, 1998.

Schwarz, Fred. *You Can Trust the Communists (to Be Communists).* Englewood Cliffs, N.J.: Prentice-Hall, 1960.

Sears, David O., and Jack Citrin. *Tax Revolt: Something for Nothing in California.* Cambridge, Mass.: Harvard University Press, 1982.

Segers, Mary C., and Timothy A. Byrnes, eds. *Abortion Politics in American States.* Armonk, N.Y.: M. E. Sharpe, 1995.

Selcraig, James Truett. *The Red Scare in the Midwest, 1945–1955: A State and Local Study*. Ann Arbor, Mich.: UMI Research Press, 1982.

Shibley, Mark A. *Resurgent Evangelicalism in the United States: Mapping Cultural Change since 1970*. Columbia: University of South Carolina Press, 1996.

Smith, Chuck. *Future Survival*. Costa Mesa, Calif.: Word for Today, 1980.

———. *What the World Is Coming To*. Costa Mesa, Calif.: Word for Today, 1980.

Smith, Chuck, and Tal Brooke. *Harvest*. Old Tappan, N.J.: Chosen Books, 1989.

Starr, Kevin. *Material Dreams: Southern California through the 1920s*. New York: Oxford University Press, 1990.

———. *Endangered Dreams: The Great Depression in California*. New York: Oxford University Press, 1996.

Steinfels, Peter. *The Neoconservatives: The Men Who Are Changing America's Politics*. New York: Simon and Schuster, 1979.

Stormer, John A. *None Dare Call It Treason*. Florrissant, Mo.: Liberty Bell Press, 1964.

Strevey, Tracy E., and associates. *Fulfilling Retirement Dreams: The First Twenty-five Years of Leisure World, Laguna Hills*. Laguna Hills, Calif.: Leisure World Historical Society of Laguna Hills, 1989.

Strozier, Charles B. *Apocalypse: On the Psychology of Fundamentalism in America*. Boston: Beacon Press, 1994.

Suall, Irwin. *The American Ultras: The Extreme Right and the Military-Industrial Complex*. New York: New America, 1962.

Sugrue, Thomas J. *The Origins of the Urban Crisis: Race and Inequality in Postwar Detroit*. Princeton, N.J.: Princeton University Press, 1996.

Swerdlow, Amy. *Women Strike for Peace: Traditional Motherhood and Radical Politics in the 1960s*. Chicago. University of Chicago Press, 1993.

Synan, Vinson. *The Holiness-Pentecostal Tradition: Charismatic Movements in the Twentieth Century*. Grand Rapids, Mich.: William B. Eerdmans, 1997.

Tanner, Don, ed. *The Silent Scream: The Complete Text of the Documentary Film with an Authoritative Response to the Critics*. Comp. by Donald S. Smith. Anaheim, Calif.: American Portrait Films, 1985.

Taylor, Larry. *What Calvary Chapel Teaches: A Brief Explanation of the Doctrine of the Calvary Chapel Movement*. Twin Peaks, Calif.: Calvary Chapel Bible College, 1994.

Thayer, George. *The Farther Shores of Politics: The American Political Fringe Today*. New York: Simon and Schuster, 1967.

Thorne, Melvin J. *American Conservative Thought since World War II: The Core Ideas*. New York: Greenwood Press, 1990.

Tilly, Charles. *From Mobilization to Revolution*. Reading, Mass.: Addison-Wesley, 1978.

Trilling, Lionel. *The Liberal Imagination: Essays on Literature and Society*. Garden City, N.Y.: Doubleday, 1953.

Tyack, David B, ed. *Turning Points in American Educational History*. Waltham, Mass.: Blaisdell, 1967.

Valdez, A. C., with James F. Scheer. *Fire on Azusa Street*. Costa Mesa, Calif.: Gift Publications, 1980.

Viguerie, Richard A. *The New Right: We're Ready to Lead*. Falls Church, Va.: Viguerie, 1981.

Voskuil, Dennis. *Mountains into Goldmines: Robert Schuller and the Gospel of Success*. Grand Rapids, Mich.: William B. Eerdmans, 1983.

Walker, Brooks R. *The Christian Fright Peddlers*. Garden City, N.Y.: Doubleday, 1964.

Weber, Francis J. *His Eminence of Los Angeles: James Francis Cardinal McIntyre*. Mission Hills, Calif.: Saint Francis Historical Society, 1997.

Weisbrot, Robert. *Freedom Bound: A History of the America's Civil Rights Movement*. New York: Norton, 1991.

Welch, Robert. *The Politician*. Belmont, Mass.: Belmont, 1963.

———. *The Blue Book of the John Birch Society*. Belmont, Mass.: Western Islands, 1961.

Wells, Tom. *The War Within: America's Battle over Vietnam*. Berkeley: University of California Press, 1994.

Whitaker, Robert, ed. *The New Right Papers*. New York: St. Martin's Press, 1982.

White, F. Clifton, with William Gill. *Suite 3505: The Story of the Draft Goldwater Movement*. New Rochelle, N.Y.: Arlington House, 1967.

White, Richard. *"It's Your Misfortune and None of My Own": A History of the American West*. Norman: University of Oklahoma Press, 1991.

White, Theodore H. *The Making of the President, 1964*. New York: Atheneum, 1965.

———. *The Making of the President, 1968*. New York: Atheneum, 1969.

Wilcox, Clyde. *God's Warriors: The Christian Right in Twentieth-Century America*. Baltimore: Johns Hopkins University Press, 1992.

Wiley, Peter, and Robert Gottlieb. *Empires in the Sun: The Rise of the New American West*. New York: Putnam, 1982.

Wills, Garry. *Nixon Agonistes: The Crisis of the Self-Made Man*. Boston: Houghton Mifflin, 1970.

Wood, Samuel E., and Alfred E. Heller. *The Phantom Cities of California.* Sacramento: California Tomorrow, 1963.

Wuthnow, Robert. *The Restructuring of American Religion: Society and Faith since World War II.* Princeton, N.J.: Princeton University Press, 1988.

Young, Perry Deane. *God's Bullies: Native Reflections on Preachers and Politics.* New York: Holt, Rinehart and Winston, 1982.

Zwier, Robert. *Born-Again Politics: The New Christian Right in America.* Downers Grove, Ill.: InterVarsity Press, 1982.

ARTICLES AND ESSAYS

Agran, Larry. "Orange County Populism and the Politics of Growth." *Journal of Orange County Studies* 1 (fall 1998): 6–8.

Ammerman, Nancy T. "North American Protestant Fundamentalism." In *Fundamentalisms Observed*, edited by Martin E. Marty and R. Scott Appleby. Vol. 1. Chicago: University of Chicago Press, 1991.

Anderson, Totton J. "The 1958 Election in California." *Western Political Quarterly* 10 (March 1959): 276–300.

———. "The 1962 Election in California." *Western Political Quarterly* 14 (March 1963): 393–414.

Anderson, Totton J., and Eugene C. Lee. "The 1964 Election in California." *Western Political Quarterly* 18 (June 1965): 451–74.

———. "The 1966 Election in California." *Western Political Quarterly* 20 (June 1967): 535–54.

Batman, Richard Dale. "Anaheim Was an Oasis in a Wilderness." *Journal of the West* 4 (January 1965): 1–21.

———. "Gospel Swamp . . . The Land of Hog and Hominy." *Journal of the West* 4 (April 1965): 231–57.

———. "Great Cities Grow on Citrus Lands." *Journal of the West* 4 (October 1965): 553–76.

Bell, Daniel. "The Dispossessed." In *The Radical Right*, edited by Daniel Bell. Garden City, N.Y.: Doubleday, 1963.

Bibby, Reginald. "Why Conservative Churches Really Are Growing." *Journal for the Scientific Study of Religion* 17 (June 1978): 129–37.

Brandmeyer Gerald A., and R. Serge Denisoff. "Status Politics: An Appraisal of the Application of a Concept." *Pacific Sociological Review* 12 (spring 1969): 5–11.

Brinkley, Alan. "The Problem of American Conservatism." *American Historical Review* 99 (April 1994): 409–29.

Broyles, J. Allen. "The John Birch Society: A Movement of Social Protest of the Radical Right." *Journal of Social Issues* 19 (April 1963): 51–62.

Clayton, James L. "Defense Spending: Key to California's Growth." *Western Political Quarterly* 15 (June 1962): 280–93.

———. "The Impact of the Cold War on the Economies of California and Utah, 1946–1965." *Pacific Historical Review* 36 (November 1967): 449–73.

Clouse, Robert G. "The New Christian Right, America, and the Kingdom of God." In *Fundamentalism and Evangelicalism*, edited by Martin E. Marty. Munich: K. G. Saur, 1993.

Costantini, Edmond, and Kenneth H. Craik. "Competing Elites within a Political Party: A Study of Republican Leadership." *Western Political Quarterly* 22 (December 1969): 879–903.

Elms, Alan C. "Psychological Factors in Right-Wing Extremism." In *The American Right Wing: Readings in Political Behavior*, edited by Robert A. Schoenberger. New York: Holt, Rinehart and Winston, 1969.

Freeman, Joshua. "Putting Conservatism Back into the 1960s." *Radical History Review* 44 (1989): 94–99.

Gayk, William. "The Changing Demography of Orange County." *Journal of Orange County Studies* 3–4 (spring 1990): 13–18.

Gottdiener, M., and George Kephart. "The Multinucleated Metropolitan Region: A Comparative Analysis." In *Postsuburban California: The Transformation of Orange County since World War II*, edited by Rob Kling, Spencer Olin, and Mark Poster. Berkeley: University of California Press, 1991.

Guth, James L. "The New Christian Right." In *The New Christian Right: Mobilization and Legitimation*, edited by Robert C. Liebman and Robert Wuthnow. Hawthorne, N.Y.: Aldine, 1983.

Hass, Lisbeth. "Grass-Roots Protest and the Politics of Planning: Santa Ana, 1976–1988." In *Postsuburban California: The Transformation of Orange County since World War II*, edited by Rob Kling, Spencer Olin, and Mark Poster. Berkeley: University of California Press, 1991.

Hadden, Jeffrey K. "Religious Broadcasting and the Mobilization of the New Christian Right." In *Fundamentalism and Evangelicalism*, edited by Martin E. Marty. Munich: K. G. Saur, 1993.

Heale, M. J. "Red Scare Politics: California's Campaign Against Un-American Activities, 1940–1970." *Journal of American Studies* 20 (April 1986): 5–32.

Hofstadter, Richard. "Pseudo-Conservatism Revisited: A Postscript." In *The Radical Right*, edited by Daniel Bell. Garden City, N.Y.: Doubleday, 1963.

Hunter, Allen. "In the Wings: New Right Ideology and Organization." *Radical America* 15 (spring 1981): 113–38.

Jenkins, J. Craig. "Resource Mobilization and the Study of Social Movements." *Annual Review of Sociology* 9 (1983): 527–53.

Kazin, Michael. "The Grass-Roots Right: New Histories of U.S. Conservatism in the Twentieth Century." *American Historical Review* 97 (February 1992): 136–55.

Kazin, Michael, and Maurice Isserman. "The Failure and Success of the New Radicalism." In *The Rise and Fall of the New Deal Order, 1930–1980*, edited by Steve Fraser and Gary Gerstle. Princeton, N.J.: Princeton University Press, 1989.

Kleppner, Paul. "Politics without Parties: The Western States, 1900–1984." In *The Twentieth-Century West: Historical Interpretations*, edited by Gerald D. Nash and Richard Etulain. Albuquerque: University of New Mexico Press, 1989.

Kling, Rob, Spencer Olin, and Mark Poster. "The Emergence of Postsuburbia: An Introduction." In *Postsuburban California: The Transformation of Orange County since World War II*, edited by Rob Kling, Spencer Olin, and Mark Poster. Berkeley: University of California Press, 1991.

Lewis, L. David. "Charles Fuller." In *Twentieth-Century Shapers of American Popular Religion*, edited by Charles H. Lippy. New York: Greenwood Press, 1989.

Lienesch, Michael. "Right-Wing Religion: Christian Conservatism as a Political Movement." *Political Science Quarterly* 97 (fall 1982): 403–26.

Lipset, Seymour Martin. "Three Decades of the Radical Right: Coughlinites, McCarthyites and Birchees." In *The Radical Right*, edited by Daniel Bell. Garden City, N.Y.: Doubleday, 1963.

Marty, Martin E. "The Revival of Evangelicalism and Southern Religion." In *Varieties of Southern Evangelicalism*, edited by David Edwin Harrell Jr. Macon, Ga.: Mercer University Press, 1981.

McCarthy, J. D., and M. N. Zald. "Resource Mobilization and Social Movements." *American Journal of Sociology* 82 (1977): 1212–41.

Melching, Richard. "The Activities of the Ku Klux Klan in Anaheim, California, 1923–1925." *Southern California Quarterly* 56 (summer 1974): 175–96.

Moore, Leonard. "Good Old-Fashioned New Social History and the Twentieth-Century American Right." *Reviews in American History* 24 (1996): 555–73.

Nichelson, F. Patrick. "Non-Protestants in Southern California." In *The American West and Religious Experience*, edited by William Kramer. Los Angeles: Will Kramer, 1975.

Olin, Spencer C. "Globalization and the Politics of Locality: Orange County, California, in the Cold War Era." *Western Historical Quarterly* 22 (May 1991): 143–61.

———. "Intraclass Conflict and the Politics of a Fragmented Region." In *Postsuburban California: The Transformation of Orange County since World War II*, edited by Rob Kling, Spencer Olin, and Mark Poster. Berkeley: University of California Press, 1991.

Pritchard, Robert L. "Orange County during the Depressed Thirties: A Study in Twentieth-Century California Local History." *Southern California Quarterly* 50 (June 1968): 191–207.

Ribuffo, Leo P. "Why Is There So Much Conservatism in the United States and Why Do So Few Historians Know Anything about It?" *American Historical Review* 99 (April 1994): 439–41.

Rieder, Jonathan. "The Rise of the 'Silent Majority.'" In *The Rise and Fall of the New Deal Order, 1930–1980*, edited by Steve Fraser and Gary Gerstle. Princeton, N.J.: Princeton University Press, 1989.

Roozen, David A., and C. Kirk Hadaway. "Denominations Grow as Individuals Join Congregations." In *Church and Denominational Growth*, edited by David A. Roozen and C. Kirk Hadaway. Nashville, Tenn.: Abingdon Press, 1993.

Rose, Susan. "Christian Fundamentalism and Education in the United States." In *Fundamentalisms and Society: Reclaiming the Sciences, the Family, and Education*, edited by Martin E. Marty and R. Scott Appleby. Chicago: University of Chicago Press, 1993.

Schiesl, Martin J. "Designing the Model Community: The Irvine Company and Suburban Development, 1950–1988." In *Postsuburban California: The Transformation of Orange County since World War II*, edited by Rob Kling, Spencer Olin, and Mark Poster. Berkeley: University of California Press, 1991.

Schuparra, Kurt. "Barry Goldwater and Southern California Conservatism: Ideology, Image and Myth in the 1964 California Republican Presidential Primary." *Southern California Quarterly* 74 (fall 1992): 281–98.

Simmons, Jerold. "The Origins of the Campaign to Abolish HUAC, 1956–1961: The California Connection." *Southern California Quarterly* 64 (summer 1982): 141–57.

Stone, Barbara J. "The John Birch Society: A Profile." *Journal of Politics* 36 (February 1974): 184–87.

Sweet, Leonard I. "The 1960s: The Crisis of Liberal Christianity and the Public Emergence of Evangelicalism." In *Evangelicalism and Modern America*, edited by George Marsden. Grand Rapids, Mich.: William B. Eerdmans, 1984.

Toy, Eckard V. "Spiritual Mobilization: The Failure of an Ultra-Conservative Ideal." *Pacific Northwest Quarterly* 61 (April 1970): 77–86.

———. "The Conservative Connection: The Chairman of the Board Took LSD before Timothy Leary." *American Studies* 21 (fall 1980): 65–77.

Van Halen, Nelson. "The Bolsheviki and the Orange Growers." *Pacific Historical Review* 22 (1953): 39–51.

Walker, Richard. "California Rages against the Dying of the Light." *New Left Review* 209 (January/February 1995): 42–75.

Westin, Alan F. "The John Birch Society: 'Radical Right' and 'Extreme Left' in the Political Context of Post World War II–1962." In *The Radical Right*, edited by Daniel Bell. Garden City, N.Y.: Doubleday, 1963.

Wilson, James Q. "A Guide to Reagan Country: The Political Culture of Southern California." *Commentary* 43 (May 1967): 37–45.

———. "Party Organization: The Search for Power." In *The Challenge of California*, edited by Eugene C. Lee and Willis D. Hawley. Boston: Little, Brown, 1970.

Wolfinger, Raymond E., and Fred I. Greenstein. "The Repeal of Fair Housing in California: An Analysis of Referendum Voting." *American Political Science Review* 62 (September 1968): 753–69.

———. "Comparing Political Regions: The Case of California." *American Political Science Review* 63 (March 1969): 75–81.

Wolfinger, Raymond E., Barbara Kaye Wolfinger, Kenneth Prewitt, and Sheilah Rosenhack. "America's Radical Right: Politics and Ideology." In *The American Right Wing: Readings in Political Behavior*, edited by Robert A. Schoenberger. New York: Holt, Rinehart and Winston, 1969.

Wollenberg, C. "*Mendez v. Westminster*: Race, Nationality, and Segregation in California Schools." *California Historical Quarterly* 53 (winter 1974): 317–33.

THESES AND DISSERTATIONS

Bernhagen, Robert. "The Magnolia School District, A Case Study in Neo-McCarthyism." Master's thesis, California State College, Fullerton, 1966.

Cocoltchos, Christopher N. "The Invisible Government and the Viable Community: The Ku Klux Klan in Orange County, California, during the 1920s." Ph.D. diss., University of California, Los Angeles. 1979.

Gerston, Larry N. "The California Democratic Council and Political Reform: Promise and Performance." Ph.D. diss., University of California, Davis, 1975.

Griffith, Duff Witman. "Before the Deluge: An Oral History Examination of Pre-Watergate Conservative Thought in Orange County, California." Master's thesis, California State University, Fullerton, 1976.

Grupp, Frederick W., Jr. "Social Correlates of Political Activists: The John Birch Society and the ADA." Ph.D. diss., University of Pennsylvania, 1968.

Hansen, Janna. "The Role for Which God Created Them: Women in the United States Religious Right." Bachelor's thesis, Harvard University, 1997.

Hertel, Michael M. "Community Associations and Their Politics: An Evaluation of Twelve Community Associations on the Irvine Ranch." Ph.D. diss., Claremont Graduate School, 1971.

Johnson, William C. "The Volunteer Republicans." Ph.D. diss., Claremont Graduate School, 1965.

Larson, Eric Christopher. "The Issue of Birchism in the 1962 California Republican Gubernatorial Primary." Master's thesis, California State University, Fullerton, 1975.

Moffit, Leonard. "Community and Urbanization." Ph.D. diss., University of California, Irvine, 1967.

Reccow, Louis. "The Orange County Citrus Strikes of 1935–1936: The Forgotten People in Revolt." Ph.D. diss., University of Southern California, 1971.

Spooner, Denise. S. "The Political Consequences of Experiences of Community: Iowa Migrants and Republican Conservatism in Southern California, 1946–1964." Ph.D. diss., University of Pennsylvania, 1992.

Stone, Barbara Shell. "The John Birch Society of California." Ph.D. diss., University of Southern California, 1968.

Wollenberg, C. "All Deliberate Speed." Ph.D. diss., University of California, Irvine, 1976.

Wong, Robert Seng-Pui. "A Study of Population Growth and Its Impact in Orange County, California." Ph.D. diss., University of California, Irvine, 1974.

Index

POLITICS AND SOCIETY IN TWENTIETH-CENTURY AMERICA